THE NEW AMERICAN IMMIGRATION

GARLAND REFERENCE LIBRARY
OF SOCIAL SCIENCE
(Vol. 376)

THE NEW AMERICAN IMMIGRATION
Evolving Patterns of
Legal and Illegal Emigration
A Bibliography of Selected References

Francesco Cordasco

GARLAND PUBLISHING, INC. • NEW YORK & LONDON
1987

© 1987 Francesco Cordasco
All rights reserved

Library of Congress Cataloging-in-Publication Data

Cordasco, Francesco, 1920–
The New American immigration.

(Garland Reference Library of Social Science;
v. 376)
Includes index.
1. United States—Emigration and immigration—
Bibliography.   2. Aliens, Illegal—United States—
Bibliography.   I. Title.   II. Series.

Z7164.I3C58 1987 [JV6450] 016.32573 86-31971
ISBN 0-8240-8523-X (alk. paper)

Printed on acid-free, 250-year-life paper
Manufactured in the United States of America

In Memory of

Giovanni Cordasco (1883–1953)

and

Carmela Madorma Cordasco (1883–1962)

who were part of the great migrations

"The United States, it seems, remains the permanently unfinished country. Created by immigrants--though we call those who came before the United States was established 'pioneers' or 'settlers'--we have for a hundred years struggled with the question of 'whom shall we welcome,' to use the title of a major report on immigration policy, issued in 1953 by a commission appointed by President Truman. In 1985, it is clear we will be struggling with the question for many years to come. Our most substantial effort in recent years to forge a new immigration policy, one responsive to a variety of needs and appealing, it was hoped, to the largest possible consensus of American opinion, failed in 1984. In the wake of that failure, the broadest and largest stream of immigrants since the 1920's continues to flow into the United States. And opinion is confused and uncertain as to whether this adds to our strength or our weakness, as well as whether it demonstrates our openness and generosity, or our simple incapacity to forge a national policy on the key question of who shall be allowed to become an American, along with our helplessness before the decisions of cynical nations trying to rid themselves of unwanted people."

Nathan Glazer, *Clamor at the Gates* (1985)

CONTENTS

PREFACE

American immigration policy is one of the critical issues
facing the United States. Nathan Glazer has sharply defined
its focus:

> The United States, it seems, remains the permanently
> unfinished country. Created by immigrants—though we
> call those who came before the United States was estab-
> lished "pioneers" or "settlers"—we have for a hundred
> years struggled with the question of "whom shall we
> welcome," to use the title of a major report on immigra-
> tion policy, issued in 1953 by a commission appointed
> by President Truman. In 1985, it is clear we will be
> struggling with the question for many years to come.
> Our most substantial effort in recent years to forge a
> new immigration policy, one responsive to a variety of
> needs and appealing, it was hoped, to the largest pos-
> sible consensus of American opinion, failed in 1984.
> In the wake of that failure, the broadest and largest
> stream of immigrants since the 1920s continues to flow
> into the United States. And opinion is confused and
> uncertain as to whether this adds to our strength or our
> weakness, as well as whether it demonstrates our openness
> and generosity, or our simple incapacity to forge a
> national policy on the key question of who shall be
> allowed to become an American, along with our helpless-
> ness before the decisions of cynical nations trying to
> rid themselves of unwanted people.[1]

Forging a national policy for immigration to the United
States has resulted in a continuing debate, both controversial
and acrimonious. The debate reflects what may be a central
contradiction of America, which has traditionally welcomed the
downtrodden, if sometimes only because their labor is (and was)
needed, but often recoils from the cultural baggage immigrants
bring. A hundred years ago, when "Liberty Enlightening the
World" was dedicated, 90 percent of the immigrants came from
Europe. More than half were still coming from Europe in
1965, when Congress prompted a new influx by lowering immigra-

tion barriers that had been based on national origins. As a
result, only 5 percent of the legal immigrants last year came
from Europe. Asians--primarily Filipinos, Koreans, Vietnamese
and Indians--accounted for nearly half of the 570,000 legally
admitted newcomers, according to the Immigration and Naturalization Service. Migration from Latin America, mainly Mexico,
made up roughly 40 percent. While public debate has focused
on illegal immigration, the majority of immigrants today
arrive quite legally. More are expected in the 1980s than in
any decade in American history except for 1900-10, about 6
million, as against 4 million in the 1970s. If illegal immigration is included--estimated at from 300,000 to 500,000
people a year--the figure could be even higher than the record
8.8 million admitted in the first decade of this century.

The public debate (very often tendentious) has spawned a
huge literature which unremittingly continues to be produced.
The New American Immigration selectively records this literature. Intended as a guide to the enormous literature which
has developed since the Immigration Act of 1965 (Hart-Celler
Act), it is a bibliography of over 2000 entries with descriptive annotations whose structure defines its coverage.[2]
Part I (American Immigration Before 1965: History and Backgrounds) is a very selective list of materials which put the
contemporary patterns into a meaningful historical focus;
Part II (American Immigration After 1965: General Studies and
Related References) includes a corpus of essential studies
which dimensionally describes and comprehensively defines the
major questions and concerns of contemporary American immigration policy; adjunctive to Part II is Part III (Illegal Immigrants in the United States) which includes (1) General Works
and Specialized Studies; and (2) Law Journals and Reviews.
"Undocumented" is a euphemism often preferred to "illegal."
I understand the term "illegal migrants" or simply "illegals"
to refer to individuals entering the United States without
valid immigration papers. The term encompasses those migrants
who are simply undocumented in the sense that they do not hold
any entry permit, those who have obtained fraudulent documents,
as well as those who have been granted temporary entry permits,
the terms of which have been violated by overstaying the
designated time and by engaging in work; Part IV (Miscellanea)
has allowed the inclusion of items not strictly appropriate
to other categories, and has afforded as well the opportunity
to incorporate entries on immigrant socialization, acculturation, immigrant and bilingual education, and other factors
and processes vitally an integral part of the immigrant experience. Continuing current information may be found in the
International Migration Review, a quarterly scientific journal
studying sociological, demographic, historical, and legislative
aspects of migration.

In the Appendix, I have included the Introduction and the Recommendations from *U.S. Immigration Policy and the National Interest* (1981), the final report of the Select Commission on Immigration and Refugee Policy which was established by the Congress in 1978 and charged with the task of studying and evaluating "existing laws, policies, and procedures governing the admission of immigrants and refugees to the United States," and formulating "appropriate legislative recommendations." Whatever form American immigration policy takes in the near future, its genesis will lie in the cogent deliberations and recommendations (however modified) of the Select Commission.[3]

Some final observations are in order. This bibliography is *selective*, and no pretense to complete coverage is made: others may have made different selections and adopted different formats for entry inclusion; I hope that no critically important items have been missed. Errors are inevitable, and for these I ask indulgence, but I am comforted by Lord Macaulay's plaintive lamentation that "Error, unhappily, leaves its sly imprimatur in every book."

Francesco Cordasco
West New York, N.J.
September 1986

NOTES

1. Nathan Glazer, ed. *Clamor at the Gates: The New American Immigration* (San Francisco: Institute for Contemporary Studies, 1985), p. 3.

2. Puerto Rican migration to the United States mainland has been an important part of the migratory experience of recent years. Puerto Ricans are, of course, American citizens and technically migrants, not immigrants. I have not included references to this group primarily because the literature is conveniently available elsewhere: Francesco Cordasco, *Puerto Ricans on the Mainland: A Bibliography of Reports, Texts, Critical Studies and Related Materials* (Totowa, N.J.: Rowman & Littlefield, 1972); Paquita Vivó, *The Puerto Ricans: An Annotated Bibliography* (New York: R.R. Bowker, 1973); and Diane Herrera, ed., *Puerto Ricans and Other Minority Groups in the Continental United States: An Annotated Bibliography*. With a New Foreword and Supplemental Bibliography by Francesco Cordasco (Detroit: Blaine-Ethridge, 1979).

3. For insightful historical antecedents in the origins and development of immigration law, see Kitty Calavita, *U.S.*

Immigration Law and the Control of Labor, 1820-1924 (Orlando: Academic Press, 1984). Calavita examines the evolution of immigration policies from 1820 to 1924, when more than 35 million immigrants, mostly Europeans, came to the United States. Immigrants were actively recruited in the 1820s to facilitate the development of industrialization, in marked contrast to the 1920s, after the development of monopoly capital, when immigrants were almost completely excluded. Calavita demonstrates that the motivations for the creation of immigration laws in this hundred-year period were much more complex than the naive altruism of providing refuge, on the one hand, or racist exclusion, on the other hand. She seeks to explain immigration laws on the basis of the labor function of immigrants in general, and as industrial labor in particular.

INTRODUCTION

In 1978, the U.S. Congress passed a law providing for a worldwide immigration cap of 290,000 created by combining both hemispheres, with a preference system and 20,000-per-country limit. The reforms begun in 1965 were now complete. Why had reform been so strong a force in immigration policy by the mid-1960s? Vernon M. Briggs, Jr., has observed:

The overt racism of the national-origins admission system could not be sustained in a nation that was already multiracial and multicultural in its composition and that boasted to the world of these attributes. Thus, the movement in the 1950s and early 1960s to overhaul the U.S. immigration system gradually accumulated sufficient momentum to accomplish most of its goals. The capstone of this drive occurred on October 3, 1965, when President Lyndon Johnson signed into law the Immigration and Nationality Amendments of 1965, or the Hart-Celler Act (hereafter referred to as the Immigration Act of 1965). Technically speaking, the legislation was a lengthy series of amendments to the Immigration and Nationality Act of 1952, but in terms of its policy significance it has been called "the most far-reaching revision of immigration policy" since the imposition of the first numerical quotas in 1921. Since its passage, immigration to the United States has changed dramatically both quantitatively and qualitatively.[1]

In another frame of reference, David M. Reimers (who has called the Immigration Act of 1965 "a cautious reform") reminds us that

Eradicating discrimination against Third World countries was not the focal point of those who disapproved of American immigration policies. Rather, critics urged a number of reforms, several of which would have benefited potential migrants from Third World nations, but the center of their critique was the national origins system embedded in the McCarran-Walter Act. Both Harry S. Truman and Dwight D. Eisenhower criticized policies

xiii

established by the McCarran-Walter Act. In his veto
message Truman declared, "The basis of this quota system
was false and unworthy in 1924. It is even worse now.
At the present time, this quota system keeps out the
very people we want to bring in. It is incredible to
me that, in this year of 1952, we should again be enact-
ing into law such a slur on the patriotism, the capacity,
and the decency of a large part of our citizenry."[2]

For almost a century, American immigration policy was restrictionist. In the 1880s the Congress began an active role
in the administration and control of immigration, and this
new role was evident in the passage of the Chinese Exclusion
Act of 1882 which suspended entry of Chinese workers for ten
years and barred all foreign-born Chinese from acquiring
citizenship. In 1885, Congress enacted the Foran Act which
prohibited unskilled laborer recruitment with prepaid passage
and advance contracting, and in 1888 Congress ordered deportation of all alien contract laborers within one year of entry.

Betwen 1890-1921 (a period Vernon M. Briggs, Jr., has
called "The Era of Screening Without a Numerical Ceiling")
Congress attempted to impose literacy requirements to restrict
immigration. Four literacy bills were debated in Congress
between 1896 and 1917; the Congress passed three literacy
acts, each of which received a presidential veto. In 1907,
legislation established an Immigration Commission whose ap-
pointment President Theodore Roosevelt had called for. The
Commission was chaired by Senator William P. Dillingham (Rep.,
Vermont). The Commission published its *Report* (see Entry No.
69) in 1911 in 41 volumes, and Oscar Handlin called it "one
of the most ambitious social science research projects in the
nation's history up to then, barring only the censuses";[3]
but the *Report* was restrictionist in its basic recommendations,
and Vernon M. Briggs, Jr., has succinctly characterized it as
"neither impartial or scientific." The Commission had spent
over a million dollars, had convened a staff of three hundred,
and taken over three years in its deliberations, but (as
Briggs further observes):

> The Dillingham commission found that the new immigrants
> differed significantly from the nation's older immi-
> grants. It deemed the new immigrants to be "inferior"
> and to possess attributes that would make it difficult
> for them to assimilate. It argued that a slower rate
> of expansion--a rate that emphasized the ability of
> immigrants to adapt to their new surroundings--would
> be preferable to a rapid and uncontrolled rate, which
> imperiled the prevailing wages and employment opportuni-
> ties of American citizens. Laced throughout the com-

missioner's argument were pseudo-scientific theories pertaining to "superior" and "inferior" persons. The mixture of economic and ethnic arguments in the commission's report has plagued all efforts to discuss and to legislate immigration reform impartially since that time.[4]

In 1917, over a presidential veto, an Immigration Act was passed which required of immigrants over 16 years of age literacy (in English, or any other language); and in 1921 the Johnson Act introduced a system of national quotas, determined as the percentage of the number of immigrants from the country in question at a designated census. The 1921 Act (which had been vetoed by President Woodrow Wilson earlier but signed into law when Warren Harding took office) limited the annual number of immigrants of each admissible nationality to 3 percent of the foreign-born of that nationality as recorded in the U.S. Census of 1910, and set a limit on European immigration at 350,000.

When the Johnson Act expired in 1924, Congress passed the Johnson-Reed Act which set national quotas at 2 percent of the 1890 population, and also provided that as of July 1, 1927, the quota limit would be 150,000, allocated on the base of the estimated national origins distribution of the continental U.S. population in 1920; postponed twice, this latter provision became effective in 1929, and

> Between 1929 and 1968, quotas were determined by the "national origins" formula which provided that the annual quota equal one-sixth of 1 percent of the number of white inhabitants in the continental United States, less Western Hemisphere immigrants and their descendants. The annual quota for each nationality was then determined by the same ratio to 150,000 as the number of inhabitants of each nationality living in the continental United States in 1920 to the total inhabitants, although a minimum quota for any nationality was 100.[5]

Various other pieces of restrictionist legislation were passed by the Congress in the period following the Johnson-Reed Act of 1924; the only piece of major immigration legislation passed was the McCarran-Walter Act (Immigration and Nationality Act) of 1952 which changed the formula for computing the annual quotas of any country to one-sixth of 1 percent of the numbers of persons of that national origin in the United States in 1920 as computed for the 1924 Quota Act. As Reimers notes:

> The McCarran-Walter Act basically reinforced the tough immigration restrictions of the 1920s. That law re-

affirmed the national origins quotas and added security
provisions designed to make it almost impossible for
suspected subversives to enter the United States.
Liberals generally saw the 1952 immigration act as
containing unduly harsh security provisions and as
racist because of its inclusion of national origins
quotas that gave the vast bulk of immigrant slots to the
people of northern and western Europe. President Truman
agreed with the liberal position and vetoed the bill,
but Congress overrode his veto by a vote of 278 to 113
in the House and 57 to 26 in the Senate.[6]

The McCarran-Walter Act, however,

could not survive changes at home and abroad. At home
the immigrants of the great wave from Eastern and
Southern Europe, and their children growing to maturity,
were becoming more and more effective politically,
developing greater resources economically, becoming
bolder in asserting their wishes against a weakening
nativism. Abroad, crises that produced waves of refugees from Communism—in Hungary in 1957, in Cuba in
1960 and later—were also changing public opinion about
immigration. Perhaps more potent in changing these
attitudes was the fading of fears of depression, as
post-war prosperity continued, marred only by occasional
recessions. Perhaps most potent was the radical change
in American attitudes on race that accompanied the rise
of the civil rights movement. The attempt to freeze
the composition of the American people by favoring
Northwestern Europe was increasingly seen as basically
immoral and wrong.[7]

By 1965, it was clear that the national origins system
had to be changed:

In addition to the fact that the prevailing immigration
system had been rendered obsolete, it is also true that
the nation's attitudes toward race and ethnic background
had changed dramatically by the early 1960s. The Civil
Rights movement, which had begun in earnest in 1957
with the Montgomery, Alabama, bus boycott, had culminated
in passage of the Civil Rights Act of 1964 and the
Voting Rights Act of 1965. Thus, it has been observed:
"The 1965 immigration legislation was as much a product
of the mid-sixties and the heavily Democratic 89th
Congress which produced major civil rights legislation
as the 1952 Act was a product of the Cold War period
of the early 1950s." Just as overt racism could no
longer be tolerated in the way citizens treated their

fellow citizens, neither could it be sanctioned in the laws that governed the way in which noncitizens were considered for immigrant status.[8]

The Hart-Celler Act of 1965 eliminated national origins as the basis for selection of immigrants to the United States. Instead, it established an annual limit of 170,000 aliens (and a per country quota of 20,000) who could enter the United States as immigrants. It set a ceiling of 120,000 on immigration from the western hemisphere, thus allowing (with the annual limit of 170,000 elsewhere) for the admission of 290,000 immigrants a year. The Act, further, established a system whereby immigration visas would be distributed according to a seven-point preference list that favored close relatives of U.S. citizens and those with special occupational skills. The definition of refugees was broadened to include those who were victims of natural calamities, as well as the victims of religious and/or political persecution. Three categories of exclusion were established: (1) people with mental diseases and drug and alcohol addictions; (2) criminals, prostitutes, and those with contagious diseases; (3) subversives and some twenty other categories of aliens. Continuing immigration reforms included the passage of legislation for the admission and resettlement of refugees, mainly from the Soviet Union, Southeast Asia, and Cuba, *e.g.*, the Indochinese Refugee Resettlement Program which allowed the admission of 200,000 Indochinese refugees. In 1980, the Refugee Act established an overall policy for the admission and resettlement of refugees.

The Immigration Act of 1965 had unanticipated consequences:

> The United States was giving itself the moral satisfaction of passing a nondiscriminatory immigration act that it expected would in no substantial way change the sources or volume of American immigration. The people who were fighting for the bill were Jews, Italians, Greeks, Poles, who hoped their relatives, their fellow countrymen, and their co-religionists would have an easier time getting in, and the bill itself favored strongly the principle of family unification. But the prophets were wrong. It turned out the chief beneficiaries of the new immigration regime were Asians and Latin Americans. Starting from a modest base, the numbers of Asian immigrants increased rapidly; and as they increased family reunification played a greater and greater role in enabling immigration and resulted in steadily larger numbers of immigrants from Hong Kong and Taiwan, the Philippines, Korea, and India. The disaster in Vietnam added Vietnamese, Cambodians, and

Laotians. In the decade of the 1970s, astonishingly,
the number of Asians in the United States doubled to
three-and-a-half million. It will undoubtedly double
again in the course of the 1980s. In 1984 six out of
the first seven countries, by size of number of immigrants sent to the United States, were Asian. But the
first was Mexico. And that, too, was not foreseen by
the reformers of 1965. Thus a bill that had been expected to remove discrimination against the countries
of Southern and Eastern Europe, that had been passed
by the political weight of immigrants from those countries and their children and grandchildren who had become warp and woof in the United States, benefited
others and was taken advantage of by others. For
Europe, too, was benefiting from postwar prosperity.
There was no longer any strong demand from Europe to
enter the United States. Europe's standards of living
approached and in some countries surpassed that of the
United States, its social benefits certainly surpassed
that of the United States, class boundaries there were
increasingly a thing of the past, and educational opportunities expanded and abounded. What need for the United
States?[9]

In the 1970s, continuing concerns over various immigration
issues led to mounting criticisms and demands for reform.
Illegal immigration was the paramount concern, but other related issues (*e.g.*, the status of temporary foreign workers
and refugee accommodation) continued to be controversial.

The intensity of the debate surrounding the "new immigration" is indicated in the somber observations of Raymond A.
Mohl:

Indeed, the twentieth century remains a great uncharted
wilderness for immigration and ethnic historians. The
great surge of new immigrants and refugees since 1960,
in particular, has yet to be placed in the larger context
of immigration history. In many ways, the new immigration of the past few decades has been reshaping some of
the major U.S. metropolitan areas. For instance, in
1983 *Time* magazine reported that the Los Angeles metropolitan area was home not only for over two million
Mexican-Americans, but also for hundreds of thousands of
other new immigrants. These included 200,000 Salvadorans,
200,000 Iranians, 175,000 Japanese, 150,000 Chinese,
150,000 Koreans, 150,000 Filipinos, 130,000 Arabs, and
smaller but still sizeable concentrations of Israelis,
Samoans, Colombians, Hondurans, Guatemalans, Cubans,
Vietnamese, Pakistanis, and East Indians. Similarly,

New York City has become a magnet for Asian, Caribbean,
Hispanic, and other new immigrants and refugees. Huge
concentrations of Haitians, Dominicans, Colombians,
West Indians, and the like have created new ethnic
neighborhoods in areas formerly populated by the
Italians, Jews, Germans, Scandinavians, and Irish. As
the *New York Times* observed in 1981, "Immigrants are
coming to New York City from virtually every country
on the globe, creating a city more diverse in race,
language and ethnicity than it was at the turn of the
century when immigrants from Europe poured through
Ellis Island." Reflecting this new surge of immigration,
the foreign born made up about 25 percent of New York
City's population in 1980. The incredible dimensions
of the new immigrant flood are just beginning to be
sketched out. According to a careful study by Douglas
S. Massey, new immigration to the United States during
the 1970s totaled more tha seven million persons—a
figure surpassing the previous record high of about 6.3
million during the first decade of the twentieth century.
Some specialists estimate that at the present rate,
35 million additional immigrants and refugees will
come to the United States by the year 2000. It is not
too early for ethnic historians to begin studying this
late-twentieth-century immigration.[10]

In 1978, Congress established a Select Commission on
Immigration and Refugee Policy to make a major study of immigration and recommend changes; the sixteen-member Commission
(including Congressional representatives and senators, Cabinet
officials, and presidential appointees) was chaired by Father
Theodore Hesburgh, president of Notre Dame University and its
work directed by Professor Lawrence Fuchs of Brandeis University. The Commission's *Report*[11] was submitted to the Congress in March 1981; its recommendations were that the basic
immigration system be kept intact, with more flexibility,
adjustments in preferences, and increases in immigration to
assist in easing backlogs in certain nations. Its recommendations on illegal (undocumented) aliens proved very controversial,[12] but it became the basis for immigration reform legislation now pending in the Congress.

In speaking of the Commission and its *Report*, Father
Hesburgh noted in the March 20, 1986, *New York Times*:

The essential recommendation was that America ought to
open the front door of legal immigration a bit wider
while shutting the back door of illegal immigration.
While maintaining a generous policy toward those in an
impoverished world who wish to come here, we cannot

accommodate everyone and must regain control of our
borders. To face this moral dilemma, I undertook my
role as commission chairman by asking: Why should immigration be a problem? Why not let down the barriers
and let people move freely? After our two years of
study, the question answered itself. It is not enough
to sympathize with the aspirations and plight of illegal aliens. We must also consider the consequences
of not controlling our borders. What about the aspirations of Americans who must compete for jobs and whose
wages and work standards are depressed by the presence
of large numbers of illegal aliens? What about aliens
who are victimized by unscrupulous employers and who die
in the desert at the hands of smugglers? Unfortunately,
nothing has happened in the last five years to alleviate
the conditions that cause illegal immigration. The commission concluded that the key to curtailing the flow
was to remove the magnetic lure of jobs in this country.
The cornerstone of the immigration reform bill passed
by the Senate last fall, and the one now under consideration in the House, is a provision that would penalize
employers who hire undocumented workers. Under present
law, it is illegal for an undocumented alien to be in
this country, but it is not illegal to hire one. It
was also the commission's strong, compassionate opinion
that aliens who have been law-abiding residents for a
reasonably long time should be granted the opportunity
to legalize their status. Alternatives are limited.
Failure to act quickly and responsibly to control the
flow of illegal immigrants will lead to drastic solutions no one wants. No responsible proponent of reform
wants immigration stopped. Controlled, legal immigration
can continue to be beneficial to the nation. But as
Representative Peter W. Rodino, Jr., Democrat of New
Jersey, chief sponsor of the House bill, has observed:
"It is a mistake to let this problem go unaddressed.
What's going to happen if we don't act is that a
psychology will develop that says, 'Don't let anybody
in, or, have the military round up those here illegally
and push them across the border.' During the next 15
years, assuming a persistently strong economy, the
United States will create about 30 million new jobs.
Can we afford to set aside more than 20 percent of them
for foreign workers? No. It would be a disservice to
our own poor and unemployed to try."

In 1984 different versions of the Simpson-Mazzoli Bill,
entitled the Immigration Reform and Control Act of 1982,
passed both houses of the Congress. Its major provisions

would impose civil and criminal penalties against employers who knowingly hire illegal aliens; require national identity cards for all legal aliens; grant permanent residence status to illegal aliens who could prove continuous residence in the United States since January 1, 1977, and temporary residence status to those who could prove continuous residence in the United States since January 1, 1980; and establish a new ceiling for the number of legal aliens who would be allowed to enter each year. Before it can be sent to the President for approval or veto, an agreement on key issues must be reached by a joint committee of the House and the Senate. On June 25, 1986 (with Congressman Peter Rodino, Chairman of the House Judiciary Committee taking a major role), for the third time in five years, the House Judiciary Committee approved a comprehensive bill to revise the nation's immigration laws and to curtail the influx of illegal aliens. The bill will probably go later this year to the floor of the House, where a long and bitter debate is expected. The Senate passed a generally similar bill last September by a vote of 69 to 30, and the Reagan Administration supports it. The House and Senate bills would both prohibit employers from hiring illegal aliens. In addition, they would offer legal status to many illegal aliens already in the United States. But the two measures differ in many important details.

For example, the Senate bill would establish a new government program under which farmers could bring up to 350,000 aliens into the United States to harvest perishable fruit and vegetables. The workers could stay for up to nine months in any one year. By contrast, the bill approved by the House Judiciary Committee would permit certain foreign workers to become residents of the United States, with most of the rights of citizens. Under the House bill, the Attorney General would grant lawful permanent resident status to any illegal alien who could prove that he had been working in American agriculture for at least 60 days in the period from May 1, 1985, to May 1, 1986. The plan calls for the admission of additional aliens if they are needed to work on farms in subsequent years; they, too, could qualify for permanent resident status. The Senate passed comprehensive immigration bills in 1982, 1983, and 1985. The House passed a bill in 1984 by a five-vote margin, but the measure died when the House and Senate could not work out their differences.

The present status of immigration reform is best described in a *New York Times* editorial (May 9, 1986), entitled "Peter Rodino and Special Interests":

> Immigration reform, says Brooklyn's Representative Charles Schumer, is a "metaphor for governance....
> Can the general interest transcend the specific in-

terest?" And how! is the answer Senate Finance Chairman Bob Packwood has just given for tax reform. The same could still be true for immigration reform--except that the movement is backward. This was the week the bill was supposed to go to the House. What it produced instead was five suspicious weeks of more delay. This balanced, bipartisan bill embodies the general interest. It would enable America to be just in deciding which of the clamoring millions around the world it will admit. It would enable America to be humane in its treatment of those who, having sneaked in, now live under a cloud of exploitation. Yet the bill remains pinned between growers determined not to run short of farmhands to pick their crops and union leaders who fear that poor foreign workers will undercut wages. As tax reform came finally to depend on a Senate Republican chairman from the West, immigration reform now depends on a House Democratic chairman from Newark: Peter Rodino. Peter Rodino, child of Italian immigrants, a Congressman for 37 years and chairman of the Judiciary Committee, knows the importance of immigration reform better than anyone. In the 1970s, he twice won House passage of reform bills only to see them die in the Senate. Now the dragging shoe is on the other foot. The Senate has passed reform three times and the House has repeatedly dithered. It finally passed once but then died in conference. Would he let that happen again? No, he said, not if President Reagan personally reaffirmed his commitment. The President did that, in March. Okay, said the chairman; we'll mark up the legislation in early May and get the bill to the floor. This was to be the week. Now, Mr. Rodino has again gone along with a request for more time. Representatives Schumer and Leon Panetta and Howard Berman of California are trying to negotiate agreement between growers and labor. Their delay may mask shrewd tactics, avoiding torpedoes later. But the negotiators have already been at it for five months. Considering how dyspeptic the House's Democratic leaders have been about this bill, a five-week delay this late in the session is cause for alarm. If Mr. Rodino wants immigration reform to curdle and die, he is, like Speaker O'Neill and Majority Leader Wright, a canny parliamentarian who knows how to strangle without leaving fingerprints. But if he wants it to pass, he also knows what to do. In his 19 terms in the House, Peter Rodino has traveled some historic paths; he chaired the Nixon impeachment hearings in 1974. Now immigration reform may be his biggest remaining milestone. How he'll be remembered depends on which way he is headed when he goes by.

NOTES

1. Vernon M. Briggs, Jr., *Immigration Policy and the American Labor Force* (Baltimore: Johns Hopkins University Press, 1984), p. 61.

2. David M. Reimers, *Still the Golden Door: The Third World Comes to America* (New York: Columbia University Press, 1985), p. 63.

3. Oscar Handlin, *Race and Nationality in American Life* (New York: Doubleday, 1957), p. 80.

4. Briggs, *op. cit.*, p. 37.

5. *Statistical Abstract of the United States, 1984.* 104th Edition (Washington, D.C.: U.S. Department of Commerce, Bureau of the Census, 1983), p. 104.

6. Reimers, *op. cit.*, p. 20.

7. Nathan Glazer, ed., *Clamor at the Gates: The New American Immigration* (San Francisco: Institute for Contemporary Studies, 1985), p. 6.

8. Briggs, *op. cit.*, p. 62.

9. Glazer, *op. cit.*, pp. 7-8.

10. *Immigration History Newsletter*, 16 (May 1984): 1.

11. It is tempting to compare the Select Commission's 1981 *Report* with the 41-volume 1911 *Report* of the Dillingham Commission:

> During its deliberations the Select Commission had access to the work of its own staff as well as that of the staff of several congressional committees; the advice of "dozens of consultants who participated in 21 special consultations"; and the opinions of "over 700 witnesses who testified at 12 regional public hearings." The commission funded a limited amount of research on a few specialized subjects, but because the original deadline for its report was October 1, 1980 (later extended to March 1, 1981), it did not undertake any ambitious research projects that would add to the meager store of knowledge that was available. For most of its inputs, therefore, it drew upon the existing literature on the subject. Unlike the Dillingham commission, which did initiate massive research projects (but, as discussed in Chapter 2, largely ignored the results of this research when preparing its final report), the Select Commission on Immigration and Refugee Policy did not even pretend to follow such a course. In all fairness

it should be noted that at the time the Dillingham commission was appointed very little relevant information was available. By the late 1970s, however, the nation had amassed volumes of wisdom on the topic. Unfortunately, this store of knowledge was (and still is) limited and often contradictory. The Select Commission therefore based its findings largely upon what was known. It added very little that was new. (Briggs, *op. cit.*, p. 88)

12. Select Commission on Immigration and Refugee Policy. *U.S. Immigration Policy and the National Interest* (Washington, D.C.: U.S. Government Printing Office, 1981), pp. 302-314.

POSTSCRIPT

On October 9, 1986, in a dramatic reversal, the U.S. House
of Representatives approved a comprehensive bill to overhaul
the nation's immigration law and curtail the influx of illegal
aliens. The vote was 230 to 166. Voting for the bill were
168 Democrats and 62 Republicans. Sixty-one Democrats and
105 Republicans voted against it. The U.S. Senate passed its
version of the immigration bill by a vote of 69 to 30 in
September 1985.

On October 14, 1986, House and Senate negotiators reached
agreement, reconciling all differences between the Senate and
House bills; and on October 17, 1986, the Congress gave final
approval to the landmark immigration bill as it moved toward
adjournment. By a vote of 63 to 24, the Senate agreed to the
compromise bill, clearing the measure for action by President
Reagan. The chief sponsor of the legislation, Senator Alan K.
Simpson, Republican of Wyoming, said President Reagan "awaits
this bill and has agreed to sign it." President Reagan proposed similar legislation in 1981 to tighten control of the
borders and to curtail the influx of illegal aliens.

The Immigration Reform and Control Act of 1986 marks a
historic change in American immigration policy. Under current law, illegal aliens may be deported, but it is generally
not illegal for employers to hire them. Under the new bill,
employers who hired illegal aliens would be subject to civil
penalties ranging from $250 to $10,000 for each such alien.
The aliens bill, a product of nearly a decade of work in Congress, would make the biggest changes in immigration law in at
least 20 years. Senator Phil Gramm, Republican of Texas, led
the opposition. He denounced the bill's amnesty for illegal
aliens. In addition, he said it was "outrageous" that under
one section, illegal aliens who had done only 90 days of agricultural work in this country could eventually become permanent
residents. "I want to do what the founding fathers envisioned
the Senate would do," Senator Gramm said. "I want to have a
real debate on this." The provisions granting legal status
to foreign agricultural workers were drafted by Representative
Charles E. Schumer, Democrat of Brooklyn. They were adopted by

the House and accepted by a House-Senate conference committee. The provisions were part of a delicately balanced compromise that revived the bill after it was pronounced dead just three weeks before. The bill had broad bipartisan support. It was sponsored in the House by Representatives Peter W. Rodino, Jr., of New Jersey and Romano L. Mazzoli of Kentucky, both Democrats.

The number of illegal aliens in the United States is disputed. Jeffrey S. Passel, a demographer at the Census Bureau, has stated that the Bureau estimated there were 2.5 million to 3.5 million illegal aliens who had their usual residence in the United States at the time of the last census in 1980. The Bureau estimates that the number of illegal aliens has grown since then by 100,000 to 300,000 a year, so the total now probably stands at three million to five million. These figures do not include the thousands of illegal aliens who go back and forth across the border, working in the United States but returning to permanent residences in Mexico or other countries.

The Immigration Reform and Control Act of 1986 is a milestone in the history of American immigration policy. In Colonial times, immigration was generally encouraged. The first Federal restriction on immigration was not adopted until 1875, when Congress barred the admission of prostitutes and convicted criminals. The new bill ranks in importance with the Quota Act of 1921, which established the first numerical restrictions on immigration, and the Immigration and Nationality Act of 1952, the McCarran-Walter Act, which listed dozens of ideological and other reasons for excluding aliens. Under the bill, aliens in the United States illegally could apply for legal status in the one-year period starting six months after the bill becomes law. Then, after 18 months as lawful temporary residents, the aliens could apply for status as permanent residents, and after another five years they could apply for citizenship. If the illegal aliens did not seek legal status, they would remain subject to deportation. Members of Congress and lobbyists said that two factors added impetus to the drive for a comprehensive immigration bill this year. First, they said, liberals feared that any such bill adopted by the next Congress would be more restrictive and less generous to illegal aliens. In addition, in the last few months, the Reagan Administration has argued that the bill was needed to help combat drug smuggling. Immigration officials said that many illegal aliens and smugglers of aliens were involved in illicit drug traffic.

Main Provisions of the
Immigration Reform and Control Act
of 1986

• Employers would be forbidden to hire illegal aliens. The ban would apply to all employers, even those with just a few employees. For a first offense, the employer would be subject to a civil penalty of $250 to $2,000 for each illegal alien hired. For subsequent offenses, the employer would be subject to civil penalties as high as $10,000 for each.

• For a "pattern or practice" of violations, the employer would be subject to criminal penalties, up to a $3,000 fine and six months' imprisonment.

• Employers would have to ask all job applicants for documents, such as a passport or a birth certificate and driver's license, to confirm that they were either citizens or aliens authorized to work in the United States. The employer is not required to check the authenticity of the document. The bill says it does not authorize issuance or use of national identification cards.

• The Government would offer legal status to aliens who entered the United States illegally before January 1, 1982, and have resided here continuously since then. For five years, they would be ineligible for welfare, food stamps and most other Federal benefits, with some exceptions.

• The Federal Government will set aside $1 billion a year for four years to reimburse state governments for providing public assistance, health care and education to illegal aliens who gain legal status.

• Under a special program, illegal aliens who worked in American agriculture for at least 90 days in the period from May 1, 1985, to May 1, 1986, could become lawful temporary residents of the United States. After two years in that status, they could become permanent residents, eligible for American citizenship after five years more.

• If there is a shortage of seasonal farm workers, the Government could admit additional aliens in the fiscal years 1990 through 1993. They would have to work in agriculture and, after three years as temporary residents, could become permanent residents.

• Immigration officers could not enter a farm without a search warrant or the owner's permission if they wanted to question a person believed to be an alien.

• Employers would be forbidden to discriminate against legal aliens because of their national origin or citizenship status. A new office would be established in the Justice Department to investigate complaints of such discrimination.

• States would generally have to verify, through records of the Immigration and Naturalization Service, the legal status of aliens seeking welfare benefits, Medicaid, unemployment compensation, food stamps, housing assistance or college aid under Federal programs.

• To improve enforcement, the Immigration and Naturalization Service would receive $422 million more in the current fiscal year and $419 million extra next year. The agency's budget last year was $593.8 million, of which $379.7 million was for enforcement.

The bill also envisions a 50 percent increase in Border Patrol personnel although there is no guarantee Congress would actually provide money for the increase. At present, the Border Patrol has 3,694 officers. President Ronald Reagan signed the Immigration Reform and Control Act of 1986 into law on November 6, 1986.

The New American Immigration

I. AMERICAN IMMIGRATION BEFORE 1965: HISTORY AND BACKGROUNDS

1. Abbott, Edith. *Historical Aspects of the Immigration Problem. Select Documents.* Chicago: University of Chicago Press, 1926.

   Covers the period of the "old immigration" before 1882, when the control of immigration was assumed by the federal government.

2. ———. *Immigration: Select Documents and Case Records.* Chicago: University of Chicago Press, 1924. Reprint. New York: Arno Press, 1969.

   Documents related to passage, admission, exclusion, and expulsion of aliens, and domestic migration problems, many of them involving women from a wide range of European countries. All aspects of immigration are examined by an eminent sociologist, who served as dean of Chicago's School of Social Service Administration.

3. Archdeacon, Thomas J. *Becoming American: An Ethnic History.* New York: The Free Press, 1983.

4. Bennett, Marion T. *American Immigration Policies: A History.* Washington, D.C.: Public Affairs Press, 1963.

5. Bernard, William S., ed. *Americanization Studies: The Acculturation of Immigrant Groups into American Society* [Commissioned by the Carnegie Corporation, 1920-1921]. Reprint. Montclair, N.J.: Patterson Smith, 1971. 10 vols.

   Vol. I: *Schooling of the Immigrant.* By Frank V. Thompson, with a general introduction to the republished studies by William S. Bernard and a new introduction by Clarence Senior; Vol. II: *America via the Neighborhood.* By John Daniels, with a new introduction by Florence G. Cassidy; Vol. III: *Old World Traits Transplanted.* By William I. Thomas, together with Robert E. Park and

3

Herbert A. Miller, with a new introduction by Donald R.
Young; Vol. IV: *A Stake in the Land*. By Peter A. Speek,
with a new introduction by Rabel J. Burdge and Everett M.
Rogers; Vol. V: *Immigrant Health and the Community*. By
Michael M. Davis, Jr., with a new introduction by Raymond
F. O'Dowd; Vol. VI: *New Homes for Old*. By Sophonisba P.
Breckinridge, with a new introduction by William S. Bernard;
Vol. VII: *The Immigrant Press and Its Control*. by Robert E.
Park, with a new introduction by Read Lewis; Vol. VIII:
Americans by Choice. By John Palmer Gavit, with a new
introduction by William S. Bernard; Vol. IX: *The Immi-
grant's Day in Court*. By Kate Holladay Claghorn, with a
new introduction by Ann S. Petluck; Vol. X: *Adjusting
Immigrant and Industry*. By William M. Leiserson, with a
new introduction by Gerd Korman. See review of series,
Milton Gordon, *Social Forces* 54 (December 1975): 470-474.

6. Berthoff, Rowland T. *British Immigrants in Industrial
    America, 1790-1950*. Cambridge, Mass.: Harvard University
    Press, 1953.

    A history of how English, Scottish, and Welsh immigrants
    have fared economically and socially in the United States
    based entirely on primary source materials. The British
    immigrants, as skilled workers, soon filled the higher
    paid jobs in textiles, iron, and steel and moved on to
    management and ownership when other immigrants took their
    place. Since they spoke the same language as the native-
    born, the assimilation was easier and quickly leveled
    social barriers.

7. Blegen, Theodore. *Norwegian Migration to America*. 2 vols.
    Northfield, Minn.: Norwegian-American Historical Associa-
    tion, 1931-1940. Reprint. New York: Arno Press, 1969.

    A massive history encompassing all facets of Norwegian
    immigration to the United States with considerable material
    on the Norwegian immigrant family.

8. Boody, Bertha. *A Psychological Study of Immigrant Chil-
    dren at Ellis Island*. Baltimore: Williams & Wilkins,
    1926. Reprint. New York: Arno Press, 1970.

    An examination of immigrant children in 1922 (August
    and September) and 1923 (July and August) with review of
    procedures at Ellis Island, literature on immigrant testing,
    and application of conclusions to Immigration Law of 1924.
    Conclusion: "The smaller number of immigrants arriving,
    the more careful selection at the source, the lower quotas
    for races which have come to this country in the last

few years, in numbers impossible of assimilation, the
opportunity for more intensive physical and mental examination on arrival, and for greater leisure in getting
the facts necessary to determine the fitness of the
individual, all give promise of the establishment of
improved conditions throughout the country." Originally,
Ph.D. dissertation, Johns Hopkins University, 1924.

9. Bowers, David F., ed. *Foreign Influences in American
    Life.* Princeton, N.J.: Princeton University Press,
    1944.

    Foreign contributions to American values and institu-
    tions. See, particularly, Stow Persons, "The Americaniza-
    tion of the Immigrant." Essays largely concern the im-
    pact of immigrants on American society.

10. Brace, Charles Loring. *The Dangerous Classes of New York
    and Twenty Years Among Them.* 3rd ed. New York:
    Wynkoop and Hallenbeck, 1880.

    Charles Loring Brace (1826-1890), one of the founders
    of the Children's Aid Society, describes his work among
    the poor (largely the immigrant Irish) of the city,
    "classes with inherited pauperism and crime." See also
    Emma Brace, *The Life of Charles Loring Brace, Chiefly
    Told in His Own Letters* (1894), and Charles R. Henderson,
    *Introduction to the Study of Dependent, Defective and
    Delinquent Classes* (2nd ed., 1901).

11. Buenker, John D., and Nicholas C. Burckel. *Immigration
    and Ethnicity: A Guide to Information Sources.* Detroit,
    Michigan: Gale Research, 1977.

12. Carpenter, Niles. *Immigrants and Their Children.* U.S.
    Bureau of the Census, Census Monograph, No. 7. Wash-
    ington, D.C. Government Printing Office, 1927.

    Statistical analysis of the distribution of immigrants,
    spatial demography, residence, national origins, race,
    sex, language, age, marriage patterns, citizenship,
    occupations. See also E.P. Hutchinson, *Immigrants and
    Their Children* (1956), an updating of the Carpenter data.
    Reference should also be made to *Catalogs of the Bureau
    of the Census Library* (Washington, D.C.), which include
    some 323,000 cards. (Boston: G.K. Hall, 1976-1981.)
    20 vols.

13. Chotzinoff, Samuel. *A Lost Paradise.* New York: Alfred
    A. Knopf, 1955.

Immigrant life in the Lower East Side (New York City) Jewish community. Extraordinarily rich in the details of everyday life and one of the most important immigrant memoirs.

14. Commons, John R. *Races and Immigrants in America*. New York: Macmillan, 1907.

Surveys the historical evolution of the American demography and analyzes the role of immigrants in industry, labor, crime, poverty, and politics. Illustrates the assimilationist outlook of many prominent intellectuals and reformers of the era.

15. Cordasco, Francesco, ed. *A Bibliography of American Immigration History: The George Washington University Project Studies*. Fairfield, N.J.: Augustus M. Kelley, 1977.

Includes "An Introductory Bibliography for the History of American Immigration, 1607-1955"; and "An Annotated Bibliography on the Demographic, Economic and Sociological Aspects of Immigration."

16. ———. "Charles Loring Brace and the Dangerous Classes. Historical Analogues of the Urban Black Poor." *Journal of Human Relations*, 20 (3rd Quarter, 1972): 379-386.

On Charles Loring Brace (1826-1890), one of the founders of the Children's Aid Society, and the author of *The Dangerous Classes of New York and Twenty Years Work Among Them* (1872).

17. ———. "The Children of Immigrants in the Schools: Historical Analogues of Educational Deprivation." *Journal of Negro Education*, 42 (1973): 3-12.

"In the effort to respond to the immigrant child, it is important to note at the outset that no overall programs were developed to aid any particular immigrant group. Although there was little agreement as to what Americanization was, the schools were committed to Americanize (and to Anglicize) their charges. Ellwood P. Cubberley's *Changing Conceptions of Education* (1909), which Lawrence A. Cremin characterizes as 'a typical progressive tract of the era,' saw the new immigrants as 'illiterate, docile, lacking in self-reliance and initiative, and not possessing the Anglo-Teutonic conceptions of law, order, and government ...' and the school's role was (in Cubberley's view) 'to assimilate and amalgamate.'"

18. ──────. *Immigrant Children in American Schools: A
    Classified and Annotated Bibliography. With Selected
    Source Documents.* Fairfield, N.J.: Augustus M. Kelley,
    1976.

    Incorporates some 1,500 entries in a classified plan:
    (I) Basic References, General History, and Immigration;
    (II) The Immigrant Child and His World; (III) Selected
    Source Documents: Edward L. Thorndike, The Elimination
    of Pupils from School (1908); The Education of the Immi-
    grant (1913); State Americanization (1919); The Problem
    of Adult Education (1920). See Review, S.M. Tomasi,
    International Migration Review, 12 (Summer 1978): 277-278.

19. ──────. *The Immigrant Woman in North America: An Anno-
    tated Bibliography of Selected References.* Metuchen,
    N.J.: Scarecrow Press, 1985.

    An introductory bibliography on immigrant women from
    the vast number of titles that exist on the immigrant
    experience in the United States. The 1200 entries come
    from most disciplines and reach across a wide socio-
    historical spectrum. Contents include: I. Bibliography
    and General Reference, interpreted broadly to include
    major ethnic group studies. II. Autobiographies, Biog-
    raphies, and Reminiscences, allowing immigrant women to
    tell their own stories. III. The Workplace and Political
    Encounters. IV. The Immigrant and Progressive Reformers,
    in which immigrant women assume the veiled but dynamic
    roles that explain the industrial expansion of America
    and illuminate the wellsprings of the humanitarian reform
    movements in the United States, with its organized phil-
    anthropy, charity agents, and Settlement House reformers.
    V. The Family, Immigrant Child, and Educational Influences,
    a focal point for themes of assimilation and enforced
    acculturation better measured (in the long view) in the
    immigrant child's encounters with the larger society and
    its schools. VI. Miscellanea, a collection of inter-
    related entries that cut across categorical lines. With
    a Foreword by Rose Basile Green.

20. ──────. *Jacob Riis Revisited: Poverty and the Slum in
    Another Era.* New York: Doubleday, 1968.

    Selections from three books by the Danish immigrant
    social reformer, Jacob August Riis (1849-1914): *How the
    Other Half Lives* (1890); *The Children of the Poor* (1892);
    and *A Ten Years' War: An Account of the Battle with the
    Slums in New York* (1900). Includes considerable material
    on the immigrant family, particularly Irish and Italian.

See also Louise Ware, *Jacob A. Riis* (New York: D. Apple-
ton-Century, 1939). The Jacob A. Riis Collection, Museum
of the City of New York, is a rich collection of memora-
bilia of the era.

21. ————. *"Street Arabs and Gutter Snipes."* *Journal of
     Human Relations,* 20 (3rd Quarter, 1972): 387-390.

On George C. Needham's *Street Arabs and Gutter Snipes*
(1884), slum life in the late nineteenth-century American cities, the immigrant family, and neglected and desti-
tute children.

22. ————, and David N. Alloway. *American Ethnic Groups:
     The European Heritage. A Bibliography of Doctoral
     Dissertations Completed at American Universities.*
     Metuchen, N.J.: Scarecrow Press, 1981.

A bibliography of over 1400 dissertations which deal
with American ethnic groups of European origin. The
ethnic groups included are identified in the conceptual
design which sets up two major geographical areas of
origin, *i.e.,* (I) Western and Northern Europe; (II) Central, Southern, and Eastern Europe. Some of the included
groups are the Irish, French, Portuguese, Dutch, Norwegian,
Swedish, Danish, Finnish, German, Hungarian, Italian,
Greek, Polish, Russian, Jewish, and other Slavic-language
groups. Beyond the two geographical areas of origin
(each with appropriate subdivisions), the volume includes
sections on (III) Multi-Group, Interethnic, and Related
Studies; (IV) Emigration/Immigration: History, Politics,
Economics and Policy; (V) Miscellanea; and (VI) A Checklist of Selected Published Bibliographies. An Index of
Names and a Subject Index are provided, both are keyed to
entry numbers (continuous throughout) assigned to the
dissertations arranged alphabetically by author in each
of the sections. The bibliographical information for
each dissertation is as follows: author, title; conferring university; year; pagination; and (when available)
the *Dissertation Abstracts* volume and page number.
Most entries are annotated.

23. ————, and Eugene Bucchioni. *The Italians: Social
     Backgrounds of an American Group.* Clifton, N.J.:
     Augustus M. Kelley, 1974.

Sources drawn from the period circa 1880-1940. Part
I: Emigration: The Exodus of a Latin People; Part II:
Italian Communities in America. *Campanilismo* in the
Ghetto; Part III: Responses to American Life; Part IV:

Employment, Health, and Social Needs; Part V: Education:
The Italian Child in the American School. Includes 16
contemporary photographs and an annotated bibliography.

24.   ———, and Rocco G. Galatioto. "Ethnic Displacement in
       the Interstitial Community: The East Harlem Experience."
       Phylon: The Atlanta University Review of Race & Culture,
       31 (Fall 1970): 302-312.

   "East Harlem [New York City] is an interesting area.
   Most minority groups have lived there at one time or
   another; however, the ideal melting pot never melted
   substantially. The immediate scope of this paper is to
   trace the movement of the largest ethnic groups through
   this area from 1900 to 1960. These groups are Italians,
   Jews, Puerto Ricans, and Negroes. The aim of this paper
   is to document and establish probable reasons for the
   change in East Harlem from a 'Little Italy' to a so-called
   Spanish Harlem, and eventually to an extension of Negro
   Harlem. East Harlem housed during the 1920s the largest
   Italian immigrant community in the United States. We
   will attempt to explain and trace the growth of the
   Italian population and its replacement by Puerto Ricans
   and Negroes, with some notice of the Jewish subcommunity
   which slowly withdrew from the area."

25.   ———, and Thomas M. Pitkin. *The White Slave Trade
       and the Immigrants*. Detroit, Michigan: Blaine Ethridge,
       1981.

   Delineates the historical contents (largely from contemporary sources) in which the white slave trade existed
   in the period of the great migrations to the United
   States. The account begins in 1902 and includes a source
   document, "Importation and Harboring of Women for Immoral Purposes." A select bibliography and note on immigration literature are included.

26.   Davis, Allen F., and Mark H. Haller, eds. *The Peoples
       of Philadelphia: A History of Ethnic Groups and Lower-
       Class Life, 1790-1940*. Philadelphia: Temple University
       Press, 1973.

   Includes "The Immigrant and the City: Poles, Italians,
   and Jews in Philadelphia, 1870-1920"; "Philadelphia's
   Jewish Neighborhoods"; and "Philadelphia's South Italians
   in the 1920's."

27.   Diner, Hasia R. *Erin's Daughters in America: Irish Im-
       migrant Women in the Nineteenth Century*. Baltimore:

The Johns Hopkins University Press, 1983.

Described here are thousands of Irish women who saw in
America the chance to utilize the energy, ambition, and
ability that would otherwise have been stifled by the
poverty and social inflexibility of their native land.
Erin's Daughters in America follows these women from an
Ireland devastated by the Great Famine of the 1840s to
their new homes in the United States. Hasia Diner explores their post-immigration family life, their work
and education, their battles against poverty, alcoholism,
and mental illness, and the network of formal and informal
ethnic organizations that developed to help them adjust
to a different way of life. Diner also discusses the
stress that the immigrant women's newly found social and
economic independence put on already frail relationships
with Irish men. In terms of marriage, work, educational
achievement, and upward mobility, Irish women were very
different from--and much more successful than--other
female immigrants. Diner describes that success in detail, but her primary emphasis is on the qualities that
enabled Irish women to prosper in a new and challenging
world. The origins of those qualities, she argues, can
be found only in Ireland, in a cultural tradition that
the immigrant women could neither live within nor leave
behind them.

28. Dinnerstein, Leonard, Roger L. Nichols, and David M.
      Reimers. *Natives and Strangers: Ethnic Groups and the
      Building of America.* New York: Oxford University
      Press, 1979.

    Integrates the experiences of racial, religious, and
    ethnic minorities into the mainstream of American history.
    See review, F. Cordasco, *The Annals*, 444 (July 1979);
    178-179.

29. ———, and David M. Reimers. *Ethnic Americans: A His-
      tory of Immigration and Assimilation.* New York: Harper
      & Row, 1975.

    Concentrates on non-English immigrants, with particular
    emphasis on the period after 1840. Important materials
    on ethnic conflict and immigration restriction; ethnic
    background of the American population; and provisions
    of major U.S. immigration laws and programs.

30. Divine, Robert A. *American Immigration Policy, 1924-1952.*
      New Haven, Connecticut: Yale University Press, 1957.
      Reprint. New York: DaCapo, 1972.

31. Ehrlich, Richard L., ed. *Immigrants in Industrial
     America, 1850-1920*. Charlottesville: University Press
     of Virginia for the Eleutherian Mills-Hagley Foundation
     and Balch Institute, 1977.

     The major theme is the persistence of pre-migration
     patterns, habits, and values in an American setting.
     Moreover, the family emerges as the primary mechanism
     for perpetuating the pre-migration culture. Immigrant
     groups differed in their family structure, in their
     attitude toward daughters and wives working outside the
     home, and in the appropriate economic contribution of
     children. In coping with the urban, industrial setting,
     the immigrants employed strategies which minimized the
     upheavals in their family networks and values. At the
     same time, family and kinship ties displayed a remarkable
     ability to adapt to changing needs. The essays by Golab
     on Philadelphia Poles; Yans-McLaughlin on Buffalo
     Italians; Hareven on Manchester, New Hampshire French-
     Canadians; and Carole Groneman on Irish and German women
     in New York emphasize the importance of the family in
     the migration process.

32. Glazer, Nathan, and Daniel Patrick Moynihan. *Beyond the
     Melting Pot: The Negroes, Puerto Ricans, Jews, Italians,
     and Irish of New York City*. 2nd ed. Cambridge, Mass.:
     M.I.T. Press, 1970.

     An influential study of American ethnic groups with
     special reference to the twin themes of the persistence
     of ethnicity in the United States and the emergence of
     the "new ethnicity." Appeared originally in 1963; the
     1970 edition incorporated a 90-page introduction, "New
     York City in 1970."

33. Goddard, Henry M. "Mental Tests and the Immigrant."
     Journal of Delinquency, 2 (1917): 253-277.

     See also the author's *Feeble-Mindedness and Immigration*
     (Training School Bulletin, vol. 9, no. 6, 1912): and
     Human Efficiency and Levels of Intelligence (Princeton
     University Press, 1920). Goddard served as director of
     studies of hereditary feeblemindedness at the Training
     School at Vineland, N.J. See also Goddard's *The Kallikak
     Family: A Study in the Heredity of Feeblemindedness*
     (1912); and his *School Training of Defective Children*
     (1914). In a study for the U.S. Public Health Service at
     Ellis Island in 1912, Goddard reported that, based upon
     his examination of the "great mass of average immigrants,
     83 percent of Jews, 80 percent of Hungarians, 79 percent

of Italians, and 87 percent of Russians were feeble-
minded." ["The Binet Tests in Relation to Immigration,"
Journal of Psychoanalysis, 18 (1913): 105-117].

34. Hale, Frederick, ed. *Danes in North America*. Seattle:
     University of Washington Press, 1984.

     Documents the stories of Danes who left their European
     homeland, mostly in the latter half of the nineteenth
     century, for the promise of America. In little-explored
     archives and repositories throughout Denmark, Hale has
     searched for and translated letters written by Danes
     (both men and women) in America to friends, family, and
     hometown newspapers in Denmark. Although collections
     of both Swedish and Norwegian immigrant correspondence
     have long been valuable standard works in the field, no
     similar compilation of Danish immigrant experience, as
     told in scores of personal letters, has been available.
     Each chapter addresses a major theme or aspect of life
     in nineteenth-century America. Through letters, Danes
     share their observations and opinions of the New World.
     They tell of crossing the Atlantic in crowded ships,
     the summer heat of Iowa, having picnics in Chicago's
     magnificent parks, reaching the Mormon "Zion" in Utah,
     championing Bryan against McKinley in 1896, and traveling
     with small children to join a husband on the vast
     Canadian plains.

35. Handlin, Oscar. *Boston's Immigrants*. Cambridge, Mass.:
     Harvard University Press, 1941; rev. ed., 1959. New
     York: Atheneum, 1968.

     Actually a study of acculturation, with emphasis on
     the Irish immigrant community.

36. ———. *The Uprooted: The Epic Story of the Great Migra-
     tions That Made the American People*. Boston: Little,
     Brown, 1951; 2nd ed., 1973.

     The immigrant urban experience and its background with
     perceptive assessments of immigrant family adjustment.
     An epic narrative of the life of immigrants; the ocean
     crossing, work, religion, generational differences,
     conflict/acculturation, and restriction.

37. ———, Carl Wittke, and John Appel, advisory eds. *The
     American Immigration Collection*. 41 vols. New York:
     Arno Press/New York Times, 1969.

     A massive reprint program of basic materials on the
     history of American immigration. Also (Series II), Victor

Greene, Oscar Handlin, and John Appel, advisory eds., *The American Immigration Collection*, 33 vols. (1970).

38. Hansen, Marcus Lee. *The Immigrant in American History.* Cambridge, Mass.: Harvard University Press, 1941.

Also, Hansen's influential *The Problem of the Third Generation Immigrant* (Rock Island, Ill.: Augustana Historical Society, 1938); and Eugene L. Bender and George Kagiwada, "Hansen's Law of 'Third Generation Return' and the Study of American Religio-Ethnic Groups," *Phylon*, 29 (Winter 1968): 360-370.

39. ————. *The Problem of the Third Generation Immigrant.* Rock Island, Ill.: Augustana Historical Society, 1938.

A historical interpretation of migration with special reference to the problems confronting the historian in his study of the third-generation immigrant. The third-generation immigrants develop a spontaneous and almost irresistible interest in their common heritage. Hansen was concerned with how to direct this interest toward the development of the receiving country.

40. Harney, Robert F., and J.V. Scarpaci, eds. *Little Italies in North America.* Toronto: The Multicultural History Society of Ontario, 1981.

The essays in this volume were originally prepared for a conference in the spring of 1979 under the auspices of the University of Toronto's Ethnic and Immigration Studies Program and the Multicultural History Society of Ontario. The American Little Italies discussed were those of Chicago, New York, Philadelphia, Baltimore, the canal town of Oswego in upstate New York, Tampa, New Orleans, and St. Louis. For Canada, Little Italies in Toronto, Montreal, and Thunder Bay were described. The cities were chosen to show some of the variety of settlement in the United States and Canada as well as to contrast the Italian-Canadian and Italian-American experiences. The editors were interested in seeing if they "could limn more precisely the ways in which such variables as the size of each Italian colony, the predominant *paesi* of origin of the settlers in each, and the magnitude and nature--in ethnic groups--and the attitude toward immigrants of the host city or regional ecosystem, affected immigrant settlements and the subsequent Italian ethno-culture."

41. Hartmann, Edward. *The Americanization of the Immigrant.*
     New York: Columbia University Press, 1948.

     A study of the "Americanization Crusade" initiated at
     the opening of World War I and continuing into the post-
     war era which drew its leadership from the intelligentsia,
     the educators and social workers, the industrialists,
     and from business and civic groups generally. Invaluable
     data on urban immigrant subcommunities. Massive bibliog-
     raphy and documentation.

42. Higham, John. *Send These to Me: Immigrants in Urban
     America.* Baltimore, Maryland: The Johns Hopkins Uni-
     versity Press, 1984.

43. ————. *Strangers in the Land: Patterns of American
     Nativism, 1860-1925.* Corrected with a new Preface.
     New York: Atheneum, 1973.

     American attitudes toward immigrants and immigration.
     See also the author's *Send These to Me: Jews and Other
     Immigrants in Urban America* (1975), much broader than
     its title suggests, and particularly, "Chapter 10: Ethnic
     Pluralism in Modern American Thought" (pp. 196-230),
     which includes an incisive commentary on family adapta-
     tion.

44. Hoglund, A. William. *Finnish Immigrants in America.*
     Madison: University of Wisconsin Press, 1960.

     Basic source on the Finnish community in America. A
     full portrait of the Finnish immigrant community (with
     valuable vignettes of women's roles) and its evolving
     acculturation.

45. ————. *Immigrants and Their Children in the United
     States: A Bibliography of Doctoral Dissertations,
     1885-1982.* New York: Garland Publishing, 1986.

46. Howe, Irving. *World of Our Fathers: The Journey of the
     East European Jews to America and the Life They Have
     Found and Made.* New York: Harcourt Brace Jovanovich,
     1975.

     The East European Jews in the United States, 1880 to
     the present. See the review of Theodore Solotaroff,
     New York Times Book Review, February 1, 1976. A vast
     panoramic portrait of the immigrant community. A social
     and cultural history of the East European Jewish community
     in New York City. See a critique-essay review by Leon
     Wieseltier, *New York Review of Books,* July 15, 1976.

47. Hutchinson, E.P. *Legislative History of American Immigration Policy, 1798-1965.* Philadelphia: University of Pennsylvania Press, 1981.

Intended to be a reference source on Congressional attitudes toward immigration from 1798-1965. Presents a chronological account of all bills dealing with aliens that were brought before the Congress and provides summaries of the discussion surrounding them and their final disposition. Covers an immense amount of material. The scope requires that discussions be limited. Although it is not definitive, the book serves as a useful guide to anyone seeking to identify the major areas of Congressional concern. Prior to the second half of the nineteenth century, policy governing immigration was primarily in the hands of the states. State law determined the restrictions governing alien entry into the United States. The area where federal policy first impinged on immigrants' naturalization is identified. Uniform national policies for acquiring citizenship long preceded Congressional regulation of the flow of foreigners into the country. There was also a body of national law governing the conditions of travel for immigrants generally known as "steerage legislation." The problem of state versus federal jurisdiction was not resolved until 1882 when national responsibility for immigration law was clearly established. The federal government then embarked on an elaborate system of regulation. Criminals and those likely to become public charges were among the excludable classes since colonial days. The latter part of the nineteenth century saw the expansion of this category to include mental defectives, prostitutes, polygamists, and others deemed morally unfit. Race becomes a basis for exclusion during this period as do political beliefs thought to be subversive. The latter has remained a constant in immigration law since that time. Regulation of immigration led to restriction in the period following World War I. Ceilings on immigration appeared in the 1920s along with the national quota system that remained until 1965. By 1929, "Congress had developed a quite highly evolved legislative structure for the regulation and numerical restriction of immigration, supplemented with the selective exclusion of certain classes of aliens and provision for the deportation of aliens considered undesirable."

48. Jones, Maldwyn Allen. *American Immigration.* Chicago: University of Chicago Press, 1960; rev. ed., 1970.

A richly textured history, and one of the best intro-
ductions to the history of the migrations to America.

49. Joseph, Samuel. *History of the Baron De Hirsch Fund:
     The Americanization of the Jewish Immigrant*. New
     York: Baron De Hirsch Fund, 1935. Reprint. With a
     new Introduction by Philip S. Cohen and Francesco
     Cordasco. Fairfield, N.J.: Augustus M. Kelley, 1976.

     A documented account of a half-century of a philan-
     thropic program aimed at "the adjustment and assimilation
     of the immigrant Jewish population ... [through] relief,
     temporary aid, promotion of suburban industrial enter-
     prises, removal from urban centers, land settlement,
     agricultural training, trade and general education."
     Illustrations and texts of documents.

50. ————. *Jewish Immigration to the United States, 1881-
     1910*. New York: Columbia University Press, 1914.

     The fullest study of its kind. Invaluable data and
     sources on the Jewish immigrant community and patterns
     of acculturation and adjustment.

51. Kastrup, Allan. *The Swedish Heritage in America: The
     Swedish Element in America and American-Swedish Rela-
     tions in Their Historical Perspective*. Minneapolis:
     Swedish Council of America, 1975.

     The contributions and major events in the American-
     Swedish experience. A massive (863 pp.) catalogue of
     broad themes and detailed narrative, with detailed
     notices of the immigrant family.

52. Kessner, Thomas. *The Golden Door: Italian and Jewish
     Immigrant Mobility in New York City, 1880-1915*. New
     York: Oxford University Press, 1977.

     Compares the social and residential mobility patterns
     of the two groups and finds that, while Jews fared
     better than Italians, both groups experienced significant
     progress over two generations. Also discusses similari-
     ties and difference between New York and other cities
     with regard to evolving social mobility. See review,
     F. Cordasco, *Educational Studies*, 9 (Spring 1978): 86-89.

53. Kraut, A.M. *The Huddled Masses: The Immigrant in American
     Society, 1880-1921*. Arlington Heights, Illinois: Harlan
     Davidson, Inc., 1982.

54. Miller, Wayne C., et al. *A Comprehensive Bibliography for the Study of American Minorities*. New York: New York University Press, 1976. 3 vols.

    Includes 29,300 entries, the most comprehensive biblio-graphical coverage of American ethnic groups extant, and includes references to more specialized bibliographies for every ethnic group. Vol. 3 assembles the historical-bibliographical essays preceding each section on in-dividual groups. See review, F. Cordasco, *Contemporary Sociology*, 6 (September 1977): 594-595.

55. Mindel, Charles H., and Robert W. Habenstein, eds. *Ethnic Families in America: Patterns and Variations*. New York: Elsevier Scientific Publishing, 1976.

    This collection is designed to fill a gap in the literature on ethnic and other minority group family styles in America. Most of the contributors are members of the group about which they are writing. In addition to brief introductory and concluding chapters by the editors, consists of fifteen original essays, of which only two appear in other books. Of the four sections of the book, the first, "early ethnic minorities," contains essays by Helena Z. Lopata on the Polish; Harry H.L. Kitano and Akemi Kikumura on the Japanese; Francis X. Femminella and Jill S. Quanago on the Italians; Ellen Horgan Biddle on Irish-Catholics; and Lucy Jen Huang on the Chinese. The second section, "recent and continuing ethnic minorities," contains essays by Abdo A. Elkholy on the Arabs; George A. Kourvetaris on the Greeks; and Joseph P. Fitzpatrick on Puerto Ricans. The third sec-tion, "historically subjugated but volatile ethnic minorities," includes essays by Robert Staples on Blacks; John N. Price on North American Indians, and David Alverez and Frank Bean on Mexicans. The concluding section, "socioreligious ethnic minorities," is comprised of essays by Gertrude Enders Huntington on the Amish; Laurence French on the French; Bernard Farber, Charles H. Mindel, and Bernard Lazerwitz on the Jews; and Bruce L. Campbell and Eugene E. Campbell on the Mormons.

56. Neidle, Cecyle S. *American Immigrant Women*. Boston: G.K. Hall, 1975. Reprint. New York: Hippocrene Books, 1976.

    Surveys the contribution of immigrant women to American social and political development. Beginning in the colonial period, the author details the deeds of wives and daughters of the British settlers. In later chapters focuses on groups from continental Europe and concludes with a brief treatment of successful professional women in the mid-twentieth century. Chapters, which cover the peak period of European immigration, record the activities of mainly Irish and Jewish women in the trade-union movement.

57. Pitkin, Thomas M. *Keepers of the Gate: A History of Ellis Island*. New York: New York University Press, 1975.

Ellis Island (one of the islets off the New Jersey shore of the Upper Bay of New York City) was the principal gateway for millions of immigrants to America. Formally inaugurated as a federal immigration station on January 1, 1892, it continued to function until March 4, 1955. Pitkin's history is the "administrative side of the Ellis Island story." See review, F. Cordasco, *Italian Americana*, 2 (Autumn 1975): 121-125. See also Ann Novotny, *Strangers at the Door: Ellis Island, Castle Garden, and the Great Migration to America* (Riverside, Conn.: Chatham Press, 1971); Ludovico Caminata, *Nell'Isola delle Lagrime: Ellis Island* (New York: Stabilimento Tipografico Italia, 1924); Edward Corsi, *In the Shadow of Liberty: The Chronicle of Ellis Island* (New York: Macmillan, 1937); and B. Severn, *Ellis Island: The Immigrant Years* (New York: Simon and Schuster, 1971).

58. Riis, Jacob A. *How the Other Half Lives: Studies Among the Tenements of New York*. New York: Charles Scribner's Sons, 1890.

A panorama of urban destitution and the social world of the immigrant child by the Danish immigrant social reformer, Jacob August Riis (1859-1914). An edition of *How the Other Half Lives* (New York: Dover Press, 1951) includes 100 photographs (taken by Riis) from the Jacob A. Riis Collection of the Museum of the City of New York, and should be consulted. Since printers had not yet perfected the halftone process of reproducing photographs in 1890, Riis's photographs in *How the Other Half Lives* and in his other books were redrawn by artists.

59. Rischin, Moses, ed. *Immigration and the American Tradition*. Indianapolis: The Bobbs-Merrill Company, 1976.

60. Roberts, Peter. *The New Immigration: A Study of the Industrial and Social Life of Southeastern Europeans in America*. New York: Macmillan, 1912.

The "new" immigration was that movement to America of the peoples of Southern Europe, which began in a small way in the early eighties and continued unabated until the imposition of immigration restrictions in the 1920s. Deals with the inducements that led to emigration and first impressions of the immigrant; industrial life; community conditions (with special attention to the immigrant woman and family); social relations; assimilation and hindrances.

61. Saveth, Edward N. *American Historians and European Immigrants, 1875-1925.* New York: Columbia University Press, 1948. Reprint. New York: Russell & Russell, 1965.

The development of racism in America with special references to immigrants. Ideas of racial superiority which were developed in the nineteenth century and traced in writings of Theodore Roosevelt, Woodrow Wilson, and twentieth-century historians. Bibliographies include (1) writings by historians; (2) writings about historians; (3) general references. See also Saveth, "Race and Nationalism in American Historiography: The Late Nineteenth Century," *Political Science Quarterly*, 64 (September 1939): 421-441.

62. Seller, Maxine S., ed. *Immigrant Women*. Philadelphia: Temple University Press, 1981.

The only comprehensive sourcebook on the American immigrant woman. The book's strength lies in the use of primary source materials: "Using documents written by immigrant women themselves, or by others who knew them intimately, *Immigrant Women* offers a different perspective, a woman-centered perspective on American immigration history" (Intro.). Contents: I. Why They Came; II. Surviving in a New Land; III. Work; IV. Family; V. Community Life; VI. Education; VII. Social Activists; VIII. Daughters and Granddaughters; Bibliographical Essay.

63. ———. *To Seek America: A History of Ethnic Life in the United States.* Englewood, N.J.: Jerome S. Ozer, 1977.

A history of immigrant life in America. Particularly Chapter 6: "The Urban Ghetto: Immigrants in Industrial America, 1880-1924"; and Chapter 7: "Progressive America: Home, School, and Neighborhood," which includes a section on the immigrant woman. Excellent bibliographical essay.

64. Taylor, Philip. *The Distant Magnet: European Immigra-
    tion to the U.S.A.* New York: Harper & Row, 1972.

    Both a history and an analysis of the patterns and
    significance of American immigration, with attention to
    evolving patterns of acculturation.

65. Thernstrom, Stephan, ed. *Harvard Encyclopedia of
    American Ethnic Groups.* Cambridge, Mass.: Harvard
    University Press, 1980.

    A guide to the history, culture, and distinctive char-
    acteristics of the more than 100 ethnic groups who live
    in the United States. The origins, history, and present
    situation of each ethnic group is described in detail.
    Not only the immigrants and refugees who came voluntarily,
    but also those already in the New World when the first
    Europeans arrived, those whose ancestors came involun-
    tarily as slaves, and those who became part of the Ameri-
    can population as a result of conquest or purchase and
    subsequent annexation are examined. The group entries
    are at the heart of the book, but it contains, in addi-
    tion, a series of thematic essays that illuminate the
    key facets of ethnicity. Some of these are comparative,
    some philosophical, some historical, and others focus
    on current policy issues or relate ethnicity to major
    subjects such as education, religion, and literature.
    American identity and Americanization, immigration policy
    and experience, and prejudice and discrimination in U.S.
    history are discussed at length. Several essays probe
    the complex interplay between assimilation and pluralism--
    perhaps the central theme in American history--and the
    complications of race and religion.

66. Thomas, William I., and Florian Znaniecki. *The Polish
    Peasant in Europe and America.* 5 vols. Boston:
    Richard G. Badger, 1918-1920. Reprint. Ed. by Eli
    Zaretsky. Urbana: University of Illinois Press, 1984.

    A classic work which alleges a disintegration of the
    Polish family in America. Essential for study of the
    Polish immigrant woman and family in America. See Her-
    bert Blumer, "Critiques of Research in the Social Sciences:
    An Appraisal of Thomas and Znaniecki's *The Polish Peasant
    in Europe and America*" (New York: Social Sciences Re-
    search Council, Bulletin 44, 1939); and Konstantin
    Symmons-Symonolewicz, "The Polish-American Community--
    Half a Century After *The Polish Peasant*," *The Polish
    Review*, 11 (Summer 1966): 67-73.

67. Tolzmann, Don Heinrich. *German Americana*. Metuchen,
     N.J.: Scarecrow Press, 1975.

     A comprehensive bibliography on most aspects of Ger-
     man-American history and life (including women and fam-
     ily). Includes listing of archives containing material
     on German-Americans.

68. U.S. Congress. Senate. *Report on the Condition of
     Women and Children Wage-Earners in the United States*.
     61st Cong. 2d sess. Senate doc. nos. 86-104. Wash-
     ington, D.C.: Government Printing Office, 1912. 19
     vols.

     An invaluable repository of data on "industrial,
     social, moral, educational, and physical condition" of
     women and children. Begun in 1907. The nineteen volumes
     are entitled as follows: 1. *The Cotton Textile Industry*;
     2. *Men's Ready-Made Clothing Industry*; 3. *The Glass In-
     dustry*; 4. *The Silk Industry*; 5. *Wage-Earning Women in
     Stores and Factories*; 6. *The Beginning of Child Labor
     Legislation*. Prepared by Elizabeth L. Otey; 7. *Conditions
     Under Which Children Leave School to Go to Work*;
     8. *Juvenile Delinquency and Its Relation to Employment*;
     9. *History of Women in Industry in the United States*.
     Prepared by Helen L. Sumner; 10. *History of Women in
     Trade Unions*. Prepared by John B. Andrews and W.D.P.
     Bliss; 11. *Employment of Women in Metal Trades*. Prepared
     by Lucian W. Chaney; 12. *Employment of Women in Laundries*.
     Prepared by Charles P. Neill; 13. *Infant Mortality and
     Its Relation to the Employment of Mothers*; 14. *Causes of
     Death Among Women and Child Cottonmill Operatives*. Pre-
     pared by Arthur R. Perry; 15. *Relation Between Occupation
     and Criminality of Women*. Prepared by Mary Conyngton;
     16. *Family Budgets of Typical Cottonmill Workers*. Pre-
     pared by Wood F. Worcester and Daisy W. Worcester;
     17. *Hookworm Disease Among Cottonmill Operators*. Prepared
     by Charles W. Styles; 18. *Employment of Women and Children
     in Selected Industries*; 19. *Labor Laws and Factory Con-
     ditions*.

69. United States Immigration Commission. *Report of the
     Immigration Commission*. (61st Congress, 2nd and 3rd
     Sessions). Washington: Government Printing Office,
     1911. 41 vols.

     Abstracts, vols. 1-2. Includes statistical review of
     immigration; emigration conditions in Europe; dictionary
     of races and peoples; immigrants in industries; immigrants
     in cities, occupations of immigrants; fecundity of

immigrant women; children of immigrants in schools;
immigrants as charity seekers; immigration and crime;
steerage conditions; physical characteristics of descendants of immigrants; federal immigration legislation;
state immigration and alien laws; other countries, statements and recommendations. *The Index of Reports of the
Immigration Commission* (S. Doc. No. 785, 61st Congress,
3rd Session) was never published. The *Report* was restrictionist in its basic recommendations, and the
chairman of the Commission was Senator William P. Dillingham. The *Report* is summarized in Jeremiah W. Jenks and
W. Jett Lauck, *The Immigration Problem: A Study of Immigration Conditions and Needs* (New York: Funk & Wagnalls,
1912; 6th ed., 1926). Isaac A. Hourwich, *Immigration
and Labor: The Economic Aspects of European Immigration
to the United States* (New York: G.P. Putnam Sons, 1912;
2nd ed., 1922), subsidized by the American Jewish Committee, was a statistical attack on the Commission's
Report.

70.   ———. *Report of the Immigration Commission.* 41 vols.
       Washington: Government Printing Office, 1911. *The
       Children of Immigrants in Schools*, vols. 29-33. Repub-
       lished with an introductory essay by Francesco Cordasco.
       Metuchen, N.J.: Scarecrow Reprint Corp., 1970.

       The five-volume report is a vast repository of data on
       immigrant children (analyses of backgrounds, nativity,
       school progress, home environments, etc.). In all,
       2,036,376 school children are included (in both public
       and parochial schools in 37 cities). Also, data on
       32,882 students in higher education and 49,067 public
       school teachers. "The purpose of the investigation was
       to determine as far as possible to what extent immigrant
       children are availing themselves of educational facilities
       and what progress they make in school work."

71.   Vecoli, Rudolph J. "European Americans: From Immigrants
       to Ethnics." *International Migration Review*, 6 (Winter
       1972): 403-434.

       An analysis of immigration historiography. Also, with
       some change, in William H. Cartwright and Richard L.
       Watson, eds., *The Reinterpretation of American History
       and Culture* (1973), pp. 81-112.

72.   Wheeler, Thomas C., ed. *The Immigrant Experience: The
       Anguish of Becoming an American.* New York: Dial, 1971.

       Immigrant narratives in conflict and acculturation and
       the maintenance of cultural identity.

73. Wirth, Louis. *The Ghetto*. Chicago: University of Chicago Press, 1928.

    A classic study of Jews in Chicago. See also Albert J. Reiss, Jr., ed., *Louis Wirth on Cities and Social Life* (1964); and Amitai Etzioni, "The Ghetto--A Re-evaluation," *Social Forces*, 37 (March 1959): 255-262, which uses Wirth's *Ghetto* to explore the shift of ethnicity from a basis in the ecological community to a reference group concept.

Immigrant Archives and Collections

74. The Balch Institute. (18 South Seventh St., Philadelphia, Pa. 19106).

    An educational institution devoted to North American immigration, ethnic, racial, and minority group history. The Institute comprises a museum and library whose seven-point program includes: (1) library programs; (2) exhibitions; (3) educational programs; (4) outreach programs; (5) internal research; (6) information coordination; (7) Bicentennial planning. The Institute plans to assemble the nation's most comprehensive collection of books, manuscripts, and printed materials concerning all national groups who came to North America. Plans call for a library of 400,000 volumes; 20 million manuscripts; 20,000 reels of microfilm; and large numbers of ethnic and minority group newspapers. The Institute is supported by the late Mrs. Emily Swift Balch and her sons, Edwin Swift Balch and Thomas Willing Balch.

75. Center for Migration Studies. (209 Flagg Place, Staten Island, New York, N.Y. 10304).

    A specialized library on migration and a card catalogue of books, articles, and dissertations on migration. Particularly strong (at the present time, it is the most comprehensive collection) in Italian-American materials. Publishes *The International Migration Review*, a scientific journal studying sociological, demographic, historical, and legislative aspects of migration. Maintains connections with Centro Studi Emigrazione (Via Dondolo, 58, Roma, Italia), a Center staffed by the Society of St. Charles, a religious order ministering to migrants since 1887, which publishes *Studi Emigrazione*.

76. ———. (Brooklyn College, City University of New York).

    Organized to "assist scholars in the social sciences, education, humanities, and related fields in the collection, preservation, and anaylsis of primary and secondary materials for the study of the migration processes." The Archives of Migration "will solicit manuscripts, photographs and taped autobiographies and interviews with significant persons involved in various aspects of migration."

77. Immigration History Research Center. University of Minnesota (826 Berry Street, St. Paul, Minnesota 55114).

    An international center for the collection and preservation of the historical records of immigrants who came to the United States and Canada. See Rudolph J. Vecoli, "The Immigrant Studies Collection of the University of Minnesota," *American Archivist*, 32 (April 1969): 139–145.

78. Museum of the City of New York. (Fifth Ave. at 103rd St., New York City, N.Y. 10029).

    A very rich collection of memorabilia, photographs, and other materials, particularly strong for the period 1880 through 1920. Includes the Jacob A. Riis Collection and the Byron Collection, rich photographic archives of immigrant life in New York City. Many of the photographs of the Riis Collection have appeared in editions of Riis's books (q.v.). Many of the Byron photographs are reproduced in Grace M. Mayer, *Once Upon a City* (1958); Roger Whitehouse, New York: *Sunshine and Shadow* (1974); John A. Kowenhoven, *The Columbia Historical Portrait of New York* (1953); and Oscar Handlin, *Statue of Liberty* (1971).

79. New York Public Library. (Fifth Avenue and 42nd St., New York, N.Y. 10018).

    The general collections contain extensive materials on American ethnic groups. Invaluable for New York City immigrant archives; also, collections of papers and letters in the Library's Manuscript Division, *e.g.*, the papers and letters of Gino Charles Speranza (1872–1927), a major figure in the early history of the Italian immigrant community; the letterbooks and scrapbooks of Joseph Barondess, a Jewish immigrant leader who in 1904 ran unsuccessfully as a candidate for Congress; the papers of the social reformer Lillian Wald (1867–1940); and the unpublished manuscripts of the Italian political reformer Carlo Tresca.

II. AMERICAN IMMIGRATION AFTER 1965:
GENERAL STUDIES AND RELATED REFERENCES

80. Abrams, Elliott, and Franklin S. Abrams. "Immigration Policy--Who Gets in and Why." *The Public Interest*, 80 (Winter 1975): 3-29.

81. Abrams, Franklin S. "American Immigration Policy: How Strait the Gate?" *Law and Contemporary Problems*, 45 (Spring 1982): 107-135.

82. Adler, Jerry. "The New Immigrants." *Newsweek* (July 7, 1980): 26-31.

83. Aguirre, Benigno E. "Differential Migration of Cuban Social Races." *Latin American Research Review*, 11 (1976): 103-124.

84. ———, et al. "The Residential Patterning of Latin American and Other Ethnic Populations in Metropolitan Miami." *Latin American Research Review*, 15 (1980): 35-63.

85. "Aid to Cuban Refugees." *Interpreter Releases*, 38 (April 27, 1961): 110-113.

86. Alba, Francisco. "Mexico's International Migration as a Manifestation of Its Development Pattern." *International Migration Review*, 12 (Winter 1978): 502-513.

   Summarizes the views on the broader structural determinants of the illegal flow held by Mexican scholars. In the first section, some of the aspects of the country's economic and technological structures are examined; in the second, certain features of the modernization process are dealt with; in the third, an analysis is made of one component of the Mexican migratory flow into the United States; in the last, the migratory flow, seen in the context of the system of "peripheral" and "central" economies, is discussed.

87. ——. *La población de México: Evolución y dilemas.*
    México City: El Colegio de México, 1977.

    Describes the characteristics and the development of
    the Mexican population and society. Chapter 3 deals with
    emigration to the United States and Chapter 5 with in-
    ternal migration and urban concentration.

88. Alcantara, R. *Sakada: Filipino Adaptation in Hawaii.*
    Lanham, Maryland: University Press of America, 1981.

89. Alisky, Marvin. "U.S.-Mexican Relations: More Than Wet-
    backs, Drugs, Tourists, and Spicy Food." *Intellect*
    (February 1978): 292-94.

90. Allen, D.G. MacDonald. "Entry into the United States of
    America." *Solicitors Journal*, 127 (October 21, 1983):
    690-692.

91. Allen, James P. "Recent Immigration from the Philip-
    pines." *Geographical Review*, 67 (1977): 195-208.

    Traces the changes in Filipino immigration in the
    1970s, noting its more recent professional composition.
    Most immigrants are close relatives of people already in
    the United States and are welcomed into tightly-knit com-
    munities not generally visible to other Americans.
    California is the preferred settlement site.

92. Allman, James. "Estimates of Haitian International Migra-
    tion for the 1950-1980 Period." *Occasional Papers
    Series*, Dialogue No. 2, Miami: Latin American and
    Caribbean Center, Florida International University,
    March 1981. Pp. 1-20.

93. ——. "Haitian Migration: 30 Years Assessed." *Migra-
    tion Today*, 10 (1982): 7-12.

94. Amaro, Nelson, and Alejandro Portes. "Una sociología
    del exilio: Situación de los grupos Cubanos en Estados
    Unidos." *Aportes: La revista de Estudios Latino-
    americanos*, 23 (January 1972): 6-24.

95. Andersen, K. "The New Ellis Island." *Time* (June 13,
    1983): 18-26.

    Describes Los Angeles as America's new melting pot.
    More than 90,000 foreign immigrants settled there during
    1982, and since early 1970, more than 2 million, mostly
    Hispanic, Asian and Middle Eastern.

96. Anderson, Jervis. "A Reporter at Large: The Haitians of New York." *New Yorker* (March 31, 1975): 50-75.

     An overview of "The Silent Minority" in New York City, looking into their distrust of any government and their fear for relatives left in Haiti. Haitian culture and characteristics are explored through discussions of a recent Haitian Cultural Festival at the American Museum of Natural History and interviews with various Haitian immigrants. Discusses the policy of immigration officers in New York who are arresting Haitians and the problems of housing, jobs, and language which most Haitians face.

97. Archdeacon, Thomas J. "Problems and Possibilities in the Study of American Immigration and Ethnic History." *International Migration Review*, 19 (Spring 1985): 112-134.

     In the study of the history of immigration and ethnicity scholars very often write about their own ethnic groups. That pattern has led to an overemphasis on the new immigrants of the early twentieth century, a limitation of focus to the experiences of the first and second generations of individual immigrant groups, and a disinterest in immigration and ethnicity as processes. Efforts to produce comparative studies of various kinds and to use survey data as a source of primary information about later generations may help correct those shortcomings.

98. Archor, Shirley. *Mexican Americans in a Dallas Barrio.* Tucson: University of Arizona Press, 1978.

     Presents an interesting model of "cultural responses" to the ecology of culture in the larger community. The model, a two-by-two table, simplifies the dynamics of the process of mobilization, insulation, alienation, and accommodation.

99. Arguelles, Lourdes. "Cuban Miami: The Roots, Development, and Everyday Life of an Emigré Enclave in the U.S. National Security State." *Contemporary Marxism*, 5 (Summer 1982): 27-43.

100. Arizpe, Lourdes. "The Rural Exodus in Mexico and Mexican Migration to the United States." *International Migration Review*, 15 (Winter 1981): 626-649.

     In the 1950s, labor conditions in the United States attracted Mexican migrants, mostly from rural areas, in

sharply fluctuating patterns of active recruitment,
laissez-faire or repatriation. Because these two movements have varied simultaneously and because they are
interrelated, it has been assumed that the rural exodus
in Mexico generally explains the flow of migrants across
the border to the United States. Argues that they must
be analyzed instead as two distinct movements. Data
presented show that most of the migrants created by the
prevailing conditions in Mexican rural villages settle
within Mexico, and that only specific types of migrants
are attracted over the border.

101. Ashabranner, B. *The New Americans: Changing Patterns
     in U.S. Immigration.* New York: Dodd, Mead & Company,
     1983.

     Written for young readers. Describes the changing
     patterns in U.S. immigration and discusses their impor-
     tance now and in the years ahead. Primarily, however,
     the book offers an in depth look at today's immigrants
     in America, including refugees and illegal aliens, often
     using direct quotations.

102. Ashmun, L.F. *Resettlement of Indochinese Refugees in
     the United States: A Selective and Annotated Bibliog-
     raphy.* Occasional Paper No. 10. DeKalb: Northern
     Illinois University, Center for Southeast Asian
     Studies, 1983.

     Bibliography is an extensive resource guide that
     serves both lay persons and scholars concerned with
     the resettlement of Indochinese refugees in the United
     States. Variety of printed material from 1975 to 1981
     is included.

103. Azicri, Max. "The Politics of Exile: Trends and Dy-
     namics of Political Change Among Cuban-Americans."
     Cuban Studies, 11-12 (July 1981-January 1982): 55-73.

104. Bach, Robert L., et al. "The Flotilla 'Entrants':
     Latest and Most Controversial." Paper presented at
     Population Association of America Annual Meeting,
     Washington, D.C., March 26-28, 1981.

     Presents information on the individual and social
     backgrounds of the latest Cuban emigrants. Examines
     the public perception of these "entrants," the number
     and nature of those who admitted to having a prison
     record, and compares this group to the previous waves of
     Cuban exiles.

105. ————. "Mexican Immigration and the American State." *International Migration Review*, 12 (Winter 1978): 536-558.

An attempt to place the contemporary situation in historical perspective, showing how the American state permitted and indeed had to permit illegal immigration to meet its various commitments to different sectors of capital and labor. Outlines the historical dialectics which made illegal immigration the direct consequence not of the weakness but of the strength of U.S. organized labor.

106. ————. "Mexican Immigration and U.S. Immigration Reforms in the 1960's." *Kapitalistate*, 7 (1978): 63-80.

107. ————. "The New Cuban Exodus: Political and Economic Motivations." *Caribbean Review*, 11 (Winter 1982): 22-25, 58-60.

108. ————. "The New Cuban Immigrants: Their Background and Prospects." *Monthly Labor Review*, 103 (October 1980): 39-46.

109. Baker, R.P., and David S. North. *The 1975 Refugees: Their First Five Years in America*. Washington, D.C.: New TransCentury Foundation, 1984.

Using the data of "The 1975 Indochinese Evacuee Master File," Alien Registration Numbers issued by INS and Alien Registration Cards filed by refugees in 1978-1980, the authors explore in depth the characteristics of the 1975 Cohort and their experiences in the U.S.

110. Baldwin, B.C. *Capturing the Change: The Impact of Indochinese Refugees in Orange County: Challenges and Opportunities*. Santa Ana, California: Immigrant and Refugee Planning Center, 1982.

Report of a project of the Fluor Foundation to help Indochinese refugees find employment in Orange County, California, to become self-reliant, financially secure, and accepted into the American community.

111. ————. *Patterns of Adjustment: A Second Look at Indochinese Resettlement in Orange*. Orange, California: Immigrant and Refugee Planning Center, 1985.

Presents a comprehensive insight into the progress of refugee settlement in Orange County. The results of

interviews with employers, residents, and refugees were
compiled in four critical areas of study: employment;
education; welfare dependency; and Americanization/
community adjustment.

112. Balseiro, Jose Agustin, ed. *Presencia Hispanica en la
     Florida.* Miami: Ediciones Universal, 1976.

113. Barkan, E.R. "Whom Shall We Integrate? A Comparative
     Analysis of the Immigration and Naturalization Trends
     of Asians Before and After the 1965 Immigration Act
     (1951-1978)." *Journal of American Ethnic History*, 3
     (1983): 29-57.

     Asks whom we have integrated within America culturally,
     socially, civically, and in terms of national identifi-
     cation. Focuses on selected demographic characteristics
     of Asians (Middle Easterners, Far Easterners and Indians)
     --the regional group that went from 5 percent of all new
     citizens in fiscal year 1951 to 39 percent in 1978.

114. ————, and R.M. O'Brien. "Naturalization Trends Among
     Selected Asian Immigrants, 1950-1976." *Ethnic Forum*,
     4 (Spring 1984): 91-108.

     Studies the naturalization patterns since 1958 among
     Asian immigrants who were permitted to become citizens
     in less than the usual five years because of special
     familial circumstances or as a result of joining the
     U.S. armed forces.

115. Beegle, J. Allan, et al. "Demographic Characteristics
     of the United States-Mexico Border." *Rural Sociology*,
     25 (1960): 107-62.

116. Bender, Lynn Darrell. "The Cuban Exiles: An Analytical
     Sketch." *Journal of Latin American Studies*, 5 (Novem-
     ber 1973): 271-278.

117. ————. "The Cuban Exiles: *Gusanos* or *Mariposas*?"
     Revista/Review Interamericana, 9 (Fall 1979): 331-334.

118. Bennett, Marion T. *American Immigration Policies: A
     History.* Washington, D.C.: Public Affairs Press, 1963.

119. Bentley, J. *American Immigration Today: Pressures,
     Problems, Policies.* New York: Julian Messner, 1981.

     Explains the current immigration law and shows how it
     works in practice. Stories of recent immigrants reveal

the difficulties and challenges. Reviews pending legislation proposals and explores the personal and economic
effects.

120. Bentz, T. *New Immigrants: Portraits in Passage*. New
York: The Pilgrim Press, 1981.

Records the stories of eleven immigrant families and
two Americans who work with immigrants. Gerard Jean-
Juste, a priest, speaks of Haitian poverty and brutality
of Haitian dictator Jean-Claude Duvalier and of the
Haitians' adjustment to life in the United States.
Stories are recorded of immigrants from Cuba, Mexico,
Chile, Korea, China, Vietnam, Laos, the Philippines,
and Samoa.

121. Bernard, T.L. "United States Immigration Laws and the
Brain Drain." *International Migration*, 8 (1970):
31-38.

One of the many factors which have stimulated the
immigration of Brain Drain personnel into the United
States has been the enactment of the Immigration and
Nationality Act of 1965. In place of the national
quotas, the new immigration laws have substituted a
series of "preference categories," each of which has
set numerical limitations. The one most pertinent
from the Brain Drain point of view is the "third preference" category, which "consists of qualified immigrants
who are members of the professions or who, because of
their exceptional ability in the sciences or the arts,
will substantially benefit the national economy, the
cultural interests or the welfare of the United States."

122. Bernard, William. "Immigrants and Refugees: Their
Similarities, Difference and Needs." *International
Migration*, 14 (1976): 267-281.

123. Bogre, Michelle. "Haitian Refugees: [Haiti's] Missing
Persons." *Migration Today*, 7 (September 1979): 9-13.

124. Boiston, Bernard G. "The Simpson-Mazzoli Bill—The
First Major Immigration Bill in Thirty Years." *Ohio
State Bar Association Report*, 55 (October 11, 1982);
1738.

125. Bonacich, Edna, et al. "Koreans in Business." *Society*,
14 (1977): 54-59.

Observes that Koreans are the third largest group of

immigrants, just behind Mexicans and Filipinos. Unlike
the Asian immigrants of the past, they are well educated,
have often lived in cities and run small businesses, and
are intent on making use of a highly organized network
of compatriots.

126. ————. "The Political Economy of the New Immigration
      from Asia." Paper presented at the Seventy-fifth
      Annual Meeting of the American Sociological Associa-
      tion, New York, August 27, 1980.

      Presents an overall model of immigration to developed
      capitalist countries and then develops a checklist of
      things that need to be looked at in analyzing the new
      immigration from Asia to the United States.

127. Boodhoo, Ken I. "The Problems of Haitian Refugees in
      the United States." *Occasional Papers Series*, Dia-
      logue No. 6. Miami: Latin American and Caribbean
      Center, Florida International University, August 1982.
      Pp. 23-31.

128. Borjas, George J. "The Labor Supply of Male Hispanic
      Immigrants in the United States." *International
      Migration Review*, 17 (Winter 1983/84): 653-671.

      Studies have begun the systematic analysis of the
      labor market characteristics of Hispanics in the United
      States. Research has focused on two related issues:
      (a) how the immigration and assimilation experience
      affects Hispanic earnings; and (b) the measurement of
      wage differentials between Hispanics and non-Hispanics.
      The main findings of this research are that the earnings
      of (some) Hispanic immigrants rise rapidly after immigra-
      tion; and that the wage differential between Hispanics
      and non-Hispanic whites is generally due to differences
      in observable skill characteristics. This article ex-
      tends previous research by focusing on another market
      characteristic: the labor supply of Hispanic immigrants.

129. Boswell, Thomas D. "In the Eye of the Storm: The Con-
      text of Haitian Migration to Miami, Florida." *South-
      eastern Geographer*, 23 (November 1983): 57-77.

130. ————. "The New Haitian Diaspora: Florida's Most Re-
      cent Residents." *Caribbean Review*, 11 (Winter 1982):
      18-21.

131. ————, and James R. Curtis. *The Cuban-American Ex-*

perience: Culture, Images and Perspectives. Totowa,
N.J.: Rowman and Allanheld, 1984.

Contents: *Cubans in Contemporary American Society*:
Cuban Americans as an Ethnic Minority; A National View
of Cuban-Americans • *Cuba: Revolution and Change*: A
Historical Perspective; The Period of Spanish Domina-
tion; The Period of United States Influence; The Castro
Revolution; Major Social Changes Since Castro • *History
of Cuban Migration to the United States*: The Early
Trickle; Period of the "Golden Exiles"; Missile Crisis
Hiatus; Period of Freedom Flights; The Interlude from
1973 to 1980; The Flood from Mariel; Summary of Historical Trends • *Cuban Settlement in the United States:
Patterns and Processes*: Concentration in a Few States
and Large Cities; The Return Flow to Miami; Ethnic
Segregation • *Miami: Cuban Capital of America*: Growth
and Expansion of the Cuban Population; An Economic En-
clave; The Cultural Landscape of Little Havana • *A Demo-
graphic Profile of the Cuban-American Population*: Cuban-
Americans, Spanish-Americans, and Non-Spanish Americans;
Florida, New Jersey, New York and Other Origins • *Lan-
guage and Religion* • *Cuban-American Artistic Expression*:
Music; The Visual Arts; Creative Literature; Theater and
Dance • *Cuisine and Foodways*: Historical Roots of Cuban
Cuisine; The Cuban-American Diet; Grocery Stores and
Restaurants • *Politics and Ideology*: Exile Politics;
United States Politics; Cuban Municipalities in Exile •
*The Cuban-American Family and Youth: Acculturation and
Assimilation*: The Cuban-American Family; Cuban-American
Youth; The Question of Assimilation.

132. Bouvier, Leon F. *Immigration and Its Impact on U.S.
Society*. Washington, D.C.: Population Reference
Bureau, 1981.

133. ————. *The Impact of Immigration on U.S. Population
Size*. Washington, D.C.: Population Reference Bureau,
1981.

This report examines how future U.S. population size
might vary according to different levels of net immigration, also taking into account varying possible trends
in future fertility. The results should be of value to
decision-makers concerned with U.S. immigration and
population policy. During the nineteenth and much of
the twentieth century, natural increase accounted for a
substantial portion of all population growth. Recently,
the contribution of net immigration has increased con-

siderably. If both legal and illegal entries are included, close to half of all growth can now be attributed
to net immigration. This is even greater than the impact
of immigration on U.S. population growth in the late
nineteenth century and first decade of this century,
when waves of European immigrants arriving in the United
States in search of a new life totaled as high as one
million in some years.

134. Boyd, Monica. "The Changing Nature of Central and
      Southeast Asian Immigration to the United States:
      1961-1972." *International Migration Review*, 8 (Winter
      1974): 507-519.

135. ————. "Immigration Policies and Trends: A Comparison
      of Canada and the United States." *Demography*, 13
      (1976): 83-104.

      Outlines some of the similarities and differences.
      Despite a common emphasis on labor needs and the desira-
      bility of reuniting families, the two countries differ
      in the importance they place on immigration's economic
      contribution. Canada gives preference to job prepara-
      tion, while the United States assigns most of its
      numerical limit to family members. The United States
      limits its immigration, letting people in if they fit
      into a permitted category. Canada uses immigration as
      an important part of its economic programs, raising and
      lowering the limits as conditions change. Canada's im-
      migration policy and administration are relatively cen-
      tralized, but the United States assigns responsibilities
      to several offices and agencies.

136. ————. "Occupations of Female Immigrants and North-
      American Immigration Statistics." *International
      Migration Review*, 10 (1976): 73-80.

137. ————. "Oriental Immigration: The Experience of the
      Chinese, Japanese, and Filipino Populations in the
      United States." *International Migration Review*, 5
      (Spring 1971): 48-61.

138. Bracker, Milton. "Bitter, Frustrated, Divided: Cuba's
      Refugees." *New York Times Magazine* (April 21, 1963):
      7, 106-109.

139. ————. "Cuba's Refugees Live in Hope--and Despair."
      New York Times Magazine (September 30, 1962): 21,
      84-87.

140. Bradshaw, Benjamin S., and W. Parker Frisbie. "Poten-
      tial Labor Force Supply and Replacement in Mexico and
      the States of the Mexican Cession and Texas: 1980-
      2000." *International Migration Review*, 17 (Fall 1983):
      394-409.

      Efforts to anticipate and account for future migration
      patterns hinge on an examination of the potential for
      the supply, demand, and replacement of labor. In
      Mexico, the projected number of males entering the labor
      force will be about 48 percent larger in the 1980s than
      in the 1970s, and entrants will outnumber departures by
      a labor force replacement ratio of 407 to 100—a fifty-
      year high. Fertility declined significantly in Mexico
      in the 1970s, and the number of new entrants to the labor
      force ages in the 1990s will decline; the replacement
      ratio is projected to be about 330 to 100—a decrease
      of 19 percent. It seems very unlikely, even allowing
      for renewed rapid growth in Mexico's economy, that new
      job opportunities can be created to accommodate such an
      enormous influx to the job market. Accommodations may
      be made more difficult because of increasing expectations
      of workers.

141. Brana-Shute, Rosemary. *A Bibliography of Caribbean
      Migration and Caribbean Immigrant Communities*.
      Gainesville, Florida: University of Florida Center
      for Latin American Studies, 1983.

      Containing 2,585 citations and 339 pages, this book
      is an attempt to bring together pertinent historical and
      contemporary literature dealing with the massive migra-
      tion of peoples into, within, and out of the Caribbean
      region. The physical area covered, defined geographically
      and culturally, includes the Caribbean archipelago and
      its linguistic groups, as well as the mainland terri-
      tories of Belize, Guyana, Suriname, and French Guiana.
      Citations include references to books, anthologies,
      articles in the academic and popular press, and govern-
      mental reports in the following languages: English,
      French, Spanish, Dutch, German, Italian, Slovak, Polish,
      and Welsh. Both published and unpublished work are cited.
      An attempt has been made to reference all disciplines
      and topics, including international migration, intra-
      regional migration, the impact of migration on the
      sending and receiving societies, rural out-migration
      and urbanization. Works dealing with the African slave
      trade have been excluded. Arranged alphabetically by
      author. There are four appendices providing cross

references for second authors, origins of migrants, destinations of migrants, and a topical index. Two additional appendices list the data bases searched and the journal titles cited.

142. "Bridling at a U.S. Immigration Bill." *Business Week* (February 28, 1983): 43-44.

143. Briggs, Vernon M., Jr. "Alien Migration from Mexico: The Search for an Appropriate Theory and Policy." Paper presented at the Southern Economic Association, Atlanta, Georgia, November, 1976.

"Reviews some of the theoretical explanations, offered by economists to explain the increasing participation of alien workers in the United States labor force and to evaluate critically the policy recommendations that flow from each such explanation."

144. ———. *Chicanos and Rural Poverty.* Baltimore, Maryland: The Johns Hopkins University Press, 1973.

145. ———, et al. *The Chicano Worker.* Austin, Texas: University of Texas Press, 1977.

In their effort to identify the characteristics of the Chicano population, the authors draw from an impressive array of source material as well as available Census data. To list a few of the major points of interest, the reader is provided with an historical perspective of habitation in the United States, an identification of the cultural differences of the subject population, a breakout of incomes from several perspectives, and a solid interpretation of educational biases.

146. ———. "Employment Trends and Contemporary Immigration Policy." In Nathan Glazer, ed. *Clamor at the Gates: The New American Immigration.* San Francisco, California: Institute for Contemporary Studies, 1985. Pp. 135-160.

"The absence of any serious effort to forge an immigration policy based upon labor market consideration means that immigration policy today functions as a 'wild card' among the nation's array of key labor market policies. Unlike all other elements of economic policy (*e.g.*, fiscal policy, monetary policy, employment and training policy, education policy, and anti-discrimination policy) where attempts are made by policymakers to orchestrate the diverse policy elements into a harmony of action to

accomplish particular objectives, immigration policy
has been allowed to meander aimlessly. This is a situation that no sensible nation can allow to continue."

147. —————. "Immigration." *Labor Law Journal,* 28 (August
1977): 495–500.

148. —————. *Immigration Policy and the American Labor Force.*
Baltimore, Maryland: The Johns Hopkins University
Press, 1985.

Since the late 1970s and early 1980s, the United
States has been in the midst of the largest influx of
immigrants in its history. During this period, argues
Vernon Briggs, political considerations have dominated
contemporary immigration policy, with little concern
for their labor market implications. Charts the evolution of U.S. immigration policies toward all types of
immigrants—legal immigrants, illegal immigrants,
refugees, non-immigrant workers, border commuters—and
analyzes the impact of these policies upon American
labor practices. Calls for a comprehensive policy
reform and proposes a number of alternative options,
including the establishment of immigration ceilings
that are flexible and responsive to the nation's employment trends and a return to occupational preferences
as the basis for allowing immigrants to enter the country. "The real issue, which is the thesis of this work,
is that the immigration policy of the United States has
been allowed to function without regard to its economic
consequences."

149. —————. *Mexican Migration and the U.S. Labor Market.*
A Mounting Issue for the Seventies. Austin, Texas:
Center for the Study of Human Resources and the Bureau
of Business Research of the University of Texas,
1975.

Analysis of the effects of U.S. labor, immigration,
and border policies, along with their effect on employment and labor problems of the seventies and suggestions
for alternative courses of action. An expanded version
of a paper presented at the First International Conference on Migrant Workers sponsored by the International
Institute of Management of Berlin, Federal Republic of
Germany, in December 1974. Statistics indicate the
magnitude of Mexican migration over time. Includes an
examination of characteristic features of the two categories, legal immigrants and illegal aliens.

150.   ──────, and Marta Tienda, eds. *Immigration Issues and
        Policies*. Salt Lake City, Utah: Olympus Publishing
        Co. [1985].

        The proceedings of a 1984 conference on immigration
        and the American economy sponsored by the National Coun-
        cil on Employment Policy. Included are contributed
        papers by Robert Bach, George Borjas, Vernon Briggs, and
        Marta Tienda as well as discussant comments by Philip
        Martin, Douglas Massey, and Michael Piore.

151.   Brintnall, D. "Guatemalan Refugees in the United
        States: An Overview." Paper presented at American
        Anthropological Association. 83rd Annual Meeting.
        Denver, Colorado, November 14-18, 1984.

        There are an estimated 55,000 Guatemalan refugees in
        the United States and more coming. Based on interviews
        with refugees, as well as a review of relevant litera-
        ture, presents an overview of the Guatemalan refugee
        situation in the United States, including the underground
        railroad, church sanctuary, threat of deportation, living
        conditions and social organizations. Examines the ques-
        tion of emerging ethnic relations in the new context of
        U.S. society.

152.   Brom, Thomas. "Haitians Jam the Gears at INS." *In
        These Times* (April 7-13, 1982): 7.

153.   Brook, K. "Patterns of Labor Force Participation and
        Employment in the U.S.-Mexican Border Countries,
        1970-1980." Paper presented at Western Social Science
        Association 26th Annual Meeting. San Diego, California,
        April 28, 1984.

        Examines the changing patterns of labor force partici-
        pation and employment in twenty-five counties located
        along the southeast border of the United States. It
        examines the data derived from the Census of the Popula-
        tion and concludes that the total and civilian partici-
        pation rates on the border remain below the national
        figures.

154.   Brookings Institution──El Colegio de Mexico. *Structural
        Factors in Mexican and Caribbean Basin Migration*.
        Proceedings of Brookings/Colegio Symposium, The
        Brookings Institution, Washington, D.C., 1978.

155.   Brown, Peter G., and Henry Shue, eds. *The Border That
        Joins: Mexican Migrants and U.S. Responsibility*.
        Totowa, N.J.: Rowman and Allanheld, 1983.

Hundreds of thousands of Mexican citizens now travel illegally back and forth across the 1,945-mile border stretching from the Pacific Ocean to the Gulf of Mexico, leaving home to seek work. U.S. treatment of these Mexican migrants has taken on enormous importance for both national governments and, of course, for the Mexican workers themselves and those Americans who may resist or welcome their coming. One of the most prominent suggestions is that the United States respond to the current illegal flow by legitimizing it through the creation of temporary worker programs. Are temporary worker programs desirable or feasible? How many workers should be permitted to come, and for how long? What benefits and protections should temporary workers be granted? What corresponding obligations should they incur? Controversial questions raised by proposed U.S.-Mexican temporary worker programs are examined in light of historical precedents, current labor patterns and conditions in both countries, and philosophical analyses of human rights and international obligations. Multidisciplinary experts drawn from Mexico, the United States, and Europe consider recent proposals against a background of seemingly similar programs, such as the *bracero* program earlier in this century and the European *Gastarbeiter* experience.

156. ———, and ———, eds. *Boundaries: National Autonomy and Its Limits.* Totowa, N.J.: Rowman and Littlefield, 1983.

Controversial questions raised by proposed U.S.-Mexican temporary worker programs are examined in light of historical precedents, current labor patterns and conditions in both countries, and philosophical analyses of human rights and international obligations. Rural development and unemployment in Mexico are analyzed as they bear upon the dimensions and direction of the migratory flow. Economists debate the impact of temporary worker programs on the American economy and on the employment prospects of America's own least-advantaged workers. And philosophers explore the basic moral principles that place ethical constraints on any proposed visa program.

157. Bruce, J. Campbell. *The Golden Door: The Irony of Our Immigration Policy.* New York: Random House, 1954.

158. Bruck, Connie. "Springing the Haitians." *The American Lawyer,* 4 (September 1982): 35-40.

159. Bruno, E. *Acculturation Difficulties of the Khmer in
       New York City*. New York: The Cambodian Women's Pro-
       gram, American Friends Service Committee, 1984.

       Provides a historical and cultural overview of the
       Khmer refugee movement and outlines in some detail the
       problems the refugees face upon resettlement in New York
       City. The focus is on the difficulties of the transi-
       tion of a people from Southeast Asia to the United States.

160. Bryce-Laporte, Roy S. "Archbishop McCarthy Defends
       Haitian Refugees." *Latin American Documentation*, 9
       (1979): 7-14.

161. ————. *The New Migrants: Their Origin, Visibility and
       Challenge to the American Public--Impact of the Immi-
       gration Act of 1965*. Washington, D.C.: Smithsonian
       Institution, Research Institute on Immigration and
       Ethnic Studies, 1976.

162. ————. "New York City and the New Caribbean Immigra-
       tion: A Contextual Statement." *International Migration
       Review*, 13 ((1979): 214-234.

       Calls New York City the Mecca of Caribbean immigrants
       and tourists. In 1976, almost 68 percent of the Domini-
       cans, 66 percent of the Haitians, and 53 percent of the
       Jamaicans settled in New York City. Suggests that New
       York's position as port of entry, its access to travel
       to the rest of the country, its supply of various job
       levels, and its image as a place relatively hospitable
       to blacks make it especially attractive.

163. ————, ed. *Sourcebook on the New Immigration*. New
       Brunswick, New Jersey: Transaction Books, 1980.

       Contains forty-three essays. Main essays are modified
       versions of a conference held by the Research Institute
       on Immigration and Ethnic Studies. They begin with a
       section which puts U.S. immigration patterns and policy
       into an historical context and end with a chapter on
       theoretical and methodological considerations. Inter-
       vening chapters develop implications for host societies
       and the immigrants themselves. More specified sub-
       divisions such as diplomatic, political, occupational,
       and public service concerns of the established sectors
       of the host society as distinguished from the concerns
       which relate to the native minorities are presented.
       Papers are grouped to deal with various reports on
       adaptations as distinct from examples of inter- and

intra-ethnic conflicts among the immigrants. The set of appendices includes proceedings of two public panels held at the conference and a background commentary.

164.   ————. "Visibility of the New Immigrants." *Society*, 14 (1977): 18-22.

Traces a "strong ethnocentric or racial bias among dominant groups in American society." Observes that new immigrants from the Orient and the Caribbean can hardly become invisible among Caucasian Americans. White native Americans tend to group them with other members of their race. Believes that their visibility will affect their life chances and choices.

165.   ————, and S.R. Couch. *Exploratory Fieldwork on Latino Migrants and Indochinese Refugees*. Washington, D.C.: Smithsonian Institution, 1976.

Deals with problems and kinds of research sponsored by RIIES (Research Institute on Immigration and Ethnic Studies). First section explores the kinds of data available from service organizations, the problems using it, as well as the problems and tensions faced by Latino migrants in California. The papers call for major efforts by researchers to collect primary data about migrants from the migrants themselves and a type of research centering on organizations. Section Two focuses on the problems of data collection among the "distinctive" Indochinese refugees at Camp Pendleton, California.

166.   ————, and Delores M. Mortimer. *Caribbean Immigration to the United States*. Washington, D.C.: Smithsonian Institution, 1976.

Provides a glimpse of the range of thought and concern of many Caribbean immigrant scholars. Section One includes four papers prepared by members of the Institute staff or participants in its seminars. Part Two contains solicited papers and commentaries by some of the Caribbean-originated scholars now involved in on-going research about West Indian immigrants or related subjects, and Part Three is a selective bibliography of recent works in the field.

167.   Buchanan, Susan H. "Language and Identity: Haitians in New York City." *International Migration Review*, 13 (1979): 298-313.

Of the some 300,000 Haitians living and working in the
New York City area, most have arrived after 1968. Since
only 2 to 5 percent of the people in Haiti speak French,
most of the New York Haitians speak Creole. These two
languages are mutually unintelligible. Since French-
speaking people generally hold high status in Haiti,
the language difference mirrors and reinforces class
distinctions. In New York, language differences continue to divide Haitians in even more complex subgroup-
ings.

168. ————. "Scattered Seeds: The Meaning of Migration for
      Haitians in New York City." Unpublished Ph.D. disser-
      tation, New York University, 1980.

169. Buffenstein, D.R. "The Proposed Immigration Reform and
      Control Act of 1982: A New Epoch in Immigration Law
      and a New Headache for Employers." *Employee Relations
      Law Journal*, 8 (Winter 1982-3): 450-462.

170. Burton, Eve. "Surviving the Flight of Horror: The Story
      of Refugee Women." *Indochina Issues*, 34 (1983).
      Whole Issue.

171. Bushnell, John A., and Stephen E. Palmer, Jr. "Haitian
      Migration to the U.S." U.S. Department of State.
      Current Policy, No. 191 (June 17, 1980): 1-6.

172. Bustamente, Jorge. "Commodity Migrants: Structural
      Analysis of Mexican Immigration to the United States."
      In Stanley R. Ross, ed., *Views Across the Border: the
      U.S. and Mexico*. Albuquerque, New Mexico: University
      of New Mexico Press, 1978. Pp. 183-203.

173. ————. "Mexican Migration: The Political Dynamics of
      Perceptions." In *U.S.-Mexican Relations: Economic
      and Social Aspects*. Edited by C.W. Reynolds and
      C. Tello. Stanford, California: Stanford University
      Press, 1983. Pp. 259-276.

      Focuses on the public perception both in Mexico and
      the United States of the phenomenon of undocumented
      Mexican migration to the United States.

174. ————. "The Mexicans Are Coming: From Ideology to
      Labor Relations." *International Migration Review*, 17
      (Summer 1983): 323-341.

      In spite of the progress made in the identification
      and quantification of the socioeconomic characteristics

of the Mexicans migrating to the United States and the fact that there is a general consensus among the scientific community of both countries that the research findings of the last ten years have destroyed many of the myths surrounding this migratory phenomenon, there is still an enormous gap between the consensus of the researchers and public opinion as reflected in the mass communication media of both countries.

175. ——, and J.D. Cockroft. "Unequal Exchange in the Binational Relationship: The Case of Immigrant Labor." In *Mexican U.S. Relations: Conflict and Convergence.* Edited by Carlos Vásquez and Manuel Garcia y Griego. Los Angeles: University of California, Chicano Studies Research Center, 1983. Pp. 309-324.

In spite of recent changes, the underlying pattern of Mexican migration to the United States persists: strong demand for temporary immigrant labor by certain U.S. employers and an abundant supply of such labor in specific regions of Mexico. Explores the reasons for this and studies the results.

176. Butler, E.W., et al. "Migration to Baja California: 1900-1980." Paper presented at Western Social Science Association. 26th Annual Meeting. Denver, Colorado, November 14-18, 1984.

Presents an historical examination of migration patterns within the Republic of Mexico to Baja California. It utilizes data from 1900-1980 Republic of Mexico Censuses. Concludes that the only major policy impact on growth of Baja has been the *Bracero* program.

177. The Cabinet Committee on Opportunities for Spanish Speaking People. *The Spanish Speaking in the United States: A Guide to Materials.* With an Introduction by Francesco Cordasco. Detroit: Blaine Ethridge Books, 1975.

A compact bibliography and bibliographical guide to the literature on Spanish-speaking peoples in the United States. The bibliography includes 1,139 entries; a register of several hundred dissertations; a selected list of state and federal documents; a useful list of audio-visual materials, producers, and distributors; a list of currently published serials; a state-by-state listing of Spanish language radio and TV stations and programs; and a subject index.

178. Camposeco, J. "Guatemalans as Migrant Laborers in
      Florida." Paper presented at American Anthropological
      Association. 83rd Annual Meeting. Denver, Colorado,
      November 14-18, 1984.

      An estimated 55,000 (as of 1984) Guatemalan refugees
      have entered the United States illegally. Based on
      the author's experiences as a Guatemalan Indian and
      his work with Guatemalan refugees in the United States,
      the paper lays out a framework for understanding the
      immigration of Guatemalans to the United States via
      Mexico and then within the United States from centers
      in the Southwest to Florida, where work is available.
      Focuses on the conditions of the Guatemalan refugee
      migrant laborers in Florida, including relations with
      other Hispanic groups, other migrant laborers, and the
      dangers of capture and deportation by the Immigration
      and Naturalization Service.

179. Carballo, Manuel. "A Socio-Psychological Study of
      Acculturation/Assimilation: Cubans in New Orleans."
      Unpublished Ph.D. dissertation. New Orleans: Tulane
      University, 1970.

180. Cardenas, Gilberto. "Public Data on Mexican Immigra-
      tion into the United States: A Critical Evaluation."
      In W.B. Littrell and G. Sjoberg, eds., *Current Issues
      in Social Policy.* London: Sage Publications, 1976.
      Pp. 127-144.

      Critical evaluation of the "methodological and prac-
      tical problems associated with data collected and utilized
      by the Immigration and Naturalization Service on the
      migration of Mexicans into the United States, focusing
      on the difficult issues surrounding the data about the
      flow of illegal aliens." Suggests that "the data of
      the INS are collected, analyzed, and utilized in accor-
      dance with the social and political goals of the agency.
      If one accepts this orientation, then social scientists
      must examine alternative sources of data in order to
      interpret the data of the INS and to provide data to
      policy makers that suggest alternative ways to estimate
      the amount and the potential impact of Mexican immigra-
      tion into the United States."

181. ————. "United States Immigration Policy Toward
      Mexico: An Historical Perspective." *Chicano Law
      Review*, 2 (1975): 66-89.

182. *Caribbean Refugee Crisis: Cubans and Haitians.* Hearing
     before the Committee on the Judiciary, U.S. Senate,
     96th Congress, 2nd Session, May 12, 1980. Washington,
     D.C.: U.S. Government Printing Office, 1980.

     Includes the testimony of Bishop Edward A. McCarthy
     of Miami, Msgr. Walsh of Miami's Catholic Charities,
     Donald Hohl of U.S.C.C. Migration and Refugee Services,
     Ambassador Victor Palmieri, the U.S. Coordinator for
     Refugee Affairs and a spokesman for the Haitian refugees
     in Miami. Appendix I: "Report on the Status of Human
     Rights in Haiti"; Appendix II: "Violations of Human
     Rights in Haiti--1980" by the Lawyers Committee for
     International Human Rights; Appendix III: "Report of
     Department of State Study Team on Haitian Refugees,
     June 19, 1979."

183. Carlson, Alvar W. "Filipino and Indian Immigrants in
     Detroit and Suburbs, 1961-1974." *Philippine Geographic
     Journal* (Manila), 19 (1975): 199-209.

     A critical overview of how Filipino and Indian immi-
     grants (some undocumented) are changing the demography,
     composition, and character of the Detroit, Michigan,
     metropolitan area.

184. ————. "Recent Immigration, 1961-1970: A Factor in
     the Growth and Distribution of the United States
     Population." *Journal of Geography*, 72 (December 1973):
     8-18.

185. Carpenter, Margaret. "Addressing the Needs of Women
     Refugees." *World Refugee Survey*, 2 (1981): 42-44.

186. Casal, Lourdes. "Cubans in the U.S." *Nueva Generacion*,
     3-4 (December 1972): 6-20.

187. ————. "Cubans in the United States." In Martin Wein-
     stein, ed. *Revolutionary Cuba in the World Arena.*
     Philadelphia: Institute for the Study of Human Issues,
     1979. Pp. 109-136.

188. ————, and Andrés R. Hernández. "Cubans in the U.S.:
     A Survey of the Literature." *Cuban Studies*, 5 (July
     1975): 25-51.

189. Castelli, Jim. "Special Report: The Year of the Immi-
     grant." *Christian Century* (November 12, 1975): 1031-
     33.

190. Castro, Janice. "For 1,800 Haitians—Freedom." *Time*,
      120 (July 26, 1982): 14.

191. Castro, M.G., et al. *Women and Migration: Latin
      America and the Caribbean: A Selective Annotated
      Bibliography*. Gainesville, Florida: Center for Latin
      American Studies, University of Florida, February 1984.

      Introduction explains the considerations adopted in the
      compilation process and the importance of gender in
      migration studies. References are organized in alpha-
      betical order by author's last name and numbered. An
      index is included which contains a variety of subject
      topics, origin of migrants, and the methodology used.

192. Cattau, Daniel. "Lost Hope Among Haitian Refugees."
      Christian Century, 99 (October 6, 1982): 974-975.

193. Center for International Policy. *A Guide for Helping
      Indochinese Refugees in the United States*. Washing-
      ton, D.C.: Center for International Policy, 1980.

      Explains problems faced by Indochinese refugees as
      they settle in the United States and lists resources
      they can contact for help in resolving problems, in-
      cluding the many voluntary agencies involved in sponsor-
      ing refugees.

194. *Central American Refugees: Regional Conditions and
      Prospects and Potential Impact on the United States*.
      Report to the Congress of the United States by the
      Comptroller General of the United States. Gaithers-
      burg, Maryland: General Accounting Office, July 20,
      1984.

      Discusses the policies and extent of assistance given
      to Central American refugees by the U.N. High Commis-
      sioner for Refugees and other international organizations,
      refugees' living conditions and prospects in asylum
      countries, and U.S. and asylum government policies
      toward refugees. It also examines (1) the link between
      assistance and asylum opportunities available to refu-
      gees in the region and the possible future migration
      of refugees to the United States and (2) the potential
      impact of such migration.

195. Centro nacional de información y estadísticas del
      Trabajo (CENIET). "Encuesta nacional de emigración
      a la frontera norte del país y a los Estados Unidos
      (ENEFNEU)." Secretaria del trabajo y previsión social
      México, D.F., 1980.

A four-stage field study culminating in a nationwide
sample survey of 62,500 Mexican households. Fieldwork
for the final stage was completed in January 1979.
Final report completed in 1980.

196. Chambers, F. *Haiti*. World Bibliographical Series.
      Santa Barbara, California: ABC Clio Inc., 1983.

      Annotated bibliography of over 550 citations.
      Divided into 37 categories covering every aspect of
      Haiti, past and present, including its foreign relations
      with the colonial powers, the United States, and the
      Caribbean states. Material has been selected with the
      English reader in mind, but foreign language works are
      provided as balance or where no equivalent work in
      English exists. Intended for both the specialist stu-
      dent and the general reader. The author offers an im-
      pression of Haiti which will make the island republic
      and its citizens more widely known and better understood.

197. Chandrasekhar, S., ed. *From India to America: A Brief
      History of Immigration; Problems of Discrimination;
      Admission and Assimilation*. La Jolla, California:
      Population Review Publications, 1982.

      Intended to be an "introductory" volume "on the his-
      tory and growth of the slender Indian immigration to
      the United States and the small pockets of Indian immi-
      gration communities.... The numerical growth and growing
      'visibility' of this ethnic group during the second
      half of this century, particularly following the massive
      influx of Indian immigrants, consequent upon the 'liberal'
      amendment of the U.S. immigration law in 1965, has
      generated fresh research interest in the study of its
      history, adjustment patterns and distinctive attributes."

198. Chaney, Elsa M. "Colombian Migration to the United
      States: Part II." In Interdisciplinary Communications
      Program, Smithsonian Institution, *The Dynamics of
      Migration: International Migration*. Pp. 87-141.
      Washington, D.C.: Smithsonian Institution, 1976.

199. ————. "Colombian Outpost in New York City." *Society*
      (September-October, 1977): 60-64.

200. ————. "The World Economy and Contemporary Migration."
      International Migration Review, 13 (1979): 204-211.

201. ————, and C.L. Sutton, eds. "Caribbean Migration to
      the U.S." *International Migration Review*, 13 (Summer
      1979). Special issue of *Review*.

202. Chao, R. *Chinese Immigrant Children*. New York: City
      University of New York, 1977.

      A comparative study of elementary-school-level Chinese
      children living in and outside New York's Chinatown, who
      emigrated to the United States recently to determine
      the adjustment process of these children in the school,
      in the home, and in the community. Findings are based
      primarily upon first-hand observations, interviews, and
      knowledge of the researchers about the community.

203. Chaze, William L. "Now It's Haiti's Boat People Coming
      in a Flood." *U.S. News and World Report* (December 3,
      1979): 64-66.

204. Chierici, R., and S. Roark-Calnek. "Two Models for the
      Construction of Experience Among Haitian Immigrants."
      Paper presented at American Anthropological Association.
      83rd Annual Meeting. Denver, Colorado, November 14-18,
      1984.

      Oral histories of upwardly mobile Haitian immigrants
      in western New York are examined in terms of two models
      of how immigrants construe personal agency and social
      identity. Social action model presents actors as making
      instrumental use of religious affiliations, kin networks,
      and status markers to move across social boundaries.
      The second model grounds action in culturally constituted
      "primordial attachments" to place, family, and sacred
      beings; action is expressive or ritually participatory.
      Both models have antecedents in Haitian culture and both
      have adaptive functions for immigrants to America.

205. Chiswick, Barry R., ed. *Conference on U.S. Immigration
      Issues and Policies*. *Report*. Chicago: University of
      Illinois at Chicago Circle, 1980.

206. ————. "The Economic Progress of Immigrants: Some Ap-
      parently Universal Patterns." In Barry R. Chiswick,
      ed. *The Gateway: U.S. Immigration Issues and Policies*.
      Washington, D.C.: American Enterprise Institute, 1982.
      Pp. 119-158.

      On the basis of assumptions regarding the international
      transferability of skills and the favorable self-selection
      of migrants, hypotheses are generated regarding the
      progress of economic migrants and refugees in comparison
      with the native born. These hypotheses are found to be
      consistent with data from the United States (by racial
      and ethnic groups) and other countries. Data on males

from the 1970 Census of Population indicate that, although economic migrants initially have an earnings
disadvantage in comparison with the native born, their
earnings rise sharply with post-immigration labor market
experience, and they reach earnings equality with native-
born men of the same ethnic group and the same demographic characteristics for those in the United States in
about eleven to fifteen years. Economic migrants in
the United States for more than fifteen years tend to
have higher earnings than the native born. Refugees
have lower earnings than economic migrants or the native
born with the same characteristics, but the large differential shortly after immigration narrows with the
duration of residence. The earnings of refugees approach
but do not overtake those of the native born. The sons
of immigrants are found to earn 5 to 10 percent more
than the sons of native-born parents with the same demographic characteristics.

207. ———. *The Employment of Immigrants in the United
States*. Washington, D.C.: American Enterprise Institute, 1983.

208. ———, ed. *The Gateway: U.S. Immigration Issues and
Policies*. Washington, D.C.: American Enterprise Institute, 1982.

Contains the proceedings of a conference, "U.S. Immigration Issues and Policies," cosponsored by the
American Enterprise Institute for Public Policy Research
and the College of Business Administration, University
of Illinois at Chicago Circle (UICC). The conference
was held April 10-11, 1980, at the UICC campus. "The
conference was organized in part because of the importance
of immigration and immigration policy to a wide range of
U.S. domestic economic and social issues, as well as
relations with other countries. Immigrants have an impact on nearly all aspects of domestic life, including
wages and employment, population growth, housing prices,
and intergroup relations. Immigration policy is also
linked to foreign policy, not only with Mexico but also
more recently with countries in the Caribbean, Asia,
and Eastern Europe and in coming decades with sub-
Saharan Africa." Contents: Part One: The Supply and
Demand for Immigrants, with papers by David M. Reimers,
Michael J. Greenwood and John M. McDowell, and Jagdish
N. Bhagwati; Part Two: The Progress of Immigrants, with
papers by Barry R. Chiswick, Andrew M. Greeley, and
Walter Fogel; Part Three: The Economic Impact of Immi-

grants, with papers by Jeffrey G. Williamson, Barry R. Chiswick, and Julian L. Simon; Part Four: Alternative Immigration Policies, with papers by Larry C. Morgan and Bruce L. Gardner, and Robert S. Goldfarb. Each part also contains commentaries and discussion of the papers.

209.   ————. "Immigrants and Immigration Policy." In William Fellner, ed., *Contemporary Economic Problems 1978*. Washington, D.C.: American Enterprise Institute, 1978. Pp. 285-325.

210.   ————. "The Impact of Immigration on the Level and Distribution of Economic Well-Being." In Barry R. Chiswick, ed. *The Gateway: U.S. Immigration Issues and Policies*. Washington, D.C.: American Enterprise Institute, 1982. Pp. 289-313.

Based on two-factor and three-factor (high-level man-power, low-level manpower, and capital) aggregate produc-tion functions. It shows that immigration tends to raise the income of the native population but to change the distribution of this income. The different impacts of high-skilled and low-skilled immigrants are con-sidered. A dynamic element is introduced when the model allows for changing impacts as the relative skills of immigrants increase with their duration of residence. When an income transfer system (welfare, social services, and social overhead capital financed prior to the im-migration) is introduced, income redistribution programs can make all native-born groups at least as affluent as before the migration. This cannot occur, however, if the immigrants themselves are substantial net recipients of these transfers. It could not occur, for example, if the immigrants were low-skilled workers and had equal access to the income transfer system as native-born low-skilled workers. An immigrant tax (large visa fee or immigrant income tax surcharge) that captures some of the economic rent that visa recipients receive would raise the aggregate income of the native population and increase the annual number of visas that the United States would be willing to issue. Such a scheme would still provide opportunities for refugee and family re-unification migration.

211.   ————. "Sons of Immigrants: Are They at an Earnings Disadvantage?" *The American Economic Review*, 6 (Feb-ruary 1977): 376-380.

Examines the effect of foreign parentage on the earn-ings of native-born white men age 25 to 64 who worked in

1969. The study was restricted to whites as they comprise 97 percent of the persons of foreign parentage and to men because the problems of estimating labor market experience for women require that they be dealt with separately. In addition, persons born in Puerto Rico or an outlying area of the United States are excluded from the data.

212. Clark, Juan M. "The Cuban Escapees." *Latinamericanist*, 6 (November 1, 1970): 1-4.

213. ————. *Hispanics in Dade County: Their Characteristics and Needs*. Miami: Office of Dade County Manager, 1980.

214. ————, et al. *The 1980 Mariel Exodus: An Assessment and Prospect*. Washington, D.C.: Council for Inter-American Security, 1981.

215. Clark, Victor S. "Mexican Labor in the United States." *Bulletin of the Department of Labor*, 78 (September 1980); 470-474.

216. Cockrum, D., and J.M. Redondo. "*Norteños* as *Pachos*: A Psychological Phenomenon?" Paper presented at Western Social Science Association. 26th Annual Meeting. San Diego, California, April 28, 1984.

Norteños (citizens of northern Mexico) are said to be *pachos* ("bleached") by their exposure to the United States. Does this bleaching extend to psychological constructs? Two studies were performed, one using managers from Guadalajara, Chihuahua, Texas, and Chicago. Study measured need for achievement, need for affiliation, and need for power. Second study used business owners, founders, and managers from Mexico City, Chihuahua, and assessed Internal-External Locus of Control and Traditional Family Ideology. Results showed that *norteños* were psychologically unique but were not uniformly more similar to businessmen in the United States than to businessmen in the interior of Mexico. On each psychological construct the borderlands businessmen scored in the direction that would be most associated with business success. Appears that the borderlands businessmen, living on the border between two cultures, adopt those psychological characteristics from both cultures that are most associated with business success.

217. Cohen, Lucy M. "The Female Factor in Resettlement."
      Society, 14 (1977): 27-30.

      About two thirds of Central and South American new-
      comers are women. Women have established families in
      their native countries and left them with kin as they
      venture to the United States to earn money. Generally
      less educated than men, they experience less job
      mobility in the United States and earn less than their
      male counterparts. Concludes with an appeal for more
      attention to female immigration.

218. Cohodas, Nadine. "The Haitians: Seeking Asylum in the
      U.S." *Congressional Quarterly Weekly Report*, 40
      (August 14, 1982): 1966-1967.

219. Colbert, Lois. "Haitian Aliens--A People in Limbo."
      The Crisis, 87 (August-September 1980): 235-238.

220. Community Council of Greater New York. *New Immigrants
      in New York City. Summaries of Research in Progress
      and Recent Reports*. Interim Report. New York: Com-
      munity Council of Greater New York, [October], 1979.

      Includes research in progress, recent reports, and
      bibliographies on new immigrants.

221. Congressional Research Service, Library of Congress.
      "Review of U.S. Refugee Settlement Programs and Poli-
      cies." Washington, D.C.: U.S. Government Printing
      Office, 1980.

      Prepared at the request of Senator Edward M. Kennedy,
      Chairman, Committee on the Judiciary, United States
      Senate, updates an earlier study on U.S. refugee re-
      settlement programs and reviews the evolution of U.S.
      refugee law and policy in order to give some perspective
      to "The Refugee Act of 1980." Charts and tables.

222. ———. "Selected Reading on U.S. Immigration Policy
      and Law." A compendium prepared for the use of The
      Select Commission on Immigration and Refugee Policy.
      Washington, D.C.: U.S. Government Printing Office,
      1980.

      A collection of a full range of background readings
      and opinions on American immigration policy. Besides
      presenting various views on current immigration problems
      also gives an historical perspective. Deals with the
      issues of what nation's immigration goals ought to be
      and what to do about illegal immigration.

223.   ————. *Summary of Hearings Held by the Senate
       Judiciary Subcommittee on Immigration and Refugee
       Policy, July 1981-April 1982.* Washington, D.C.:
       U.S. Government Printing Office, 1983.

The focus of the hearings was on the need for or re-
gaining control of the various forms of immigration.
The hearings addressed five basic aspects of immigration: (1) legal permanent immigration, the subject of
two days of hearings; (2) refugee admission and resettlement, considered in two hearings; (3) mass asylum
and the related issues of adjudication, considered in
three hearings; (4) illegal immigration, including work
authorization, legalization, and temporary worker programs, considered in four hearings; and (5) nonimmigrants, the subject of two hearings.

224.   ————. *Temporary Worker Programs: Background and
       Issues.* Washington, D.C.: U.S. Government Printing
       Office, 1980.

Prepared at the request of Senator Edward M. Kennedy,
Chairman of the Committee on the Judiciary of the U.S.
Senate, for the use of the Select Commission on Immigration and Refugee Policy. Reviews the problems, history,
and options involved in establishing a temporary worker
program.

225.   ————. *U.S. Immigration Law and Policy: 1952-1979.*
       Washington, D.C.: U.S. Government Printing Office,
       1979.

Prepared at the request of Senator Edward M. Kennedy,
Chairman of the Committee on the Judiciary, U.S. Senate,
upon the formation of the Select Commission on Immigration and Refugee Policy. Previewed legislation and
major developments in the immigration field over the
past three decades.

226.   ————. "World Refugee Crisis: The International Com-
       munity's Response." Washington, D.C.: U.S. Government
       Printing Office, 1979.

Prepared at the request of Senator Edward M. Kennedy,
Chairman, Committee on the Judiciary, United States
Senate, reviews issues concerning the world refugee
problem and the scope and dimension of refugee movements. A team of more than twenty researchers has
worked to complete this up-to-date, comprehensive review
of international refugee problems—their numbers, needs,
problems, as well as what more needs to be done.

227. Connor, Walker, ed. *Mexican-Americans in Comparative
      Perspective.* Washington, D.C.: The Urban Institute
      Press, 1985.

      What are the effects of immigration by people of
      Mexican origin on the economic, educational, social,
      political, and linguistic systems of the United States?
      To answer this question, authors of the conference
      papers presented here use a comparative method to pro-
      vide objective information about the Mexican-American
      presence in the United States during the 1980s. *Con-
      tents:* Who Are the Mexican-Americans? A Note on Com-
      parability; Assimilation in the United States: The
      Mexican-Americans; Conflict and Accommodation: Mexican-
      Americans in the Cosmopolis; Ethnicity and Stratifica-
      tion: Mexican-Americans and the European *Gastarbeiter*
      in Comparative Perspective; Transborder People; Migra-
      tion Theory and Practice; Political Distinctiveness of
      the Mexican-Americans; Mexican-American Political
      Mobilization and the Loyalty Question; Political Mobili-
      zation in the Mexican-American Community; Language Poli-
      cies: Patterns of Retention and Maintenance; National
      Language Profile of the Mexican-Origin Population in
      the United States; Ethnic Revival in the United States:
      Implications for the Mexican-American Community; Con-
      clusions: Through a Comparative Prism Darkly.

228. Conroy, M.E., et al. *Socio-economic Incentives for
      Migration from Mexico to the United States: Cross-
      Regional Profiles, 1969-78.* Austin, Texas: Population
      Research Center, The University of Texas, 1980.

      Presents evidence of the magnitude of current real
      wage differentials for low-skill laborers across regions
      within Mexico and throughout the southwestern United
      States. Trend in wage differentials in recent years
      is presented and specific attention is given to the
      effect of devaluations of the Mexican peso. Analysis
      shows non-monetary socio-economic incentives and sug-
      gests policy implications with respect to Mexican migra-
      tion to the United States in the context of broader
      interrelationships between the two countries.

229. Coon, Deborah L., and Rita M. Edmonds, eds. *Indochinese
      Refugees: Adjustment Patterns and Resettlement Stra-
      tegies.* Provo, Utah: Brigham Young University, 1982.

230. Cooney, Rosemary Santana, and Maria Alina Contreras.
      "Residence Patterns of Social Register Cubans: A Study

of Miami, San Juan, and New York SMSAs." *Cuban Studies*, 8 (July 1978): 33-49.

231. Copeland, Ronald. "The Cuban Boatlift of 1980: Strategies in Federal Crisis Management." *Annals of the American Academy of Political and Social Science*, 467 (May 1983): 138-150.

232. Cordasco, Francesco. [Review] Gianfausto Rosoli. *Un Secolo di Emigrazione Italiana, 1876-1976* (Roma: Centro Studi Emigrazione, 1978). *American Historical Review*, 85 (December 1980): 1230-1231.

233. ————. [Review] June Helm, ed. *Spanish Speaking People in the United States* (Seattle: University of Washington Press, 1968). *Journal of Negro History*, 54 (July 1969): 308-310.

234. ————, and David N. Alloway. "Spanish Speaking People in the United States: Some Research Constructs and Postulates." *International Migration Review*, 4 (Spring 1970); 76-79.

"Adequate, and reasonably current, research information on specific ethnic groups is a constant problem to the diligent social science researcher. All too often the studies containing adequate or current data on minority groups tend to treat them collectively, superficially, or in passing, and many specialized studies often lack the kind of useful real specificity that is sought. In addressing itself to this problem, the American Ethnological Society has done a great service to the academic world by publishing the papers and proceedings of the annual meetings, illustrative of which is the 1968 *Proceedings* dealing with the Spanish-speaking people in the United States."

235. Cordova, Fred. *Filipinos: Forgotten Asian Americans*. Dubuque, Iowa: Kendall/Hunt Publishing Company, 1983.

236. Cornelius, Wayne A. "America in the Era of Limits: Migrants, Nativists, and the Future of U.S.-Mexican Relations." In *Mexican-U.S. Relations: Conflict and Convergence*. Edited by C. Vásquez and M. Garcia y Griego. Los Angeles: University of California, Chicano Studies Research, 1983. Pp. 371-396.

Describes the main feature of the public opinion climate in the United States in which the current debate over immigration, especially illegal (undocumented) immigration from Mexico is occurring. Sketches the public's specific perceptions and attitudes toward immigration, as well as some of the broader social, economic, and political forces operating in the United States today which condition mass attitudes toward immigrants.

237.   ———. "The Future of Mexican Immigrants in California: A New Perspective for Public Policy." *Working Papers in U.S.-Mexican Studies*, No. 6, February 1980. [Los Angeles, California, 1980]

238.   ———. "The Future of Mexican Immigrants in California: A New Perspective for Public Policy." *Working Papers in U.S.-Mexican Studies*, No. 6, La Jolla, California: Center for U.S.-Mexican Studies, University of California, San Diego, 1981.

Reports on second stage of a field study initiated in nine rural sending communities in the Los Altos region of Jalisco, Mexico and completed in 10 receiving cities in California and Illinois. Fieldwork in the United States completed in 1978. Based primarily on 185 interviews conducted in the United States receiving cities.

239.   ———. *Immigration, Mexican Development Policy, and the Future of U.S.-Mexican Relations*. Working Papers in U.S.-Mexican Studies, University of California, San Diego, 1981.

Examines the magnitude of the unemployment/underemployment problem in Mexico and the prospects for solving it. Explores the economic growth and job creation possibilities for 1980–2000, discusses the various push factors behind migration and how they might be reduced, and poses policy options.

240.   ———. *Immigration and U.S.-Mexican Relations*. Working Papers in U.S.-Mexican Studies, No. 1. Program in U.S.-Mexican Studies, University of California, San Diego, 1981.

An abridged transcript of a conference on Mexican immigration. Purpose of the conference was to develop an agenda of high-priority knowledge producing knowledge-disseminating activities that could be supported by the Rockefeller Foundation and/or other private foundations. It identified a range of options for research and educational activities.

241. ————. *Mexican and Caribbean Migration to the United States: The State of Current Knowledge and Priorities for Future Research.* Monographs in U.S.-Mexican Studies, No. 1. La Jolla, California: Center for U.S.-Mexican Studies, University of California, San Diego, 1982.

242. ————, et al. "Mexican Immigrants and Southern California: A Summary of Current Knowledge." *Working Papers in U.S.-Mexican Studies*, No. 36. La Jolla, California: Center for U.S.-Mexican Studies, University of California, San Diego, 1982.

243. ————. *Mexican Migration to the United States: Causes, Consequences, and U.S. Responses.* Cambridge, Massachusetts: Center for International Studies, Massachusetts Institute of Technology, 1978.

244. ————. *Mexican Migration to the United States: The Limits of Government Intervention.* Working Papers in U.S.-Mexican Studies, No. 5. Program in U.S.-Mexican Studies, University of California, San Diego, 1981.

Questions the view that Mexican immigration could be reduced significantly by government action and concentrates instead on the limits of government intervention on the U.S. side.

245. ————, et al. "Project on Local-Level Impacts of Mexican Immigration, with Special Reference to Health Problems and Health Service Utilization" [1982].

Based in the Center for U.S.-Mexican Studies and the School of Medicine, University of California, San Diego. Multi-method study including interviews with 2,500 Mexican immigrants (males and females) who live or work regularly in San Diego County. Field interviewing commenced February 1981; was completed March 1982.

246. ————. "The Reagan Administration's Proposals for a New U.S. Immigration Policy: An Assessment of Potential Effects." *International Migration Review*, 15 (Winter 1981): 769-778.

"The Reagan Administration's attempt to grapple with the complex and emotional issues surrounding the immigration policy of the United States has yielded a set of proposals which essentially reaffirm policies advocated by the Ford and Carter Administrations, while adding some new elements tailored to the concerns of various groups within the Reagan Administration's support

base. Staunch 'law-and-order' advocates, many of whom
see undocumented immigrants as just another criminal
class whose law-breaking behavior must not be condoned
nor rewarded, have been given an 'amnesty' proposal
that is so restrictive and punitive in its details that
it could not possibly be embraced by any of the major
groups concerned with immigrants' rights that have advocated amnesty for undocumented aliens who are long-term
residents of the United States."

247.   ————. "Simpson-Mazzoli vs. the Realities of Mexican
        Immigration." In Wayne A. Cornelius and Ricardo
        Anzaldna Montoya, eds. *America's New Immigration
        Law: Origins, Rationales and Potential Consequences.*
        San Diego, California: Center for U.S.-Mexican Studies,
        1983. Pp. 142-156.

248.   ————, and Juan Diez-Canedo. *Mexican Migration to the
        United States: The View from the Rural Sending Communi-
        ties.* Cambridge, Massachusetts: Massachusetts Insti-
        tute of Technology, Migration and Development Study
        Group, 1976.

        On the "preliminary findings of a study of the causes
        and consequences of out-migration from rural communities
        in Mexico, which has been in progress for 15 months.
        The data for this paper were drawn from interviews with
        the residents, a population census, local birth and death
        records, participant observation, and archival research
        in Mexican and United States government documents."

249.   ————, and ————. "Rural Change and Emigration: Im-
        pact of Mexico and the U.S." Paper presented at
        American University, Washington, D.C., March 18, 1976.

250.   ————, and Ricardo A. Montoya, eds. *America's New
        Immigration Law: Origins, Rationales, and Potential
        Consequences.* San Diego: Center for U.S.-Mexican
        Studies, University of California, 1983.

        A volume of essays and edited commentary summarizes
        the proceedings of the Fourth Annual Earl Warren Memorial
        Symposium on the evolution of U.S. immigration policy
        held in November 1982.

251.   Cortés, Carlos E., ed. *Cuban Exiles in the United
        States.* New York: Arno Press, 1980.

        Provides a variety of perspectives on the Cuban exile
        experience in the United States, such as the differences

between the "old" and "new" waves of exiles, the Cuban
elderly, experiences of Cubans in U.S. cities, adjustment to life in the United States, and problems and
opportunities encountered by different groups of professionals.

252.   ————, ed. *Cuban Refugee Programs*. New York: Arno
Press, 1980.

Examines Cuban refugee programs from several different
viewpoints. Consisting of a special report to the
President and transcripts of the 1961-62 hearings before
the Senate subcommittee on refugee problems, the first
three entries reveal diverse opinions that developed
within government during the early years of Cuban refugee immigration. The refugee programs themselves are
then examined, followed by studies focusing on the
special problems faced by unaccompanied Cuban children.

253.   ————, ed. *Latinos in the United States*. New York:
Arno Press, 1980.

254.   Corwin, Arthur F. "Causes of Mexican Emigration to the
United States: A Summary View." *Perspectives in
American History*, 7 (1973): 557-635.

255.   ————. "Historia de la emigración Mexicana, 1900-1970,
literatura e investigacion." *Historia Mexicana*, 22
(October/December 1972): 188-220.

Examination of historical and sociological studies on
Mexican migration; a survey of Mexican literature on
migration; the opportunities for research in the field
of Mexican migration.

256.   ————, ed. *Immigrants and Immigrants: Perspectives on
Mexican Labor Migration to the United States*. Westport, Connecticut: Greenwood Press, 1978.

257.   ————. "Mexican Emigration History, 1880-1970: Literature and Research." *Latin American Research Review*,
8 (1973): 3-24.

258.   Cowan, Rachel. "For Hispanics It's Still the Promised
Land." *New York Times Magazine* (June 22, 1975): 9-10.

259.   Craig, A.L. *Mexican Immigration Changing Terms of the
Debate in the United States and Mexico*. Working Papers
in U.S.-Mexican Studies, No. 4. Program in United

States-Mexican Studies, University of California, San
Diego, 1981.

Summary of briefing session organized by the Program
in U.S.-Mexican Studies helps to "demystify" the political process through which both the United States and
Mexico will arrive at new policies bearing upon Mexican
immigration to the United States in the 1980s and of the
forces which affect the range of policy choices.

260.   Crewdson, John. *The Tarnished Door: The New Immigrants
       and the Transformation of America*. New York: New York
       Times Book Co., 1983.

Upwards of a million illegal immigrants are caught
trying to enter this country each year, and countless
others succeed.   John Crewdson, whose reporting on the
new American immigrants for *The New York Times* won him
a Pulitzer Prize, guides us on their very special journey; from Key West during the Cuban refugee invasion to
Miami's Little Haiti, from the silent Arizona desert
at midnight to the nation's big-city barrios.   It is a
situation, as Crewdson reports, that is made more urgent
by competition for jobs and living space, by a new and
disturbing strain of racism, and by the often nightmarish
policies of the Immigration and Naturalization Service.
"Not intended to be a scholarly or definitive study.   It
is, rather, an account of what I saw and heard and thought
during my journeys around the United States.   For that
reason, I have avoided the use of footnotes and citations.
Whenever a particular fact or number is included without
attribution, the reader may assume that it either is
generally accepted or else represents a consensus; in
most cases where facts are in dispute, conflicting views
have been noted."

261.   Cross, Harry E., and James A. Sandos. *Across the Bor-
       der: Rural Development in Mexico and Recent Migration
       to the United States*. Berkeley, California: Institute
       of Governmental Studies, University of California,
       1981.

Despite the much-heralded Green Revolution and the
considerable expenditure of money and effort on agrarian
reform and agricultural development by the Mexican government since 1920, hundreds of thousands of Mexicans have
continued to migrate to the United States; 70 percent
originate in just six states.   This sending region, the
states of Durango, Guanajuato, Jalisco, Michoacán, San
Luis Potosi, and Zacatecas, has played this role during

much of the twentieth century. The Mexican Revolution
benefited the region little, and subsequent governmental
agricultural policy decisions exacerbated rather than
ameliorated conditions in the region. Agrarian reform
created minifundios; irrigation works were built elsewhere; income redistribution favored others; and credit
was too scarce or too dear. The Green Revolution bypassed
the ordinary farmer, for its technological and fiscal
requirements were beyond his means. Predictably, residents of the region have been "pushed" out of their
homelands into large Mexican cities, especially on the
border with the United States, or into the United States,
sometimes after a sojourn in such border cities as
Tijuana. The book focuses on Mexico, but the authors
also examine the impact of Mexican migration on the
United States and make policy recommendations for both
the Mexican and United States governments.

262. Cruz, Carmen Inés, and Juanita Castaño. "Colombian
     Migration to the United States; Part I." In Interdis-
     ciplinary Communications Program, Smithsonian Institu-
     tion, *The Dynamics of Migration: International Migra-
     tion*, pp. 41-86. ICP Occasional Monograph Series,
     vol. 2, no. 5. Washington, D.C.: Smithsonian Institu-
     tion, 1976.

263. Cuddy, D.L., ed. *Contemporary American Immigration:
     Interpretive Essays (European). Contemporary American
     Immigration: Interpretive Essays (Non-European).*
     2 vols. Boston: Twayne Publishers, 1982.

     Volumes consist of collections of essays by leading
     figures in their respective areas. Deal with migration
     to the United States since World War II. Each essay
     includes six primary points of reference: (1) the history
     of the migration; (2) motives for leaving the homeland;
     (3) reasons for selecting the United States; (4) initial
     impressions of this country; (5) later satisfaction or
     dissatisfaction with life in the United States; and
     (6) possible return migration to the homeland.

264. Cué, R.A., and R.L. Bach. "The Return of the Clandestine
     Worker and the End of the Golden Exile: Recent Mexican
     and Cuban Immigrants in the United States." In R.S.
     Bryce-La Porte, ed., *Sourcebook on the New Immigration.*
     New Brunswick, N.J.: Transaction Books, 1980.

265. Cummings, Judith. "Indochinese Women Find Life in America
     Fraught with Barriers." *The New York Times*, 84 (Novem-
     ber 1, 1984): C1, C12.

An overview of the difficulties faced by women from
Southeast Asia "struggling with special barriers to a
smooth resettlement in the United States." Notices of
Vietnamese, Cambodian, and Laotian women.

266. Cummings, S. *Immigrant Minorities and the Urban Working
Class*. New York: Irvington, 1983.

267. Dade County, Florida. *Community and Economic Profile:
Little Havana Target Area*. Miami: Dade County Office
of Economic Development, 1977.

268. ―――. *Cuban/Haitian Needs Assessment, 1981*. Miami:
Metro-Dade County Department of Human Resources, 1981.

269. ―――. *Cuban and Haitian Refugees, Miami SMSA, 1980*.
Miami: Metro-Dade County Planning Department, 1981.

270. ―――. *Dade County Characteristics*. Miami: Dade
County Department of Human Resources, 1983.

271. ―――. *Needs Assessment Study: Terrorism in Dade
County, Florida*. Miami: Dade-Miami Criminal Justice
Council, 1979.

272. ―――. *Profile of the Latin Population in the Metropolitan Dade County Area*. Miami: Office of the County
Manager, 1976.

273. ―――. *Social and Economic Problems among Cuban and
Haitian Entrant Groups in Dade County, Florida*. Miami:
Dade County Department of Human Resources, 1981.

274. Daniels, Roger. "The Japanese Experience in North
America: An Essay in Comparative Racism." *Canadian
Ethnic Studies/Études ethniques du Canada*, 9 (1977):
91-100.

Examines the similarities and differences in the experiences of Japanese immigrants who settled in the
United States and Canada from the 1960s to the 1970s.
Japanese immigrants and their descendants experienced
the same kinds of problems whether they settled in the
northwest part of the United States or in British
Columbia. Differences encountered depended more on
size of the Japanese communities than on institutional
differences between the countries.

275. ————. *Racism and Immigration Restriction*. St. Louis: Forum Press, 1975.

276. Danilov, D.P. "Immigration into the United States Today." *Practical Lawyer*, 23 (December 1977): 57-61.

277. Darasz, Kathy A. "Cuban Refugees in Miami: Patterns of Economic and Political Adjustment." Unpublished M.A. thesis, Florida Atlantic University, 1982.

278. Da Vanzo, J. "Repeat Migration in the U.S.: Who Moves Back and Who Moves On?" Santa Monica, California: The Rand Corporation, 1982.

Focuses on repeat moves and inquiries into how previous migrants choose among moving on to a new location, returning to a previous location, and staying put.

279. David, Charles, and Jorge Uribe Navarrete. "Haiti's Forgotten Refugees." *World Press Review*, 27 (August 1980): 25-27.

280. Davis, C., et al. "U.S. Hispanics: Changing the Face of America." Washington, D.C.: *Population Bulletin*, 38 (June 1983): 1-44.

With relatively high fertility and growing legal and illegal immigration, the U.S. Hispanic population increased by some 265 percent from an estimated 4 million in 1950 to 14.6 million and 6.4 percent of the total population counted in the 1980 census. By 2020 they could number some 47 million and displace blacks as the largest U.S. minority if immigration were to continue at the recent estimated level of one million a year (legal plus illegal, Hispanics plus all others). Self-identified as persons who trace their heritage to Spanish-speaking countries, Hispanics consist of Mexican-Americans (60 percent of the total), still concentrated in the Southwest; Puerto Ricans, living mainly in New York and New Jersey; Cubans headquartered in Florida; and the second largest, most scattered "Other Hispanic" group from 16 other Latin American countries and Spain, plus some Mexican-Americans established many generations in the U.S. Southwest. Fully 88 percent of Hispanics, compared to 75 percent of the general population, live in metropolitan areas. Except for Cubans, Hispanics are younger than the U.S. average (a median of 23 years versus the general median of 30 in 1980) and have higher fertility (an estimated 2.5 versus 1.8 births per woman),

though their life expectancy may not equal that of all
U.S. whites. They are also more likely to be divorced
or separated and live in female-headed families. Hispanic occupational status and educational attainment
will lag far behind the U.S. average, unemployment is
40-50 percent higher, and Hispanic families average 70
percent of the median income and 2.7 times the poverty
rate of all U.S. white families. But younger Hispanics
and Cubans in particular are beginning to catch up, as
is likely also for future generations of U.S. Hispanics.
However, with their common language and large numbers
(including a large, if unknown, number of "undocumented"
aliens), assimilation into the U.S. "melting pot" may
take longer for Hispanics than it did for other immigrant
ethnic groups before them.

281. Davison, Lani. "Women Refugees: Special Needs and Pro-
        grams." *Journal of Refugee Resettlement*, 1 (1981):
        16-26.

        Summarizes the main findings of a study, undertaken
        by the Equity Policy Center with support from the Asia
        Foundation, which identifies the major problems facing
        Indochinese refugee women being resettled in the United
        States, reviews programs available to them, and suggests
        changes in current programs.

282. DeCew, Judson M., Jr. "Hispanics." In J. Dauer Manning,
        ed., *Florida's Politics and Government*. Gainesville,
        Florida: University of Florida Press, 1980. Pp. 321-
        330.

283. Deckelbaum, Yetta. "Little Haiti: The Evolution of a
        Community." Unpublished M.A. thesis, Florida Atlantic
        University, 1983.

284. de Conde, Eulalia D. "Haitian Refugees: A Dilemma for
        the United States." *SAIS Review* (Summer 1981): 71-79.

285. DeForest, M.E. "Mexican Workers North of the Border."
        Harvard Business Review, 59 (May/June, 1981): 150-157.

286. de la Garza, Rodolfo. "Mexican Americans, Mexican
        Immigrants, and Immigration Reform." In Nathan
        Glazer, ed. *Clamor at the Gates: The New American
        Immigration*. San Francisco, California: Institute
        for Contemporary Studies, 1985. Pp. 93-105.

287. de la Puente, Manuel, and Marc Bendick, Jr. *Employment and Training Programs for Migrant and Refugee Youth: Lessons from the United States Experience.* Washington, D.C.: The Urban Institute, 1983.

288. de Man, Elaine. "Haiti's Refugees." *Oceans*, 16 (January–February 1983): 30–35.

289. Dernis, Martin M. "Haitian Immigrants: Political Refugees or Economic Escapees?" *University of Miami Law Review*, 31 (1976–1977): 27–41.

290. Deutsch, H.D. *Getting into America.* New York: Random House, 1978.

291. Diaz Briquets, Sergio. "Demographic and Related Determinants of Recent Cuban Emigration." *International Migration Review*, 17 (Spring 1983): 95–119.

Highlights some of the principal demographic determinants of recent Cuban emigration, while also considering how these demographic variables interact with other social and economic determinants, utilizing a broad conceptualization of emigration. It also makes reference to Cuban military activities abroad. Conclusions suggest that labor migration is more responsive to demographic factors than some theorists assume.

292. ————, and Melinda J. Frederick. "Colombian Emigration: A Research Note on Its Probable Quantitative Extent." *International Migration Review*, 18 (Spring 1984): 99–110.

Has two objectives. One is to provide a brief overview of quantitative estimates of Colombian emigration, including formal attempts to estimate the volume of net emigration. The second objective is to update the existing estimates with more recent data (in a highly speculative fashion). The goals of the note are modest. Attempts to summarize existing evidence while providing a brief discussion of how the estimates were prepared. Some of the estimates discussed involve a very laborious methodology impossible to summarize in a few paragraphs. The ultimate goal of the exercise is to derive a "plausible" estimate of the extent of Colombian net emigration in 1980 although no claim is made that this estimate is correct or final. A more definitive estimate will not be available until after the careful and detailed evaluation of the 1980 round of censuses although even these

data will fail to yield answers to many questions related to the volume of Colombian emigration.

293. Dinerman, Ina R. *Migrants and Stay-at-Homes: A Com-
      parative Study of Rural Migration from Michoacán,
      Mexico.* La Jolla, California: Center for U.S.-
      Mexican Studies, University of California, San Diego.
      Monographs in U.S.-Mexican Studies, No. 5, 1982.

      Ethnographic and survey study of two sending communi-
      ties in the state of Michoacán (one of which is Huecorio),
      based on fieldwork completed in 1980.

294. ———. "Patterns of Adaptation Among Households of
      U.S.-Bound Migrants from Michoacán, Mexico." *Inter-
      national Migration Review*, 12 (Winter 1978): 485-501.

      Provides a close-range study of conditions leading to
      illegal migration from a rural village in Mexico. It is
      one of the few available studies of illegal migration
      at its point of origin. Its primary concern is not in-
      dividual psychological traits but the social network of
      relationships and mutual obligations conditioning the
      decision to migrate.

295. Doi, M., C. Lin, and I. Vohra-Sahu. *Pacific Asian
      American Research: An Annotated Bibliography.* Chi-
      cago: Pacific/Asian American Health Research Center,
      1981.

      First volume in a bibliography series from Documenta-
      tion Center where information on Pacific/Asian-American
      populations is collected, classified, and disseminated.
      Some 556 items are included in the abstracts.

296. Dominguez, Virginia R. "Defining Refugees: Haitians
      and Cubans." *Cubatimes*, 1 (Fall 1980): 11-15.

297. ———. *From Neighbor to Stranger: The Dilemma of
      Caribbean Peoples in the United States.* New Haven,
      Connecticut: Yale University. Antilles Research
      Program Occasional Papers, 5, 1975.

      Deals with the migration of Caribbean peoples--Puerto
      Ricans, Cubans, Dominicans, Haitians, and others--to
      the United States in recent decades. Varying adaptations
      of these newcomers to North American life is considered
      from legal, educational, occupational, and other per-
      spectives. Fifty-five tables summarize much of what is
      known about migrants.

298. Dougé, Daniel. *Caribbean Pilgrims: The Plight of the Haitian Refugees*. New York: Exposition Press, 1982.

299. Eastman, C. "Immigration Reform and New Mexico Agriculture." Paper presented at Western Social Science Association. 26th Annual Meeting. San Diego, California, April 28, 1984.

   Intended to help provide factual background for the national debate on immigration and refugee policy. "Not only have the kinds of agriculture work and the rate of compensation been identified, there is also an attempt to present the basic expectation and perspective of both the employers and the undocumented workers."

300. "The Efficiency Bill in a Nutshell." *Immigration Journal*, 5 (March-April 1982): 6-7.

301. Egerton, John. *Cubans in Miami: A Third Dimension in Racial and Cultural Relations*. Nashville, Tennessee: Race Relations Information Center, 1969.

302. Elgass, James A. "Federal Funding of United States Refugee Resettlement Before and After the Refugee Act of 1980." *Michigan Yearbook of International Legal Studies* (Annual 1982): 179-196.

303. Enders, Thomas O. "Cuban and Haitian Migration." *Department of State Bulletin*, 81 (October 1981): 78-79.

304. Erhlich, Paul R., et al. *The Golden Door: International Migration, Mexico and the United States*. New York: Ballantine Books, 1979.

   Focus is on the Mexican immigration problem in its historical and cultural context; examines the possible consequences of various policies aimed at dealing with it. The problem is not viewed as a unique dilemma, however, but as part of a continuing pattern woven through the centuries, a pattern of mass movements as old as humanity itself. Is thus not only about Mexico and the United States but about human migration in general. Presents an overview of migration in history and as a contemporary worldwide phenomenon. The relationship between Mexico and the United States is examined in detail. The options open to both the United States and Mexico are described and the possible consequences of adopting them evaluated.

305.   Espenshade, Thomas J., and Tracy Ann Goodis. *Recent Immigrants to Los Angeles: Characteristics and Labor Market Impacts*. Washington, D.C.: The Urban Institute, 1985.

306.   "Estimates of Cubans and Haitians Who Entered the United States Between April 1, 1980 and October 1, 1980." *Federal Register*, 47 (October 1, 1982): 43414-43415.

307.   Fagen, P.W. *Applying for Political Asylum in New York: Law, Policy and Administrative Practice*. New York: Center for Latin American and Caribbean Studies, New York University, April, 1984.

       Examines national policies related to political asylum determinations and the implementation of those practices at the local level in New York City.

308.   Fagen, Richard R. "So Distant from God, So Close to the United States." *Across the Board*, 14 (1977): 47-57.

       Believes that development programs in Mexico have helped the wealthier residents while leaving the poor to look north for aid. Estimates as many as four million illegal Mexicans are in the United States at any one time and their remittances to families who stayed behind exceed the amounts Mexico gains from tourism. Concludes that the United States must find ways to support forces in Mexico working for social justice. Both countries would gain from such changes.

309.   ————, and Richard A. Brody. "Cubans in Exile: A Demographic Analysis." *Special Problems*, 11 (April 1964): 389-401.

310.   ————, and ————. *Cubans in Exile: Disaffection and the Revolution*. Stanford, California: Stanford University Press, 1968.

       The Cubans constitute a group of refugees who were not fleeing because their lives were endangered, or because their homes had been destroyed, or because they were displaced by a rearrangement of political borders.... This group was composed of self-imposed political exiles. They chose to become refugees rather than live under conditions which they found intolerable. This book studies "who these refugees are, why they left Cuba, and what they believe."

311. Fallows, James. "Immigration: How It's Affecting Us."
     The Atlantic (November 1983): 45-68, 85-106.

     Surveys the changes in American immigration laws, the
     contemporary migratory flows, the origin and volume of
     new immigrants to the United States, and the best-known
     myths about today's immigration. Four parts of the
     article (Money, Language, Race, The Law) try to answer
     the "unspoken question about the immigrants: What are
     they doing to us? Will they divide and diminish the
     nation's riches? Will they accept its language? Will
     they alter racial relations? Will they respect the
     thousand informal rules that allow this nation of many
     races to cohere?"

312. Fauriol, G. *U.S. Immigration Policy and the National
     Interest.* Washington, D.C.: Center for Strategic
     International Studies, 1983.

     "Reflects the basic parameters within which the CSIS
     Immigration Policy Project is to evolve: namely, an
     assessment of the breakdown in the management of U.S.
     immigration and refugee policies, the apparent fluidity
     in border control, and its implications for the national
     interest."

313. Fawcett, J.T., et al. *Asia Pacific Immigration to the
     United States.* Honolulu: East-West Population Insti-
     tute, 1985.

     A report on the conference on Asia-Pacific immigration
     to the United States held in Honolulu on September 20-25,
     1984. Includes the highlights and conclusions of the
     conference, the abstracts of the papers presented, a
     selected bibliography on policies on population movement
     in selected Asian countries.

314. Fernandez, R.A. *The United States-Mexico Border: A
     Politico-Economic Profile.* South Bend, Indiana: Uni-
     versity of Notre Dame, 1977.

315. Finnan, C.R. "A Community Affair: Occupational Assimila-
     tion of Vietnames Refugees." *Journal of Refugee Re-
     settlement,* 1 (1981): 8-14.

     How Vietnamese in Santa Clara County, California,
     adjust to new occupations, suggesting that successful
     occupational assimilation depends on ability and willing-
     ness to identify with a particular occupation.

316. Fitzpatrick, Joseph P. "Hispanics in New York: An
      Archdiocesan Survey." *America*, 148 (March 1983):
      185-188.

      Summarizes the two-volume report, "Hispanics in New
      York: Religious, Cultural and Social Experiences"
      (Archdiocese of New York: Office of Pastoral Research,
      1982). The three-year study based on in-depth inter-
      views with a sample of 1,000 subjects confirms the
      achievements of past pastoral effects and identifies
      new resources and challenges for the Church. Three
      other components to the study: (1) a demographic profile,
      (2) some case studies to provide a more concrete illus-
      tration of the religious experience of Hispanics and
      (3) a series of background papers.

317. ————, and Lourdes Travieso Parker. "Hispanic-Americans
      in the Eastern United States." *Annals of the American
      Academy of Political and Social Science*, 454 (March
      1981): 98-110.

318. Flanigan, James. "North of the Border: Who Needs Whom?"
      Forbes (April 15, 1977): 37-41.

319. Fleitas, Roberto F. "Adjustment Without Assimilation:
      The Cubans in the United States, 1959-1976." Unpub-
      lished M.A. thesis, University of Miami, 1976.

320. Florida State Commission on Hispanic Affairs. *Fourth
      Annual Report, 1979-1980*. Tallahassee: State of
      Florida, 1980.

321. ————. *Fifth Annual Report, 1981*. Tallahassee: State
      of Florida, 1981.

322. ————. *The Impact of Crime and the Criminal Justice
      System on Florida's Hispanics*. Tallahassee: State
      of Florida, 1981.

323. Fogel, Walter. *Education and Income of the Mexican-
      Americans of the Southwest*. Mexican-American Project.
      Los Angeles, California: University of California,
      1966.

324. ————. "Twentieth-Century Mexican Migration to the
      United States." In Barry R. Chiswick, ed. *The Gate-
      way: U.S. Immigration Issues and Policies*. Washington,
      D.C.: American Enterprise Institute, 1982. Pp. 193-
      221.

Believes that contemporary migration from Mexico is quite different from migration in the 1920s and 1950s, two decades with high rates of immigration from Mexico. Mexico's population is 70 million, compared with 25 million in 1950 and 16 million in 1920. Thus, the number of potential immigrants is much larger. Similarly, the Mexican-American population of the United States is 8 to 10 million compared with under 3 million in 1950. The larger Mexican population of the United States provides a cultural and knowledge environment that facilitates additional migration. Argues that the current migration is not very sensitive to shifts in the demand for labor in the United States but, more than in the past, is driven by population and labor-force growth in Mexico. Believes the analysis of the data on Mexican migration is consistent with this conclusion although the available data do not permit definitive results. These findings have important implications for the United States because Mexican immigrants have much lower earnings than other immigrants, and their offspring fail to catch up with other native-born white Americans. The current large migration from Mexico amounts to a rapid enlargement of a disadvantaged group.

325. Foner, Nancy. "Jamaican Journey: Race and Ethnicity Among Jamaican Migrants in New York City." Paper presented at the Conference on Immigration and the Changing Black Population in the United States, University of Michigan, 1983.

326. ————. *Jamaican Migrants: A Comparative Analysis of the New York and London Experience.* New York: Center for Latin American and Caribbean Studies, New York University, 1983.

A comparative study of the migration process. Focus is on Jamaican migrants, and the comparison is between Jamaicans who have moved to London and those who have come to New York City. Analyzes and tries to explain the contrasts as well as the similarities in the experiences of Jamaicans in these two different settings.

327. ————. "Sex Roles and Sensibilities: Jamaican Women in New York and London." In Rita J. Simon and Caroline B. Bettrell, eds. *International Migration: The Female Experience.* Totowa, N.J.: Rowman & Allanheld, 1986. Pp. 133-151.

328.   Fong, Hiram L. "Immigration and Naturalization Laws:
        Today's Need for Naturalization Law Reform." *Inter-*
        national Migration Review, 5 (Winter 1971): 406-418.

        "The immigration and nationality aspects of our law
        must be considered in juxtaposition to one another.
        They go hand in hand. One cannot talk about the one
        without viewing the other. Together, these laws embrace
        our regard for the alien. The immigration and nationality
        laws, together, set forth the conditions for admission
        of aliens to our country and then, once they are within
        the country, the conditions for transition from the
        status of alien to the status of citizen, through
        naturalization. Today, the immigration and nationality
        laws are embodied in the Act of October 3, 1965 (79
        Stat. 911). This Act amended the Immigration and
        Nationality Act (Act of June 27, 1952-66 Stat. 163)
        and, at long last in our history, eliminated the dis-
        crimination therein based upon race and national origins."

329.   Forbes, S. *Medical Assistance for Refugees: Options*
        for Change. Washington, D.C.: Refugee Policy Group,
        February, 1984.

        Identifies and analyzes alternatives to and improve-
        ments on the current refugee medical assistance financing
        system.

330.   ————. *Residency Patterns and Secondary Migration of*
        Refugees: A State of the Information Paper. Washing-
        ton, D.C.: Refugee Policy Group, April, 1984.

        Synthesizes available research regarding the residence
        patterns of refugees in the United States, tracing the
        evolution of U.S. policy and outcomes from 1945 to the
        present.

331.   ————, and P.W. Fagen. *Unaccompanied Refugee Children:*
        The Evolution of U.S. Policies, 1939 to 1984. Wash-
        ington, D.C.: Refugee Policy Group, August, 1984.

332.   "Foreign Workers: Dimensions and Policies." Special Re-
        port (34). Washington, D.C.: National Commission for
        Manpower Policy, March, 1979.

        Lays out a set of policy options with respect to the
        temporary importation of foreign labor to the United
        States and with reference to evaluating these options.

333. Fornaro, Robert J. "Asian-Indians in America: Acculturation and Minority Status." *Migration Today*, 12
(1984): 28-32.

334. Foster, D.W., ed. *Sourcebook of Hispanic Culture in the
United States*. Chicago: American Library Association,
1982.

Presented in three sections: Mexican-Americans, Puerto
Ricans and Cuban-Americans, each essay establishing the
problems, controversies, and concerns of the group along
with the trends and general conclusions that have
emerged. Following each essay is an annotated bibliography of the most important monographs, essays, journals,
and reports on the topic.

335. Foster, S. *Economic Development in the U.S.-Mexico
Border Region: A Review of the Literature*. Monticello,
Illinois: Vance Bibliographies, 1981.

Lists literature concerned with the balance of commercial trade between U.S. and Mexican border cities,
the participation of Mexican nationals in the U.S. labor
markets of the border region, and the effects of
Mexico's Border Industrialization Program.

336. Fouron, Georges E. "The Black Immigrant Dilemma in the
U.S.: The Haitian Experience." *Journal of Caribbean
Studies*, 3 (March 1982): 242-265.

337. Fox, G. *Organizing the New Immigrants: The Hispanic
Trade Unionists' Perspectives*. New York: Center for
Latin American and Caribbean Studies, New York Univer-
sity, May 1983.

Explores the experiences and perceptions of live Hispanic trade unionists, using the format of detailed and
transcribed interviews. Through it, an unusually vivid
understanding of the interviewees' opinions and goals
is transmitted, contributing greatly to understanding
of Hispanic migrants' relationship to the trade union
movement.

338. Fragomen, Austin T., Jr. "Administrative Developments."
[Cuban Refugees] *International Migration Review*, 10
(Winter 1976): 527-529.

"On September 16, 1976, the Immigration and Naturalization Service announced that Cuban refugees in the United
States may become permanent resident aliens without

having to wait for visa numbers to become available
under the Western Hemisphere quotas. Cuban refugees
who in the past were paroled into the United States are
now eligible to apply for adjustment of status after
maintaining parole status for a minimum of two years,
subject to the numerical limitation of 120,000 persons
per year for natives of the Western Hemisphere. This
results in delays of approximately two and one-half
years and expends 30,000 to 40,000 of the 120,000 numbers
available to qualify immigrants from the Western Hemisphere per year. Henceforth, Cuban refugees will be
able to adjust status in the United States outside the
Western Hemisphere numerical limitation."

339.   ———. "The Final Report and Recommendations of the
        Select Commission on Immigration and Refugee Policy:
        A Summary." *International Migration Review*, 15
        (Winter 1981): 758-768.

        On March 1, 1981, the Select Commission on Immigration
        and Refugee Policy submitted its report to the President
        and each House of Congress. The Commission had been
        authorized by law to conduct a study that would take into
        account both the statutory provisions of the Immigration
        and Nationality Act and the practical implementation
        of these provisions, their impact upon political,
        social and economic trends in the United States--and
        upon human life, the lives of not only those persons
        whose native land is the United States but also those
        nationals of other countries who desire to live in the
        United States, either temporarily or permanently. "The
        Commission has addressed itself to the causes and con-
        sequences of undocumented/illegal aliens, many of whom
        enter this country in search of economic opportunity.
        Although precise information regarding the impact un-
        documented aliens have on social services, depression of
        wages and overall effect of United States society is not
        available, there is little question that United States
        citizens and residents competing for low-paying or
        minimum wage jobs have been displaced by undocumented
        aliens. There are additional adverse consequences, since
        undocumented aliens will fail to report crimes, health
        hazards, or violations of the labor law."

340.   ———. "Immigration and Nationality Act of 1981."
        International Migration Review, 16 (Spring 1982):
        206-222.

        Highlights the Immigration and Nationality Act Amend-
        ments of 1981 (Pub. L. No. 97-116). During the past

session of the Ninety-seventh Congress, the bill, which
was referred to as the "efficiency bill," passed the
House by a voice vote on October 13, 1981 and was received in the Senate on October 14, 1981. Its purpose
is to improve the efficiency of the Immigration and
Naturalization Service, to provide clarification of
certain provisions of the Immigration and Nationality
Act, and, in some cases, to eliminate the need for
Congress to consider private immigration bills. With
the exception of a few provisions relating to students,
foreign medical students, and the retention of fees by
naturalization courts, the new law went into effect
December 29, 1981.

341. ————. "Legislative and Judicial Developments."
International Migration Review, 6 (Fall 1972): 296-302.

[Illegal Aliens]. "Within the past two years, Congress
has focused on the topic of illegal aliens--those persons who either entered the United States surreptitiously
or, after gaining lawful admission to the United States,
violated the terms of their nonimmigrant status. Illegal
aliens were first recognized as a 'problem' approximately
five years ago because of their adverse economic impact
upon U.S. workers in towns along the Mexican border.
At that time, it was concluded in a study conducted by
the Trancentury Corp. on contract to the U.S. Department
of Labor that illegal aliens flowing over the border
from Mexico into the southwestern areas of the United
States were a primary cause of depressed wages and working
conditions and grinding poverty in that area of the
country. Both the Immigration and Nationality Subcommittee of the House and the House Education and Labor
Committee as well as the Senate Subcommittee on Migratory
Labor and the Senate Subcommittee on Refugees and Escapees became involved in attempting to find a solution
to this grave economic situation. Within the past year,
it has become apparent that Congress now considers the
problem of 'illegal aliens' to be national in nature,
whereas, previously, the problem was viewed as uniquely
southwestern."

342. ————. "Permanent Resident Status Redefined." *International Migration Review*, 9 (Spring 1975): 63-68.

On November 25, 1974 the United States Supreme Court
in the case of *Saxbe v. Bustos*, 43 L.W. 4017 held that
permanent resident aliens residing abroad and commuting
to work in the United States, on either seasonal or daily

basis, are entitled to maintain their status as permanent residents and may be admitted to the United States
without further documentation with the exception of
evidence to show their status as permanent resident
aliens of the United States. The Immigration and
Naturalization Service has for a number of years permitted aliens who have their homes in Canada or Mexico
the privilege of commuting daily to places of employment
in the United States. Moreover, it has permitted aliens
residing abroad to do so on a seasonal basis as well.
The question before the Court was whether the practice
of permitting aliens to reside abroad and to work in
the United States either daily or seasonally conforms
with the Immigration and Nationality Act. The essential
question was whether alien commuters were immigrants
who were "lawfully admitted for permanent residence"
and were "returning from a temporary visit abroad" when
they entered the United States and were, thus, "special
immigrants" under the Immigration and Nationality Act.
It had long been an administrative construction of the
statute in the context of commuter aliens to permit
such a practice. Mr. Justice Douglas delivered the
opinion of the Court in the 5-4 decision.

343.   ————. "The Refugee: A Problem of Definition." *Case
        Western Reserve Journal of International Law*, 3
        (Winter 1970): 45-70.

In the context of the increased number of refugees
since WW II and the importance of a definition for the
policy of any body, the article examines the primary
definition in the international area and the definition
utilized by the United States under its national laws,
with a view toward enlarging the personal scope of
both by incorporating the following basic elements:
"The term 'refugee' means any person, (I) who owing to
a well-founded fear of being persecuted for reasons of
race, religion, nationality, membership in a particular
social group, or political opinion, is outside his usual
place of abode and is unable or, owing to such fear,
unwilling to return there, or (II) who owing to natural
calamity or military operations is outside his usual
place of abode and is unable to return there."

344.   ————, and A.J. Del Rey, Jr. "The Immigration Selec-
        tion System: A Proposal for Reform." *San Diego Law
        Review*, 17 (1979): 1-36.

Reviews the historical background of present immigration law and analyzes the policy goals of the present

immigration law in light of major contemporary issues
that bear directly on the immigration act: population
growth, the requirements of the labor force, family reunion, illegal immigration, and refugee admission.

345. Francis, N.C. "Haitian Entrant Relocation in Philadel-
phia." Paper presented at American Anthropological
Association. 83rd Annual Meeting. Denver, Colorado,
November 14-18, 1984.

Given their noneligibility (as a group) for "refugee"
status, Haitian entrants have had little or no recourse
to federal funds and organizations for aid. They rely
on individuals and themselves for help in coping with
U.S. institutional and social systems. Preliminary
research shows that amongst the Haitians themselves,
there is no unified support system. There is a difficulty in their joining together, which is exacerbated
by the subconscious manifestation of social stratification that exists in Haiti. Studying the entrants' social
networking patterns reveals what they do to live not
only amongst native-born and other U.S. residents but
also amongst each other.

346. Frank, M. *Newcomers to the United States: Children and
Families*. New York: The Haworth Press, 1983.

347. Fuchs, Lawrence H. "The Search for a Sound Immigration
Policy: A Personal View." In Nathan Glazer, ed.
Clamor at the Gates: The New American Immigration
(San Francisco: Institute for Contemporary Studies,
1985). Pp. 17-48.

Fuchs served as executive director of the Select Commission on Immigration and Refugee Policy established
by the U.S. Congress in 1978. "After nearly two years
of thoroughly bipartsian work, the commission made its
report to Congress and President Reagan as specified by
law. Subsequently, the Simpson-Mazzoli Immigration
Reform Act of 1981 was introduced, embodying many of the
most important recommendations of the Select Commission.
As former director of the staff of the commission, I
often have been involved in defending its recommendations
and supporting the Simpson-Mazzoli bill. Rarely have I
been asked how I would disagree with or improve either,
and I welcome this opportunity to do so."

348. Galarza, Ernesto, et al. *Mexican Americans in the
Southwest*. Santa Barbara, California: McNally &
Lofton, 1970.

Trade unionism, community and national organizations, black and brown affinities and frictions, intellectuals, research, and the Office of Economic Opportunity programs are topics treated from the authors' personal involvements.

349. Gallagher, Patrick Lee. *The Cuban Exile: A Socio-Political Analysis.* New York: Arno Press, 1980.

350. Gann, L.H., and Peter J. Duignan. *The Hispanics in the United States: A History.* Boulder, Colorado: Westview Press, 1986.

A large-scale survey covering the history, politics, and culture of all major Hispanic groups (including Cubans, Mexicans, Puerto Ricans, and Chicanos) in the United States. Begins by examining the Spanish legacy of the Southwest, the beginnings of large-scale Mexican immigration into the borderlands after the turn of the century, socioeconomic changes brought about by World War I, and changes in the demographic composition of the nation as a result of later immigration. Discusses in detail the national debate over immigration, asking whether immigrants compete for jobs and social services, whether the Immigration and Naturalization Service is capable of handling the flow of immigrants, and whether employer sanctions are just. Describes the immigrants themselves--their educational levels, occupational backgrounds, and experiences in adapting to life in the United States--stressing the difference between the various groups in these areas. Looks at Hispanic culture, including politics, education, sports, and social problems. This study argues that immigration is a positive experience for both the newcomers and the local communities into which they immigrate.

351. Garcia, John A. "Political Integration of Mexican Immigrants: Explorations into the Naturalization Process." *International Migration Review,* 15 (Winter 1981): 608-625.

Examines the significant influx of Mexican immigrants to the United States since 1920 and represents an examination of one dimension of political integration, naturalization, in terms of the contributing factors that affect Mexican immigrants to pursue (or not) U.S. citizenship. "Within the context of this article, the use of the term, immigrant, refers to the movement of Mexican nationals into the United States. Scholars of

Mexican-origin populations have characterized them as
an indigenous population that were conquered because
of America's manifest destiny efforts. Therefore, they
should not be categorized as an immigrant population.
The author does not deal with the various ideological
interpretations of Mexican people but limits the discussion to the movement of Mexican persons into the
United States as immigrants."

352. Garcia y Griego, M. *El volumen de la migración de
Mexicanos no documentados a los Estados Unidos: Nuevas
hipótesis.* Centro Nacional de Información y Estadisticas del Trabajo, México, D.F. La Jolla, California:
Center for U.S.-Mexican Studies, University of California, San Diego, 1980.

353. Garkovich, L.E. "A Pilot Study of the Dispersal and
Assimilation of Indochinese Refugees." Unpublished
Ph.D. dissertation, University of Missouri, 1976.

Interviewed 128 refugees resettled in three areas of
the central United States: a large metropolitan community;
a medium-sized metropolitan area; and a group of non-
metropolitan communities. In addition, 29 sponsors and
representatives of agencies involved in the resettlement
process were consulted. Purpose was twofold: to assess
the success and impact of the dispersal policy and to
evaluate the initial stages in the assimilation of the
refugees. The theoretical framework has rested on three
assumptions: (1) adjustment and assimilation are processes which revolve around on-going changes in the refugees'
symbolic map of the world, their values, behaviors, and
psychological identifications; (2) these processes require differing periods of time to accomplish, and possibly may not fully occur at all; and finally, the size
and type of resettlement community will influence the
nature and pace of these processes.

354. Garrison, Vivian, and Carol I. Weiss. "Dominican Family
Networks and United States Immigration Policy: A Case
Study." *International Migration Review,* 13 (1979):
264-283.

One of the major objectives of the 1965 law is the
reunification of families, that is, of parents, spouses,
siblings, and children. The law neglects godparents,
godchildren, aunts, nephews, and "assumed relatives"
who, under Dominican traditions, are important. In
order to reunite Dominican-defined families after one

member has immigrated to the United States, a whole
arsenal of subterfuges is employed. Describes one
family's history and concludes that if the United States'
policy were more open to the realities of "family" in
the Dominican Republic, fewer people would need to re-
sort to illegal means to immigrate.

355. Garver, S., and P. McGuire. *Coming to North America
     from Mexico, Cuba and Puerto Rico*. New York: Dela-
     corte, 1981.

     Tells, through detailed histories, personal accounts,
     primary sources and photographs, the human side of the
     experience of Latin Americans in North American society.

356. Gerber, Stanford N., and Gregg E. Whitman. "Notes on
     Recent Immigrants to the United States Virgin Islands."
     International Migration Review, 5 (Fall 1971): 357-62.

357. Gergosian, Edward M. "Significant Development in the
     Immigration Laws of the United States 1980-1981."
     South Dakota Law Review, 19 (Winter 1981): 195-231.

358. "Getting Their Slice of Paradise." *Time* (May 2, 1977):
     26-27+.

359. Gibson, Campbell. "The Contribution of Immigration to
     the U.S. Population Growth: 1790-1970." *International
     Migration Review*, 9 (1975): 157-176.

360. Gibson, Lay James, and Alfonso Corona Renteria, eds.
     *The United States and Mexico: Borderland Development
     and the National Economies*. Boulder, Colorado:
     Westview Press, 1985.

     Addressing the economic aspects of ties between the
     United States and Mexico, looks at the structural char-
     acteristics of the border region and the flow of goods,
     services, capital, and people between the two countries.
     The contributors describe the cultural, economic, and
     demographic dimensions of the borderlands and focus
     on specific issues critical to the region, among them
     environmental pollution, migration, territorial issues,
     and the implications of border-zone industrial growth.
     Considers how these issues affect the national economies
     and relations between the two countries.

361. Gil, V.E. "The Personal Adjustment and Acculturation
     of Cuban Immigrants in Los Angeles." Unpublished

Ph.D. dissertation. Los Angeles: University of California, 1976.

362. Girling, R.K. "The Migration of Human Capital from the Third World: The Implications and Some Data on the Jamaican Case." *Social and Economic Studies*, 32 (March 1974): 84-96.

363. Girordet, E. "Refugee Crisis: Helping the World's Homeless." *The Christian Science Monitor*, November 18-21, 25-26, 28, 1980.

Surveys the worldwide refugee situation, sees some hope; describes refugee movements from the Huguenots to the Haitians including Vietnamese boat people and Afghanistan refugees; echoes "neglected African cries for help," and samples the situations of refugees in Europe and the United States.

364. Glaessel-Brown, Eleanor E. "The Role of Blue-Collar Migrants from Colombia in New England Labor Markets for Light Manufacturing Industry." Unpublished Ph.D. dissertation, Massachusetts Institute of Technology, 1983.

Open-ended interviewing conducted in four Massachusetts cities and one Colombian city, including extensive interviews with employers.

365. Glantz, Oscar. "Native Sons and Immigrants: Some Beliefs and Values of American Born and West Indian Blacks at Brooklyn College." *Ethnicity*, 5 (1978): 189-202.

Compares the attitude toward work and the American legal system of English-speaking West Indians who arrived in New York in 1971-1972 with those of American-born blacks. West Indians are generally more optimistic about their chances and see the police as fairer and are convinced that hard work rather than violence will pay off.

366. Glazer, Nathan, ed. *Clamor at the Gates: The New American Immigration*. San Francisco: Institute for Contemporary Studies, 1985.

Contents: Lawrence H. Fuchs, "The Search for a Sound Immigration Policy: A Personal View"; Harris N. Miller, "The Right Thing to Do: A History of Simpson-Mazzoli"; Edwin Harwood, "How Should We Enforce Immigration Law?";

Rodolfo O. de la Garza, "Mexican Americans, Mexican Im-
migrants, and Immigration Reform"; Thomas Muller, "Eco-
nomic Effects of Immigration"; Vernon M. Briggs, Jr.,
"Employment Trends and Contemporary Immigration Policy";
Ivan Light, "Immigrant Entrepreneurs in America: Koreans
in Los Angeles"; Peter I. Rose, "Asian Americans: From
Pariahs to Paragons"; Nathan Glazer, "Immigrants and
Education"; Peter Skerry, "The Ambiguity of Mexican
American Politics"; Michael S. Teitelbaum, "Forced
Migration: The Tragedy of Mass Expulsions"; Peter H.
Schuck, "Immigration Law and the Problem of Community."

367.   ————. "Immigrants and Education." In Nathan Glazer,
        ed. *Clamor at the Gates: The New American Immigration*
        (San Francisco, California: Institute for Contemporary
        Studies, 1985). Pp. 213-239.

        "One would think that if any schools were adapted to
        the education of vast numbers of immigrant children it
        would be American urban schools. But when, after a
        period of forty years in which immigration, radically
        reduced by immigration restriction acts, depression,
        war, and continued restriction in the postwar period,
        began to rise in the mid-1960s (in 1966 immigration
        passed 300,000 for the first time since 1924), a great
        number of things had changed. The education of immi-
        grants today is as controversial as it ever has been,
        indeed more controversial than it was during the great
        age of mass immigration that ended in 1924."

368.   Glick, Nina Barnett. "The Formation of a Haitian Ethnic
        Group." Unpublished Ph.D. dissertation, Columbia Uni-
        versity, 1975.

369.   Goldfarb, Robert S. "Occupational Preferences in the
        U.S. Immigration Law: An Economic Analysis." In Barry
        R. Chiswick, ed. *The Gateway: U.S. Immigration Issues
        and Policies*. Washington, D.C.: American Enterprise
        Institute, 1982. Pp. 412-448.

        After a description of current immigration law, argues
        that the provisions limit skilled immigration but fail
        (because of illegal immigrants) to limit unskilled
        immigration effectively. A number of conceivable economic
        rationales for such provisions are identified, and the
        relevance of each rationale is explored. "Aggregate
        output" rationales viewing immigration as a way of
        maximizing an objective such as national output or per
        capita income are found to be relevant, while rationales

focusing on special conditions in specific occupations (labor shortages, monopoly elements, etc.) are not considered a useful basis for a general immigration policy. As part of the discussion, the U.S. use of immigration to ameliorate the so-called doctor shortage is described and evaluated. Broad policy implications of the aggregate output rationale are explored, with simple models. Optimal immigration levels do exist and vary with the precise policy objective. The current system's ability to apply an aggregate output rationale effectively is then investigated. Sources of difficulty include the inability to set numerical limits on immigration by occupation group and the lack of incentives for selecting "high-quality" potential immigrants. Finally, there is the issue of who gets the "economic rents" generated by the nonprice rationing system. Argues that there is at present no mechanism for the native population to capture some of these economic rents and that probably a substantial proportion of these rents not retained by the immigrants are received by immigration lawyers or are otherwise dissipated in misallocations of resources designed to increase the probability of receiving a visa.

370. Gollobin, Ira. "Haitian 'Boat People' and Equal Justice Under Law: Background and Perspective." *Migration Today*, 7 (September 1979): 40-41.

371. Gonzales, Diana H. "Sociocultural Adaptation Among Cuban Emigré Women in Miami, Florida." Paper presented at the annual meeting of the Caribbean Studies Association, 1980.

372. Gonzales, Juan L. *Mexican and Mex-American Farm Workers: The California Agricultural Industry*. New York: Praeger, 1985.

373. Gonzalez, Esther B. *Annotated Bibliography of Cubans in the United States, 1960-1976*. Miami: Florida International University, 1977.

374. González, Gustavo R. "The Migration of Latin American High-Level Manpower." *International Labor Review*, 98 (December 1968): 551-569.

375. Gonzalez, L.S. "La cooperación international en la migración." *International Migration*, 14 (1976): 200-208.

"International co-operation is indispensable in the
migration field, if the migrants are to become culturally
and economically integrated in the country of reception
and to contribute to the social welfare of the local
community and, reciprocally, if local environment and
community are to penetrate the migrants and transmit to
them all aspects of the native culture--i.e. if the
integration process is to be achieved."

376. González, Nancie L. "Multiple Migratory Experiences
     of Dominican Women." Paper presented at West Chester
     State College Ethnic Studies Conference, December 4,
     1976.

     "An analysis of sex as a discriminatory factor in the
     migratory process leads to a consideration of the larger
     implications of Dominican migration in relation to the
     political economy of the Caribbean. It is suggested that
     prostitution, domestic service, and--more recently--work
     in the United States garment industry, are among the few
     avenues open to lower-class Dominican women seeking to
     improve their situations. Regardless of her social
     class, however, a Dominican woman's residence in the
     United States offers her opportunities not available at
     home. The extensive outmigration from the Dominican
     Republic can be seen as being related to the increasing
     urban unemployment rate and to the decreasing availability
     of land for small agricultural pursuits."

377. ————. "Multiple Migratory Experiences of Dominican
     Women." Anthropological Quarterly, 49 (1976): 36-44.

378. ————. "Peasants' Progress: Dominicans in New York."
     Caribbean Studies, 10 (1970): 154-171.

379. Goodwin, G.G.S. International Law and the Movement of
     Persons Between States. New York: Oxford University
     Press, 1978.

380. Gordon, Linda W. "New Data on the Fertility of South-
     eastern Asian Refugees in the United States."
     P/AAMHRC Research Review, 2 (1983): 3-6.

381. ————. "Southeast Asian Refugee Migration to the
     United States." Paper presented at the Conference
     on Asia-Pacific Immigration to the United States,
     East-West Population Institute, Honolulu, Hawaii,
     1984.

382. Gordon, M.H. *The Selection of Migrant Categories from the Caribbean to the United States: The Jamaican Experience.* New York: Center for Latin American and Caribbean Studies, New York University. May 1983.

    Focuses on the process through which categories of immigrants have been selected from the Commonwealth Caribbean to the United States in two different time periods--pre-1940 (early immigrants) and post-1960 (recent immigrants).

383. Goza, F. "Income Attainment Among Native and Immigrant Asians in the United States, 1960 to 1980." CDE Working Paper 84-19. Madison, Wisconsin: Center for Demography and Ecology, University of Wisconsin-Madison [1985].

    Examines earnings differentials between Asian origin men and native whites using the 1960, 1970 and 1980 U.S. Bureau of the Census Public Samples. The extent of income heterogeneity among five Asian groups as well as the degree of dissimilarities between the native- and foreign-born ethnics are demonstrated via examination of socioeconomic and demographic characteristics.

384. Grau, Kenneth. "Immigration Law." *Annual Survey of American Law* (June 1982): 865-900.

385. Gray, Richard B. "Aid to Cuban Refugees in Florida." *Governmental Research Bulletin* (Florida State University), 1 (March 1964): 1-4.

386. Grebler, Leo. *Mexican Immigration to the United States: The Record and the Implications.* Los Angeles, California: Mexican-American Study Project. University of California, 1966.

387. Greeley, Andrew M. "Immigration and Religio-Ethnic Groups: A Sociological Reappraisal." In Barry R. Chiswick, ed. *The Gateway: U.S. Immigration Issues and Policies.* Washington, D.C.: American Enterprise Institute, 1982. Pp. 159-192.

    Considers the sociological concept of "social disorganization" elaborated by W.I. Thomas, especially in his *Polish Peasant* volumes. Thomas argued that the trauma of immigration destroyed the old agricultural values of the Polish peasant and provided him with no new set of values with which to cope with the demands of urban industrial life in the United States. The

result was a collapse of the intimate social structures
that make life possible and success achievable. Believes
that the social disorganization theory, sometimes dras-
tically oversimplified, has had enormous impact on both
policy makers and educated Americans. A consideration
of the history of the Polish-Americans whom Thomas
described suggests that he may well have confused the
pathology of a minority with the culture of the majority
of the group. Using data from the General Social Surveys and other sources, Greeley shows that Polish-
Americans rapidly acculturated into American life,
achieving educational, occupational, and income parity
in a relatively brief period of time without necessarily
shedding many of their Polish cultural characteristics.
Greeley believes that the success of Polish Americans
and other European Catholics raises serious questions
about the claims that other "disorganized" groups cannot be successful in American life. Some preliminary
data on several ethnic groups presented by Greeley from
another analysis indicate that there may be many different roads to economic success. Some immigrants first
acquire high income and then high levels of schooling,
while others seem to use large investments in schooling
as a path to high incomes.

388. Greene, Sheldon L. "Wetbacks, Growers and Poverty."
      The Nation (October 20, 1969): 403-6.

389. Greenwood, Michael J., and John M. McDowell. "The
      Supply of Immigrants to the United States." In
      Barry R. Chiswick, ed. *The Gateway: U.S. Immigration
      Issues and Policies.* Washington, D.C.: American
      Enterprise Institute, 1982. Pp. 54-85.

      A short-run perspective by analyzing a cross section
of international migration flows to the United States
from as many origin countries as the available data
allow. Develops and estimates a model to explain the
international distribution of emigration from each of
several countries of origin around the world to the receiving countries. A major conclusion emerging from
this analysis is that observed emigration from many
countries to the United States is substantially less
than is predicted by the model, suggesting that U.S.
immigration law is a binding constraint. If entry
barriers were removed, Western Hemisphere nations appear
most likely to supply the United States with large
increases in immigrants. Examines immigration to the
United States from the perspective of the United States;

that is, using U.S. data on immigration, analyzes migration to the United States from various countries of origin. Model includes variables designed to capture the influences of differential economic advantage and variables intended to reflect the costs of transferring skills to the United States from abroad (as measured by the similarity of occupational structure). Distance and the earnings differentials appear to be important factors affecting the rate of migration from various countries to the United States. Another factor decreasing the rate of immigration is a higher level of economic development in the sending country. Similarly, the availability of social security for the aged in the countries of origin discourages migration by the aged. Finally, the ability of prospective immigrants to transfer their occupational knowledge from their native country to the U.S. labor market is also an important influence on U.S. immigration rates.

390. Griffin, E. "Help Mexican Workers at Home." *Nation*, 238 (March 3, 1984): 250-252.

391. Grimond, J. "New York, 1980, Los Angeles 1980." *Economist*, 283 (April 3, 1982): 10-12.

392. Grindle, M.S. *Issues in U.S.-Mexican Agricultural Relations: A Binational Consultation*. San Diego: Center for U.S.-Mexican Studies, University of California, 1983.

   Summarizes the proceedings of a Binational Consultation on U.S.-Mexican Agricultural Relations held at the University of California at San Diego in February 1981. "The consultation sought to define the nature, causes, and consequences of flows of labor, capital, technology, and agricultural commodities across the U.S.-Mexican border and to identify fruitful areas for additional research. This agenda required not only analysis of the trade relationships between the countries but also discussion of socioeconomic changes occurring in both countries and related public policies that could be identified as causes or consequences of binational concerns."

393. Gross, Gary. "Openup America." (Refugees). *Human Rights*, 10 (Spring 1982): 26.

394. Haas, L. *The Bracero in Orange County, California: A Work Force for Economic Transition*. Working Papers

in U.S.-Mexican Studies No. 29. Program in United
States-Mexican Studies, University of California, San
Diego, 1981.

Studies the relationship between the *Bracero* program
and the industrialization of Orange County.

395. Haines, David W. "Family and Community among Vietnamese
Refugees." *International Migration Review*, 15 (Spring/
Summer 1981): 310-319.

Focuses on the maintenance, extent, and structure of
family and community ties among Vietnamese refugees in
the United States. The findings from a series of field
efforts in northern Virginia indicate the continuing
and pervasive importance of both family and community.
The family, in particular, extends well beyond the
boundaries of the household and is capable of furnishing
significant amounts of emotional and practical support.

396. ————. "Mismatch in the Resettlement Process: The Vietnamese Family Versus the American Housing Market."
Journal of Resettlement, 1 (1980): 15-19.

Explores one area of mismatch between American and
Vietnamese societies—kinship and family. The nature
of kinship in Vietnam and Vietnamese in the United States
is described to show the lack of proper housing in the
United States for Vietnamese families.

397. ————, ed. *Refugees in the United States: A Reference
Handbook*. Westport, Connecticut: Greenwood Press,
1985.

Since the 1979 mimeographed edition of the Department
of Health and Human Services' *Refugee Resettlement in
the U.S.*, there has been no compendium of information
on refugees recently resettled in America. This collection spans the gap and provides a comprehensive
description of main refugee waves that have come to the
United States during the past twenty-five years. The
book is divided into two parts—a general introduction
written by the editor and a series of specialized essays
on particular refugee groups written by contributors,
some of whom are well-known analysts of the refugee
adjustment process.

398. ————. "Vietnamese Refugee Women in the U.S. Labor
Force: Continuity or Change?" In Rita J. Simon and
Caroline G. Brettell, eds. *International Migration:*

The Female Experience. Totowa, N.J.: Rowman & Allanheld, 1986. Pp. 62-75.

399. "Haitian Leaders, NAACP Join Protest Moves over Refugees." *The Crisis,* 88 (December 1981): 504.

400. "Haitian Refugees: Reprieved." *The Economist* (July 3,
1982): 25-26.

401. "Haitian Requests for Asylum." *Interpreter Releases,*
51 (May 23, 1974): 138-140.

402. "Haitians, Stay Home!" *America,* 144 (May 16, 1981):
398.

403. Hampton, Ellen. "Little Haiti: The City Within."
Miami Herald, Tropic Magazine (July 3, 1983): 7-26.

404. Hansen, Niles M. *The Border Economy: Regional Development in the Southwest.* Austin, Texas: University of
Texas Press, 1981.

Although examining regional development issues on
both sides of the border in their respective contexts,
devotes primary attention to the U.S. side. Analyzes
the border economy in terms of the historical role of
Mexican labor in the Southwest and finds that Mexican
labor, whether legal or undocumented, has been a valuable
asset in the growth and development of the economy of
the Southwest. Special consideration is also given to
the social and economic status of Mexican-Americans.
Presents evidence suggesting that the prospects of this
historically disadvantaged minority have been improving.
Represents a synthesis of much of the existing secondary
literature on immigration and extensive primary research.
Major attention is given to a wide range of border
theories, to the significance of the new international
division of labor, and to European guest worker experiences, all of which have relevance to the Mexico-
U.S. borderlands.

405. Harbolt, Pat. "Cuban Refugees." *Access: A Human Services Magazine,* 3 (June-July 1980): 13-15, 36.

406. ————, and Danny Pietrodangelo. "The Haitian Refugees."
Access: A Human Services Magazine, 3 (June-July 1980):
16-19.

407. Hartley, W. "Reform in the Restrictionist Tradition:
      The Immigration Act of 1965." *Research Studies*, 37
      (September 1969): 194-207.

408. Harwood, Edwin. "Alienation: American Attitudes Toward
      Immigration." *Public Opinion* (June/July 1983): 49-51.

409. ———. "Can Immigration Laws Be Enforced?" *Public
      Interest*, 72 (Summer 1983): 107-123.

410. ———. "The Crisis in Immigration Policy." *Journal
      of Contemporary Studies*, 6 (Fall 1983): 47-52.

411. ———. "How Should We Enforce Immigration Law?" In
      Nathan Glazer, ed. *Clamor at the Gates: The New
      American Immigration* (San Francisco: Institute for
      Contemporary Studies, 1985). Pp. 73-91.

      "When he declared that America had 'lost control over
      its borders,' the Reagan administration's Attorney
      General, William French Smith, was merely stating a
      truism familiar to all. References to the 'revolving
      door' at our southern border or, more generally, to the
      'immigration crisis' have become stock cliches. They
      refer to a breakdown in immigration enforcement that
      began during the late 1960s, accelerated during the
      1970s, and continues to the present time. Although the
      number of illegal aliens living in the United States is
      not known, a conservative estimate of from three to six
      million is accepted by most scholars. Estimates of the
      net annual influx of illegal immigrants coming to the
      United States range from 200,000 to 500,000. Whether
      the level of illegal immigration constitutes a 'social
      problem' for our society is hotly disputed by scholars.
      Economists and policy analysts can be found on both
      sides of the fence. What is not in dispute is that the
      Immigration and Naturalization Service (INS) can no
      longer effectively deter illegal immigration."

412. Haskins, J. *The New Americans: Cuban Boat People*.
      Hillsdale, New Jersey: Enslow, 1982.

      Tells the story of the Cuban refugees who fled to the
      United States. Beginning with a factual account of
      Cuba's tumultuous history, traces the journey of the
      refugees across the Straits of Florida in fishing boats
      and deals with the reaction of the U.S. government to
      the refugees' plight and to the Cuban government.

413. Hawthrone, L., ed. *Refugee: The Vietnamese Experience.* Oxford: Oxford University Press, 1982.

Refugees tell their own stories in their own words, beginning at the time when their lives and futures in Vietnam seemed relatively peaceful, even hopeful. The refugees tell about their "ordinary" lives in South Vietnam before the communist victory in 1975, life in their country under the new regime and, finally, the ordeals of flight and resettlement.

414. Hayes, A.M. "Away from Tax Home Guidelines--Foreign Citizens." *CPA Journal*, 53 (November 1983): 80-81.

415. Heer, David M. "The Socioeconomic Status of Recent Mothers of Mexican Origin in Los Angeles County: A Comparison of Undocumented Migrants, Legal Migrants, and Native Citizens." Paper presented at the meeting of the International Union for the Scientific Study of Population, Manila, the Philippines, December, 1981.

First report of findings from a study based in part on interviews with nondetained undocumented Mexican women who gave birth in Los Angeles County in 1980-81. The sampling frame consisted of all official birth records for that period. The project was sponsored by the Population Research Laboratory, University of Southern California.

416. Hendricks, Glenn. *The Dominican Diaspora: From the Dominican Republic to New York City. Villagers in Transition.* New York: Teachers College Press, 1974.

Describes the social processes triggered by the migration and consequent culture context of the population from Sabana de Corona, Dominican Republic, in New York City, through the variables of the cultural experience in the sending society, the legal and social mechanisms involved in the process of entering the United States, and the socio-economic niche they have come to occupy in the receiving society. Assumes that the experience of these immigrants is "proto-typical" of a fairly sizable number of the current immigration population of New York City. Shows that technology, "both in modes of transportation and communication, makes an understanding of the sending society an essential element in any attempt to explicate immigrant behavior."

417. Henkin, A.B., and L.T. Nguyen. *Between Two Cultures:*
      The Vietnamese in America. Palo Alto, California:
      R & E Research Assoc., Inc., 1981.

418. Hernández, Andres, ed. *Cuban Minority in the United*
      States: Final Report on Need Identification and Pro-
      gram Evaluation. Washington, D.C.: Cuban National
      Planning Council, 1974.

419. Hernandez, José, et al. "Census Data and the Problem
      of Conceptually Defining the Mexican American Popula-
      tion." *Social Science Quarterly,* 53 (March 1973):
      671-87.

420. Hersh, B.R. "Ethical Considerations of the Immigration
      Lawyer." *Florida Bar Journal,* 51 (January 1977):
      18-25.

421. Hirabayashi, L.R. *Asian American Community Studies:*
      Selected References. Council of Planning Librarians,
      No. 94. Chicago: CPL Bibliographies, 1982.

      Organized in terms of the major Asian-American groups,
      provides an overview of recent Asian-American community
      studies.

422. *Hispanics: Challenges and Opportunities.* New York: Ford
      Foundation, June 1984.

      Working paper examines the demographic, economic,
      social, and political situation of Hispanics in the
      United States and the Ford Foundation's initiatives to
      address the needs and impact of this growing population.

423. Ho, C. "Transnational Networks Among Caribbean Immi-
      grants in the United States." Paper presented at
      American Anthropological Association. 83rd Annual
      Meeting. Denver, Colorado, November 14-18, 1984.

      Caribbean immigration, as a component of the "New
      Immigration" to the United States, may be distinguished
      by kinship and friendship networks that transcend
      national boundaries. Such networks affect the patterns
      of migration by recruiting new immigrants, maintaining
      close ties with the country of origin, and sustaining
      cultural persistence. Findings were made during field-
      work among black immigrants from Trinidad to Los Angeles.
      Multicultural and multiracial facets of the "New Immigra-
      tion" present a formidable challenge to social scientists
      of the assimilation school.

424. Hofstetter, Richard R., ed. *U.S. Immigration Policy.*
     Durham, North Carolina: Duke University Press, 1984.

     Text originally published as vol. 45, No. 2, of the
     journal *Law & Contemporary Problems.* Contents: Martin
     Bronfenbrenner, "Hyphenated Americans--Economic Aspects";
     Philip L. Martin and Marion F. Houstoun, "European and
     American Immigration Policies": Richard R. Hofstetter,
     "Economic Underdevelopment and the Population Explosion:
     Implications for U.S. Immigration Policy"; William P.
     Travis, "Migration, Income Distribution, and Welfare
     Under Alternative International Economic Policies":
     Franklin S. Abrams, "American Immigration Policy: How
     Strait the Gate"; Maxine S. Seller, "Historical Perspec-
     tives on American Immigration Policy: Case Studies and
     Current Implications": Alex Stepick, "Haitian Boat
     People: A Study in the Conflicting Forces Shaping U.S.
     Immigration Policy"; Roger Waldinger, "The Occupational
     and Economic Immigration Policy"; Roger Waldinger, "The
     Occupational and Economic Integration of the New Immi-
     grants"; Arthur F. Corwin, "Estimates of Illegal Aliens
     in the United States, 1970-1981."

425. Hohl, Donald G. "Attempts at Immigration Reform: 94th
     Congress." *International Migration Review*, 10 (Winter
     1976): 523-525.

     "The last major revision of the United States immigra-
     tion laws was approved on October 3, 1965. Two amend-
     ments had far-reaching effects, especially in the
     Western Hemisphere. Section 212 (a)(14), as amended,
     required labor certifications for aliens coming to the
     United States to take up employment unless specifically
     exempted. In addition, for the first time in history,
     a numerical limitation was placed on Western Hemisphere
     immigration. The annual numerical ceiling, which was
     set at 120,000, became effective on July 1, 1968. When
     the 94th Congress convened ten years later, the disas-
     trous effects of these amendments on Western Hemisphere
     immigration was clearly evident. Immigration of native-
     born Canadians, traditionally that of skilled workers,
     dropped from 27,662 in 1968 to 7,308 in 1975. The enact-
     ment of the new labor certification provision played a
     major role in this decline. Hemisphere-wise, due to the
     lack of a preference system and the low numerical ceil-
     ing, a backlog quickly developed to the point that there
     was a waiting period of over two and one-half years
     before an immigrant visa became available. The illegal
     alien influx increased, certainly due in part to the

long waiting period, and many persons simply crossed a
border or overstayed a visa in order to reside with
husbands, wives, and children until lawful immigration
was possible."

426.   ————. "The Indochinese Refugee: The Evolution of
United States Policy." *International Migration Review*,
12 (Spring 1978): 128-132.

"In the weeks prior to the collapse of the South Vietnamese government on April 30, 1975, elaborate plans
were made whereby large numbers of Vietnamese would be
evacuated when the United States withdrew its personnel
from that country. This group consisted of close family
members of U.S. citizens, individuals (and their families) who had worked for the U.S. government or U.S.
firms conducting business there, and certain special
cases ('high risk') whose lives would be endangered if
they remained behind. Unfortunately, due to a variety
of circumstances including the sudden demise of that
government, very few of those selected were able to get
out during the air-sea evacuation. In all, a total of
nearly 130,000 evacuees were taken to temporary haven
on Guam and Wake Island and later transferred to the
processing centers located in California, Arkansas,
Pennsylvania, and Florida. The resettlement process was
undertaken following the traditional pattern by which
the voluntary agencies were to find homes and jobs for
the refugees with limited financial assistance from the
government. The program of clearing the camps terminated
on December 29, 1975, but the resettlement of these
refugees still continues."

427.   ————. "Proposed Revisions of U.S. Western Hemisphere
Immigration Policies." *International Migration Review*,
8 (Spring 1974): 69-76.

The House of Representatives Subcommittee on Immigration, Citizenship and International Law on March 28,
1973, opened hearings on revision of the Western Hemisphere immigration system. The emphasis was to create
a preference system to regulate the flow of the 120,000-
ceiling immigrants who were admitted from that hemisphere
each year.

428.   ————. "U.S. Congress on Immigration." *International
Migration Review*, 10 (Summer 1976): 249-251.

429.   ————. "U.S. Immigration Legislation--Prospects in the

94th Congress." *International Migration Review,* 9
(Spring 1975): 59-62.

In the absence of the per-country limitation, Mexican
immigration under the ceiling has risen to 45,247 in
1974 followed by the Dominican Republic with 11,924 and
Jamaica with 10,422 (Cuban immigration was 17,583, but
none of these applicants came directly from Cuba). Due
to the close proximity of these countries to the United
States it is entirely possible that the presence of a
U.S. born or lawful resident alien child gives an advantage to the parents from these countries not enjoyed
by others from more distantly located countries.
During the 93rd Congress the House again held extensive
hearings as it became apparent the number of illegal
aliens in the United States was increasing dramatically
and their employment no longer was restricted to agricultural occupations as in the past but many were now
engaged in semi-skilled and skilled jobs in urban areas.
The increase in population especially among Western
Hemisphere nations was not matched by a corresponding
increase in employment opportunities. The answer for
many to keep body and soul and family together was to
seek employment legally or illegally in this country.
The problems created by the presence in the United
States of untold numbers of illegal aliens are many and
varied, ranging from the economic and the moral to the
impact on our international relations. The solution to
the problem once again as viewed by the House of Representatives in the 93rd Congress was to penalize the
employer and thus remove the economic incentive for these
aliens to seek employment. On May 3, 1973 the House
again passed a bill (H.R. 982) to impose sanctions upon
employers, but again the Senate failed to act.

430.   ————, and Michael G. Wenk. "Current U.S. Immigration
Legislation: Analysis and Comment." *International
Migration Review,* 5 (Fall 1971): 339-356.

431.   Holborn, Louise W. *Refugees: A Problem of Our Time.
The Work of the United Nations High Commissioner for
Refugees, 1951-1972.* 2 vols. Metuchen, N.J.: The
Scarecrow Press, Inc., 1975.

432.   Hong, Lawrence K. "Recent Immigrants in the Chinese-
American Community: Issues of Adaptations and Impacts."
International Migration Review, 10 (Winter 1978);
509-514.

"Over half a million people of Chinese ancestry now
live in the United States. This number represents more
than a 300 percent increase in the past twenty-five years.
One of the major factors that has contributed to this
dramatic growth is the influx of immigrants from Taiwan
and Hong Kong in recent years. In fact, approximately
50 percent of the Chinese-Americans today are immigrants
who came to the United States after the implementation
of the 1965 immigration law. Some obvious questions
readily come into mind when a demographic change of such
magnitude has occurred. How are the immigrants adapting
to their new environment? What is the response of the
established members of the Chinese-American community to
the new immigrants? The purpose of this note is to
call attention to these issues which arose from an exploratory study in Los Angeles and San Francisco.
Specifically, it seeks to point out the need to investigate the effect of migration patterns on adaptation,
the effect of community organization on adaptation and
the impact of immigrants in the social economic life of
Chinatown."

433. Hossain, Mokkerom. "South Asians in Southern California:
      A Sociological Study of Immigrants from India, Pakistan,
      and Bangladesh." *South Asia Bulletin*, 2 (1982): 73-83.

434. Houstoun, Marion F., et al. "Female Predominance in
      Immigration to the United States Since 1930: A First
      Look." *International Migration Review*, 18 (Winter
      1984): 908-959.

      After a brief comparative discussion of postwar inter-
      national migration flows, analyzes U.S. statistics on
      the characteristics of immigrants to the United States,
      by sex; discusses the reasons for the predominance of
      female immigrants since 1930; and lays the statistical
      groundwork for future analyses of its implications
      for the United States.

435. ————, and David S. North. *"The New Immigration" and
      the Presumptions of Social Policy.* Washington, D.C.:
      Linton & Co., 1975.

436. Hune, S. *Pacific Migration to the United States: Trends
      and Themes in Historical and Sociological Literature.*
      Washington, D.C.: Smithsonian Institution, 1977.

      American perspectives of immigration with particular
      emphasis on Pacific migration. Examines how historians

and social scientists have viewed the Asian American
experience and the impact of their perspectives on the
literature. Certain assumptions, biases, and interests
held by historians and social scientists have shaped
the parameters for studying Asian-American experiences.
The first three parts of the essay consist of a review
of selected Pacific migration literature covering the
late nineteenth century to the 1960s. Part four explores
the recent literature which has appeared since the
emergence of Asian-American Studies programs.

437. Hurh, Won Moo, and Kwang Chung Kim. "Adhesive Socio-
      cultural Adaptation of Korean Immigrants in the U.S.:
      An Alternative Strategy of Minority Adaptation."
      International Migration Review, 18 (Summer 1984):
      188-216.

      Adhesive adaptation is conceptualized as a particular
      mode of adaptation in which certain aspects of the new
      culture and social relations with members of the host
      society are added on to the immigrants' traditional cul-
      ture and social networks, without replacing or modifying
      any significant part of the old. In light of this con-
      ceptual framework, various patterns of Korean immigrants'
      adaptation in the United States are examined. For data
      collection, 615 Korean immigrants in the Los Angeles
      area were interviewed in 1979. Findings indicate that
      the immigrants' strong and pervasive ethnic attachment
      is unaffected by their length of residence in the United
      States, socioeconomic status, and cultural and social
      assimilation rates. The adhesive mode of adaptation
      is thus empirically confirmed by this study. Theoretical
      and practical implications of this adhesive adaptation
      are discussed in the conclusion.

438. Hurlich, M.G., and N.D. Donnelly. "Social Tension and
      the Development of a Public Ethnic Identity: Hmong
      Refugees from Laos." Paper presented at American
      Anthropological Association. 83rd Annual Meeting.
      Denver, Colorado, November 14-18, 1984.

      The public identity of the Hmong from Laos has changed
      in America *vis-à-vis* their public identity in Laos. In
      the United States the Hmong have experienced significant
      loss of control over basic areas of their lives as com-
      pared with their circumstances before U.S. military
      involvement in Southeast Asia. These changes in public
      identity involve perceptions of Hmong occupational com-
      petence, economic productivity, the importance of

patrilineality, access and use of medical curing, distinctive features of material culture. The consequences
of these changes are reflected in interactions within
the Hmong community.

439. Hurt, Harry, III. "The Cactus Curtain." *Texas Monthly*
     (August 1977): 94-107.

440. Hurth, W.M., and K.C. Kim. *Korean Immigrants in America:
     A Structural Analysis of Ethnic Confinement and Ad-
     hesive Adaptation.* Cranbury, New Jersey: Fairleigh
     Dickinson University, 1984.

441. Hutchinson, Edward P. *The New Immigration.* Philadel-
     phia: American Academy of Political and Social Science,
     1966.

442. Huyck, E.E., and L.F. Bouvier. "The Demography of Refu-
     gees." *The Annals of the American Academy,* 467 (May
     1983): 39-61.

     Focuses on the number of refugees in the world by
     major areas. Gives some background on refugee movements
     and characteristics in order to suggest parameters of
     future movements, especially those that may have impli-
     cations for the United States with respect to (1) assis-
     tance programs in situ, or (2) acceptance of refugees
     into the United States.

443. Hyman, J. Patton. "Immigration: The Status of Cuban
     Refugees in the United States." *University of Florida
     Law Review,* 21 (Summer 1968): 73-84.

444. "Immigrants and Refugees: The Caribbean and South
     Florida." *Occasional Papers Series,* Dialogue No. 2.
     Miami: Latin American and Caribbean Center, Florida
     International University, March 1981.

445. "Immigration: Another Effort." *Economist,* 282 (March 27,
     1982): 45.

446. "Immigration Bill: Its Last Hurrah? (Simpson-Mazzoli)."
     Economist, 292 (August 4, 1984): 20-21.

447. "The Immigration Bill's Political Price." *Business
     Week* (July 2, 1984): 9.

448. "Immigration Compromise?" *Engineering News-Record,* 210
     (May 26, 1983): 203.

449. "Immigration and the Randomness of Ethnic Mix." *New York Times*, October 3, 1984.

450. "Immigration: The Untouchable Topic (Simpson-Mazzoli Immigration Bill)." *Economist*, 289 (October 8, 1983); 22.

451. [Institute for Research in History]. *Ethnic and Immigration Groups: The United States, Canada and England.* New York: The Institute for Research in History and The Haworth Press, 1983.

The primacy of the North American experience is the point of departure for this issue of the *Trends in History* series. The essays deal with the political aspects of ethnicity, the current debate over acculturation and pluralism in American society, immigrant women, immigrants from Asia and Latin America, the Canadian experience, and immigrant groups from India who have settled in England since World War II.

452. *International Migration Policies and Programmes: A World Survey.* New York: Unipub, 1983.

453. Jackson, J.A., ed. *Migration.* New York: Cambridge University Press, 1969.

454. Jacobson, Gaynor I. "The Refugee Movement: An Overview." *International Migration Review*, 11 (Winter 1977): 514-523.

"While international migration has often furthered human rights, led to the enhancement of human dignity, relieved population pressures, helped in the development and enrichment of receiving nations and facilitated cultural interchange, hindrances to such international movement have just as often led to social injustice and the demeaning of various peoples at various points in history. In fact, to impede migratory movement is a violation of human rights which can lead to uncircumscribed human suffering such as that which existed during the Nazi hegemony over Europe, when escape routes were blocked."

455. Jamail, Milton H. *The United States-Mexican Border: A Guide to Institutions, Organizations, and Scholars.* Tucson: University of Arizona, Latin American Center, 1980.

456. Jean-Juste, Gerard. "Stranger in Miami." In Thomas
     Bentz, ed. *New Immigrants: Portraits in Passage.*
     New York: Pilgrim Press, 1981. Pp. 33–60.

457. Jenkins, J. Craig. "The Demand for Immigrant Workers:
     Labor Scarcity or Social Control?" *International
     Migration Review,* 12 (Winter 1978): 514–535.

     Recent analyses of the economic role of immigrant
     workers from Mexico in U.S. labor markets have been
     advanced from two divergent interpretations—a labor
     scarcity argument and a social control thesis. Analyzes
     the two perspectives, finding little evidence to support
     the labor scarcity argument. Immigrant workers are in-
     stead argued to be tied to social control functions in
     the peripheral sectors of the U.S. economy. Detail from
     the historical experience of farm workers in Southwestern
     agriculture are drawn upon to illustrate the argument.

458. ———. "Push/Pull in Recent Mexican Migration to the
     U.S." *International Migration Review,* 11 (Summer
     1977): 178–89.

459. Jorge, Antonio. "Perspectives on Recent Refugees and
     Immigrant Waves into South Florida." *Occasional
     Papers Series,* Dialogue No. 6. Miami: Latin American
     and Caribbean Center, Florida International University,
     August 1982.

460. ———, and Raul Moncarz. "Cubans in South Florida: A
     Social Science Approach." *Metas,* 1 (Fall 1980): 37–87.

461. Kane, Parsons & Associates, Inc. *A Survey of Public
     Attitudes Towards Refugees and Immigrants. Report of
     Findings.* New York: American Council for Nationalities
     Service, April 1984.

     To improve the base of knowledge on public opinion
     regarding refugees, the U.S. Committee for Refugees
     undertook a telephone survey in February 1984 using a
     sample of 750 adults supplemented with one hundred blacks
     and one hundred Hispanics. The major findings: (1) con-
     trary to the perception that the U.S. public is solidly
     antagonistic, there is substantial public sentiment to
     admit both refugees and immigrants; (2) most members of
     the public do not know the difference between refugees
     and other immigrants, the numbers in the various cate-
     gories of people who come from elsewhere to live in the
     U.S., or where they are coming from; (3) the more accurate

knowledge a person has regarding refugee/immigrant issues, the more willing the person is likely to be to
support a generous refugee/immigrant admissions policy;
and (4) regardless of a person's attitudes concerning
generous or restrictive admissions policy, the overwhelming majority of those interviewed considered the
issue as one of moderate to low importance compared with
other major national policy issues.

462. Kass, Scott. "Haitians: A List of All *Miami Herald*
Articles About Haitians in Miami from 1979–June, 1984."
Mimeo. Miami: Florida International University
Libraries, 1984.

463. Keely, Charles B. "Effects of the Immigration Act of
1965 on Selected Population Characteristics of Immigrants to the United States." *Demography*, 8 (May 1971);
157–169.

Changes in immigration law have affected the characteristics of immigrants coming to the United States.
Changes in immigration policy contained in the 1965
Immigration Act, which amended the McCarron-Walter Act
of 1952, concerned the abolition of the quota system,
preference system, and labor clearances for certain
classes of immigrants. Effects of these policy changes
on two controversial characteristics of immigrants,
their country of origin and occupational levels, are
traced. Law led to clear changes in origin of immigrants.
Southern Europe, Asian, and Caribbean immigrants make
up a larger proportion of immigrants than previously.
Although the volume of immigration increased, the distribution of occupational groups shifted to some extent,
especially the professional level from Asian countries.

464. ———. "Effects of U.S. Immigration Law on Manpower
Characteristics of Immigrants." *Demography*, 12 (1975):
179–191.

Explains how the 1965 law increased immigration. In
addition to setting a higher numerical limit (290,000
rather than 150,000), the new law increased the number
of groups exempted from the ceilings. By repealing the
national origins system, the law opened up immigration
to countries where the interest was greater. Under the
old law, many nations of Northern Europe did not fill
their yearly quota, but under the new law, countries of
Southeast Asia regularly did. Different pooling provisions had an impact, because they permitted unused

categories to be picked up by people lower on the
preference list. The 1965 law did not just swell numbers, it also changed the occupational composition.
The blue-collar segment increased slightly, while that
of farm-related occupations declined.

465. ————. "The Estimation of the Immigration Component
      of Population Growth." *International Migration Re-*
      view, 8 (Fall 1974): 431-437.

466. ————. *Global Refugee Policy: The Case for Development-*
      Oriented Strategy. New York: The Population Council,
      1981.

      Offers a overview of the global refugee situation and
      the problems involved in an effective international re-
      sponse. Reviews the international definition of a
      refugee, the issues created by it, and its implications
      for assistance activities. Includes an overview of
      current number, location, and origin of the world's
      refugees and the history of international response to
      refugees.

467. ————. "The Immigration Act of 1965: A Study of the
      Relationship of Social Science Theory to Group In-
      terest and Legislation." Unpublished Ph.D. disser-
      tation, Fordham University, 1970.

468. ————. "Immigration Composition and Population Policy."
      Science (August 16, 1974); 587-93.

469. ————. "Immigration Policy and Population Growth."
      Paper presented at Annual Meeting of the Population
      Association of America, April 1972, Toronto, Ontario.

      From an evaluation of the Commission on Population
      Growth's report, (1) there seems to have been some con-
      fusion between net civilian immigration and alien immi-
      gration due to dropping the word "civilian" in the
      Population Commission's interim report; (2) there is a
      large group of non-immigrants who are not accounted for
      in the "net civilian immigration" category; (3) the
      400,000 figure as the input of immigrants to population
      growth is inappropriate; (4) to focus on the percentage
      contributed by net civilian increase to population
      growth may not be the most appropriate course when
      natural increase is declining. The analysis concludes
      that eliminating alien immigration seems impossible and,
      from the point of view of national needs and foreign
      policies, undesirable at present.

470. ————. "Immigration Recommendations of the Commission on Population Growth and the American Future." *International Migration Review*, 6 (Fall 1972): 290-294.

"The single word that best characterizes the handling of the topic of immigration by the Commission on Population Growth and the American Future is surprise. The commission and its staff were left floundering when they realized the possible impact of current levels of immigration on population growth: The *Interim Report* of the Commission, issued in March, 1971, stated: Right now about 80 percent of our annual population growth results from natural increases—the amount by which births exceed deaths. About 20 percent of our current growth is due to net immigration; the number has been averaging about 400,000 annually. Historically speaking, that is not many. In the years just before World War I, the figures ran to twice that, at a time when the United States had less than half the number of people it has now. Even so, the long-term effects of immigration are large. This is partly because most immigrants enter the country in young adulthood, at an age when their childbearing is at its peak. If the average family (including immigrants) had two children, and immigration continued at 400,000 per year, the survivors and descendants of immigrants in the next 30 years would number 16 million in the year 2000, and would have accounted for one fourth of the total population increase during that period. Over the next 100 years immigrants and their descendants would account for nearly half of the increase in population from 204 to 340 million. (Commission on Population Growth and the American Future, *Interim Report*, 1971, 8-9.)"

471. ————. "Measuring the Effect of Labor Certification." *International Migration Review*, 4 (Spring 1970): 87-92.

"The amendments to the Immigration and Nationality Act signed into law on October 3, 1965 were aimed at major reform in the immigration policy of the United States. The 1965 act contained three major policy changes—phasing out the national origins quota system, emphasizing family reunion as a basis for granting an immigrant visa preference, and introducing a system of individual labor certification for certain classes of immigrants. These three changes acting in concert could be expected to bring about significant modifications in the national

origin, use of preferences, and levels of skill of immigrants. During debate on the bill in Congress were
projections for these changes, but no one was really
sure what the changes would bring. The purpose of this
paper is to document any changes in the occupational
skill levels of immigrants after the 1965 Act took effect
and to explain how the provisions of the 1965 Act affected the labor characteristics of immigrants."

472.   ———. "Philippine Migration: Internal Movements and
       Emigration to the U.S." *International Migration
       Review*, 7 (Summer 1973): 117-187.

473.   ———. "Politics, Policy and Refugee Movements."
       Paper presented at Population Association of America.
       Annual Meeting, Minneapolis, May 3-5, 1984.

       Review of theory development outlines the framework
       relating conflict, refugee flows, and refugee outcomes
       and discusses specific interviewing variables connected
       with assistance and trade and their roles in refugee
       movements.

474.   ———, and Ellen Kraly. "Recent Net Alien Immigration
       to the U.S.: Its Impact on Population Growth and Native
       Fertility." *Demography*, 15 (1978): 267-284.

475.   Kelley, D. "Open Society, Open Borders: The U.S.
       Stands to Gain, Not Lose, from Immigration." *Barrons*,
       65 (March 11, 1985): 11.

476.   Kelly, Gail Paradise. *From Vietnam to America: A Chron-
       icle of the Vietnamese Immigration to the United
       States*. Boulder, Colorado: Westview Press, 1978.

       The first study of the exodus and of the transforma-
       tion from refugees to immigrants, first in the camps to
       which they were sent, and subsequently in the communities
       which accepted them. The author spent 18 months with
       the refugees in the Fort Indian Town Gap, Pennsylvania,
       camp.

477.   Kelly, O. "The Great Immigration Nightmare." *U.S. News
       and World Report*, June 22, 1981. Pp. 27-31.

       "A flood of newcomers to the U.S. threatens to swamp
       one of Uncle Sam's most troubled bureaucracies--the
       immigration service."

478. Kennedy, Edward M. "The Immigration Act of 1965."
     *Annals of the American Academy of Political and Social
     Science: The New Immigration*, 367 (September 1966):
     140-144.

479. ————. "Refugee Act of 1980." *International Migration
     Review*, 15 (Spring/Summer 1981): 141-156.

     Traces the legislative history of the Refugee Act of
     1980, identifies the goals Congress intended to achieve,
     discusses its implementation in relation to the recent
     influx of Cuban refugees, and shows how it can be
     utilized "beneficially in the future."

480. Kessner, Thomas, and Betty Boyd Caroli. *Today's Immi-
     grants: Their Stories. A New Look at the Newest
     Americans.* New York: Oxford University Press, 1981.

     An overview of the American immigration experience
     since the 1965 Immigration Act. Historical analysis
     combined with oral history (recent immigrants to New
     York City). See review, D.M. Reimers, *International
     Migration Review*, 16 (Winter 1982): 900.

481. Kilpatrick, J.J. "A Time for Statemanship." *Nation's
     Business*, 71 (December 1983): 4.

482. Kim, Chin, and Bok Lim C. Kim. "Asian Immigrants in
     American Law: A Look at the Past and the Challenge
     Which Remains." *American University Law Review*, 26
     (1977): 373-407.

483. Kim, Hyung-Chan, ed. "Class and Ethnicity: Korean Immi-
     grants in America." Paper presented at American
     Anthropological Association. 83rd Annual Meeting.
     Denver, Colorado, November 14-18, 1984.

     Most of the research done on the topics of immigration
     and ethnicity overlooks the importance of understanding
     the class background of the immigrant population. The
     predominantly middle-class background of Korean immi-
     grants in America serves as a significant factor in the
     formation and maintenance of their ethnic identity. The
     process with which Korean immigrants align their socio-
     economic existence with the American capitalist system
     is analyzed in terms of the interplay between class back-
     ground and ethnic identity and the emergence of conflicting
     class interests within the ethnic group is also explored.

484.   ———. *The Korean Diaspora: Historical and Sociologi-
       cal Studies of Korean Immigration and Assimilation in
       North America.* Santa Barbara, California: American
       Bibliographical Center-Clio Press, 1977.

       A collection of fourteen assorted studies by ten con-
       tributors about Koreans in the United States and
       Hawaii, with a mention or two about a 1905 band of
       Koreans in Mexico. In the book's first section, two
       articles examine factors related to immigration around
       1900, and another four discuss Korean activities relative
       to churches, community organizations, and economic enter-
       prises and present demographic data about the most re-
       cent influx since 1968.

485.   ———. "Some Aspects of Social Demography of Korean
       Americans." *International Migration Review*, 8 (Spring
       1974): 23–42.

       Presents an historical survey of the emigration of
       Korean people to the United States of America from 1901
       to 1971. The major emphasis of the study, however, is
       focused on a critical analysis of two major aspects of
       social demography of Korean minority in America:
       (1) general trends of Korean immigrants to the USA from
       1959 to 1971, and (2) ascribed characteristics of
       Koreans in America as reported in the 1970 census.
       Included in the analysis of the ascribed characteristics
       is the composition of age and sex of the native-born
       Koreans compared with that of the foreign-born Koreans
       in America.

486.   Kim, Illsoo. "Immigrants to Urban America: The Korean
       Community in the New York Metropolitan Area." Un-
       published Ph.D. dissertation, City University of New
       York, 1979.

487.   ———. *New Urban Immigrants: The Korean Community in
       New York.* Princeton, New Jersey: Princeton University
       Press, 1981.

       Across the 1970s the number of Koreans in the United
       States increased five times—from about 70,000 in 1970
       to 355,000 in 1980. The majority of this rapidly in-
       creasing immigration group is concentrated in major
       metropolitan areas, such as Los Angeles, New York, and
       Chicago. According to Kim, some 80,000 Korean immigrants
       have settled in the New York metropolitan region.
       Unlike the early immigrants who were largely uneducated
       laborers from rural Korea in the beginning of the

twentieth century, a majority of the recent Korean immigrants are highly educated urban middle-class people.
Kim's general theoretical framework for his book is thus
the modern pattern of urban-to-urban migration in contrast to the traditional model of rural-to-urban migration.

488. Kim, Kwang Chung. "Ethnic Resources Utilization of
     Korean Immigrant Entrepreneurs in the Chicago Minority
     Area." *International Migration Review*, 19 (Spring
     1985): 82-111.

     A high proportion of Korean immigrants are engaged in
     self-employed small business in the United States. In
     light of their business proliferation, this study has
     empirically investigated Korean immigrant entrepreneurs'
     ethnic resources utilization. Findings indicate that
     the Korean entrepreneurs rely heavily on their ethnic
     resources for both business preparation and operation.
     While such ethnic resources utilization facilitates the
     immigrants' business entry and gives them competitive
     advantage, the same mechanism poses serious problems;
     intra-ethnic business competition and precarious position
     as a middle-man minority. Implications of these findings
     are discussed and suggestions are made for future re-
     search.

489. Kiser, George C., and Martha W. Kiser, eds. *Mexican
     Workers in the United States: Historical and Political
     Perspectives*. Albuquerque: University of New Mexico
     Press, 1979.

490. Kitagawa, Joseph M., ed. *American Refugee Policy:
     Ethical and Religious Reflections*. Washington, D.C.:
     Winston Press, 1985.

     Although this volume in the area of the ethics and
     practice of U.S. refugee policy does not provide much
     concrete information about the antecedents or numbers of
     the worldwide refugee problem, it is an èxcellent intro-
     duction to the issues and variety of views surrounding
     refugees and U.S. public policy, and it is an outstanding
     example of the promise, peril, and frustration of moral
     discourse in the public arena. Consists of edited
     selections from the proceedings of a conference held in
     Washington, D.C. (1983), with participants from govern-
     ment, religious, and academic communities. H. Eugene
     Douglas, coordinator for refugee affairs in the Reagan
     administration, sees the solution to the refugee problem

in containment of the USSR and the promotion of American-
style economies throughout the world; Marc Tannenbaum
ties the dignity and sanity of the human race to the
refugee problem. Joseph Kitagawa's closing essay is
particularly helpful in providing an ethical and practical perspective.

491. Kleinmann, Howard H., and James P. Daniel. "Indochinese
      Resettlement: Language Education and Social Services."
      International Migration Review, 15 (Spring/Summer
      1981): 239-245.

      "Proposes that the Monitor Model adequately predicts
      the problem of teaching English as a second language
      (TESL) to the previously uneducated and can indicate a
      solution. The basic problem is managerial and does not
      indicate a lack in the underpinnings of the TESL field.
      The key is to integrate the ESL program with the larger
      resettlement program."

492. Knapp, Elaine S. "Refugee Woes Dumped on States."
      State Government News, 23 (August 1980): 11-13.

493. Knoll, T. *Becoming Americans: Asian Sojourners, Immi-
      grants, and Refugees in the Western United States.*
      Portland, Oregon: Coast to Coast Books, 1982.

      Portrays the immigration of all Asians to America
      from the Chinese of the 1850s to the Vietnamese of the
      1980s, describing trends and individual experiences
      from the view of both Asian and American history. Traces
      people from each nationality from homeland to U.S.
      citizenship.

494. Kolm, Richard, ed. *Bibliography of Ethnicity and
      Ethnic Groups.* Bethesda, Maryland: National Institute
      of Mental Health, 1973.

495. Konvitz, M.R. *Civil Rights in Immigration.* Westport,
      Connecticut: Greenwood, 1977.

496. Koo, H., and E.Y. Yu. "Korean Immigration to the
      United States: Its Demographic Pattern and Social
      Implications for Both Societies." No. 74. Honolulu:
      East-West Population Institute, 1981.

      Drawing on immigration statistics and secondary
      survey data, attempts to delineate dominant patterns of
      post-1965 Korean immigration to the U.S., to analyze
      its effects on both societies, and to evaluate the world
      economic system approach to migration.

497. —————, and —————. "Korean Immigration to the United States: Its Structural Sources and Implications." Paper presented at the Annual Meetings of the American Sociological Association, New York, August 27-30, 1980.

Focuses primarily on recent immigration to the United States. Its purposes are: (1) to delineate, through the use of existing materials, the dominant patterns of Korean immigration; (2) to analyze its impact on both societies; and (3) to use this case to critically evaluate, as well as contribute, to those recent efforts that have theorized about international migration within the world economic system.

498. Koral, R.L. "Keep Your Tired, Your Poor, Your Huddled Masses." *Human Rights*, 7 (Fall 1978): 31-5.

499. Koss, Margo, and Harry Hatry. *Human Services Needs and Resources in Long Beach*. Urban Institute Report to the City of Long Beach, California. Washington, D.C.: The Urban Institute, 1985.

500. Kossoudji, Sherrie A., and Susan I. Ranney. "The Labor Market Experiences of Female Migrants: The Case of Temporary Mexican Migration to the U.S." *International Migration Review*, 18 (Winter 1984): 1120-1143.

In spite of the public debate surrounding Mexican migration to the United States, little is known about the labor market activities of the female component of this flow. This article, using a Mexican national survey, provides a characterization of the labor market activities of temporary female migrants. The roles of schooling, work experience, origin region in Mexico, and legal status are discussed in comparing female and male migrants' working experiences.

501. Krajick, Kevin. "Refugees Adrift: Barred from America's Shores." *Saturday Review* (October 27, 1979): 17-20.

502. Kritz, Mary M., ed. *United States Immigration and Refugee Policy*. Lexington, Massachusetts: Lexington Books, 1983.

503. Ladner, Robert A. *Demography, Social Status, Housing and Social Needs of the Haitian Population of Edison-Little River*. Miami: Behavioral Sciences Research Institute, 1983.

504. LaFontaine, Pierre-Michel. "Haitian Immigrants in Bos-
     ton." In Roy S. Bryce-LaPorte and Delores M. Morti-
     mer, eds., *Caribbean Migration to the United States*
     (Washington, D.C.: Smithsonian Institution, 1976).
     Pp. 111-129.

505. Laguerre, Michel S. *American Odyssey: Haitians in New
     York City*. Ithaca, New York: Cornell University Press,
     1984.

     Presents the results of extensive fieldwork in New
     York's Haitian community. Laguerre contends that
     Haitian ethnicity has intensified as a result of the
     migration experience. As Laguerre puts it, "The racist
     structure of American society compels them to use
     ethnicity in their adaptation process." More specifical-
     ly, the Haitians have used ethnicity "in a tactical
     manner to maintain and protect individual and group
     interests." Thus, as with earlier white immigrants,
     family, religion, language, culture, and traditional
     values and beliefs have not only been transplanted but
     strengthened by the migration process. Contends that
     some 800,000 Haitians and American-born Haitian children
     reside in the United States as of 1984. Perhaps 450,000
     of these live in New York City and another 90,000 or so
     in South Florida. The Haitian migration first took on
     sizeable proportions after 1957, when François Duvalier
     came to power. The brutal Duvalier regime made exiles
     of many from the urban elite and professional classes.
     During the 1960s, these Haitian immigrants created new
     communities in New York, Montreal, Boston, Philadelphia,
     Washington, and Miami. The Haitian exodus swelled in
     the 1970s after the installation of Jean-Claude Duvalier
     as President-for-Life, but now the exiles included the
     urban working class and the rural peasantry.

506. ———. *The Complete Haitiana: A Bibliographic Guide to
     the Literature, 1900-1980*. 2 vols. Millwood, New York:
     Kraus International Publications, 1982.

507. ———. "Haitian Americans." In Alan Harwood, ed.,
     Ethnicity and Medical Care. Cambridge, Massachusetts:
     Harvard University Press, 1981. Pp. 172-210.

508. ———. "Haitian Immigrants in the United States: A
     Historical Overview." In Arnaud F. Marks and Hebe M.C.
     Vessuri, eds., *White Collar Migrants in the Americas
     and the Caribbean*. Leiden, Netherlands: Department of
     Caribbean Studies, Royal Institute of Linguistics and
     Anthropology, 1983. Pp. 119-169.

509. ————. "The Haitian Niche in New York City." *Migration Today*, 7 (September 1979): 12-18.

510. ————. "Haitians." In Stephan Thernstrom, ed., *Harvard Encyclopedia of American Ethnic Groups*. Cambridge, Massachusetts: Harvard University Press, 1980. Pp. 446-449.

511. Lampley, James. "Uncharted Future for Haitian Boat People." *Africa*, 117 (May 1981): 60-61.

512. Lanphier, C. Michael. "Refugee Resettlement: Models in Action." *International Migration Review*, 17 (Spring 1983): 4-33.

      A model of refugee resettlement containing two axes is proposed: volume of refugee intake and emphasis on economic or cultural adaptation. The resultant fourfold scheme yields three types of resettlement activities which can be sustained over a protracted period of time: large volume/primacy on economic adaptation; moderate volume/primacy on economic adaptation; moderate volume/ primacy on cultural adaptation. Large volume/emphasis on cultural adaptation, however, is a type which is structurally unstable and in practice would modify into another form. Refugee resettlement practices of three major receiving countries, Canada, France, United States, reflect principles derived from these three stable types. France and Canada exemplify moderate intake with emphasis on economic adaptation although Quebec uniquely demonstrates moderate intake/emphasis on cultural adaptation. Practices in the United States overwhelmingly correspond to large volume/emphasis on economic adaptation.

513. Laraque, Franck. "Haitian Emigration to New York." *Migration Today*, 7 (September 1979): 28-32.

514. "Latest Wave of Immigrants Brings Problems to U.S." *U.S. News and World Report* (April 5, 1976): 25-29.

515. Latortue, P., et al. "Haitian Migration and the Haitian Economy." Gainesville, Florida: Center for Latin American Studies, University of Florida, Occasional Paper No. 3, February 1984.

      Deals with three separate topics: (1) the Haitian economy in historical perspective; (2) geographic and socioeconomic aspects of the recent Haitian migration to South Africa; and (3) Haitian migrants in U.S. agriculture.

516. Lernoux, Penny. "The Miami Connection." *The Nation*
      (February 18, 1984): 186-198.

517. Levin, N. "Soviet Jewish Immigrants in Philadelphia,
      1972-1982." *Soviet Jewish Affairs*, 14 (November 1984);
      15-29.

      Discusses Soviet Jews in Philadelphia—their character-
      istics, the Jewish organizations that assisted them, the
      problems they faced, absorption, and the immigrants'
      contributions to American Jewish life.

518. Levine, Daniel B., ed. *Immigration Statistics: A Story
      of Neglect*. Panel on Immigration Statistics.
      National Research Council. Washington: National
      Academy Press, 1985.

      Sponsored by the National Research Council, the report
      is the result of an intensive two-year study of immigra-
      tion information by the Panel on Immigration Statistics.
      Policy decisions without adequate factual information
      are major concerns of the research panel and staff.
      Report sections include the perspective and recommenda-
      tions of the panel, a historical view of U.S. immigra-
      tion policy, a call for reliable and complete information,
      and a concern for improved cooperation and coordination
      among the many agencies involved. Panel recommendations
      are stratified by the major agencies and data sources
      used.

519. Li, Gertrude Roth. *The Vietnamese: The Challenge of
      Sponsorship*. Nyack, New York: World Relief Corp.,
      1982.

520. Lieberman, Leslie Sue. "The Impact of Cuban and Haitian
      Refugees on State Services: Focus on Health Service
      Problems in Cross-Cultural Contexts." Gainesville,
      Florida: University of Florida Library, 1982.

521. Light, Ivan. "Immigrant Entrepreneurs in America:
      Koreans in Los Angeles." In Nathan Glazer, ed.
      Clamor at the Gates: The New American Immigration.
      San Francisco, California: Institute for Contemporary
      Studies, 1985. Pp. 161-178.

      "However, as the underutilized human capital of immi-
      grants has risen, a function of their middle and upper-
      middle class social origins, their motives and capability
      for entrepreneurship have also risen. Even if the path
      of small business owners is harder now, contemporary

immigrants are better prepared for entrepreneurship than were the unskilled, uneducated immigrants of the prewar epoch. Therefore, new immigrants surmount business hurdles that still obstruct the social mobility of low status blacks, whites, and Hispanics. When the *Wall Street Journal* wondered why Cubans in Miami could open numerous businesses whereas blacks in Miami could not, the newspaper concluded that the question unfairly ignored the money, Latin American import-export connections, and bourgeois social origin of at least a substantial minority of Miami's Cubans. This conclusion underscores the hazard of assuming that intergroup differences in rates of entrepreneurship reflect only ethnic resources. Ethnic resources do affect entrepreneurship, but before their effect can be identified in empirical cases, one must discount intergroup differences in class resources."

522. Lindborg, K., and C.J. Ovando. *Five Mexican-American Women in Transition: A Case Study of Migrants in the Midwest.* San Francisco, California: R & E Research Associates, 1977.

Mexican American migrant women's attitudes and experiences regarding such aspects of life as courtship, love, marriage, motherhood, women's rights, and education are explored. Not an analysis of Mexican American culture and society as a whole from the point of view of the migrant woman but rather a consideration of certain domains of Mexican American life considered of significance by the women themselves. Focuses on four Mexican Americans from migrant farmworker backgrounds and one Mexican recently immigrated from Mexico.

523. Liu, William T., et al. *Transition to Nowhere: Vietnamese Refugees in America.* Nashville, Tennessee: Charter House, 1979.

A study by the Asian Mental Health Research Center to examine the Vietnamese refugees in the United States and the impact of flight and resettlement on their mental health. This study focuses on the early stages of the refugee career: flight, transit, sojourn in the holding camp, sponsorship out, and immediate resettlement.

524. ————, and Alice K. Murata. "The Vietnamese in America: Refugees or Immigrants?" *Bridge: An Asian American Perspective,* 5 (Fall 1977): 31-39.

525. ———, and ———. "The Vietnamese in America, Part
      II: Perilous Flights, Uncertain Future." *Bridge: An
      Asian American Perspective*, 5 (Winter 1977): 42-50.

526. ———, and ———. "The Vietnamese in America, Part
      III: Life in the Refugee Camps." *Bridge: An Asian
      American Perspective*, 6 (Spring 1978): 36-46.

527. ———, and ———. "The Vietnamese in America, Part
      IV: Mental Health of the Refugees." *Bridge: An Asian
      American Perspective*, 6 (Summer 1978): 44-49.

528. Llanes, José. *Cuban Americans: Masters of Survival.*
      Cambridge, Massachusetts: Abt Books, 1982.

529. Loescher, Gilburt, and John Scanlan. "Human Rights,
      U.S. Foreign Policy, and Haitian Refugees." *Journal
      of Interamerican Studies and World Affairs*, 26
      (August 1984): 313-356.

530. ———, and ———. "Mass Asylum and U.S. Policy in
      the Caribbean." *The World Today*, 37 (October 1981):
      387-395.

531. Louie de Irizarry, Florita Z. *U.S. Women of Spanish
      Origin in the Employment Sector: A Selected Bibliog-
      raphy.* Monticello, Illinois: Vance Bibliographies,
      1982.

532. Lowenthal, D. "New York's New Hispanic Immigrants."
      The Geographical Review, 99 (1976): 90-92.

533. Lucas, I. *The Browning of America, The Hispanic Revo-
      lution in the American Church.* Chicago, Illinois:
      Fides/Claretian, 1981.

      Shows how Hispanics view their faith, country, and
      heritage, bringing to the forefront the question of the
      American church's neglect of its Hispanic members. Ex-
      plains the reasons behind the movement to revolutionize
      the Hispanics in the church.

534. "Lure of New York." *The Economist* (March 22, 1975):
      67-68.

535. Luytjes, Jan B. *Economic Impact of Refugees in Dade
      County.* Miami: Bureau of Business Research, Florida
      International University, 1982.

536. MacCorkle, L., ed. *Cubans in the United States: A Bibliography for Research in the Social and Behavioral Sciences: 1960-1983*. Westport, Connecticut: Greenwood Press, 1984.

Is intended to bring together the dispersed and growing literature on Cuban exiles. Compiles a portion of what is available. Only English-language material is cited: creative literature is excluded. Included are articles from both academic journals and popular periodicals, books, theses, unpublished papers, and government documents completed after 1950 that are directly concerned with Cubans living in the United States.

537. MacEoin, G., and N. Riley. *No Promised Land, American Refugee Policies and the Rule of Law*. Boston, Massachusetts: Oxfam America, 1982.

The United States has in recent years been confronted with an influx of refugees from Haiti, El Salvador, and Guatemala. Examines both the conditions which have compelled such large numbers of people to flee their home countries and the situation which awaits them on arrival in the United States. Concludes that I.N.S. treatment of these refugees has been at variance not only with U.S. domestic law but also with our national responsibilities as a signatory to the United Nations Convention Relating to the Status of Refugees.

538. McBride, R.N., ed. *Mexico and the United States*. Englewood Cliffs, New Jersey: Prentice-Hall, Inc., 1981.

Presents the background papers discussed October 30-November 2, 1980 by the American Assembly, established by Dwight D. Eisenhower to provide information, stimulate discussion, and evoke independent conclusions in matters of vital public interest. Former Ambassador to Mexico (1969-1974) Robert H. McBride authored the chapter, "The United States and Mexico: The Shape of the Relationship" and edited the volume which covers the topics of energy, trade, investment, and tourism. Chapters on immigration, undocumented Mexican workers in the United States and a U.S.-Mexican temporary workers program are by Wayne A. Cornelius, Guido Belsasso and David D. Gregory.

539. McCarthy, K.F. *Immigration and California: Issues for the 1980s*. Santa Monica, California: Rand Corporation, 1983.

Considers how immigration is currently reshaping the
profile of California, why these trends are likely to
continue, and what these changes imply for business, the
private sector, and, ultimately, for the social fabric
of the state.

540. McClellan, G.D., ed. *Immigrants, Refugees and U.S.
     Policy.* New York: H.W. Wilson Company, 1981.

     One of The Reference Shelf series. Contains reprints
     of articles, excerpts from books, and addresses on
     current issues and social trends in the United states
     on the topics of emigration, immigration, and refugees.
     Reprints are grouped in four parts and after an individual
     editor's introductory address: American reactions to
     world problems; the special needs of varied groups;
     questions of language and culture in Americanization;
     and the designing of a policy for the future.

541. Entry deleted.

542. McCoy, Clyde B., et al. "Cuban and Other Latin Immigra-
     tion to Florida." *Florida Economic Indicators,* 12
     (1980): 1-4.

543. ———, and Diana H. Gonzalez. "Florida's Foreign-Born
     Population: A Growing Influence on Our Economy."
     Business and Economic Dimensions (University of Florida),
     18 (1982): 25-36.

544. McCoy, Terry L. "A Primer for U.S. Policy on Caribbean
     Emigration." *Caribbean Review,* 8 (1979): 1015.

     United States immigration policies encourage illegal
     immigration from the Western Hemisphere and exacerbate
     relations between the countries involved. Notes that
     the strongest impetus for changing policy on immigration
     comes from the federal government.

545. McGlauflin, Deborah. "Mainstreaming Refugee Women's
     Economic Development." In Lucy M. Cohen and Mary Ann
     Grossnickle, eds., *Immigrants and Refugees in a
     Changing Nation: Research and Training.* Washington,
     D.C.: Catholic University, 1983. Pp. 142-168.

546. McInnis, K. "Secondary Migration Among the Indochinese."
     Journal of Refugee Resettlement, 1 (May 1981): 36-42.

547. McLennan, K., and M. Lovell, Jr. "Immigration Reform:

An Economic Necessity." *The Journal of the Institute for Socioeconomic Studies*, 6 (Summer 1981): 38-52.

"If immigration is not increased, the American labor force will in all possibility not be sufficient by the end of the century to maintain the present level of social benefits afforded our elderly population." Points out "that in 19 years the ratio of elderly to overall population will be 1 in 5 (in 1965 it was 1 in 10). Since those now working are paying the pensions of those retired, working immigrants could help pay the pensions; that in increasing the numbers of legal immigrants, preference be given to specific skilled workers and professionals by increasing the temporary worker program. Control must come through the workplace and welfare system by means of a national identification system."

548. McWilliams, Carey. *North from Mexico*. New York: Greenwood Press, 1968.

A classic portrayal of Mexican-Americans, their past and present. Agriculture in the Southwest and further North has needed seasonal labor in large quantities since before 1900 and the Mexican or Mexican-American has been willing to accent this kind of work. The consequences of the movement that followed and the contemporary scene are delineated in: Chapter X, "The Second Defeat," Chapter XI, "The Mexican Problem," Chapter XII, "The Pattern of Violence," and Chapter XIII, "Blood on the Pavements." These chapters detail the growth of unionism, political awareness, urbanization, patterns of employment, and violence during World War II.

549. Mahoney, Larry. "Los Haitianos." *Miami Mensual*, 2 (September 1982); 34-43.

550. Maidens, M., ed. *Immigration: New Americans, Old Questions*. New York: Facts on File, 1981.

Contains editorials, chosen from major newspapers in all 50 states and Canada, that deal with the problems of immigration, illegal aliens, and refugee resettlement. Wide range of views.

551. Maingot, Anthony P. "Caribbean Migration as a Structural Reality." *Occasional Papers Series*, Dialogue No. 13. Miami: Latin American and Caribbean Center, Florida International University, January 1983.

552. ———. "The Haitians and America's Pull." *Occasional Papers Series*, Dialogue No. 2. Miami: Latin American and Caribbean Center, Florida International University, March 1981. Pp. 1-10.

553. *Making It on Their Own: From Refugee Sponsoring to Self-Sufficiency.* A Survey by Church World Service Immigration and Refugee Program. [New York, December 12, 1983].

     With a high return rate of 65 percent, results showed that: (1) over time most refugees are finding jobs; (2) refugees use of public assistance is significantly lower than is commonly believed; (3) over time most refugees are achieving self-sufficiency; and (4) CWS sponsors and congregations have contributed an estimated $133 million in cash, goods and services, and time over the past three and a half years.

554. Mann, E.S., and J. Salvo. "Characteristics of New Hispanic Immigrants to New York City: A Comparison of Puerto Rican and Non-Puerto Rican Hispanics." Paper presented at Population Association of America. Annual Meeting. Minneapolis, May 3-5, 1984.

     Using Summary Tape Files 2 and 4 of the 1980 Census, and the Public Use Microdata Samples, provides a comprehensive look at the demographic and socioeconomic characteristics of Puerto Ricans and "Other Hispanics," those non-Puerto Rican immigrants exclusive of Cubans and Mexicans, in New York City. Results show wide differences in socioeconomic status of the groups, closely related to basic disparities in fertility, labor force participation, and, most of all, family structure and composition. Moreover, an examination of the two largest "Other Hispanic" subgroups, Colombians and Dominicans, revealed differences which were, in many instances, wider than those between Puerto Ricans and all "Other Hispanics."

555. Manson, Donald M., et al. *Mexican Immigration to Southern California: Issues of Job Competition and Worker Mobility.* Washington, D.C.: The Urban Institute, 1985.

556. Maram, Sheldon L. "Hispanic Workers in the Garment and Restaurant Industries in Los Angeles County." Working Papers in U.S. Mexican Studies, No. 12. Program in United States-Mexican Studies, University of California, San Diego, 1980.

Describes the social and economic characteristics of
Hispanic workers in the garment and restaurant industries
in Los Angeles County. Provides the first comparison
based on survey research of the characteristics of undocumented workers with those of U.S. citizens and legal
immigrants who worked with them and is also the first
to be based on a large sample of undocumented workers in
specific U.S. industries.

557. Marshall, A. *Immigration in a Surplus-Worker Labor
     Market: The Case of New York.* New York: Center for
     Latin American and Caribbean Studies, New York Univer-
     sity, May 1983.

     First aim is to analyze the economic allocation of
     manual-labor immigration in the New York region and the
     change it underwent during the evolution of the immigra-
     tion process and of global labor market conditions since
     1965. The second is to discuss some of the socioeconomic
     consequences of large-scale immigration, in particular,
     the effects upon the working class at large. Pays
     special attention to the inflows of Latin American
     origin, *i.e.*, to one of the streams that showed a steady
     rhythm of immigration to New York during the 1970s
     despite the growing excess of internal labor supplies
     in the region. The discussion generally transcends the
     ethnic origin of immigrant labor and is intended to
     apply broadly to the allocation and socioeconomic conse-
     quences of manual-labor immigration as a whole.

558. Marshall, Dawn. *The Haitian Problem.* Mona, Jamaica:
     University of the West Indies, 1979.

559. ————. "The International Politics of Caribbean
     Migration." In Richard Millett and W. Marvin Will,
     eds. *The Restless Caribbean.* New York: Praeger,
     1979. Pp. 42-50.

560. Marshall, F. Ray. "Economic Factors Influencing the
     International Migration of Workers." *Views Across
     the Border.* Edited by Stanley R. Ross. Albuquerque:
     University of New Mexico Press, 1978. Pp. 63-78.

561. ————. "Immigration: An International Economic Per-
     spective." *International Migration Review*, 18 (Fall
     1984): 593-612.

     An effective American immigration policy has been com-
     plicated by the diversity of political interests and the

absence of reliable statistics to determine the magnitude of the impact on the American economy. Estimates of the number of illegal aliens in the United States range from one to twelve million. While political biases and complexities and data inadequacies complicate our analysis, some generalizations, examined in this essay, seem to be confirmed by worldwide experience.

562. Martin, Philip L. "Select Commission Suggests Changes in Immigration Policy. A Review Essay." *Monthly Labor Review*, 105 (February 1982): 31.

563. Massey, Douglas S. "Dimensions of the New Immigration to the United States and the Prospects for Assimilation." *Annual Review of Sociology*, 7 (1981): 57-85.

564. ————. "Residential Segregation of Spanish Americans in United States Urbanized Areas." *Demography*, 16 (November 1979): 553-563.

Measures residential segregation among Spanish Americans, whites, and blacks in the twenty-nine largest urbanized areas of the United States. The relative proportion of Spanish who live in a central city and the relative number of Spanish who are foreign stock are both highly related across urbanized areas to variations in the level of Spanish-white segregation.

565. ————, and Kathleen M. Schnabel. "Recent Trends in Hispanic Immigration to the United States." *International Migration Review*, 17 (Summer 1983): 212-243.

566. Matta, B.N. "Observations on the Effects of U.S. Labor Markets on Immigration." Paper presented at the Second International Meeting of the North American Economics and Finance Association, Mexico City, July 27, 1984.

Reports the results of efforts at measuring substitution between male U.S. born workers and two cohorts of male legal immigrant workers using the Survey of Income and Education 1976.

567. May, J. "The Vermont Experience Planned Clusters in Snow Country." *Journal of Refugee Resettlement*, 1 (May 1981): 31-35.

Examines the planned cluster of Laotians in St. Johnsbury, Vermont, detailing how the plan began and was carried out and how the residents of the town welcomed and helped the Laotian refugees.

568. Melendy, H. Brett. *Asians in America: Filipinos, Koreans, and East Indians.* Boston: Twayne Publishers, 1977.

Shows how the change in immigration law since 1965 has permitted a larger number of representatives from these three Asian groups to come to America and how each of these three groups has a history of migration, settlement, and problems antedating the Kennedy-Johnson liberalization. According to the author, "neither the new professional and middle class immigration nor the formal abrogation of racist statutes, occasioned by a recently renewed commitment to civil rights, has ended the issues of prejudice, discrimination, and adjustment that mark the lives of these and other Asian minorities."

569. ————. "Filipinos in the United States." *Pacific Historical Review,* 43 (November 1974): 520-547.

570. Melville, Margarita B. "Mexican Women Adapt to Migration." *International Migration Review,* 12 (Summer 1978): 225-235.

Deals primarily with the mental stress of acculturation which results from the processes of migration. Focuses on recent Mexican female migrants to the City of Houston and seeks to determine the strategies used by these migrants to cope with the stress of migration. As a principal cause of stress, the undocumented status of twenty-one out of forty-six of the respondents was revealed during the course of the interviews.

571. Meredith, William H., et al. *Nebraska Indochinese Refugee Needs Assessment. May 1981.* Lincoln, Nebraska: University of Nebraska, 1981.

572. ————, and Sheran L. Cramer. *Sponsors of Nebraska Indochinese Refugees: Meeting the Challenges "There Are No Strangers, Only Friends We Haven't Met."* Lincoln, Nebraska: University of Nebraska, 1981.

573. ————, and Bette J. Tweten, eds. *Proceedings: Helping Indochinese Families in Transition Conference, May 11-12, 1981.* Lincoln, Nebraska: College of Home Economics, University of Nebraska, 1981.

574. "The Mexican Origin Experience in the United States." *Social Science Quarterly,* 65 (June 1984). Whole Issue.

The 35 articles and research notes all deal with
Mexicans in the United States. They are arranged under
nine topics: social justice and the legal system; political access and participation; labor force experience;
the cost of being a Mexican American; undocumented migrants; language, fertility and mortality; socialization
and the family; and changing world views and cultural
perspectives.

575. Meyer, Michael C. "U.S.-Mexican Relations in the 1970s:
     The Persistent Problems of the Border." Paper pre-
     sented at a conference (Fronteras 1976: San Diego/
     Tijuana--The International Border in Community Rela-
     tions: Gateway or Barrier?), San Diego, November 19-
     20, 1976. [ERIC microfiche: ED146087].

576. [Miami]. *The Cuban Immigration, 1959-1966, and Its
     Impact on Miami-Dade County, Florida*. Miami, Florida,
     University of Miami: Center for Advanced International
     Studies, 1967.

577. "Miami: New Hispanic Power Base in the U.S." *U.S. News
     and World Report*, 86 (February 19, 1979): 66-69.

578. [Miami]. City of Miami. *Preliminary Haitian Impact
     Analysis*. Miami: City of Miami Planning Department,
     1981.

579. *The Miami Report. Recommendations on United States
     Policy Toward Latin America and the Caribbean*. Coral
     Gables, Florida [1983].

     Represents the Miami community's call for response to
     economic and political crisis. Its recommendations for
     U.S. policy on immigration are the following: (1) Support
     principles protecting the rights of potential immigrants
     and those seeking asylum; (2) Assert these principles
     by diplomatic means and in international organizations;
     (3) Enact legislation to grant residence status of un-
     documented aliens now in the United States; (4) Impose
     sanctions on those employing undocumented immigrants,
     while protecting the rights of U.S. citizens and law-
     fully admitted immigrants; (5) Establish control over
     the borders of the United States with due respect for
     the human rights of persons intercepted; (6) Establish
     a reasonable, regulated, and orderly migration process
     for the surplus populations in the Caribbean Basin,
     including the establishment of special quotas.

580. Midgley, Elizabeth. "Immigrants: Whose Huddled Masses?"
     Atlantic Monthly (April 1978): 6-26.

581. "Migration and Behavioral Deviance." *American Behavioral
     Scientist*, 13 (September-October 1969): 5-132. Whole
     Issue.

     Based on papers and discussions at the conference on
     "Migration and Behavioral Deviance." Contents: Eugene B.
     Brody, "Migration and Adaptation: The Nature of the Prob-
     lem"; Robert C. Hanson and Ozzie G. Simmons, "Differen-
     tial Experience Paths of Rural Migrants to the City";
     Lyle W. Shannon, "The Economic Absorption and Cultural
     Integration of Immigration Workers"; Elmer L. Struening,
     Judith G. Rabkin and Harris B. Peck, "Migration and
     Ethnic Membership in Relation to Social Problems";
     Robert L. Derbyshire, "Adaptation of Adolescent Mexican
     Americans to U.S. Society"; Robert J. Kleiner and
     Seymour Parker, "Social-Psychological Aspects of Migra-
     tion and Mental Disorder in a Negro Population"; Eugene B.
     Brody, "Preventive Planning and Strategies of Interven-
     tion: An Overview."

582. Miller, Harris N. "The Right Thing to Do: A History
     of Simpson-Mazzoli." In Nathan Glazer, ed. *Clamor at
     the Gates: The New American Immigration* (San Francisco,
     California: Institute for Contemporary Studies, 1985).
     Pp. 49-71.

     "It is said that Congress and the President have only
     dealt with immigration once in any generation: the post-
     World War I quotas, the post-World War II McCarran-Walter
     Act, and now Simpson-Mazzoli. Setting aside the question
     of whether immigration as a topic of legislation is in
     fact cyclical, and whether or not Simpson-Mazzoli was to
     be enacted and work as intended, it is unlikely legisla-
     tion designed to deal with people coming to our shores
     will disappear from the political screen for another
     thirty years. Economists can debate how many immigrants
     we can afford to absorb and whether they help or hurt
     our nation. Demographers can debate population growth
     and the 'push' and 'pull' factors which send people from
     other nations to our country, but the issue will not go
     away. We can only hope that when future congressional
     and executive bodies are faced with immigration issues,
     they will deal with them constructively, as they have
     on Simpson-Mazzoli, so that we will never again see the
     day when nativism and racism become the basis of immi-
     gration policy."

583. Miller Jake C. *The Plight of Haitian Refugees*. New York: Praeger, 1984.

"While the number of Haitians entering the United States in recent years has been a major cause of concern, it pales into insignificance when compared with the total number of refugees who have entered this country during the last decade. With 124,789 Cubans coming to this country during the Mariel boat lift and 600,424 Southeast Asians arriving in the United States since 1975, the 40,023 boat people from Haiti constitute only a small percentage of the total refugee population of this country. Although conceding the truth of the above, some government officials insist that the Haitian boat people are not refugees but instead are illegal aliens. However, even when considering aliens who have come to this country without acceptable documents, Haitians constitute only an insignificant percentage. While the number of such aliens is not known, the INS estimated that there were between three and five million in the United States in 1979. In appraising the impact upon this country of Haitian boat people, Professor Virginia Dominguez observed: 'By comparison to the millions of Mexicans who reside in the United States at any given point without proper documentation, this flow is totally insignificant. Even if it is compared to the number of Haitians who reside in the New York metropolitan area illegally ... the entry of Haitian boat people is insignificant.'"

584. Miller, M.J., and D.J. Yeres. *A Massive Temporary Worker Programme for the U.S.: Solution or Mirage?* Geneva: International Labour Office, World Employment Programme Research, 1979.

585. Miller, Wayne Charles. "Cuban Americans." In W.C. Miller, *A Comprehensive Bibliography for the Study of American Minorities*. 2 vols. New York: New York University Press, 1976. Vol. II, pp. 773-780.

586. Miller, W.H. "Another Stab at Immigration Reform." *Industry Week*, 218 (May 31, 1982): 19-20.

587. ————. "Immigration Reform Finally in Sight." *Industry Week*, 217 (May 30, 1983): 20-21.

588. ————. "Legislation: Immigration Qualms." *Industry Week*, 222 (July 9, 1984): 26-27.

589. Mines, Richard. *Developing a Community Tradition of Migration: A Field Study in Rural Zacatecas, Mexico, and California Settlement Areas.* La Jolla, California: Program in U.S.-Mexican Studies, University of California, San Diego, Monographs in U.S.-Mexican Studies, No. 3, 1981.

Ethnographic and survey study of migration from the community of Las Animos in Zacatecas state, Mexico, to various receiving areas in California, based on field-work completed in 1979.

590. ———, and A. De Janvry. "Migration to the United States and Mexican Rural Development: A Case Study (Los Animos)." *American Journal of Agricultural Economics*, 64 (August 1982): 444-454.

591. Mitchell, William L. "The Cuban Refugee Program." *Social Security Bulletin*, 25 (March 1962): 3-8.

592. Moerk, E. "The Acculturation of the Mexican-American Minority to the Anglo-American Society in the U.S." *Journal of Human Relations*, 20 (1972): 317-325.

From two studies conducted by the author in the Southwest of the United States in 1967 and 1970, it is evident that "Mexican-Americans have caught up in the last few years." From these findings the author concludes that "populations, even those coming from lower social classes, and from a low educational group which are very loyal to their traditional culture and religion, can change their values and attitudes relatively fast."

593. Mohl, Raymond A. "Cubans in Miami: A Preliminary Bibliography." *The Immigration History Newsletter*, 16 (May 1984): 1-10.

This "bibliography is designed to identify the chief sources upon which historians of immigration and ethnicity might rely for interpretation of the Cuban experience in the United States and particularly in Miami. It draws especially on mimeographed studies prepared by social scientists at the University of Miami, Florida International University, and Florida Atlantic University. It identifies little-known and hard-to-track-down reports on Cubans in Miami issued by the Cuban National Planning Council, the Florida State Commission on Hispanic Affairs, the National Council of Hispanic Mental Health, the Amercan Council

for Nationalities Service, the Council for Inter-
American Security, the New Transcentury Foundation, and
various agencies of the Metro-Dade County and the
Florida state governments.... Over the past 25 years,
Miami has emerged as one of the most fascinating, yet
least studied, of the new immigrant cities. The mass
immigration of Cuban exiles which began in 1959 has
made Miami as much a Latin American as an American city.
Growing numbers of immigrants and refugees from other
Caribbean and Latin American nations have altered
Miami's demographic and cultural pattern even further.
Indeed, Miami has become a truly multiethnic and
multicultural urban region."

594.   ————. "An Ethnic 'Boiling Pot': Cubans and Haitians
        in Miami." *Journal of Ethnic Studies*, 13 (Spring
        1985): 36-41.

595.   ————. "Miami: The Ethnic Cauldron." In Richard M.
        Bernard and Bradley R. Rice, eds. *Sunbelt Cities:
        Growth and Politics Since World War Two*. Austin,
        Texas: University of Texas Press, 1983. Pp. 58-99.

596.   ————. "The New Caribbean Immigration." *Journal of
        American Ethnic History*, 5 (Spring 1986): 64-71.

A review-essay. "The United States has become a
nation of immigrants once again. During the 1970s,
according to one careful study, net immigration
totaled more than 7 million people--a figure that
surpasses the previous record high of about 6.3 million
between 1900 and 1910. Some specialists estimate that
at the present rate, 35 million additional immigrants
and refugees will come to the United States by the year
2000. They are coming to America from all over the
world but especially from Asia, Central and South
America, and the Caribbean. The books under discussion
here reflect an early effort to examine the patterns
of arrival and adjustment of some of these recent immigrant groups from the Caribbean, particularly Cubans
and Haitians."

597.   ————. "The New Haitian Immigration: A Preliminary
        Bibliography." *Immigration History Newsletter*, 17
        (May 1985): 1-8.

During the past few decades, the character of American
immigration has changed dramatically. Third World
nations have replaced European countries as the chief

sources of immigrants to the United States. During the 1970s, more than seven million newcomers poured into the United States, mostly from Asia, Central and South America, and the Caribbean. Among these new immigrants are the Haitians, exiles from political repression and economic hopelessness in the western hemisphere's poorest nation.... "Because American immigration law has made it difficult for Haitians to migrate to the U.S. legally, tens of thousands of Haitians have taken to the seas in tiny, barely seaworthy sailboats. These are the 'black boat people' of the Caribbean, who have risked all in a dangerous 800-mile journey to the beaches of South Florida. No one knows how many Haitians mave made this perilous trip, but at least 40,000 have been counted on arrival since 1975. Immigration experts believe that at least an equal number perished at sea. There are thousands more who made it safely and escaped the notice of immigration officials."

598. ————. "Race, Ethnicity, and Urban Politics in the Miami Metropolitan Area." *Florida Environmental and Urban Issues*, 9 (April 1982): 23–25.

599. Molton, David. "Immigration and Nationality Law. 1984." *Annual Survey of American Law* (December 1981): 165–186.

600. Moncarz, Paul. "Effects of Professional Restrictions on Cuban Refugees in Selected Health Professions in the United States, 1959–1969." *International Migration*, 8 (1970): 22–30.

601. ————. "The Golden Cage—Cubans in Miami." *International Migration*, 16 (1978): 160–173.

602. ————. "A Model of Professional Adaptation of Refugees: The Cuban Case in the U.S., 1959–1970." *International Migration*, 11 (1973): 171–183.

603. ————. "A Study of the Effect of Environmental Change on Human Capital Among Selected Skilled Cubans." Unpublished Ph.D. dissertation, Florida State University, 1969.

604. ————, and Antonio Jorge. "Cuban Immigration to the United States." In Dennis Laurence Cuddy, ed. *Contemporary American Immigration: Interpretive Essays*. Boston: Twayne Publishers, 1982. Pp. 146–175.

605. Monroe, Gary. *Detention at Krome: Photographs of Haitian Refugees.* Miami: Miami-Dade Community College, 1982.

606. Monroy, D. "Like Swallows at the Old Mission: Mexicans and the Racial Politics of Growth in Los Angeles in the Interwar Period." *The Western Historical Quarterly,* 14 (1983): 435-458.

Examines the role the Mexican labor force played in the economic growth of Los Angeles after World War I. Analyzes the political needs of employers, social control of the group whose culture conflicted with the demands of capitalist development, and conflict at the work place and immigration.

607. Montero, Darrel. *Vietnamese Americans: Patterns of Resettlement and Socioeconomic Adaptation in the United States.* Boulder, Colorado: Westview Press, 1979.

Presents data, from the surveys of the refugees conducted by Opportunity Systems, Inc. (OST) for H.E.W., about the resettlement and adaptation of the Vietnamese refugees to life in the United States. Includes a brief history of Vietnam but the central objective is to analyze and document the background characteristics of the refugees and their progress in adjusting, economically and socially, to their new life during their first three years in America. A second objective is to develop a theory of Spontaneous International Migration (SIM) analyzing the Vietnamese experience in a broader sociohistorical content. The relatively brief text is supplemented by 125 pages of tables from the OSI surveys.

608. ————. "Vietnamese Refugees in America: Toward a Theory of Spontaneous International Migration." *International Migration Review,* 13 (1979): 624-648.

609. Montoya, R.A., and W.A. Cornelius, eds. *International Inventory of Current Mexico-Related Research.* San Diego: Center for U.S.-Mexican Studies, University of California, 1983.

Annotated bibliography presents interdisciplinary and international compendium of advanced research in progress relating to Mexico. Over 450 research projects are listed and described.

610. ————, and ————, eds. *The Report of the U.S. Select Commission on Immigration and Refugee Policy: A Critical Analysis.* San Diego, California: Center for U.S.-Mexican Studies, University of California, 1982.

Includes essays on Mexican immigration, immigration law and law enforcement, and the Chicano community. Each essay focuses on a particular set of issues raised by the Select Commission on Immigration and Refugee policy.

611. Moore, Joan W. "Mexican Americans and Cities: A Study in Migration and the Use of Formal Resources." *International Migration Review*, 5 (Fall 1971): 292-308.

Explores the circumstances under which Los Angeles Mexican-American men turn to formal or informal Mexican or non-Mexican resources. Formal sources are likely to be utilized for advice or help in dealing with the city government, second with regard to money problems, third with regard to politics, and least for personal problems. Formalization of resources is associated with length of residence in the city, but birthplace shows a different pattern. The data do not support the theoretical notion that urbanization is associated with abandonment of primary-group resources for this population. In fact, native *Angelenos*, with greater access to "cheaper" *gemeinschaft* resources, tend to adhere to them. Findings have implications for theories of urbanism as well as understanding of Mexican Americans.

612. ———, and Harry Pachon. *Hispanics in the United States*. Englewood Cliffs, New Jersey: Prentice-Hall, 1985.

613. Morgan, Larry C., and Bruce L. Gardner. "Potential for a U.S. Guest-Worker Program in Agriculture: Lessons from the Braceros." In Barry R. Chiswick, ed. *The Gateway: U.S. Immigration Issues and Policies* (Washington, D.C.: American Enterprise Institute, 1982). Pp. 361-411.

Indicates that, in dealing with the problem of illegal immigration from Mexico, neither a policy of strictly policing the border nor a policy of opening the border seems acceptable. An alternative is to permit temporary migration by Mexican guest workers. Assesses the possible consequences of this policy by analyzing the earlier experience with the *bracero* program under Public Law 78 in the 1950s and 1960s. Using an econometric model of the supply of and demand for farm labor in the seven states that received almost all the *braceros*, estimates that the *bracero* program on average reduced farm wages by about 8 percent and imposed losses

of about $140 million per year on U.S. farm workers.
The estimated gains to U.S. employers and consumers of
farm products sum to about $185 million per year, for a
net gain to the U.S. population of about $45 million per
year. The effects of the *braceros* on other aspects of
social welfare and on illegal immigration are also
discussed. Concludes that the more pessimistic warnings
about the ill effects of a guest-worker program are un-
supported by the U.S. experience with the *bracero* program.

614. Morris, M.D. *The Administration of Immigration Policy.*
     Washington, D.C.: Brookings Institution, 1984.

615. Morrison, Allan. "Miami's Cuban Refugee Crisis."
     Ebony, 18 (June 1963): 96-104.

616. Morrison, Thomas K. "International Migration in the
     Dominican Republic: Implications for Development
     Planning." *International Migration Review*, 16
     (Winter 1982): 819-836.

     The Dominican Republic represents a microcosm of all
     the major migration patterns: substantial emigration and
     immigration, sizeable return migration, and persistent
     internal rural-urban migration. The impacts of these
     various types of migration are related and have a sig-
     nificant influence on the development process. This
     study analyzes the causes of these migrations as well
     as the costs and benefits in terms of the individual
     migrants and the country as a whole. Finally, it in-
     vestigates the implications of migration for development
     planning in the Dominican Republic. A major conclusion
     of the study is that the migration issue is not an area
     distinct from the various development focuses but rather
     cuts across and is related to many of the program areas
     in which the government is involved.

617. Morse, R.A., ed. *Korean Studies in America: Options for
     the Future.* Lanham, Maryland: University Press of
     America, Inc., 1983.

     The proceedings of a conference devoted to Korean
     studies in the United States. Presented are past
     achievements in the field and suggested proposals for
     future development.

618. Moulier-Boutang, Yann, and Jean Pierre Garson. "Major
     Obstacles to Control of Irregular Migrations: Pre-

requisites to Policy." *International Migration Review*, 18 (Fall 1984): 579-592.

Examines three basic obstacles thwarting all attempts to reduce irregular migration. The first, rather well known and analyzed, underscores the dependency of all regulation of migratory flows on the system of economic and political relations between developed and developing countries. The second obstacle resides in the persistence and growth of subsequent dependent irregular migration. This obstacle also reveals the relative autonomy of population movements compared with the employment situation in the labor market. The third, generally ignored obstacle, is the role played by migration itself, particularly the discriminatory status of foreign workers in the labor market, in producing irregular migration.

619. Mueller, Charles F. *The Economics of Labor Migration: A Behavioral Analysis.* Studies in Urban Economics. New York: Academic Press, 1982.

Views migration as a choice made in each time period among alternative destinations, with the origin as one destination. The characteristics of the individual and the various potential destinations enter the decision regarding the optimal destination. Multinominal logit (MNL) procedures are used to estimate the equations. Defines a migrant as a worker who changed county of employment in 1969. The data are from the Social Security Administration's Longitudinal Employer-Employee Data file (LEED) which contains work histories from 1957 to 1969 for persons in covered employment. The file included information on the employee's age, sex, and race, as well as the location (county), industry, and wages for each job.

620. Mullaney, J. *Aiding the Desplazados of El Salvador: The Complexity of Human Assistance.* Washington, D.C.: U.S. Committee for Refugees, 1984.

Seeks to frame the problem of displaced people in El Salvador by providing (1) an overview of the development of displaced populations in El Salvador and the conditions and problems they encounter; (2) an outline of the ways that the displaced are being helped by the governments of El Salvador and the United States, the churches and PVOs, including a discussion of why the aid is interpreted as a function of the political struggle;

(3) a discussion of recent efforts to relocate large
numbers of displaced people to more peaceful areas in
the country; and (4) recommendations for future assistance.

621. Muller, Thomas. "Economic Aspects of Immigration."
     In Nathan Glazer, ed. *Clamor at the Gates: The New
     American Immigration*. San Francisco, California:
     Institute for Contemporary Studies, 1985. Pp. 109-
     133.

     "On balance, the economic benefits of immigration,
     based on our knowledge so far, tend to exceed private
     and in some areas public costs. However, serious
     research on the impact of recent immigration has
     merely begun. Further analysis may show that as a
     result of structural changes in the nation's economy,
     the effects of immigration are less positive than cur-
     rent information suggests. More likely are future
     findings showing that from an economic perspective
     immigrants are a plus to the nation. This should lead
     to a more thorough assessment of such noneconomic issues
     as social integration, language, and the environment."

622. Muller, Thomas, and Thomas J. Espenshade. *The Fourth
     Wave: California's Newest Immigrants*. Washington,
     D.C.: The Urban Institute Press, 1985.

     Places immigration to California in historical per-
     spective, and provides a profile of the recent immi-
     grants in terms of numbers and characteristics. Dis-
     cusses the effects of the recent immigration wave on
     Southern California in terms of jobs, wage levels, income
     distribution, population distribution, the public
     sector, and the Los Angeles and California economies.
     Predictions are made for the 1980s for the current
     resident population and the growth of the economy,
     population inflow from other parts of the United States,
     legal immigration, undocumented immigration, economic
     impact of projected immigration, fiscal impact, social
     impact, and, finally policy implications. *Contents:*
     Immigration in Retrospect; New Immigrants to California;
     The Mexican Living Experience in Los Angeles; Impact
     of Immigration on Jobs and Wages; Fiscal Impact of
     Mexican Immigration on California's State and Local
     Governments; The Broader Demographic, Economic, and
     Fiscal Effects of Recent Mexican Immigration; Future
     Demand for Workers in Southern California; The Fourth
     Wave; Opportunities and Challenges.

623. Murphy, E.M., and P. Cancellier. *Immigration: Questions and Answers.* Washington, D.C.: Population Reference Bureau, 1982.

624. Musgrave, Peggy B., ed. *Mexico and the United States: Studies in Economic Interaction.* Boulder, Colorado: Westview Press, 1985.

Contributors to this volume address the key issues of economic interdependence between Mexico and the U.S., including problems of capital flow and foreign dependence, the role of trade, the impact of economic fluctuations and macro policies on Mexico's economic development, and labor migration. They highlight mutual approaches to solving joint problems and illustrate that U.S.-Mexican relations cannot be viewed only in bilateral terms but most be considered in the light of a healthy world economy.

625. Nafziger, J.A.R. "Immigration Policy of Helping to Bring People to the Resources." *Denver Journal of International Law and Policy*, 8 (1979): 607-26.

626. Nalven, J., ed. "Border Perspectives on the U.S./Mexico Relationship." *New Scholar*, 9 (1984): 1-279. Whole Issue.

Among the essays gathered in this special issue, five deal specifically with migration issues: "Northern Mexican Migration and the U.S./Mexican Border Region" by E.R. Stoddard; "The U.S. Guest Worker Debate" by R. Mines and P.L. Martin; "What Drives Mexican Illegal Border-Crossers into the U.S.? A Psychological Perspective" by G.A. Barrientos, et al.; "Mexican Immigration and Petroleum: A Folkloristic Perspective" by M. Herrera-Sobek; and "American Perceptions of Undocumented Immigrants: Political Implications" by B. Loveman and C.R. Hofstetter.

627. Neil, Andrew. "America's Latin Beat: A Survey of South Florida." *The Economist*, 285 (October 16, 1982): 1-26.

628. "The New Immigration." *The Annals of the American Academy of Political and Social Science*, 377 (September 1966): Whole Issue.

629. Nicholas, M. "Protecting Aliens Is a Civilized Rite and an Economic Necessity." *Human Rights*, 9 (Summer 1981): 45-9.

630. Norquest, Carrol. *Rio Grande Wetbacks: Mexican Migrant Workers*. Albuquerque: University of New Mexico Press, 1972.

631. North, David S. *Alien Workers: A Study of the Labor Certification Program*. Washington, D.C.: U.S. Department of Labor, 1971.

632. ————. "The Canadian Experience with Amnesty for Aliens: What the United States Can Learn." Working Paper (43) [n.p.]. World Employment Programme, October 1979.

Examines the experience that the Canadian Government had as they offered amnesty, on two different occasions, to groups of aliens in Canada. Concludes that the United States can learn from the Canadian experience despite differing political settings, target population, and governing system.

633. ————. "Down Under Amnesties: Background, Programs and Comparative Insights." *International Migration Review*, 18 (Fall 1984): 524-540.

Australia, proportionately, accepts more immigrants than the United States and, consequently, immigrants and immigration policy carry a greater impact there, than in the United States. Although Australia's location limits its experience with undocumented migrants, there have been enough of them to cause Australia to conduct three alien legalization programs in 1973, 1976, and 1980. Australia's small-scale programs, by U.S. standards, provide some useful lessons to the United States.

634. ————. *Enforcing the Immigration Law: A Review of the Options*. Washington, D.C.: New TransCentury Foundation, 1980.

Consists of seven chapters. The first is a brief analysis of the apparently increasing levels of international migration to the United States. The second discusses the rationale for (and disadvantages of) changing the levels of enforcement in this area. Chapter three presents an overview of the allocation of resources to immigration law enforcement in the 1970s. The next three chapters cover the three basic areas for enforcement of the law: the flows of migrants into the nation, the population (stock) of illegal migrants in the nation, and of illegal migrants holding jobs or seeking funds from income transfer programs. The final section is a summary of the options available to policymakers. Presents an overview of the various law enforcement programs (and potential programs) which affect (or could affect) international migration to the United States. It was commissioned by the Select Commission on Immigration and Refugee Policy and is designed as a contribution to the Commissioners' decision-making process. It does *not*, therefore, reflect the views of the Commission. "One of the grave difficulties in this field is that most of those who work in it tend to use the approaches and the techniques of criminal law enforcement; most of the enforcers are armed, sometimes aided by advanced equipment (sensors, fixed-wing planes, and, at a recent count, three helicopters) as they seek to apprehend the individual, frightened blue-collar-wearing malefactor. While, as we will argue subsequently, we believe that the Border Patrol needs more of these kinds of resources, it would also be helpful if decision-makers recognized the need for systems approaches in this field, designing enforcement systems to counter systems of illegal migration, rather than simply capturing the individual illegal migrants."

635. ———. "Impact of Legal, Illegal and Refugee Migration on U.S. Social Service Programs." In Mary Kritz, ed. *U.S. Immigration and Refugee Policy* (Lexington, Massachusetts: Lexington Books, 1983). Pp. 44-63.

636. ———. *Nonimmigrant Workers in the U.S.: Current Trends and Future Implications*. Washington, D.C.: New TransCentury Foundation, 1980.

Describes nonimmigrant workers who may legally work in the U.S., but only temporarily and under other prescribed conditions. The numbers, occupations, wages and working conditions of five subclasses of such workers are analyzed: foreign students, temporary workers of distinguished merit and ability, other temporary workers, exchange visitors and intracompany transferees (multinational employees). The impacts of these workers on the microlabor markets they affect is discussed, as are demographic impacts.

637. ———. *The Virgin Islands Alien Legalization Program: Lessons for the Mainland*. Washington, D.C.: New TransCentury Foundation, 1983.

"The United States Congress, as this is written [1983], is contemplating an immigration reform package along the

lines of the Simpson-Mazzoli bills, which passed the
Senate, but not the House, last year. One of the principal elements of that package is a proposed legalization
program (or amnesty) for many aliens currently in the
nation but out of legal status. Meanwhile in a totally
separate action, the Congress last year passed the
Virgin Islands Nonimmigrant Alien Adjustment Act of 1982
(Public Law 97-271), a small-scale legalization program.
It is my belief that, although the Virgin Islands program is tiny and specialized, it can be regarded as a
trial run for alien legalization on the Mainland. In
both instances, there is a body of aliens with historical
grounds for disliking the Immigration and Naturalization
Service (INS); in both the Government has decided to
change the basic rules of the immigration game retro-
actively, and to provide a substantial benefit for an
alien population; and in both INS is working with (or
contemplating working with) voluntary agencies. Further,
the medical screening that accompanies the Virgin Islands
program is likely to be duplicated on the Mainland.
There are, of course, substantial differences, but the
similarities are such that we decided to examine the
administration of Public Law 97-271 hoping to learn some
lessons for the Mainland."

638.   ————, and Marion F. Houstoun. *The Characteristics and*
        Role of Illegal Aliens in the U.S. Labor Market: An
        Exploratory Study. Washington, D.C.: New TransCentury
        Foundation and Linton Company, 1976.

"The objectives of this study were to gather hereto-
fore unavailable data on the characteristics and labor-
market experiences of illegal aliens in the U.S. work
force, to present those data within the context of current information on illegal immigration, and to examine
the resulting policy implications, with special reference
to the question of the role and impact of illegals in
the U.S. labor market. With the financial support and
intellectual encouragement of the Office of Manpower
Research and Development, of the Department of Labor,
and the cooperation of the Immigration and Naturalization
Service (INS), of the Department of Justice, 793 apprehended illegal aliens who had worked at least two weeks
in the U.S. were interviewed in 19 sites across the
nation. In addition, with the assistance of the Catholic
Migration Service and the law firm of Fried, Fragomen,
and del Ray, supplemental interviews were conducted of
51 unapprehended illegals working in two of those sites.
In order to achieve as high a level of cooperation and

honesty as possible, a common procedure used with such surveys has been followed; all interviews were voluntary, and neither the name nor the address of any respondent were recorded."

639. ————, and Allen LeBel. *Manpower and Immigration Policies in the United States*. Special Report No. 20. Washington, D.C.: National Commission for Manpower Policy, February 1978.

An overview of the manpower policy implications of U.S. immigration policy, and of the development of immigration policy. Examines current and projected results of U.S. immigration policies and practices and the manpower consequences of these policies. Concluding chapters discuss immigration policies in other immigrant-receiving nations (Canada, Israel and Australia) and make a number of recommendations for restructuring U.S. immigration policies.

640. ————, and J.R. Wagner. *Immigration and Income Transfer Policies in the United States: An Analysis of a Non-relationship*. Washington, D.C.: Center for Labor and Migration Studies, New TransCentury Foundation, 1980.

641. ————, and W.G. Weissert. *Immigrants and the American Labor Market*. Washington, D.C.: TransCentury Corporation, 1973.

Prepared for the Manpower Administration, U.S. Department of Labor. Based primarily on an examination of documents filed by 5,000 working age immigrants who entered the nation during fiscal year 1970. The visa applications, filed prior to entry, and the alien address reports, filed in January, 1972, were tabulated and compared. In addition, interviews were conducted with some of the immigrants, with employers of immigrants and with other knowledgeable people. Principal findings of the study were that immigrants made a substantial, but uneven, impact on the labor market, that this impact is greater than previously supposed, and that immigrants are closer to the American norm, in demographic terms, than they were fifty and sixty years ago. Examines the adjustments made by immigrants as they come to terms with the U.S. labor market.

642. Office of Refugee Resettlement, U.S. Department of Health and Human Services. *Refugee Resettlement Program*. [Washington, 1985]. Report to Congress, January 31, 1985.

Covers refugee program developments from October 1,
1983, through September 30, 1984. It is the eighteenth
in a series of reports to Congress on refugee resettlement in the U.S. since 1975, and the fourth to cover an
entire year of activities carried out under the comprehensive authority of the Refugee Act of 1980.

643. Orlow, James J. "America's Incoherent Immigration
Policy: Some Problems and Solutions." *University of
Miami Law Review*, 36 (September 1982): 931-937.

644. Paganoni, A. *Migration from the Philippines*. Quezon
City: Scalabrinians, 1984.

Focuses on the world of the Filipino migrants—an econ-
nomic analysis of the Philippine manpower export industry,
Philippine overseas employment, overseas contract workers,
and migration to the Middle East.

645. Palmer, Ingrid. "Advance Preparation and Settlement
Needs of South-East Asian Refugee Women." *International
Migration*, 19 (1981): 94-101.

646. Palmer, Ransford W. "Decade of West Indian Migration
to the United States, 1962-1972: An Economic Analysis."
Social and Economic Studies, 23 (1974): 571-587.

Notes causes for the increase in West Indian immigration. While Britain made entry more difficult for
Jamaicans after they acquired independence in 1962, the
American law of 1965 provided for easier entry of skilled
workers. West Indians who come to the United States
are among the islands' best educated, causing the same
kind of brain drain that affects the Philippines.

647. Palmer, Stephen E., Jr. "Haitian Migration to the U.S."
Current Policy, No. 191 (June 17, 1980): 5-9.

648. ————. *Toward Improved U.S. Immigration and International Education Programs: Preliminary Draft*. Cambridge, Massachusetts: Center for International Affairs, Harvard University, 1974. [ERIC microfiche:
ED09556]

649. Palmieri, Victor H. "Cuban-Haitian Refugees." *Department of State Bulletin*, 80 (August 1980): 79-82.

650. Parmet, R.D. *Labor and Immigration in Industrial America*.
Boston, Massachusetts: G.K. Hall, 1981.

651. "Parole of Cuban Refugees." In *Report of the Select Commission on Western Hemisphere Immigration*. Washington, D.C.: U.S. Government Printing Office, 1968. Pp. 131-135.

652. Pastor, Robert A. "Migration and Development in the Caribbean: Relating Policies and People." *International Migration Review*, 19 (Spring 1985): 144-151.

"Throughout the twentieth century, the United States has feared that political instability in the Caribbean could be exploited by adversaries. The best way to address the causes of instability is to contribute to the region's social, economic, and political development. Therefore, the United States and the nations of the Caribbean share a compelling interest in the region's development. The dramatic increase in legal and illegal immigration to the United States from the Caribbean in the last two decades has offered an additional human reason for U.S. interest in the region. This migration has also created a new source of dependence and vulnerability for the region. Curtailment of the migration would undoubtedly affect the region, and if the effect were social and political instability, then the United States would also share those consequences. Conversely, policies that take migration into account offer the opportunity to enhance development and social-political stability."

653. ———. "U.S. Immigration Policy and Latin America: In Search of the 'Special Relationship.'" *Latin American Research Review*, 19 (1984): 35-56.

A review of the past century of U.S. immigration policy tries to identify the key decisions and ascertain their effects on Latin American migration. This essay is divided into four parts: Defining Limits, 1875-1921; The Classical Special Relationship, 1921-1964; From Special Relationship to Global Policy, 1965-1978; and The Special Case-Illegal Migration.

654. Pedraza-Bailey, Silvia. "Cuba's Exiles: Portrait of a Refugee Migration." *International Migration Review*, 19 (Spring 1985): 4-34.

Provides a portrait of Cuba's exiles that encompasses all their waves of migration while shedding light on the broader phenomenon of refugee migration. Argues that to understand the changing social characteristics of the exiles over twenty years of migration, we need to under-

stand the changing phases of the Cuban revolution.
Utilizing the Cuban exodus as data, uses Egon F.
Kunz's theoretical framework for refugee migration to shed
light on the refugees' varying experiences, while also
using the actual Cuban refugee experience to react to
Kunz's abstract model.

655. ————. "Cubans and Mexicans in the United States: The
       Functions of Political and Economic Migration."
       Cuban Studies, 11-12 (July 1981-January 1982): 79-97.

656. Peek, Peter, and Guy Standing, eds. *State Policies and
       Migration: Studies in Latin America and the Caribbean.*
       London and Canberra: Croom Helm, 1982.

       The studies of eight countries (Chile, Peru, Ecuador,
       Brazil, Mexico, Colombia, Guyana and Cuba) were part of
       a program sponsored by the ILO and focused on World
       Employment. Migration is reckoned to be a dependent
       variable and various state policies the independent
       variable, admitting, of course, that the "modes of pro-
       duction" or "social relations of production," to use the
       nineteenth century phrase, are at the root of things.
       Population dynamics are largely discounted.

657. Peirce, Neal R., and Jerry Hagstrom. "The Hispanic
       Community--A Growing Force to Be Reckoned With."
       National Journal, 11 (April 7, 1979): 548-555.

658. Pérez, Lisandro. "Cubans." In Stephan Thernstrom, ed.
       Harvard Encyclopedia of American Ethnic Groups. Cam-
       bridge, Massachusetts: Harvard University Press, 1980.
       Pp. 256-261.

659. Pessar, Patricia R. "The Linkage Between the Household
       and Workplace of Dominican Women in the U.S." *Inter-
       national Migration Review*, 18 (Winter 1984): 1188-1211.

       Explores the interdependence between the household
       and workplace in the lives of Dominican immigrant women.
       Ethnographic research documents that while women's par-
       ticipation in wage work contributes to an improvement in
       domestic social relations, these household level changes
       do not in turn stimulate modifications in female workers'
       consciousness and demands for improved working conditions.
       Paradoxically, the beliefs about immigration and work
       which are rooted in the family and the immigration goals
       that are realized through household cooperation militate
       against working class identification and organized resis-
       tance in the workplace.

660. ————. "The Role of Households in International Migration and the Case of U.S.-Bound Migration from the Dominican Republic." *International Migration Review,* 16 (Summer 1982): 342-361.

"Analysis of the role of the household in migration necessitates a theoretical framework that encompasses both variables. This study of Dominican migration contributes to this goal by exploring several propositions. Principal among these is the claim that the structure within which Dominican migration occurs is capital's requirement for a continuous stream of cheap, vulnerable labor and the need of households to reproduce themselves at an historically and culturally prescribed level of maintenance. The article's emphasis on household strategies clarifies several important issues, such as variation in the rates of migration among groups in the same peripheral area, the increased impoverishment of nonmigrant members of sending communities, and the intensified dependency of emigrant households on the core economy."

661. Peterson, M.F. "Work Attitudes of Mariel Boatlift Refugees." *Cuban Studies,* 14 (Summer 1984): 1-20.

Data concerning experienced job characteristics were collected from 135 Cuban boatlift refugees using structured and semistructured interview questions in March 1981, about 11 months after the Mariel boatlift began. Respondents described task characteristics, good performance contingencies, and work satisfactions related to their last job in Cuba. Comparing this data with parallel data for a representative sample of U.S. employees and Mexican-Americans indicates both a few differences and several notable similarities. The data concerning satisfaction and good performance contingencies imply that while refugees may be frustrated by the lack of economic rewards for good performance in the United States, they may be particularly pleased with other, noneconomic, aspects of work.

662. Philipson, Lorrin, and Rafael Llerena. *Freedom Flights: Cuban Refugees Talk About Life Under Castro and How They Fled His Regime.* New York: Random House, 1980.

663. Piore, Michael J. *Birds of Passage: Migrant Labor and Industrial Societies.* Cambridge: Cambridge University Press, 1979.

Seeks simultaneously to provide a coherent theoretical analysis of labor migrations in industrial societies and

to demonstrate the inadequacy of conventional economic
theory in accounting for structural features of the
labor market in such societies. Deals with the specificity of labor migration as a social phenomenon while
pointing the way toward its integration into a more
general macrosociology of industrial societies. Draws
from a wide range of empirical cases concerning North
America and Western Europe, some of which are founded
on the author's own previous research on both continents.
More concerned with analysis and interpretation than
with description and is therefore addressed mainly to
readers already familiar with the literature surveying
contemporary migratory trends as well as with policy and
theoretical controversies surrounding them.

664.   Plummer, G. "Haitian Migrants and Background Imperial-
       ism." *Race and Class*, 26 (Spring 1985): 35-44.

       Discusses "the structure of North American domination
       in the Caribbean, and the intensifying crisis imperialism
       has engendered as it seeks to block genuine transforma-
       tion in the area." Haiti, Haitian migration, and U.S.
       policy in this area are discussed.

665.   Poe, R. "America's Immigration Hangup." *Across the
       Board*, 21 (July/August 1984): 12-21.

666.   Poertes, Alejandro. [sic] "Dilemmas of a Golden Rule:
       Integration of Cuban Refugee Families in Milwaukee."
       American Sociological Review, 34 (August 1969): 505-
       518.

       Studies 48 refugee families in Milwaukee. Examines
       their integration as a fundamental shift from a strongly
       psychological attachment to the past to values and
       identities congruent with the new environment. It was
       found that their integration is strongly influenced by
       relative level of present socioeconomic rewards. Results
       are interpreted as consequences of "the rational-in-
       dividualistic ethic characterizing families from these
       formerly dominant sectors of Cuba."

667.   Poitras, G. *International Migration to the United
       States from Costa Rica and El Salvador*. San Antonio:
       Border Research Institute, Trinity University, 1980.

668.   ————. *Return Migration from the United States to
       Costa Rica and El Salvador*. San Antonio: Border Re-
       search Institute, Trinity University, 1980.

669. Polinard, Jerry L., et al. "Attitudes of Mexican Americans Toward Irregular Mexican Immigration." *International Migration Review*, 18 (Fall 1984): 782-799.

Focuses on the attitudes of Mexican Americans toward issues relating to current U.S. immigration policy. "This study is an expansion of research begun last year (Miller, Polinard, and Wrinkle: 1984). In the previous study the geographical focus was on Hidalgo County, situated on the Texas-Mexico border. This study offers us the additional dimension of geography as a variable influencing attitudes."

670. Portes, Alejandro, et al. "Assimilation or Consciousness: Perceptions of U.S. Society Among Recent Latin American Immigrants to the United States." *Social Forces*, 59 (September 1980): 200-204.

671. ———. "Of Borders and States: A Skeptical Note on the Legislation Control of Immigration." Paper presented for the Fourth Annual Earl Warren Memorial Symposium. "America's New Immigration Law." University of California, San Diego, November 19-20, 1982.

With the present controversy over immigration reform in the United States, points out two gaps between the intention of policy makers and daily events in the rest of society: (1) the gap between present immigration law and its implementation; and (2) the gap separating current policy debates and the structure of economic and social forces deemed in need of "reform."

672. ———. "La immigracion y el systema internacional. Algunas caracteristicas de los Mexicanos recientemente emigrados a los Estados Unidos." *Revista Mexicana de Sociologia*, 41 (1980): 1257-1277.

Analyzes the internal significance of the undocumented immigration for the sending countries as a bonus to évaluate the political proposals of the Carter Administration.

673. ———. "The New Wave: A Statistical Profile of Recent Cuban Exiles to the United States." *Cuban Studies*, 7 (January 1977): 1-32.

674. ———. "The Rise of Ethnicity: Determinants of Ethnic Perceptions Among Cuban Exiles in Miami." *American Sociological Review*, 49 (June 1984): 383-397.

Traces the evolution of perceptions of social distance and discrimination by the host society among members of a recently arrived foreign minority. Determinants of these perceptions suggested by three alternative hypothesis in this area are reviewed and their effects compared empirically. Data come from a longitudinal
study of adult male Cuban exiles interviewed at the time
of arrival in the United States and again three and six
years later. Results suggest a significant rise in perceptions of social distance and discrimination from low
initial levels and a consistent association of such perceptions with variables suggested by the ethnic resilience
perspective.

675.   ————, et al. "Six Years Later: The Process of Incorporation of Cuban Exiles in the United States, 1973-
1979." *Cuban Studies*, 11-12 (July 1981-January 1982):
1-24.

676.   ————, and Robert L. Bach. "Immigrant Earnings: Cuban
and Mexican Immigrants in the United States." *International Migration Review*, 14 (1980): 315-340.

A sample of 822 Mexicans and 590 Cubans, interviewed
in 1973-74 and again three years later. Suggests that
the two share important characteristics. Education
and knowledge of English have less effect on their incomes than occupational prestige, occupational power, and
ethnicity of co-workers. Concludes that economic enclaves employing co-ethnics might not necessarily pay
better, but they blur the usual differences between
primary and secondary labor markets, making advancement
from the bottom easier.

677.   ————, and ————. *Latin Journey: Cuban and Mexican
Immigrants in the United States*. Berkeley, California:
University of California Press, 1985.

Presents data from longitudinal survey of legally
admitted Cuban and Mexican adult males. Waves of the
survey were conducted in 1973, 1976, and 1979. As important as the data are, however, this volume's significance also lies in its carefully crafted inferences
drawn from competing theoretical perspectives. Draws
on a variety of labor market, ethnic relations, and immigration theories to develop testable hypotheses.
Notes significant theoretical gaps. Immigrants, as
opposed to ethnic groups, are included in most theories
only through analogical reasoning: in dual market theories

immigrants are more like secondary workers. In middleman theories, they are less like native-born minorities. In split labor market theories, they are more like some groups and less like others. In assimilation theories, they are less like on their way to becoming more like the native-born. Exploits contradictions and conflicting predictions to generate their hypotheses.

678. ————, and Rafael Mozo. "The Political Adaptation Process of Cubans and Other Ethnic Minorities in the United States: A Preliminary Analysis." *International Migration Review*, 19 (Spring 1985): 35–63.

Examines the patterns of naturalization, voting registration, turnout, and political orientation of this minority and compares them with those of other groups. This exercise is significant for three reasons. First, the number of Cubans already living in the United States makes the analysis of their political integration important. Second, little research has been conducted on naturalization and voting patterns of recent immigrant groups; in particular no one has examined, to our knowledge, how political refugees and other immigrants compare in this respect. Third, a comparative analysis of different minorities focused on naturalization patterns and elected behavior may offer some practical guides for those interested in promoting their participation in the political process.

679. Poulson, Barry W., and T. Noel Osborn, eds. *U.S.-Mexico Economic Relations*. Boulder, Colorado: Westview Press, 1979.

The 1980s promise a change in U.S.-Mexican relations. Some three or four million Mexicans may be illegally working in the United States, while another 100,000 work for U.S. firms in *maquiladoras*--U.S. plants located just inside Mexico. Mexico sends 60 percent of its exports to the United States, and American investment in Mexico is $4 billion, about 2 percent of the $168 billion directly invested abroad in 1978. Mexico's energy discoveries came just when the United States wanted to reduce its dependence on unstable Middle Eastern supplies.

680. Powers, Thomas. "The Scandal of U.S. Immigration: The Haitian Example." *MS Magazine* (February 1976): 62–66, 81–83.

681. Press, Robert M. "Haitians in Florida." *Christian*

Science Monitor (November 26, 1984): 3, 5; (November 27, 1984): 3-4; (November 28, 1984): 3.

682. Prohías, Rafael J., and Lourdes Casal. *The Cuban Minority in the United States*. Boca Raton, Florida: Florida Atlantic University, 1973.

683. Ragas, W.R. "Housing the Refugee: Impact and Partial Solutions to the Housing Shortages." *Journal of Refugee Resettlement*, 1 (1980): 40-48.

First presents an overview of the market forces which have contributed to the current shortage of moderate-priced housing, then reviews the impact of the Indochinese refugee flows on the existing housing stock as well as household demographic characteristics which play a part in housing refugees. Offers a series of potential partial solutions.

684. *Recent Immigration to the United States: The Literature of the Social Sciences*. Washington, D.C.: Smithsonian Institution Press, 1976.

Recently published works on immigration since W.W. II found in the social science literature. Intended to provide insight into patterns of research and publication, distribution of topics, and existing lacunae in published works. Provides some sense of direction for social science publications with regard to public policy on immigration and its various facets. Organized around such central themes as theory, trends impact, politics, and process.

685. Refugee Women's Program Development and Coordination Project. *Economic Development for Refugee Women*. Washington, D.C.: Refugee Women's Program Development, 1982.

686. "Refugees: A Dose of Bootstrap." *Economist*, 283 (April 10, 1982): 41.

687. Reichert, Josh S. "The Migrant Syndrome: Seasonal U.S. Wage Labor and Rural Development in Central Mexico." *Human Organization*, 40 (1981): 56-66.

688. ————, and Douglas S. Massey. "History and Trends in U.S.-Bound Migration from a Mexican Town." *International Migration Review*, 14 (Winter 1980); 475-491.

Examines historical trends in U.S.-bound migration
from a rural Mexican town. The data consist of detailed
migration histories collected for all town residents in
1978. From these histories, successive migrant cohorts
were constructed for the period 1940-1978. Analysis of
these cohorts indicates that prior to 1965, migration
was limited primarily to males working in the United
States as *braceros*. Since 1965, migration has been
characterized by the increased participation of women
and children and by the growing predominance of legal
U.S. residents among migrants. Trends in the size and
composition of migrant cohorts over the thirty-eight year
period are related to shifting U.S. immigration policies.

689.   ———, and ———. "Patterns of Migration from a Rural
        Mexican Town to the United States: A Comparison of
        Legal and Illegal Migrants." *International Migration
        Review*, 13 (Winter 1979): 599-623.

690.   Reimers, David M. "Recent Immigration Policy: An Analy-
        sis." In Barry R. Chiswick, ed. *The Gateway: U.S.
        Immigration Issues and Policies*. Washington, D.C.:
        American Enterprise Institute, 1982. Pp. 13-53.

Reviews the post-World War II liberalization of the
restrictive immigration legislation of the 1920s. He
shows how struggles over the Displaced Persons Law of
1948, the Immigration and Nationality (McCarran-Walter)
Act of 1952, and the various special laws of the 1950s
and early 1960s led to the 1965 amendments that abolished
the national origins quota system and the severe restrictions on Asians and substituted a preference system.
The new law, while still selective, emphasized family
unification, with a smaller role for occupational requirements and refugee status. The Refugee Act of 1980, which
increased the number of visas for refugees and introduced
other changes to facilitate refugee resettlement, was
immediately shown to be inadequate by the "unscheduled"
influx of 120,000 Cuban refugees. Congress amended the
law several times, most recently in 1980, to provide for
a uniform worldwide system of 320,000 immigrants subject
annually to numerical limitation, in addition to visas
for immediate relatives of U.S. citizens, who are not
subject to numerical limitation (now about 125,000 per
year), and "conditional" admission of refugees over and
above this limit. The changes in the law in 1965 were
accompanied by a gradual increase in immigration and
shifting patterns of immigration. After World War II,
southern and eastern Europeans began to replace northern

and western Europeans, and both in turn gave way, after
1965, to immigration from the third world. Immigration
policy responded to economic forces and fears, foreign
policy (especially the cold war), and ethnic politics.
Arguments about race and ethnicity gave way to cold war
arguments and family concerns. The old-line restrictionist groups, like the veterans and patriotic organizations, took a back seat to the growing influence of
ethnic and religious agencies and the executive branch
in shaping immigration policy. Economic interest groups
were more vociferous in discussions about the *bracero*
program (1942-1964) and the illegal alien issue.

691.   ————. *Still the Golden Door: The Third World Comes
        to America.* New York: Columbia University Press, 1985.

        Focusing primarily on the period since 1965, compre-
        hensively chronicles the waves of Indochinese, Mariel
        Cubans, Mexicans, Haitians, Salvadorans, and other
        nationalities who have come, legally and illegally, to
        the United States. Also surveys and analyzes the monu-
        mental problems these immigrants pose for policymakers.
        While not ignoring the economic foundations, emphasizes
        the relationship between immigration and foreign policy.
        In doing so, highlights the anti-Communist bias in
        Washington, which he describes as "disgraceful and
        unfair...."

692.   ————. "An Unintended Reform: The 1965 Immigration
        Act and Third World Immigration to the United States."
        Journal of American History, 3 (1983): 9-28.

        Discusses various immigration legislation which led
        to the 1965 Immigration Act, the original intentions
        of the Act and how Third World Immigrants have benefited
        from the passage of the Act.

693.   Reining, P., and I. Tinker, eds. *Population: Dynamics
        Ethics and Policy.* Washington, D.C.: American Asso-
        ciation for the Advancement of Science, 1975.

        A compendium of selected materials, appearing in
        Science from 1966 to 1975. Includes "Immigration Com-
        position and Population Policy" by Charles B. Keely
        which demonstrates that "recent changes in immigration
        policy and composition have implications for proposals
        to alter immigration."

694.   "Response of Hispanic Organizations." *Agenda* (September-
        October 1977): 22.

695. Reubens, E.P. *Immigration Problems, Limited-Visa Programs, and Other Options.* College Park, Maryland: Center for Philosophy and Public Policy, University of Maryland, 1980.

A brief report which (1) summarizes the dimensions of immigration, both legal and illegal, into the United States in recent years from all countries and particularly from Mexico; (2) reviews the forces underlying and sustaining the emigration of Mexicans and their inflows into the United States; (3) indicates the major impacts--benefits and costs--of migration; (4) outlines the range of alternative approaches for dealing with the migration; (5) sketches U.S. experience with TFW programs, specifically the "H-2 visa" operation; (6) proposes a revised and enlarged treatment of H-2 visas as a new LVFW (limited visa foreign workers) program; and (7) assesses the advantages and disadvantages of this LVFW program in comparison with alternative lines of action, and in the context of alleged rights and duties on the individual, national, and international levels.

696. ————. "International Migration Models and Policies." *American Economic Review,* 73 (May 1983): 178-182.

697. ————. *Temporary Admission of Foreign Workers: Dimensions and Policies.* A Special Report of the National Commission for Manpower Policy, Special Report No. 34. Washington, D.C.: U.S. Government Printing Office, 1979.

Illuminates the policy issues regarding H-2s (temporary foreign workers mostly other than high-level professionals), providing a factual record of the H-2 program, a structural background or conceptual framework, a survey of the policy options that are available and the relevant criteria, and an evaluation of the most feasible options in terms of their comparative benefits and costs. Evaluates not only how well these options meet the "needs for workers" and the problems of "absorbing foreign workers" but also distinguishes short-term adjustments from long-term development.

698. "Revolving Door." *Newsweek* (July 23, 1973): 24.

699. Reyes, Manolo J. *Elderly Cubans in Exile.* Working Paper, Special Committee on Aging, U.S. Senate, 92nd Congress, 1st Session. Washington, D.C.: Government Printing Office, 1971.

700. Reynolds, C.W. "Labor Market Projections for the United
     States and Mexico and Their Relevance to Current Migra-
     tion Controversies." In *Mexican-U.S. Relations: Con-
     flict and Convergence*. Edited by C. Vásquez and M.
     Garcia y Griego. Los Angeles: University of California,
     Chicano Studies Research Center, 1983. Pp. 325-369.

     Reassures the relations between the United States and
     Mexico by demonstrating current and future economic
     interdependence, particularly in the exchange of labor.
     The supply of labor in the United States is projected
     on the basis of current demographic data, and the demand
     for labor necessary to meet planned or projected levels
     of output in selected years is then calculated. The re-
     sults of comparing the supply and demand for labor in
     the two countries are sensitive to the particular parame-
     ters used, considering the wide range of predictions
     concerning sustainable rates of growth of output and
     productivity in both countries.

701. Richardson, Bonham C. *Caribbean Migrants: Environment
     and Human Survival on St. Kitts and Nevis*. Knoxville,
     Tennessee: University of Tennessee Press, 1983.

     Faced with colonial heritage and progressive ecological
     devastation, resourceful Caribbean islanders migrate to
     cities such as New York and London for work, yet maintain
     cultural ties to their homes. Richardson's study il-
     luminates the context within which a growing American
     ethnic group exists.

702. Richmond, Anthony H., and G. Lakshmana Rao. "Recent
     Developments in Immigration to Canada and Australia."
     International Journal of Comparative Sociology, 17
     (1976): 183-205.

     Finds that Australia, like Canada, has recently de-
     emphasized ethnic considerations, giving more importance
     to economic needs.

703. Richmond, M.L. "Immigrant Adaptation and Family Struc-
     ture Among Cubans in Miami, Florida." Unpublished
     Ph.D. dissertation. Florida: Florida State University,
     1973.

704. Riding, Alan. "Silent Invasion: Why Mexico Is an Ameri-
     can Problem." *Saturday Review* (July 8, 1978): 14-17.

705. Rios-Bustamente, A. *Mexican Immigrant Workers in the
     United States*. Los Angeles, California: University of
     California, Chicano Studies Program, 1980.

706. Robledo, Amado. "The Impact of Alien Immigration on
Public Policy and Educational Services on Selected
Districts in the Texas Education System." Unpublished
Ed.D. dissertation, University of Houston, 1977.

707. Rocheleau, Dianne E. "Geographic and Socioeconomic
Aspects of the Recent Cuban and Haitian Migrations
to South Florida." Gainesville, Florida: Center for
Latin American Studies, University of Florida, 1982.

708. Rochin, R.I., and O. Montufar. "Mexico's Agriculture
Along the U.S. Border: Problems and Prospects."
Paper presented at Western Social Science Association.
26th Annual Meeting, San Diego, California, April 28,
1984.

Contends that Mexico cannot generate jobs in its
border agriculture to stem the flow of workers looking
for jobs in the United States. The paper looks at
past performance, current policy, and prospects for
Mexico's agriculture and concludes that Mexico has not
dealt with crucial problems like providing adequate
water via irrigation, providing farm production incentives and dealing with its international cash flow.

709. Rockett, Ian R.H. "Immigration Legislation and the
Flow of Specialized Human Capital from South America
to the United States." *International Migration Review*,
10 (1976): 47-61.

Notes that the overall effect of the law has been
to curb arrivals from the South because of the limits
imposed on total numbers. Statistics may be misleading
because wives who enter the United States with qualified
husbands are not required to give their occupations.
Re-immigration to Latin America is high enough to offset
part of the loss.

710. Rodino, Peter W., Jr. "The Impact of Immigration on
the American Labor Market." *Rutgers Law Review*, 27
(Winter 1974): 245-74.

711. ———. "New Immigration Law in Retrospect." *International Migration Review*, 2 (Summer 1968): 56-61.

"Although immigration reform bills were introduced in
each succeeding Congress, those of us in the Congress
pledged to the repeal of the system were in the minority.
However, a period of change began on July 23, 1963,
when the late President John F. Kennedy submitted a

special message to the Congress calling for new immigration legislation. In his message President Kennedy said '... although the legislation I am transmitting deals with many problems which require remedial action, it concentrates attention primarily upon revision of our quota immigration system. The enactment of this legislation will not resolve all our important problems in the field of immigration. It will, however, provide a sound basis upon which we can build in developing an immigration law that serves the national interest and reflects in every detail the principles of equality and human dignity to which our Nation subscribed.' Notwithstanding the fact that 55 members of Congress co-sponsored this legislation, consideration of these new concepts proceeded very slowly. Substitute proposals were introduced, temporary proposals offered, spurious issues advanced-- all designed to frustrate an actual vote on the bill. Nevertheless, reform legislation was finally enacted into law. Although the Act of October 3, 1965 (P.L. 89-236), repealed the national origins system, the repeal did not become fully effective immediately because a transition or phaseout period through June 30, 1968, was contained therein. This phaseout period, unfortunately, is the cause of many of the problems that are so obvious in immigration today."

712.   Rogg, Eleanor Meyer. *The Assimilation of Cuban Exiles: The Role of Community and Class.* New York: Aberdeen Press, 1974.

"The Puerto Rican migration was basically a movement of poorer people from the island, a fact that gave rise to this question: To what extent were the problems that Puerto Ricans faced in adjusting to life on the mainland the result of their Spanish background and to what extent the result of their social class background? With the influx of thousands of middle- and upper-class Cubans to Miami and the resettlement of many of them in the New York-New Jersey area, the opportunity of exploring some answers to this question emerged. Did Cubans have similar difficulties adjusting to life in the United States?"

713.   ————. "The Influence of a Strong Refugee Community on the Economic Adjustment of Its Members." *International Migration Review*, 1 (1967): 46-57.

714.   ————. "The Influence of a Strong Refugee Community on the Economic Adjustment of Its Members." *Inter-*

national Migration Review, 5 (Winter 1971): 474-481.

Explores the economic adjustment of Cuban refugees living in West New York, New Jersey, as well as some of the factors which have helped their adjustment. Over 400,000 Cuban refugees are now living in the United States. Miami-Dade County, Florida, the point of first arrival for most Cubans, remains the area with the single largest concentration of Cubans in the United States. Nevertheless, as a result of the resettlement program set up by the U.S. government in 1965 to relieve the burdens of the concentration of so many Cubans in Miami, over half of all Cubans in the United States now live outside the greater Miami area. New York and New Jersey have accepted a large proportion of all resettled refugees. One of the densest concentrations of Cubans outside of Miami is estimated to be in West New York, New Jersey.

715. ———, and Rosemary Santana Cooney. *Adaptation and Adjustment of Cubans: West New York, New Jersey*. New York: Hispanic Research Center, Fordham University, 1980.

"This study was conducted for two reasons. First, it builds upon an earlier work carried out in the same community 11 years ago by Eleanor Rogg.... The replication of studies focusing upon the same community is a rare event in the social and behavioral sciences. When we are informed by the results of a community study conducted only at one point in time, there is a tendency to view that community as a frozen entity, historically static, and unchanging. The present study demonstrates that West New York Cubans defy such a model. Replication studies, however, are of value not only in bringing history up to date, but also because they enable the identification of patterns of continuities and discontinuities in community life. This monograph, therefore, provides an opportunity to identify structural changes in the character and life of an active, dynamic community. The second reason for conducting the study was the pressing need to understand the patterns of occupational mobility among Cuban migrants and how such patterns interrelate to a broader configuration of assimilation and adaptation variables. The effects of the occupational achievements of Cubans in the United States extend beyond their working hours and include access to quality health care, quality housing, and quality education for their children and exert an influence even on the acquisition of U.S. citizenship."

716. Roma, Thomas E., Jr. "Not My Father's Son: Obtaining
      Preferred Immigration Status Through Paternal Affilia-
      tion." *Journal of Family Law*, 20 (January 1982):
      323-335.

717. Romero, F.E. *Chicano Workers: Their Utilization and
      Development.* Monograph No. 8. Los Angeles: Univer-
      sity of California, Chicano Studies Center Publications,
      1979.

      Shows through comparative analysis of 1960 and 1970
      U.S. Census of Population data and information produced
      by other studies that Chicano human resources have neither
      been adequately prepared for nor properly utilized in
      the labor markets of the Southwest.

718. Rose, Peter I. "Asian Americans: From Pariahs to Para-
      gons." In Nathan Glazer, ed. *Clamor at the Gates:
      The New American Immigration.* San Francisco, Califor-
      nia: Institute for Contemporary Studies, 1985. Pp.
      181-212.

719. ————. "The Harbor Masters: American Politics and
      Refugee Policy." In *Social Problems and Public Policy.*
      Greenwich, Connecticut: JAI Press, 1984. Pp. 21-46.

720. ————. "Links in a Chain: Observations of the American
      Refugee Program in Southeast Asia." *Migration Today*,
      9 (1981): 6-24.

721. ————. "Some Reflections on Refugee Policy." *Dissent*
      (Fall 1984): 484-486.

722. Rosenthal, Kristine. "In the Shadow of Miami: Haitian
      Sojourn." *Working Papers Magazine*, 9 (September-
      October 1982): 18-26.

723. Rosenthal-Urey, Ina. "Church Records as a Source of
      Data on Mexican Migrant Networks: A Methodological
      Note." *International Migration Review*, 18 (Fall 1984):
      767-781.

      Discusses the methodological issues in the study of
      Mexican migration initiated by Cornelius and others.
      It addresses two problems: the need to locate strategic
      regions in Mexico before field work is begun and the
      need to develop techniques for longitudinal studies of
      migration networks.

724. Rothenberg, I.F. "Mexican-American Views of U.S. Rela-
      tions with Latin America." *The Journal of Ethnic
      Studies*, 6 (Spring 1978): 62-78.

      Presents an analysis of the attitudes, imagery, symbols,
      and arguments found in scholarly Chicano writings on the
      incipient development of the Spanish ethnic foreign
      policy lobby in the United States. Maintains that even
      a brief review of Mexican-American political history
      and thought reveals a clear ideological thrust in the
      direction of greater political identification with Latin
      America.

725. Roucek, Joseph S. "Los prolemas de los Immigrantes
      Mejicanos en los Estados Unidos." *Revista de Politica
      Social* (Madrid), 103 (July-September 1974): 85-99.

      The problems of "illegal" Mexican immigrants in the
      United States, particularly in California, Texas, and
      the cities of New York, Chicago, and Washington.

726. Ruggles, Patricia. *Immigration Status and Program
      Eligibility Issues*. Washington, D.C.: The Urban In-
      stitute, 1985.

727. ———, et al. *Profile of the Central American Popula-
      tion in the United States*. Washington, D.C.: The Urban
      Institute, 1985.

728. ———, et al. *Refugees and Displaced Persons of the
      Central American Region*. Washington, D.C.: The Urban
      Institute, 1985.

729. [Runneymede Trust]. Rynearson, Ann M., and Pamela A.
      DeVoe. "Refugee Women in a Vertical Village: Lowland
      Laotians in St. Louis." *Social Thought*, 10 (1984):
      33-48.

730. Russell, Stephanie. "Fear, Poverty Plague Haitians in
      . Florida." *National Catholic Reporter*, 17 (January 30,
      1981): 1, 16.

731. Ryan, Michael C.P. "Political Asylum for the Haitians?"
      Case Western Researve Journal of International Law,
      14 (1982): 155-176.

732. Safa, Helen I. "Caribbean Migration to the United
      States: Cultural Identity and the Process of Assimila-
      tion." In *Different People: Studies in Ethnicity and*

Education. Edited by E.B. Gumbert. Atlanta, Georgia:
Georgia State University, 1983. Pp. 47-73.

An attempt to explain why many Caribbean migrants
have clung to their cultural identity and why assimilation is not seen as a feasible goal. First section is
a discussion of the factors that hinder the assimilation
of Caribbean migrants to the United States and that have
set them apart from previous migrations, particularly
from Europe. Second part attempts to assess the prospects for assimilation of Caribbean migrants and alternatives to such a strategy. Third section examines the
formation of cultural identity among Caribbean migrants
in the United States through an analysis of the Cuban
case.

733.   ————. "The Differential Incorporation of Hispanic
Women Migrants into the U.S. Labor Force." In Delores
Mortimer and Roy Bryce-Laporte, eds. *Female Immigrants
to the United States: Caribbean, Latin American and
African Experiences.* Washington, D.C.: Research Insti-
tute on Immigration and Ethnic Studies, Smithsonian
Institution, 1981. Pp. 201-246.

734.   Salter, Paul S., and Robert C. Mings. "The Projected
Impact of Cuban Settlement on Voting Patterns in Metro-
politan Miami, Florida." *Professional Geographer,* 24
(May 1972): 123-131.

735.   Samora, Julian. "Mexican Immigration." *Mexican-Americans
Tomorrow: Educational and Economic Perspectives.* Edited
by Gus Tyler. Albuquerque: University of New Mexico
Press, 1975. Pp. 56-74.

736.   San Juan Cafferty, Patricia, et al. *The Dilemma of
American Immigration. Beyond the Golden Door.* New
Brunswick, New Jersey: Transaction Books, 1983.

Organized into three sections—history, analysis of
contemporary immigration policies, and new proposals—
the strength of this book lies in its analysis of the
history and economic impacts of immigrants. Concluding
that immigrants are good for the United States, argues
that they can be made even more valuable by selecting
to immigrate those who are most likely to be economically
productive and least likely to require income transfers.
They propose to choose by a point system managed by a
new Immigration Commission, an idea which found favor
from the research staff of the Select Commission but

which engendered only slight support among commissioners, most of whom did not want to create a new agency and who found a point system both offensive and impractical.

737. Sassen-Koob, Saskia. "Formal and Informal Associations: Dominicans and Colombians in New York." *International Migration Review*, 13 (1979): 314–332.

On the differences between two parts of what many New Yorkers perceive as the Hispanic community. Dominicans are predominantly rural, while the Colombians are urban. Rural Colombians prefer to go to Venezuela, Ecuador, and Panama. In New York both form voluntary associations but of different kinds. The Dominicans have more clubs (36 compared to 16 for the Colombians) and feature recreation as a larger part of their program. The Colombian associations come from the elite and tend to use their groups to gain political objectives for the community.

738. ————. "Immigrant and Minority Workers in the Organization of the Labor Process." *The Journal of Ethnic Studies*, 8 (Spring 1980): 1–34.

Examines the issues of (1) the effect of the recent acceleration of legal and undocumented Caribbean and South American immigration into the large Northeastern cities, leading to a significant shift in the labor market; (2) the shared characteristics between immigrant and minority workers, most significantly their disproportionate concentration in lower level occupations; and (3) the competition for jobs between immigrant and minority workers. These are discussed in the general context of the reproduction of the low-wage labor supply and the specific forms low-wage labor takes in the organization of the labor process at the work place, focusing on the organization of the labor process rather than on the immigrant and minority populations.

739. Scanlan, John A. "Asylum Adjudication: Some Due Process Implications of Proposed Legislation." *University of Pittsburgh Law Review*, 44 (Winter 1983): 261–285.

740. ————, and Gilburt Loescher. "U.S. Foreign Policy, 1959–80: Impact of Refugee Flow from Cuba." *Annals of the American Academy of Political and Social Science*, 467 (May 1983): 116–137.

741. Schaefer, R.T. "The Indochinese Refugees: Five Years Later." *New Community*, 7 (Winter 1979): 448–456.

Examines the past five years of the Indochinese refugee movement, focusing on resettlement, occupational
patterns, and assimilation.

742. Schiller, Nina Glick. "Ethnic Groups Are Made, Not
Born: The Haitian Immigrant and American Politics."
In George L. Hicks and Philip E. Leis, eds. *Ethnic
Encounters: Identities and Contexts*. North Scituate,
Massachusetts: Duxbury Press, 1977. Pp. 23-35.

743. Schuck, Peter H. "Immigration Law and the Problem of
Community." In Nathan Glazer, ed. *Clamor at the
Gates: The New American Immigration*. San Francisco,
California: Institute for Contemporary Studies, 1985.
Pp. 285-307.

The American tradition, deeply rooted in a commitment
to individual rights and equal opportunity, properly
regards any fixed or exclusive definition of community
with profound suspicion. A nation of immigrants cannot
easily justify a restrictive immigration policy. Criteria of inclusion and exclusion based upon geographical
accidents of birth, contingent events that arbitrarily
and inexorably label some individuals as insiders and
others as outsiders, run against our grain. To restrict
an individual's access to economic opportunity, physical
security, and freedom on such grounds is difficult to
justify, especially in a world in which the initial
distribution of those goods is so unequal. Instead,
a thoroughgoing individualism would invite persons to
come and go, form attachments, and live according to
their own aspirations, respecting the equal right of
others to do likewise.

744. ———. "The Transformation of Immigration Law."
Columbia Law Review, 84 (January 1984): 1-90.

745. Schultz, N., and A. Sontz. *Voyagers in the Land: A
Report on Unaccompanied Southeast Asian Refugee
Children*. Washington, D.C.: Migration and Refugee
Services, 1983.

Reviews the current situation of a sample of the
1,445 Southeast Asian refugee minors who were in 28
local programs that are affiliates of the United States
Catholic Conference. These 1,445 children formed one
half of the nation's total Southeast Asian unaccompanied
minor population. Discusses the programs and investigates
the character of the organizational framework they have
provided for the children's adaptation to their new homes.

746. Schwartz, L. "Congress to Face Stalled Immigration Bill." *Electronic News*, 30, Supp. C (November 12, 1984).

747. Selby, H.A., and A.D. Murphy. *The Mexican Urban Household and the Decision to Migrate to the United States.* Philadelphia: Institute for the Study of Human Issues, 1982.

   Mexican migration to the United States. The decision to migrate is taken by single individuals in order to gain economic advantage for themselves.

748. Seligman, Linda. "Haitians: A Neglected Minority." *Personnel and Guidance Journal*, 55 (March 1977): 409-411.

749. Seller, Maxine S. "Historical Perspectives on American Immigration Policy: Case Studies and Current Implications." *Law and Contemporary Problems*, 45 (Spring 1982): 137-162.

750. *Seven Years Later: The Experiences of the 1970 Cohort of Immigrants in the United States.* Washington, D.C.: U.S. Department of Labor, Employment and Training Administration, 1979.

751. Shadow, Robert D. "Differential Out-Migration: A Comparison of Internal and International Migration from Villa Guerrero, Jalisco (Mexico)." In *Migration Across Frontiers: Mexico and the United States.* Edited by Fernando Cámara and Robert Van Kemper. Albany, N.Y.: Institute for Mesoamerican Studies, State University of New York, Albany, 1979. Pp. 67-84.

752. Shaffer, Helen B. "Cuban Refugees." *Editorial Research Reports*, 1 (April 1, 1962): 259-276.

753. Shinoff, Paul. "Sweated Home Industry: Delancy Street in Los Angeles." *The Nation* (March 1, 1975): 240-43.

754. Simon, Julian L. "The Overall Effects of Immigrants on Natives' Incomes." In Barry R. Chiswick, ed. *The Gateway: U.S. Immigration Issues and Policies.* Washington, D.C.: American Enterprise Institute, 1982. Pp. 314-338.

   Presents estimates of the composite impact in each year following the immigrants' entry and then a present-value estimate of the entire stream of positive and negative effects in various years. The paper discusses the three most important elements. The first is the capital-dilution effect, where a new approach is sketched to estimate the proportion of the returns to capital captured by immigrants who arrive without capital. The second is the social security transfer effect, that is, the current benefits to the native population of the immigrants' social security tax contributions. Third, it considers the impact on productivity of economies of scale, the sum of learning by doing, the creation of new knowledge, and other aspects of economies of scale. Suggests that the life-cycle saving-and-transfer process has a positive effect on the income of natives and is of the same order of magnitude as his estimates of the capital-dilution effect. Assessing the effect of immigrants on productivity, together with other effects, requires a dynamic macromodel; a simple one is simulated in the paper. The results indicate that within a few years the productivity effect comes to dominate and thereafter dwarfs the capital-dilution and saving-and-transfer effects. Estimates that immigrants yield a high return on investment to the native population.

755.   ———. "What Immigrants Take from, and Give to, the Public Coffers." Paper submitted to the Select Commission on Immigration and Refugee Policy. August 15, 1980.

Aim is to estimate the amount of public service that immigrants use, including social security, unemployment, public assistance, food stamps, and education. A secondary aim of the study is to estimate the incomes of immigrant families and, from these revenues, to roughly calculate the taxes paid by immigrants.

756.   Simon, Rita J. "Refugee Families' Adjustment and Aspirations: A Comparison of Soviet Jewish and Vietnamese Immigrants." *Ethnic and Racial Studies*, 6 (Winter 1984): 492-504.

Describes the intra-family adjustments within the Soviet Jewish and Vietnamese refugee communities, with special emphasis on the relationships between parents and adolescent children.

757.   ———, and Caroline B. Brettell, eds. *International Migration: The Female Experience.* Totowa, N.J.: Rowman & Allanheld, 1986.

A collection of essays that explores the experiences of immigrant women during the post-World War II period. Its scope is international, and its overall aim is to delineate and analyze the social, economic, political, and cultural characteristics that influence female migrants both as immigrants and as women, and which therefore may differentiate their experiences from those of male migrants. The essays cover several of the important and most recent migration streams in each of the major Western receiving societies. Not only do they illustrate similarities and differences in the kinds of questions that are being asked in studies of immigrant women, but they also demonstrate a variety of research methods, ranging from statistical analyses of quantitative data to in-depth qualitative research based on case studies and/or interviews.

758. Simpson, Alan K. "Immigration Reform and Control (S529, Immigration Reform and Control Act of 1983)." *Labor Law Journal*, 34 (April 1983): 195-200.

759. ————. "The Politics of Immigration Reform." *International Migration Review*, 18 (Fall 1984): 486-504.

The United States is the target for international migration, more now than ever. Population growth and economic stagnation in the Third World are increasing the pressures for outmigration, and current immigration law is wholly incapable of responding to the ever-increasing flow of illegal immigrants. Border apprehensions of illegal aliens in the United States were up 40 percent during 1983, and total apprehensions reached 1.25 million by the year's end. Recent public opinion polls have disclosed that an overwhelming majority of the American public demands immigration reform, and yet we as a nation have been distinctly unwilling or unable to respond to this clear public sentiment. This article discusses the politics of the issue: the current "Simpson-Mazzoli" Immigration Reform and Control Act, previous immigration legislation, current counterproposals for U.S. immigration policy, and the political realities of immigration reform.

760. Skerry, Peter. "The Ambiguity of Mexican-American Politics," In Nathan Glazer, ed. *Clamor at the Gates: The New American Immigration*. San Francisco, California: Institute for Contemporary Studies, 1985. Pp. 241-257.

"For while there may be certain sociological similarities between Mexicans and the classic American ethnic
groups, there are important differences. I have already
mentioned the unique situation of the Mexican in the
American Southwest. It is also significant that Mexican
Americans today are dealing with a political and social
system vastly different from that confronting European
immigrants several generations ago. Mexican American
politicians today, for example, lack the patronage resources that earlier ethnic politicians used to lure
their countrymen into the political arena. Then, too,
Mexican Americans are raising questions about ethnic
politics and cultural pluralism at a time when the old
rules and understandings are challenged and changing."

761. Smith, Barton, and Robert Newman. "Depressed Wages Along
     the U.S.-Mexico Border: An Empirical Analysis."
     Economic Inquiry, 15 (January 1977): 51-66.

762. Smith, M. Estellie. "The Spanish-Speaking Population of
     Florida." In June Helm, ed. *Spanish-Speaking People
     in the United States*. Seattle, Washington: University
     of Washington Press, 1968. Pp. 120-133.

763. Smith, Peter C. "The Social Demography of Filipino
     Migrations Abroad." *International Migration Review*,
     10 (Fall 1976): 307-353.

"Migratory movements have always been present as an
underlying element of continuity in Philippine history.
From the earliest colonizations (Yengoyan, 1967), to the
major frontier movements of the twentieth century, long-
distance migration--often permanent, frequently disrup-
tive socially, but generally positive in its motivation--
has been the recurrent theme. One such pattern of frontier movements is the focus of this essay: the migration
of Filipinos across the borders of their nation to places
beyond. The purpose of this article is to place the
facts of Filipino migration to the United States, the
most important foreign destination, in demographic perspective. This is accomplished by setting forth the
statistical evidence in two general areas: (1) the
basic demography of Filipinos in the Philippines (emphasizing, of course, marked patterns of internal migration and redistribution); (2) the changing social and
demographic structure of the Filipino population in the
United States."

764. Smith, Richard. "The Exiles: A Mass Migration." In James N. Goodsell, ed. *Fidel Castro's Personal Revolution, 1957-1973.* New York: A. Knopf, 1975. Pp. 131-146.

765. Smyth, Maureen A. "Immigration and Nationality Law." *1980 Annual Survey of American Law* (March 1981): 237-263.

766. "Southeast Asian Refugees in the U.S.A.: Case Studies of Adjustment and Policy Implications." *Anthropological Quarterly*, 55 (July 1982): 119-188.

Special issue contains the following articles: "Refugee Resettlement and Public Policy: A Role for Anthropology," by D.R. Howell (Guest Editor); "Segmentary Kinship in an Urban Society: The Hmong of St. Paul-Minneapolis," by T. Dunnigan; "Indochinese Adaptation and Local Government Policy: An Example from Monterey," by M.K. Orbach and J. Beckwith; "The Hmong Refugee Community in San Diego: Theoretical and Practical Implications of Its Continuing Ethnic Solidarity," by G.M. Scott, Jr.; "Community Influences on the Occupational Adaptation of Vietnamese Refugees," by C.R. Finnan; and "Southeast Asian Refugees in the United States: The Interaction of Kinship and Public Policy," by D.W. Haines.

767. Squires, S.E. "Cultural Change: Asian Immigrants and Social Services in New England." Paper presented at American Anthropological Association. 83rd Annual Meeting. Denver, Colorado, November 14-18, 1984.

Investigates the interaction between recent Asian immigrants and the social service agencies providing support programs to them. Providers of services have assumed that problems of participation are based on unfamiliarity with their programs. A more fundamental cause is that the immigrants and the agencies have very different cultural expectations about appropriate mechanisms for providing social support. Effective delivery of care has required modification of the providers' model of individualized therapy to include social and cultural factors.

768. Starr, Paul D. "Troubled Waters: Vietnamese Fisherfolk on America's Gulf Coast." *International Migration Review*, 15 (Spring/Summer 1981): 226-238.

Reports on a continuing effort, initiated in late

1977, to understand the experience of Vietnamese fisherfolk who settled in communities on the Gulf Coast,
primarily in West Florida, in particular with regard to
their relationship to established local fishing interests.

769. Stein, Barry N. "Occupational Adjustment of Refugees:
     The Vietnamese in the United States." *International
     Migration Review*, 14 (1979): 25-45.

770. ———. "Refugee Research Bibliography." *International
     Migration Review*, 15 (Spring/Summer 1981): 331-393.

     "Refugee research extends across many disciplinary
     lines. The lack of an easy disciplinary fit combined
     with the common view that refugee problems are unique,
     atypical, and nonrecurring has produced both a scholarly
     neglect of refugee research possibilities and special
     research difficulties when one does undertake a project.
     Just a glance at [this] bibliography will indicate a
     great diversity of scholarly journals, governmental docu-
     ments and other resources."

771. Stencil, Sandra. "The New Immigration." *Editorial
     Research Reports* (December 13, 1974): 927-44.

772. Stepick, Alex. "Haitian Boat People: A Study in the
     Conflicting Forces Shaping U.S. Immigration Policy."
     Law and Contemporary Problems, 45 (Spring 1982):
     163-196.

773. ———. *The Haitian Informal Sector in Miami*. Miami:
     Department of Anthropology and Sociology, Florida
     International University, June 1984.

774. ———. "Haitians in Miami: An Assessment of Their
     Background and Potential." *Occasional Papers Series*,
     Dialogue No. 12. Miami: Latin American and Caribbean
     Center, Florida International University, December
     1982.

775. ———. *Haitian Refugees in the U.S.* London: Report
     No. 52, Minority Rights Group, Ltd., 1982.

776. ———. "Haitians Released from Krome: Their Prospects
     for Adaptation and Integration in South Florida."
     Occasional Papers Series, Dialogue No. 24. Miami:
     Latin American and Caribbean Center, Florida Inter-
     national University, March 1984.

777. ————. "The New Haitian Exodus: The Flight from Terror and Poverty." *Caribbean Review*, 11 (Winter 1982): 14-17, 55-57.

778. ————. "New Perspectives on Immigrant Adaptation." *Journal of Children in Contemporary Society*, 15 (1983): 15-26.

779. ————. "Root Causes of Haitian Migration." In *Immigration Reform*, Serial No. 30, Part 1, Hearings before the Subcommittee on Immigration, Refugees, and International Law of the Committee on the Judiciary, House of Representatives, 97th Congress. Washington, D.C.: Government Printing Office, 1981. Pp. 698-753.

780. ————. "Structural Determinants of the Haitian Refugee Movement: Different Interpretations." *Occasional Papers Series*, Dialogue No. 4. Miami: Latin American and Caribbean Center, Florida International University, August 1981.

781. ————. "U.S. Refugee and Immigration Policy and Its Effect on South Florida." *Occasional Papers Series*, Dialogue No. 6. Miami: Latin American and Caribbean Center, Florida International University, August 1982. Pp. 7-11.

782. Stevenson, James. "Cuban Americans: New Urban Class." Unpublished Ph.D. dissertation, Wayne State University, 1973.

783. Stoddard, E.R., et al. *Borderlands Sourcebook. A Guide to the Literature on Northern Mexico and the American Southwest*. Norman, Oklahoma: The University of Oklahoma Press, 1983.

Fifty scholars review the outstanding issues in contemporary border life and evaluate the pertinent information sources for each topic. Part One delineates the Borderlands, discusses borders and frontiers and compares the Mexican and Canadian borders. Part Two includes sections on history, archaeology, geology, the environment, economics, politics, law, demography, society, and culture. Part Three discusses Borderlands resources materials.

784. Strand, Paul J. "Employment Predictors Among Indochinese Refugees." *International Migration Review*, 18 (Spring 1984): 50-64.

The influx of Indochinese refugees into the United
States since 1975 has forced policy development in
various resettlement areas. Considerable emphasis has
been placed on employment and employment barriers.
Investigates the refugee employment process. A multivariate model is used to distinguish employed from
unemployed refugees. Early arrivals, recent arrivals,
and each of the four major ethnic groups is investigated separately.

785.   ———, and Woodrow Jones, Jr. *Indochinese Refugees in
        America: Problems of Adaptation and Assimilation.*
        Durham, North Carolina: Duke University Press, 1985.

786.   Strickland, B.K. *Analisis de la ley y de los procedi-
        mentos de immigracion en los Estados Unidos de
        America. Ensayos I.* Mexico City: Centro Nacional
        de Información y Estadisticas de Trabajo, 1978.

787.   Stuart, James, and Michael Kearney. "Causes and Effects
        of Agricultural Labor Migration from the Mixteca of
        Oaxaca to California." *Working Papers in U.S.-Mexican
        Studies,* No. 28, La Jolla, California Center for U.S.-
        Mexican Studies, University of California, San Diego,
        1981.

        Ethnographic study of Mixteca-speaking citrus workers
        from the village of San Jerónimo, state of Oaxaca,
        Mexico, to Riverside County, California. Part of a
        larger study.

788.   Sullivan, Teresa A. "The Occupational Prestige of
        Women Immigrants: A Comparison of Cubans and Mexicans."
        International Migration Review, 18 (Winter 1984):
        1045-1062.

        Analyzes the occupational prestige of women workers
        born in Cuba or Mexico who were at least 25 years of
        age at the time of their immigration to the United States.
        Dependent variable is NORC prestige scores; independent
        variables are age, U.S. experience, South residence,
        weeks worked, and schooling. Predicted prestige scores,
        controlled for social class, narrow the prestige score
        gap between Cuban and Mexican women but increase the
        gap between immigrant men and women. Data suggest that
        the social mobility process for female immigrants differs
        from the process for males, perhaps because cultural
        barriers to "pink collar" jobs of nominally higher status
        restrict women's mobility.

789. ———, and Silvia Pedraza-Bailey. *Differential Success Among Cuban-American and Mexican-American Immigrants: The Role of Policy and Community.* Springfield, Illinois: Report submitted to the Employment and Training Administration, U.S. Department of Labor, 1979.

790. Summers, Anthony. "'A Hope and a Doom': Profile of an Invasion." *Miami Magazine*, 33 (April 1982): 70-75, 139-144.

791. Sung, Betty Lee. "Changing Chinese." *Society*, 14 (1977): 44-49.

Traces Chinese immigration to the United States since 1840 and outlines the ways in which the immigrants of the 1970s differ from their predecessors. They include more women, are increasingly attracted to the East coast, and their occupational profile has shifted.

792. "Supply and Demand in California (Immigrants)." *American Demographic*, 5 (July 1983): 10.

793. Surki, A. *Indochinese Refugees: The Impact on First Asylum Countries and Implications for American Policy.* A Study Prepared for the Use of the Joint Economic Committee of the Congress of the United States. November 25, 1980. [Washington, D.C., 1980]

Examines American policy towards Indochinese refugees and possible changes in current programs. Concludes that "there are no easy alternatives to current American programs. A reduction in the American intake by itself would increase the burden on other countries—notably the first asylum states in Southeast Asia—probably jeopardize the welfare of existing refugees, and conflict with the notion that America has a commitment to aid people wishing to leave communist countries. Other alternatives to limit the flow of refugees involve a radical change in U.S. policy toward Indochina."

794. Szapocznik, José, ed. *Cuban Americans: Acculturation, Adjustment and the Family.* Washington, D.C.: National Coalition of Hispanic Mental Health, 1978.

795. Szulc, Ted. "The Refugee Explosion." *New York Times Magazine* (November 23, 1980): 136-141.

796. Taft, Julia Vadala, et al. *Refugee Resettlement in the*

U.S.: Time for a New Focus. Washington, D.C.: New TransCentury Foundation, 1979.

797. Tanton, John. *Rethinking Immigration Policy.* Washington, D.C.: Federation for American Immigration Reform, 1979.

798. Taravella, Louis, and Graziano Tassello. *Les femmes migrantes: Bibliographie internationale (1965-1982).* Rome: Centro Studi Emigrazione, 1983.

A largely annotated bibliography on migrant women (worldwide) intended to point up the state of extant research on the phenomenon. Annotations are in French, with primary attention to Europe. Includes 488 entries: "Nous avons analysé surtout des ouvrages, des essais et des articles edités en France, Italie, et dans les pays de langue anglaise."

799. Tarver, J.D., and R.D. McLeod. "Trends in the Distance of Movement of Interstate Migrants." *Rural Sociology,* 41 (Spring 1976): 119-126.

800. Teitelbaum, Michael S. "Forced Migration: The Tragedy of Mass Expulsions." In Nathan Glazer, ed. *Clamor at the Gates: The New American Immigration.* San Francisco, California: Institute for Contemporary Studies, 1985. Pp. 261-283.

"The mass expulsion of hundreds of thousands of people can no longer be viewed as the aberrational behavior of mad political leaders. To the contrary, such actions have become quite deliberate instruments of both domestic and foreign policy for various sovereign nations. In the past decade alone, literally millions have been coerced--often by their own governments--to flee their homes, sometimes onto the high seas in unseaworthy boats. Obvious examples include those of Vietnam, Uganda, and Cuba, discussed in greater detail below but other expulsions have also occurred or loom as future possibilities.... Whatever approach is taken, it seems clear enough from the experiences of the past decade that mass expulsions of citizens pose serious threats to peaceful relations among the states involved and to the human rights of the victims. The prospects for future state actions of this type are disturbingly real and, as such, the matter deserves attention at the highest levels of governments and international institutions."

801. ———. "Political Asylum in Theory and Practice." *The Public Interest*, 76 (Summer 1984), 74–86.

802. Thomas, John F. "Cuban Refugee Program." *Welfare in Review*, 1 (September 1963): 1–20.

803. ———. "Cuban Refugees in the United States." *International Migration Review*, 1 (Spring 1967): 46–57.

"On October 3, 1965, President Lyndon Johnson stated that 'those who seek refuge here in America will find it.' President Johnson was replying to an earlier statement by Fidel Castro asserting that any person who wished to leave Cuba was free to do so. The Department of State was directed by the President to seek an agreement with the government of Cuba concerning the establishment of procedures for moving refugees from Cuba to the United States.... President Johnson had stressed the fact that priority should be given to the movement of immediate relatives of Cubans already in the United States. In the 'Memorandum of Understanding' worked out between the Swiss Embassy in Havana, which represents the interests of the United States in Cuba, and the Cuban Foreign Ministry it was stipulated that priorities would be defined as follows: parents of unmarried children under the age of 21, and brothers and sisters under the age of 21. It was further agreed that the first priority would include other close relatives living in Cuba of persons now in the United States who reside in the same household as the immediate relatives, when such inclusion is required for humanitarian considerations. These cases of close relationship were designated as Priority A cases for processing purposes. Cases of more distant family relationship became known as Priority B cases."

804. ———. "Urbanization of Refugees." In *Hearings Before the National Commission on Urban Problems*. Washington, D.C.: Government Printing Office, 1967. Vol. III, pp. 332–346.

805. ———. "U.S.A. as a Country of First Asylum." *International Migration*, 3 (1965): 5–16.

806. Thompson, S.I. "Assimilation and Nonassimilation of Asian Americans and Asian Peruvians." *Comparative Studies in Society and History*, 21 (October 1979): 572–588.

Examines the primacy of internally generated attitudinal differences among Asian Americans and Asian Peruvians and the existence of situational factors which affect the attitudes of these two immigrant groups differently in the United States and in Peru.

807. Tienda, Marta. "Familism and Structural Assimilation of Mexican Immigration in the United States." *International Migration Review*, 14 (Fall 1980): 383-408.

808. ———, et al. "Immigration, Gender and the Process of Occupational Change in the United States, 1970-80." *International Migration Review*, 18 (Winter 1984): 1021-1044.

Documents the changes in the occupational allocation of native and foreign-born women between 1970 and 1980 and decomposes the observed changes into an industry shift, an intra-industry occupational recomposition shift, and an interaction of these two main effects.

809. Tomasi, Lydio F., ed. *Defense of the Alien*. Vols. 1-8. New York: Center for Migration Studies, 1978-1985.

Proceedings of the Annual National Legal Conference on Immigration and Refugee Policy sponsored by the Center for Migration Studies from 1978 to 1985. Papers contained in these proceedings are by a prominent roster of speakers including members of Congress, government representatives, national and international immigration and refugee specialists, lawyers, experienced voluntary agency representatives, social scientists, and other experts in the field. Among the various contemporary topics analyzed in these papers are: Immigration Law and Legal Representation; Rights of Aliens; Impact of Immigration Policy on U.S. Population and Labor Market; Grounds of Exclusion and Deportation; The Select Commission on Immigration and Refugee Policy and the National Interest; Refugees and Territorial Asylum; Implementation Prospects of Proposed Immigration Legislation; Refugees and Political Asylum; International Migration and Foreign Policy; Immigration Enforcement and Effects on Jobs and Businesses; Immigration and Human Rights; Refugees and Asylees.

810. Tomasi, Silvano M., and Charles B. Keely. *Whom Have We Welcomed? The Adequacy and Quality of United States Immigration Data for Policy Analysis and Evaluation*. New York: Center for Migration Studies, 1975.

After Congress passed the McCarran-Walter Act over President Truman's veto in 1952, a Presidential Commission was appointed to assess immigration policy, particularly the national origins quota concept. Their report was entitled "Whom Shall We Welcome?" The authors conclude that there are major problems in answering that question. "Because of the current federal system of data collection on annual immigration, there are serious questions about the quality and validity of immigration data. This study offers suggestions for improvement. It is the growing awareness of the continuing role of immigration that has led to closer examination of data on immigrants. A pressing need has been a method to assess the impact of legislative changes on the size and characteristics of future immigrant streams. In an attempt to meet that need, *Whom Have We Welcomed?* summarizes current policy, (Chapter 1); the question of "illegal aliens," (Chapter 3); and proposed legislative and administrative changes (Chapter 2, 4). It analyzes both the problem of estimating the demographic effects of proposed changes and the quality of immigration data available from the federal government (Chapter 5).

811. Touton, J. *Rethinking Immigration Policy*. Washington, D.C.: Federation for American Immigration Reform [FAIR], 1979.

Surveys international migration through history and discusses the brain drain and the countries of emigration and immigration as well as the long-term effects of international migration.

812. Tran, Tung. "Vietnam Refugees: The Trauma of Exile." *Civil Rights Digest*, 9 (1976): 59-62.

813. Tung, T.M. "The Indochinese Refugees as Patients." *Journal of Refugee Resettlement*, 1 (1980): 53-60.

Describes the experience of the Indochinese as patients in their home country and in the United States. Indochinese concepts of health and disease, views of medicine and medical practitioners, and experiences with medical practice in Vietnam are discussed as to how they affect Vietnamese dealing with the American medical system.

814. Turansick, Michael F. "A Critique of Proposed Amendments to the Immigration and Nationality Act." *Fordham International Law Journal*, 5 (Winter 1981-82): 213-238.

815. Ugalde, Antonio, et al. "International Migration from
      the Dominican Republic: Findings from a National Sur-
      vey." *International Migration Review*, 13 (1979): 235-
      254.

      Considers why recent Dominican migration, both legal
      and illegal, has been directed to the New York area.
      Notes that the pattern is changing: in 1965 about 78
      percent of all Dominicans in the United States lived in
      the New York/New Jersey area; by 1975 that proportion
      had decreased to 67 percent. Reviews the recent litera-
      ture on Dominican migrants and the results of a study
      undertaken in the Doninican Republic in 1974 on the
      people who left.

816. "Uncle Sam's New Citizens." *The Economist* (March 19,
      1977): 48.

817. United States Children's Bureau. *Cuba's Children in
      Exile: The Story of the Unaccompanied Cuban Refugee
      Children's Program*. Washington, D.C.: Government
      Printing Office, 1967.

818. United States Commission on Civil Rights. "Immigration
      Issues." In *Civil Rights Issues of Asian and Pacific
      Americans: Myths and Realities*. Washington, D.C.:
      U.S. Government Printing Office, 1980. Pp. 164-307.

819. ————. *The Tarnished Golden Door*. Washington, D.C.:
      U.S. Government Printing Office, 1980.

820. United States Commission on Population Growth and the
      American Future. *Population and the American Future*.
      Final Report. Washington, D.C.: Government Printing
      Office, 1972.

821. United States Committee for Refugees. "1980 World Refu-
      gee Survey." New York: U.S. Committee for Refugees,
      1980.

      Shows that the refugee total through 1980 was
      15,965,250. In addition to statistics, includes articles
      by leaders on assisting refugees and reviews specific
      refugee situations.

822. ————. *Vietnamese Boat People: Pirates' Vulnerable
      Prey*. Washington, D.C., 1984.

      States that the flow of boat people, though smaller
      than in previous years, continues at a rate of 2,000-

3,000 arrivals each month. Large numbers have been robbed, savagely beaten, or knifed. Many other refugees are killed or abandoned by pirates and fail to reach safety.

823. ————. *World Refugee Survey 1983--25th Anniversary Issue.* New York: U.S. Committee for Refugees, 1983.

824. ————. *World Refugee Survey 1984.* Washington, D.C.: U.S. Committee for Refugees, 1984.

Presents a review of the status and fate of refugees around the world. Contains some articles dealing with ethnicity as a factor in refugee flows, refugee aid and development, and U.S. refugee resettlement policy.

825. [U.S.] Comptroller General. *Improved Overseas Medical Examinations and Treatment Can Reduce Serious Diseases in Indochinese Refugees Entering the U.S.* Gaithersburg, Maryland: U.S. General Accounting Office, 1982.

826. ————. *Report to the Congress-Central American Refugees: Regional Conditions and Prospects and Potential Impact on the United States.* Gaithersburg, Maryland: U.S. General Accounting Office, 1984.

827. U.S. Congress. House. Committee on Agriculture. Immigration Reform and Control Act of 1983. *Hearing* held June 15, 1983 on H.R. 1510. Washington: Government Printing Office, 1983.

828. ————. Committee on Education and Labor. Subcommittee on Elementary, Secondary and Vocational Education. *Cuban and Haitian Refugee Education, Hearings* ... (96th Congress). Washington: Government Printing Office, 1980.

829. ————. Committee on the Judiciary. Subcommittee on Immigration, Refugees, and International Law. *Caribbean Migration.* Oversight Hearings. 96th Congress, 2d Sess. Washington: Government Printing Office, 1980.

830. ————. Committee on the Judiciary. Subcommittee on Immigration, Citizenship, and International Law. *Haitian Emigration* (94th Congress). Washington: Government Printing Office, 1976.

831. ————. Committee on the Judiciary, U.S. House of Representatives, "Immigration and Nationality Act, with

Amendments and Notes on Related Laws." 7th Edition.
Washington: U.S. Government Printing Office, 1980.

The Immigration and Nationality Act as of September 1,
1980. It also includes related provisions of the law,
information relating to the processing of immigrants and
nonimmigrants, and tables relating to the Immigration
and Nationality Act.

832.   ————. Select Committee on Population. *Immigration to
the United States. Hearings Before the Select Committee on Population.* Washington: U.S. Government Printing Office, 1975.

833.   U.S. Congress. House and Senate. Committees on the
Judiciary. Select Commission on Immigration and Refugee
Policy. *Semiannual Report to Congress.* Washington:
U.S. Government Printing Office, 1980.

Outlines some of the initial efforts of the Commission
to review U.S. immigration laws and policies and provides background information on the formation, function-
ing, and goals of the Select Commission.

834.   ————. Committees on the Judiciary. U.S. Select Commission on Immigration and Refugee Policy. *U.S.
Immigration Policy and the National Interest.* Washington: Government Printing Office, 1981. + 6 vols.
of Appendices.

As part of the 1978 law creating a worldwide ceiling
on immigration, Congress established the Select Commission on Immigration and Refugee Policy to make a
major study of immigration with recommendations for
change. The sixteen-member Commission included Congressional representatives and senators, cabinet offi-
cials, presidential appointees, and was to make its
report in March 1981. Theodore Hesburgh (Notre Dame
University) chaired the Commission and Lawrence Fuchs
(Brandeis University) served as director. Contents
[Report]: Foreword; Executive Summary; Introduction;
Section I. International Issues; Section II. Undocumented/
Illegal Aliens; Section III. The Admission of Immigrants;
Section IV. Phasing in New Programs Recommended by the
Select Commission; Section V. Refugee and Mass First
Asylum Issues; Section VI. Nonimmigrant Aliens; Section
VII. Administrative Issues; Section VIII. Legal Issues;
Section IX. Language Requirement for Naturalization;
Section X. Treatment of U.S. Territories Under U.S. Im-
migration and Nationality Laws; Appendix A. Recommenda-

tions and Votes; Appendix B. Supplemental Statements
of Commissioners; Appendix C. Action Required on Recommendations; Appendix D. Evolution of Key Provisions
Relating to Immigration; Appendix E. The Role of the
Federal Government in Immigration and Refugee Policy;
Appendix F. The U.S. Refugee Program; Appendix G. Research Contracts and Papers Prepared for the Select Commission; Appendix H. Select Commission Briefing and
Background Papers; Appendix I. Dates and Sites of Regional Hearings Held by the Select Commission; Appendix
J. Select Commission Consultations and Participants.

835. ————. *U.S. Immigration Policy and the National Interest.* "Staff Report" of the Select Commission on
Immigration and Refugee Policy. [April 30, 1981].
Washington, D.C.: U.S. Government Printing Office,
1981.

Supplement to the Final Report and Recommendations of
the Select Commission. Provides a background to the
Commission's major recommendations and strategies and
the procedures for implementing some of them. An introduction outlines the human dimensions of world migration.
Four succeeding chapters explicate the underlying principles of immigration reform--international cooperation,
the open society and the rule of law--which formed the
basis for most of the Commission's recommendations.
Two other sections spell out the background to some of
the important recommendations made by the Select Commission, dealing with the number of immigrants and
refugees to be admitted, the criteria for their selection and the enforcement of immigration policy--and the
strategies for implementing those recommendations.
Last section consists of an extensive bibliography.
Nine appendices accompany the staff report. First
seven contain compilations of papers which came to the
attention of the Select Commission, either through research it undertook or contracted for, testimony received
at public hearings, papers submitted at consultations
conducted by the Commission, or in requested agency research. Several summaries of papers published elsewhere
have been included because of their importance. Other
appendices contain additional information on public
affairs activities and summaries of Select Commission
votes.

836. U.S. Congress. Senate. Committee on the Judiciary.
"Caribbean Refugee Crisis: Cubans and Haitians."
Washington, D.C.: U.S. Government Printing Office, 1980.

Reports on the hearings before the Committee on the Judiciary. Includes opening statements by various persons, testimony by experts on the subject, prepared statements, and an appendix containing reports on human rights in Haiti.

837. —————. Committee on the Judiciary. Subcommittee on Immigration, Refugees, and International Law, *Caribbean Migration, Hearings* ... (96th Congress). Washington, D.C.: Government Printing Office, 1980.

838. —————. Committee on the Judiciary. Subcommittee to Investigate Problems Connected with Refugees and Escapees, *Cuban Refugee Problems, Hearings* ... (87th Congress, 88th Congress, and 89th Congress). Washington, D.C.: Government Printing Office, 1961-1966.

839. —————. Committee on the Judiciary. *Temporary Worker Programs: Background and Issues.* A Report prepared at the request of Senator E.M. Kennedy for the use of the Select Commission on Immigration and Refugee Policy by the Congressional Research Service of the Library of Congress, 96th Congress, Second Session, February 1980. [Washington, D.C., 1980].

Reviews U.S. and European experience with selected temporary programs, identifies the problems which have arisen under these various programs, and the lessons which may apply to any future attempt to control the illegal flow of alien workers by means of an expanded legal program. Contains an annotated bibliography on alien labor programs and alien labor, 1975-79.

840. —————. *U.S. Refugee Programs: Hearing Before the Committee on the Judiciary.* U.S. Senate, 96th Congress, 2nd Session, April 17, 1980. Washington, D.C.: U.S. Government Printing Office, 1980.

The first formal "consultation" on U.S. refugee programs required under the terms of the new refugee bill (The Refugee Act of 1980). Contains the testimonies of government representatives as well as of refugee experts. Appendixes include two reports to Congress and an overview of the world refugee situation by the State Department; two reports on the Indochinese Refugee Assistant Program by HEW; and the 1980 World Refugee Survey by the U.S. Committee for Refugees, Inc.

841. ————. Subcommittee on Immigration and Refugee Policy. *Refugee Problems in Central America*. Washington, D.C.: U.S. Government Printing Office, 1984.

The question of returning undocumented Salvadorans to El Salvador or providing them with safe haven in the United States has been the subject of debate both in Congress and in the media. The Immigration and Refugee Policy Subcommittee of the Committee on the Judiciary has monitored these humanitarian problems and nation's response to the needs of refugees and displaced persons in Central America.

842. U.S. Department of Education, Kansas City. *Refugee Materials Center Bibliography: Curricular and Supplementary Materials to Assist in the Education and Resettlement of Refugees and Immigrants*. Kansas City: U.S. Department of Education, 1984.

843. United States Department of State. *Country Reports on the World Refugee Situation: Statistics*. Report to the Congress for Fiscal Year 1985. Washington, D.C., 1984.

Based on figures provided to the Department of State by American embassies abroad. Embassies obtain the figures from foreign governments and representatives of the United Nations High Commissioner for Refugees, and other international organizations, such as the United Nations Relief and Works Agency.

844. [U.S.] General Accounting Office. *Detention Policies Affecting Haitian Nationals*. Gaithersburg, Maryland: U.S. General Accounting Office, 1983.

845. ————. *Greater Emphasis on Early Employment and Better Monitoring Needed in Indochinese Refugee Resettlement Program*. Gaithersburg, Maryland: General Accounting Office, 1983.

Reviews Indochinese refugee resettlement programs authorized by the Refugee Act of 1980, concentrating on the initial resettlement services provided by voluntary agencies under the State Department's auspices and social services funded by the Department of Health and Human Services.

846. U.S. President. "Immigration and Nationality Act Amendments of 1976." *Weekly Compilation of Presidential*

Documents, 12 (October 25, 1976): 1548.

President Ford's statement upon signing H.R. 14535
(P.L. 94-571).

847. Vázquez, Josefina Z., and Lorenzo Meyer. *The United
     States and Mexico*. Chicago: University of Chicago
     Press, 1985.

     Written by two Mexican scholars, traces concisely
     Mexican-American relations from a Mexican perspective.
     In Part 1, Vázquez covers the nineteenth century; in
     Part 2, Meyer goes from the fall of Porfirio Diaz to
     the administrations of De la Madrid and Reagan, years
     of contradictions and conflict. Designed for American
     reader. Less critical of U.S. conduct than the works
     of New Left historians, as it records Mexico's struggle
     to free itself from and create a mutually productive
     relationship with its northern neighbor.

848. Vicioso, C. "Dominican Migration to the USA." *Migra-
     tion Today*, 20 (1976): 59-72.

849. [Vietnam Resettlement]. *First, Second, Third, Fourth
     Wave Reports: Vietnam Resettlement Operational Feed-
     back*. Washington, D.C.: Opportunity Systems, 1975-
     1977.

850. Vinh, H.T. "Indochinese Mutual Assistance Associations."
     Journal of Refugee Resettlement, 1 (1980): 49-52.

     Discusses the development, nature, and potential con-
     tributions of refugee community organizations from the
     perspective of shared responsibility for integrating
     Indochinese refugees into U.S. society.

851. Viviano, Frank. "The New Immigrants." *Mother Jones*, 8
     (January 1983): 26-33, 45-46.

852. Wain, B. *The Refused: The Agony of the Indochinese
     Refugees*. New York: Simon and Schuster, 1981.

     Wain traveled to refugee camps in Asia, to the United
     Nations, and to Indochina. In recording events, he ap-
     proaches the subject thematically rather than chrono-
     logically; examines the factors that stimulated the exo-
     dus from South Vietnam, Laos, and Kampuchea, details the
     Vietnamese government's activist role, and explains
     how Hong Kong sought to deter racketeers and Hanoi from
     running refugees. Subsequent chapters deal with the
     burden imposed on neighboring countries and the results.

853. Waldinger, Roger. "The Occupational and Economic Integration of the New Immigration (U.S. Immigration Policy)." *Law and Contemporary Problems*, 45 (Spring 1982): 197-222.

854. Walsh, Bryan O. "The Boat People of South Florida." *America*, 142 (May 17, 1980): 420-421.

855. ————. "Cubans in Miami." *America*, 114 (February 26, 1966): 286-289.

856. ————. "Cuban Refugee Children." *Journal of Inter-American Studies and World Affairs*, 13 (July-October 1971): 378-414.

857. ————. "Haitian Boat People: Refugees or Gate Crashers." *The New Renaissance*, 13 (1980): 9-26.

858. ————. "Haitians in Miami." *Migration Today*, 7 (September 1979): 42-44.

859. Walter, Ingrid. *One Year After Arrival: The Adjustment of Indochinese Women in the United States, 1979-1980*. New York: Lutheran Council in the U.S., 1981.

Addresses the adjustment of Indochinese women refugees who arrived in the United States in the month of September 1979 under the sponsorship of Lutheran Immigration and Refugee Service (LIRS). Reviews situation one year after arrival as seen through their own eyes and through the eyes of Americans in the community who accepted them as new neighbors. Considers their resettlement from the family, social, emotional, English language and economic standpoints and looks at them with respect to differences in their ethnicity, age groups, and geographical locations: *i.e.*, western, central and eastern United States. In order to provide a framework to explain how and why in late 1980 they were residing in these various locations, the author begins with an examination of the U.S. refugee resettlement program, the role of voluntary agencies, and factors, such as secondary migration, which may enhance or delay the adjustment of refugees.

860. ————. "One Year After Arrival: The Adjustment of Indochinese Women in the United States (1979-1980)." *International Migration*, 19 (1981): 123-146.

861. Warren, Robert. "Recent Immigration and Current Data Collection." *Monthly Labor Review*, 100 (October 1977): 36-41.

862. ————, and Jennifer M. Peck. "Foreign-Born Emigration
      from the United States: 1960 to 1970." *Demography*,
      17 (February 1980): 71-84.

      Presents estimates of emigration of foreign-born per-
      sons by age and sex for 1960 to 1970 census counts of
      the foreign-born population, adjusted life table survival
      rates, and annual statistics on alien immigration pub-
      lished by the Immigration and Naturalization Service.
      The finding that more than one million foreign-born
      persons left the United States between 1960 and 1970,
      "has important implications for U.S. immigration policy
      and for net immigration policy and for net immigration
      data used to estimate the population of the United
      States."

863. Watson, R.J., Jr. "The Simpson-Mazzoli Bill: An Analy-
      sis of Selected Economic Policies." *San Diego Law
      Review*, 20 (1983): 97-116.

      Analyzes certain sections of the Simpson-Mazzoli bill
      in terms of the economic policies underlying them and
      concludes that any change in immigration laws should be
      drafted in such a way as to more effectively implement
      these policies.

864. Weaver, C.N., and N.D. Glenn. "The Job Performance of
      Mexican-Americans." *Sociology and Social Research*,
      54 (July 1970): 477-494.

      Mexican-American and Anglo-American workers in the
      same jobs and organizations in San Antonio, Texas, are
      compared in efficiency ratings and several objective
      indicators of job performance.

865. Weaver, Thomas, and Theodore E. Downing, eds. *Mexican
      Migration*. Tucson, Arizona: The University of Arizona,
      1976.

      Investigates the patterns of movement of migrants
      within Mexico (between states and regions) and between
      Mexico and the United States and examines the social
      and economic factors correlated with these movements
      which might assist in predicting future migrations.
      Develops a computer simulation model of migration and
      analyzes available information from private and public
      agencies and census materials.

866. Webber, Polly. "Alan Nelson Views the Tasks of INS Com-
      missioner." *Immigration Journal*, 5 (January-February
      1982): 10.

867. Weintraub, S., and S.R. Ross. "Poor United States, So Close to Mexico." *Across the Board*, 19 (March 1982): 54-61.

868. ————, and ————. *Temporary Alien Workers in the United States*. Boulder, Colorado: Westview, 1981.

869. Weissbrodt, D. *Immigration Law and Procedure in a Nutshell*. Santa Clara, California: West Publishing Co., 1984.

870. Weist, Raymond E. "Implications of International Labor Migration for Mexican Rural Development." In *Migration Across Frontiers: Mexico and the United States*. Edited by Fernando Camara and Robert V. Kemper. Albany, New York: Institute for Mesoamerican Studies, State University of New York, Albany, 1979. Pp. 85-97.

871. ————. "Wage-Labor Migration and the Household in a Mexican Town." *Journal of Anthropological Research*, 29 (Autumn 1973): 180-209.

Ethnographic study of emigration from the community of Acuitzio del Canje, state of Michoacán, Mexico, to the United States and destinations within Mexico.

872. Wenk, Michael G. "Adjustment and Assimilation: The Cuban Refugee Experience." *International Migration Review*, 3 (Fall 1968): 38-49.

Study for the U.S. Catholic Conference. Questionnaires to diocesan resettlement directors and directors of special Cuban refugee committees asking that they contact five Cuban families in their area at random and submit questionnaires to them concerning their experiences with the Cuban refugee program as well as their own adjustment to life in families. Questions concerned "family mode of living, employment, income, educational status and current schooling, their reasons for coming to the United States and evidences of success or problems in adjustment."

873. ————. "Reflections on Current United States Immigration Policy." *International Migration Review*, 4 (Spring 1970): 93-98.

"For approximately two decades, U.S. immigration policy had labored under the archaic 'National Origins' quota system. On the 3rd of October 1965, this archaic policy was eliminated and a modern substitute was born. The

Immigration Act of October 3, 1965 may be considered a
turning point; a new perspective, a new and refreshing
look at an aspect of American policy which is vital,
both culturally as well as economically, to an ever
growing and vibrant America. We are to be sure, 'A
nation of nations'! The 1965 Law preserves, and more
important, cultivates that image. It is an adaptation
of a non-discriminatory policy, directing its efforts
with both the pragmatic principle of 'first come, first
served,' as well as the humane precept of the 'reunification of families,' in mind. It is an adaptation that
provides for the admission of the professional, the
skilled, the unskilled and most important, the refugee.
In short, it is an adaptation whose entire scope and
perspective is so planned as to serve the totality--
'the human being.'"

874.   ————. "The Refugee: A Search for Clarification."
        International Migration Review, 2 (1968): 62-69.

"We will attempt a critical evaluation of at least
one of the major problem areas evident in present refugee
policy: the entity of the refugee proper. A re-appraisal
of the definition of a refugee, with an emphasis and
concentration on the 'entity' rather than the contributing
causes to that entity will serve as a tool for further
significant judgment and recommendations. The term
'refugee' has been vividly present to the international
community for many years, and still is today, a time of
repeated international crises and armed conflicts.
In general, the term implies an individual who has left
his homeland under certain pressures, be they political,
social, economic or religious in nature."

875.   Westoff, Leslie Aldridge. "A Nation of Immigrants:
        Should We Pull Up the Gangplank?" *New York Times
        Magazine* (September 16, 1973): 14-15+.

876.   Whiteford, Michael B. "Women, Migration and Social
        Change: A Colombian Case Study." *International Migra-
        tion Review*, 12 (Summer 1978): 236-247.

Contends that, for women, in particular, the process
of migration is a liberating, or freeing process.
Specifically, this paper examines the changes which take
place in the social environment of women as a result of
rural-urban migrations. The focus of the investigation
is female migrants who have moved to the city of Popayán,
Colombia. The discussion is based on data gathered in
Barrio Tulcán.

877. Williams, Dennis. "Florida's Boat People." *Newsweek* (April 2, 1979): 37-38.

878. Williamson, Jeffrey G. "Immigrant-Inequality Trade-offs in the Promised Land: Income Distribution and Absorptive Capacity Prior to the Quotas." In Barry R. Chiswick, ed. *The Gateway: U.S. Immigration Issues and Policies.* Washington, D.C.: American Enterprise Institute, 1982. Pp. 251-288.

Applies a multisectoral general-equilibrium two-factor (labor and land-capital) model to the period 1839-1966. This confirms that immigration did indeed tend to increase income inequality among the native population as well as among the labor force augmented by the immigrants. Demand forces, however, appear to have been far more important than immigrants in driving America over the increasing inequality part of the Kuznets curve after the 1830s. Believes that the timing of the immigration quotas correlates well with American experience with immigrant-absorptive capacity; political pressure in support of quotas and their subsequent enactment were a consequence of decreases in the elasticity of the demand for labor and in the supply of native labor that implied that immigration had a substantial depressing effect on wages.

879. Wilson, Kenneth L., and Alejandro Portes. "Immigrant Enclaves: An Analysis of the Labor Market Experiences of Cubans in Miami." *American Journal of Sociology,* 86 (September 1980): 295-319.

Uses data from a longitudinal sample of Cuban emigres to test competing hypotheses about the mode of incorporating new immigrants into the U.S. labor market. Causes and implications of the findings are discussed.

880. Winsberg, Morton D. "Housing Segregation of a Predominantly Middle Class Population: Residential Patterns Developed by the Cuban Immigration into Miami, 1950-74." *American Journal of Economics and Sociology,* 38 (October 1979): 403-418.

881. "Women and Migration." *Anthropological Quarterly,* 49 (January 1976): 1-80. Whole Issue.

Special issue including papers which were first presented at the 1975 Annual Meeting of the American Anthropological Association.

882. Wong, J.I. *A Selected Bibliography on the Asians in
      America.* Palo Alto, California: R & E Research Asso-
      ciates, 1981.

883. Wong, Morrison G. "The New Asian Immigrants." Occa-
      sional Papers Series. Center for International
      Studies. Durham, North Carolina: Duke University,
      1979.

      Presents a brief history of U.S. immigration policy
      in order to emphasize the impact the reform Immigration
      Act of 1965 had on Asian immigration. INS data on Asian
      immigration is analyzed to show the changes and conse-
      quences of the large influx of Asian immigrants to the
      United States, not only for the larger society but also
      for the indigenous Asian communities.

884. ————, and Charles Hirschman. "Labor Force Participa-
      tion and Socioeconomic Attainment of Asian-American
      Women." *Sociological Perspectives*, 26 (1983): 423-446.

885. Wong, Paul. "The Emergence of the Asian American Move-
      ment." *The Bridge*, 2 (1972): 32-39.

886. Woods, R.D. *Reference Materials on Mexican Americans:
      An Annotated Bibliography.* Metuchen, New Jersey:
      Scarecrow Press, 1976.

887. Wydrzynski, C.J. "Refugees and the Immigration Act."
      McGill Law Journal, 25 (1979): 154-92.

888. Wyman, D.L. *The United States Congress and the Making
      of U.S. Policy Toward Mexico.* Working Papers in U.S.-
      Mexican Studies, No. 13. Program in United States-
      Mexican Studies, University of California, San Diego,
      1981.

      Documents and explains Congressional interest in
      Mexico-related issues, analyzes how several characteris-
      tics of the Congress influence the way in which Congress
      deals with Mexico-related issues, discusses the influence
      of Congress on the outcomes of the policymaking process
      and predicts what it all is likely to mean for future
      bilateral relations.

889. Young, P.K. "Immigrant Enterprise in America: Koreans
      and Hispanics in New York City." Paper presented at
      American Anthropological Association. 83rd Annual
      Meeting. Denver, Colorado, November 14-18, 1984.

Analyzes the cultural and socioeconomic factors affecting the motivation, goals, and degree of success
of immigrant entrepreneurs by focusing on 40 Korean
owners of produce stores and 72 Hispanic owners of
grocery stores in New York City. A quantitative analysis
of an in-depth survey administered to these store owners
in their own language revealed a number of important
differences between the two groups. Among other things
Koreans in general started their own business for the
financial gain, while most Hispanics did so for reasons
of independence. Discusses these and other key differences in educational levels, work experience, degree
of competition, use of family labor, and degree of
business success and personal satisfaction.

890. Zazueta, Carlos H. "Mexican Workers in the United
States: Some Initial Results and Methodological Considerations of the National Household Survey of Emigration." Paper prepared for the Working Group on Mexican
Migrants and U.S. Responsibility. Center for Philosophy
and Public Policy. College Park, Maryland: University
of Maryland. March 1980.

891. ———, and Rodolfo Corona. *Los trabajadores Mexicanos
en Los Estados Unidos: Primeros resultados de la
encuesta nacional de emigración a la frontera norte
del país y a los Estados Unidos*. México, D.F.: Centro
nacional de información y estadísticas de trabajo,
1979.

892. [Zeisel, William, ed.] *Ethnic and Immigration Groups:
The United States, Canada, and England*. New York:
The Haworth Press, 1983.

A series of bibliographical essays. Contents: Piety
and Politics: Ethnicity and the New Political History;
Acculturation and Pluralism in Recent Studies of American
Immigration History; Immigrant Women, The Family, and
Work, 1850-1950; Recent Immigration to the United States;
Ethnic Studies in Canada; East Indians in England and
North America.

893. Zenner, Walter P. "Arabic-Speaking Immigrants in North
America as Middleman Minorities." *Ethnic and Racial
Studies*, 5 (1982): 457-477.

894. Ziegler, Benjamin, ed. *Immigration: An American Dilemma*.
Lexington, Massachusetts: D.C. Heath, 1953.

895. Zinam, Oleg. "Impact of Mexican Economic Crisis and
      Economic Conditions in the U.S.A. on Mexican Immigra-
      tion." Paper presented at Western Social Science
      Association. 26th Annual Meeting. San Diego, Cali-
      fornia, April 28, 1984.

      Summarizes the history of Mexican Americans within
      the development of the Southwest, and describes the
      Bracero Program, illegal immigrants, the Mexican Uni-
      versity and its collective action, and the interrelated-
      ness of the U.S. and Mexican economies.

896. ———. "Mexicans and Cubans." In Joseph S. Roucek
      and Bernard Eisenberg, eds. *America's Ethnic Politics*.
      Westport, Connecticut: Greenwood Press, 1982. Pp.
      253-272.

897. Zokoski, Kimberly J. "The Effects of Length of Residence
      and Stage Migration on the Demographic Characteristics
      of a Haitian Community in Miami, Florida." Unpublished
      M.A. thesis, University of Miami, 1980.

898. Zolberg, Aristide. "Migration Patterns Since World
      War II in Europe and the Americas." *Immigration
      History Newsletter*, 9 (May 1977): 1-2.

      Findings: Governmental policies are important in deter-
      mining postwar migration patterns in Europe and North
      America. Nations have routinely regulated both the exit
      of nationals—by expulsion and by forcible retention—
      and the entrance of immigrants. Political and economic
      considerations have helped to define such policies, some-
      times complementing each other and sometimes contradicting.
      In the United States between about 1920 and 1965, for ex-
      ample, economic interests dictated free entry of labor
      while political considerations encouraged the restriction
      of immigration on the grounds of national security. A
      compromise resulted from this conflict: entry became more
      difficult for Asians and Southern and Eastern Europeans,
      while Western hemisphere immigration remained almost un-
      regulated, providing a loophole which permitted the entry
      of Mexican and French Canadian laborers.

899. Zucker, Naomi Flink. "The Haitians versus the United
      States: The Courts as Last Resort." *Annals of the
      American Academy of Political and Social Science*, 467
      (May 1983): 151-162.

900. Zucker, Norman. "Refugee Resettlement in the United
      States: The Role of the Voluntary Agencies." *Michigan
      Yearbook of International Legal Studies*, annual, 1982:
      155-177.

III. ILLEGAL IMMIGRANTS IN THE UNITED STATES

(1) General Works and
Specialized Studies

901. Adams, Nathan M. "Our Mounting Wave of Illegal Immigrants." *Reader's Digest* (December 1973): 115-19.

902. "Aliens Hurting Houston Jobless (Construction)." *Engineering News-Record*, 208 (February 4, 1982): 66.

903. Alvarado, Manuel de Jesús. "Slaves or Workers? Dilemmas Affecting Undocumented Mexican Farm Workers in the U.S." University of Arizona, Tucson, Arizona, 1978. Unpublished research paper. (mimeographed)

904. American Friends Service Committee. *Undocumented Workers in the U.S. Labor Market.* Pasadena, California: American Friends Service Committee, 1980.

Based on the proceedings of a conference on the "Working Rights of Undocumented Workers: An Ethical and Moral Perspective" held in San Diego on September 22, 1979.

905. *Analisis de algunos resultados de la primera encuesta a trabajadores Mexicanos no documentados revueltas de los Estados Unidos, octubre 23-noviembre 13 de 1977. Analisis I.* Mexico City: Centro nacional de información y estadisticas del trabajo, 1979.

906. Anderson, George M. "Illegal Aliens: Refugees from Hunger." *America*, 136 (January 29, 1971): 68-72.

907. ———. "Illegal Immigration: A Sociological Unexplored Field." Unpublished paper presented at Annual Meeting (August 30-September 2, 1971, Denver, Colorado) of American Sociological Association.

908. Anker, Deborah. "Haitians' Detention Challenged in
     Court." *Immigration Journal*, 5 (January-February
     1982): 16.

909. Ardman, Harvey. "Our Illegal Alien Problem." *American
     Legion Magazine* (December 1974): 6-9.

910. Arias, Armando A., Jr. "Undocumented Mexicans: A Study
     in the Social Psychology of Clandestine Migration to
     the United States." Unpublished Ph.D. dissertation,
     University of California, San Diego, June 1981.

     Ethnographic study of undocumented Mexicans living in
     Denver, Colorado, and San Diego, California, based on
     fieldwork completed in 1980. Main source of data:
     intensive open-ended interviews with twelve key infor-
     mants.

911. "Arrests of Illegal Aliens Increase as Mexican Economy
     Falters." *New York Times*, August 27, 1982, p. A-8.

912. Baca, Reynaldo, and Dexter Bryan. *Citizenship Aspira-
     tions and Residency Rights Preference: The Mexican
     Undocumented Worker in the Binational Community.*
     Compton, California: Sepa-Option, Inc., 1980.

     Based on structured interviews with 1,414 undocumented
     Mexicans living in the Los Angeles area, 562 of whom
     are women.

913. ————, and ————. "Mexican Undocumented Workers in
     the Binational Community: A Research Note." *Inter-
     national Migration Review*, 15 (Winter 1981): 737-748.

     Researchers are finding that the Mexican undocumented
     worker population is more heterogeneous than once assumed.
     In the past, *campesinos*--male farmhands--filled the
     ranks of undocumented workers. While Mexico's agricul-
     tural workers continue to venture north in search of
     employment, illegal migration is expanding throughout
     Mexico's social structure. Today's Mexican economic
     refugees are both urban dwellers and *campesinos*, both
     men and women. The diversity of adaptation to working
     and living in the United States parallels the hetero-
     geneity of the undocumented worker population. There
     is the well-researched pattern of the migrant farmworker
     whose stay in the United States is limited to the harvest
     season. While many migrants move from state to state,
     others return each year from Mexico to the same U.S.
     agricultural center. Another pattern is common in the

twin cities of the *fronteras* or border region. Here
Mexicans work in the United States and routinely, often
daily, commute back to Mexico. Permanent settlement in
the United States is yet another pattern. The most committed of these permanent settlers will probably stay
in the United States as long as gainful economic opportunities are available for them.

914.   ————, and ————. "The Undocumented Mexican Worker:
A Social Problem?" *The Journal of Ethnic Studies*, 8
(Spring 1980): 55-70.

Proposes a redefinition of the illegal alien problem
and encourages social scientists to expand their research
beyond reactions to the economic burden themes and to
view the undocumented worker problem as one endemic to
the political economy of the United States and Mexico.

915.   Bach-y-Rita, Esther Wicab. "An Ethnographic and Psycho-
social Study of Latin American Undocumented Women
Immigrants in the San Francisco Bay Area." Unpublished
Ph.D. dissertation, University of California, Berkeley,
1986.

916.   ————. "A Study of Fifteen Undocumented Mexican Women
in a Northern California Community: A Pilot Study."
Unpublished report, Berkeley, California: Wright Institute, May 1981.

Ethnographic study of female undocumented migrants
living in a semi-rural northern California community
all of whom had had contact with the County Hospital of
the area.

917.   Bailey, Thomas. "The Influence of Legal Status on the
Labor Market Impact of Immigration." *International
Migration Review*, 19 (Summer 1985): 220-238.

Explores the labor market changes that would take
place as a result of an amnesty that would regularize
the status of undocumented workers without changing
the total size of the alien workforce. The theoretical
analysis suggests that the influence of legal status
on market wage rates and on minimum wage enforcement is
weak and that to the extent that there is an effect, it
depends on particular institutional arrangements.
Although data are not adequate for a definite measurement of these effects, those data that are available
support this conclusion. It does appear that the presence
of undocumented as opposed to resident aliens can weaken
union organizing efforts.

918. "Ban on Hiring Illegal Aliens Could Open 1 Million Jobs."
      Industry Week (March 17, 1975): 22.

919. Bean, Frank D., et al. "The Number of Illegal Migrants
      of Mexican Origin in the United States: Sex Ratio-
      Based Estimates for 1980." *Demography*, 1 (February
      1983): 99-110.

      Reports the results of applying a sex ratio-based
      method to estimate the number of undocumented Mexicans
      residing in the United States in 1980. Approach centers
      on a comparison between the hypothetical sex ratio one
      would expect to find in Mexico in the absence of emigra-
      tion to the United States and the sex ratio that is in
      fact reported in preliminary results from the 1980
      Mexican Census.

920. ————, et al. "The Sociodemographic Characteristics
      of Mexican Immigrant Status Groups: Implications for
      Studying Undocumented Mexicans." *International
      Migration Review*, 18 (Fall 1984): 672-691.

      Based on Warren and Passel's (1984) estimate that
      nearly two thirds of Mexican-born noncitizens entering
      the United States during 1975-80 and included in the
      1980 Census are undocumented immigrants, this article
      uses the 1980 Public Use Microfiles to delineate four
      Mexican origin immigrant status groups--post-1975
      Mexican-born noncitizens, pre-1975 Mexican-born non-
      citizens, self-reported naturalized citizens, and native-
      born Mexican Americans. The pattern of sociodemographic
      differences among these groups provides support for the
      idea that the first two categories contain a substantial
      fraction of undocumented immigrants. These two groups
      (especially the first) reveal characteristics that one
      would logically associate with undocumented immigrants--
      age concentration (in young adult years), high sex
      ratios, low education and income levels, and lack of
      English proficiency.

921. Biffle, Christopher. "Illegal Aliens: 'Late on a Moon-
      less Night.'" *The Nation* (January 25, 1975): 79-81.

922. Bikales, Gerda V. "The Case for a Secure Social
      Security Card." Washington, D.C.: National Parks and
      Conservation Association, 1981.

      Argues the "urgent need for more formalized identifi-
      cation" that "will screen out illegal workers and protect
      the rights of Americans--including the right to a job."

923. ————. "Illegal Immigration: An Environmental Issue."
      National Parks & Conservation Magazine (June 1978):
      2+.

924. "Bill to Curb Illegal Immigration: House Debates Reflect
      Diversity of Nation." *New York Times*, June 17, 1984,
      p. A-20.

925. Blejer, M.I., et al. "Un análisis de los determinantes
      económicos de la migración Mexicano legal e ilegal
      hacia los Estados Unidos." *Demographia & Economia*,
      11 (1979): 326-340.

926. Böhning, W.R. *Regularizing Undocumentados*. Geneva:
      International Labour Organisation, 1979.

927. Briggs, Vernon M., Jr. *Foreign Labor Programs as an
      Alternative to Illegal Immigration into the United
      States: A Dissenting View*. College Park, Maryland:
      Center for Philosophy and Public Policy, University
      of Maryland, 1980.

      Reviews some of the foreign worker programs that have
      been proposed for the United States and considers the
      case against all such proposals.

928. ————. "Illegal Aliens: The Need for a Restrictive
      Border Policy." *Social Science Quarterly*, 56 (Decem-
      ber 1975): 447-84.

929. ————. "Illegal Immigration and the American Labor
      Force." *American Behavioral Scientist*, 19 (January/
      February 1976): 351-63.

930. ————. "Methods of Analysis of Illegal Immigration
      into the United States." *International Migration
      Review*, 18 (Fall 1984): 623-641.

      A major barrier to the discussion of the scope and
      impact of illegal immigration on the American economy
      has been the inadequacy of existing data. Although data
      problems are not unique to this topic, the limited
      availability of macro-data on the size of the annual
      flows and of the accumulated stock of individuals as
      well as of macro-data on their influences on selected
      labor markets has been effectively used to forestall
      policy reform efforts.

931. Browning, H.L., and N. Rodriquez. "Mexico-U.S.A. In-
      documentado Migration as a Settlement Process and Its
      Implications for Work." Paper presented at the His-
      panic Labor Conference, University of California at
      Santa Barbara, 1982.

932. Bustamante, Jorge A. "Changing Patterns of Undocu-
      mented Migration from Mexican States in Recent Years."
      In Richard C. Jones, ed., *Patterns of Undocumented
      Migration: Mexico and the United States*. Totowa,
      N.J.: Rowman & Allanheld, 1984. Pp. 15-32.

      Reviews what is known of the characteristics of un-
      documented migration from Mexico. It is based upon a
      presentation of the findings of a survey conducted by
      the author in nine Mexican border cities, utilizing
      interviews with Mexican undocumented emigrants recently
      deported from the United States. A discussion of costs
      and benefits of the migration and some suggestions for
      solutions are also made.

933. ————. "Emigración indocumentada a los Estados
      Unidos." *Foro Internacional*, 18 (January-March
      1978): 430-63.

934. ————. "The Historical Context of Undocumented
      Mexican Migration to the United States." *Aztlan:
      Chicano Journal of the Social Sciences and Arts*, 3
      (Fall 1972): 257-81.

935. ————. *La immigracion indocumentada en los debatos
      del congreso de los Estados Unidos. Estudios I.*
      Mexico City: Centro nacional de información y
      estadisticas del trabajo, 1978.

936. ————. "More on the Impact of Undocumented Immigra-
      tion from Mexico on the U.S.-Mexico Economies:
      Preliminary Findings and Suggestions for Bilateral
      Cooperation." Paper presented at Las Fronteras
      Conference, San Diego, California, 1976.

937. ————. *So-called Wetback: The Social, Economic and
      Political Meaning of Immigration to the U.S.* Mexico
      City: Universidad nacional de Mexico, 1972.

938. ————. "Structural and Ideological Conditions of
      Mexican Undocumented Immigration to the United
      States." *American Behavioral Scientist*, 19 (1976):
      364-376.

A "theoretical outline based on Marxian analysis."
Argues that Mexican labor became a commodity to be
bought and sold, enticed and deported, as needed. Employers have historically exploited immigrant workers
and then blamed them for economic difficulties when
downswings occurred. Current attention on illegal
Mexicans is the last chapter in a long history of exploitation.

939. ————. "Structural and Ideological Conditions of
Undocumented Mexican Immigration to the United States."
In W.B. Littrell and G. Sjoberg, eds. *Current Issues
in Social Policy*. London: Sage Publications, 1976.
Pp. 145-157.

Focuses upon the conditions in which social policies
related to Mexican immigration are inextricably linked
to a class structured society. Examines a theoretical
orientation based on Marxian analysis and then relates
this to the history of immigration in the United
States and suggests how this approach relates to the
immigration of Mexicans into American society.

940. ————. "Undocumented Migration from Mexico: A Research Report." *International Migration Review*, 11
(Summer 1977): 149-178.

941. Cabral, Darien. *Illegal Aliens and Economic Development*. El Paso, Texas: The University of Texas at
El Paso, 1984.

Discusses illegal Mexican migrant laborers and the
economic development projects in the Mexican communities from which they had emigrated that, as a result
of successful American farm workers' labor actions,
were funded by the farms on which the laborers worked.
The goal of these projects was to create employment
to help mitigate the need for workers to migrate to
the United States.

942. California. State Social Welfare Board. *Position
Statement: Aliens in California*. Sacramento: Health
and Welfare Agency, Department of Social Welfare,
1973.

943. "California Tries to Dam the Alien Tide: An Estimated
1 Million Illegal Entrants Bring Crushing Social
Problems." *Business Week* (February 12, 1972): 34+.

944. Campbell, D.A., and C. Hildebrand. "Immigration Al-
     ternatives for Terminated or Laid off Aliens Working
     Temporarily in the United States (Explanation of
     Visa Holder Status)." *Personnel Administrator*, 29
     (July 1984): 73-74.

945. "Canadian Border Faces Alien Problem of Its Own."
     New York Times, April 20, 1986, p. 46.

946. Cardenas, Gilberto. "Illegal Aliens in the Southwest:
     A Case Study." In *Illegal Aliens: An Assessment of
     the Issues*. Washington, D.C.: National Council on
     Employment Policy, 1976. Pp. 42-56.

947. ————. "Manpower Impact and Problems of Mexican Il-
     legal Aliens in an Urban Labor Market." Unpublished
     Ph.D. dissertation in Labor and Industrial Relations,
     University of Illinois, Urbana, 1977.

     Interviews with 100 undocumented Mexicans living in
     San Antonio, Texas.

948. ————, and Estéven T. Flores. "Social, Economic and
     Demographic Characteristics of Undocumented Mexicans
     in the Houston Labor Market: A Preliminary Report."
     Report Prepared for the Gulf Coast Legal Foundation,
     Houston, Texas [1980].

     Based on interviews with 138 nondetailed illegal
     immigrant parents of children attending special church-
     sponsored schools for undocumented children in Houston
     as well as undocumented immigrants who were clients
     of a Houston legal counseling center.

949. ————, and Ray Flores. *A Study of the Demographic and
     Employment Characteristics of Undocumented Aliens
     in San Antonio, El Paso, and McAllen*. San Antonio:
     Avante, Inc., for the Texas Advisory Committee, U.S.
     Commission of Civil Rights, 1978.

950. Carliner, David. *The Rights of Aliens*. New York:
     Avon Books, 1977.

951. "The Carter Amnesty Proposal." *Congressional Digest*,
     56 (October 1977): 232.

952. "Carter's Plan for Illegal Aliens." *U.S. News & World
     Report* (August 15, 1977): 19-20.

953. Castillo, Leonel J. "Dealing with the Undocumented Alien--An Interim Approach." *International Migration Review*, 12 (Winter 1978): 570-577.

954. Cervera, M. *Tabla de estancia en los Estados Unidos para trabajadores Mexicanos indocumetados. Estudios 2.* Mexico City; Centro nacional de información y estadisticas del trabajo, 1979.

955. Chande, R.H., and J.A. Bustamante. "Las expulsiones de indocumentados Mexicanos." *Demografia y economia*, 13 (1979): 185-207.

Analysis and commentary on numbers of undocumented migrants caught and deported by the INS, as reported by the U.S. Department of Justice, Immigration, and Naturalization Service, Form G-23.18, in its "Monthly Report of Deportable Aliens Found in the United States by Nationality, Status of Entry, Place of Entry, Status When Found."

956. Chapman, Leonard F., Jr. "Illegal Aliens: A Growing Population." *Immigration and Naturalization Reporter*, 24 (Fall 1975): 15-18.

957. ————. "Illegal Aliens: Time to Call a Halt!" *Reader's Digest* (October 1976): 188-92.

958. ————. "The Scope and Impact of the Illegal Alien Problem in the United States." Paper presented at Population Association of America Annual Meeting, Montreal, Canada, April 29-May 1, 1976.

"In the United States there are an estimated eight million illegal aliens, nearly all of whom have entered the nation in search of employment. Although nationals of Mexico make up a large number, aliens illegally in the United States come from many countries of the world. Many are in metropolitan centers, holding jobs in industry and service. The practical solution to the problem is legislation to reduce job opportunities for illegal aliens by making it unlawful to employ them. In the absence of such legislation, with populations growing rapidly in Latin America, the number entering will continue to increase."

959. ————. "'Silent Invasion' That Takes Millions of American Jobs." *U.S. News & World Report* (December 9, 1974): 77-78.

960. Chiswick, Barry R. "Illegal Aliens in the U.S. Labor
      Market." *Proceedings*. 6th World Congress, Inter-
      national Economic Association. Mexico City, August
      1980.

961. Cifelli, A. "Business Balks at Doing the Border
      Patrol's Job (New Immigration Law)." *Fortune*, 109
      (March 19, 1984): 102.

962. Cohen, Lucy M. "Gifts to Strangers: Public Policy and
      the Delivery of Health Services to Illegal Aliens."
      Anthropological Quarterly, 46 (July 1973): 183-95.

963. "Commission Proposes Amnesty for 1 Million Undocumented
      Workers." *Restaurants and Institutions*, 89 (July 15,
      1981): 89.

964. Community Research Associates. "Undocumented Immi-
      grants: Their Impact on the County of San Diego."
      Report prepared by Community Research Associates for
      the County of San Diego, May 1980. San Diego, Cali-
      fornia: Community Research Associates, 1980.

      Multimethod study including approximately 50 inter-
      views with nondetained Mexican illegal immigrants, as
      well as analyses of samples of I-213 (apprehended alien
      records) and "Silva-Bell cases" (records of illegal
      immigrants who voluntarily reported to the INS).

965. "Conference Examines Illegal Immigration Controversy."
      National Parks & Conservation Magazine (May 1978):
      24.

966. "Congress May Place a Price Tag on Knowingly Hiring
      Illegal Aliens." *Food Service Marketing*, 43 (1981):
      22.

967. "Controversy over Proposals to Reduce the Number of
      Illegal Aliens in the United States: Pro and Con."
      Congressional Digest, 54 (January 1975). [Whole
      Issue]

968. "Controversy over Proposed Amnesty for Illegal Aliens:
      Pro and Con." *Congressional Digest*, 56 (October
      1977). [Whole Issue]

969. Coombs, Orde. "Illegal Immigrants in New York: The
      Invisible Subculture." *New York* (March 15, 1976):
      33-41.

970. Cornelius, Wayne A. *Illegal Migration to the United States: Recent Research, Findings, Policy Implications, and Research Priorities.* Cambridge, Massachusetts: Center for International Studies, Massachusetts Institute of Technology, 1977.

971. ————. "Interviewing Undocumented Immigrants: Methodological Reflections Based on Fieldwork in Mexico and the U.S." *International Migration Review,* 16 (Summer 1982): 378-411.

Discusses data collection methods and basic issues of research strategy in field studies of unapprehended illegal immigrants living in the United States. Suggests ways to increase the reliability and validity of interview responses. Necessary modifications in format and style of interviews are described. An annotated bibliography of recent field studies of undocumented immigrants is provided.

972. ————. "La migración illegal Mexicana a los Estados Unidos: Conclusiones de investigaciones recientes, implicaciones políticas y prioridades de investigación." *Foro internacional,* 18 (January–March 1978): 399-429.

973. Corwin, Arthur F. "The Numbers Game: Estimates of Illegal Aliens in the United States, 1970-1981." *Law and Contemporary Problems,* 45 (Spring 1982): 223-284.

974. Cross, H.E., and J.A. Sandos. "The Impact of Undocumented Mexican Workers in the United States: A Critical Assessment." Washington, D.C.; Battelle Human Affairs Research Centers, 1979.

Assesses primary data pertinent to Mexican migration issues: the size of the illegal stock and flow; the existence and extent of job displacement; the utilization of social services; the utilization of health care and educational facilities; and other social and cultural costs and benefits. Four appendices are attached: a critical enumeration of major research conducted in the United States and Mexico since 1969; analysis of the migratory process from origins in Mexico to destination in the United States; a directory of research scientists, study centers, and agencies contacted during the course of research for this report; and a bibliography of works consulted.

975. Cuello, José. "Curbing Illegal Immigration from
      Mexico: Obstacles to a Successful Legislative Solu-
      tion." *USA Today*, 114 (March 1986): 10-14.

      Findings: "The Congressional formula for curbing il-
      legal immigration is to legalize an undetermined per-
      centage of the undocumented aliens already residing in
      the United States, while at the same time beefing up
      the forces of the Border Patrol. What Congress ignores
      is that Mexican immigration, legal or illegal, has
      interwoven itself into the fabric of American society
      for 100 years. Patterns of behavior and mutual de-
      pendency have been deeply ingrained in both Mexican
      and American societies that will not be broken--they
      can only be modified, redirected, or channeled. The
      legalization proposed will serve only to open up a can
      of worms. It assumes most illegals are homogeneously
      intent on staying here and can prove continuous resi-
      dency for three to five years. Some will be tempted
      but will not have the documentation. Others will ob-
      tain forgeries. Many may reject the offer. Any arbi-
      trary date will break up an undetermined number of
      families and communities. Most important, the flow of
      new illegals will not be stopped."

976. Cummings, Judith. "Patrol Searches Harder as Mexicans
      Seek Easier Life in U.S." *New York Times*, August 30,
      1982, p. A-10.

977. Cuthbert, Richard W. "The Economic Incentives Facing
      Illegal Mexican Aliens in the U.S.: A Case Study at
      Hood River, Oregon." Unpublished S.M. thesis on
      Agricultural and Resource Economics, Oregon State
      University, Corvallis, August 1979.

      Interviews with 93 Mexican illegals employed by 30
      applegrowers in the Hood River Valley of north-central
      Oregon. Employers were randomly selected.

978. ————, and Joe B. Stevens. "The Net Economic Incen-
      tive for Illegal Mexican Migration: A Case Study."
      International Migration Review, 15 (Fall 1981): 543-
      550.

979. Dade County, Florida. *Human Services to Haitian Aliens*.
      Miami: Office of the County Manager, 1977.

980. Dagodag, W. Tim. "Illegal Mexican Aliens in Los
      Angeles: Locational Characteristics." In Richard C.

Jones, ed., *Patterns of Undocumented Migration: Mexico and the United States.* Totowa, N.J.: Rowman & Allanheld, 1984. Pp. 199-217.

By the 1970s, it was generally acknowledged that the Los Angeles metropolitan area had become an important destination for illegal immigrants from Mexico. Given the clandestine nature of the illegal immigration process and the alien's almost complete aversion to dealing with any agency or institution capable of gathering usable statistical information, little knowledge exists concerning the location of migrants at this destination. It is the purpose of this study to produce a much-needed estimate of the location of illegal Mexican aliens (IMAs) in metropolitan Los Angeles, thereby filling in some gaps in our knowledge of this illegal migration cycle. Several topics will be addressed in producing this estimate and in the accompanying analysis. In order of discussion, the topics are: the general background of Hispanic population increases in Los Angeles and the implications for illegal immigration; the formulation of a methodology which approximates the location of IMAs; a cartographic display of these locations; and an analysis of the locational patterns with an emphasis on ecological factors that are associated with housing, employment, and inter-racial and inter-ethnic characteristics.

981. ————. "Illegal Mexican Immigration to California from Western Mexico." In Richard C. Jones, ed., *Patterns of Undocumented Migration: Mexico and the United States.* Totowa, N.J.: Rowman & Allanheld, 1984. Pp. 61-73.

Although overlooked for decades, illegal immigration into the American Southwest from Mexico has not reached levels where considerable public interest has been evoked. Furthermore, the current scale and magnitude of illegal crossings induces a set of socioeconomic problems which beset the whole American Southwest. Concern for this topic can initiate public action involving domestic labor, which may result in the formulation of ameliorative policies dealing with labor force questions, migrant treatment, and citizenship status. This study reviews basic regional problems associated with illegal Mexican aliens. Through the use of a case study focusing on California, it generates a profile of illegal immigrants examined from several perspectives, both spatial and aspatial.

982. ———. "Source Regions and Composition of Illegal
      Mexican Immigration to California." *International
      Migration Review*, 9 (1975): 499-511.

      Finds that most illegal Mexicans come from the west
      central section of Mexico, which also furnished labor
      for the *bracero* program that employed 400,000 Mexicans
      in the United States each year from 1943 to 1964.
      Young *mestizo* men from this rural area continue to
      respond to historical patterns of legal recruitment as
      well as to illegal smugglers.

983. Dallek, G. "Health Care for Undocumented Immigrants:
      A Story of Neglect." *Clearinghouse Review*, 14 (August/
      September 1980): 407-14.

984. Davidson, C.A. "Characteristics of Deportable Aliens
      Located in the Interior of the United States." Paper
      presented at Population Association of America, Annual
      Meeting, Washington, D.C., March 26-28, 1981.

      Analysis of apprehension data was undertaken by the
      Immigration and Naturalization Service (INS) with the
      aid of the Bureau of the Census. The Service's form
      I-213, Record of Deportable Alien, is the basic data-
      collection instrument administered to known illegal
      aliens. The aim of this study is to analyze data from
      a sample of I-213 forms to determine demographic and
      economic characteristics of illegal aliens apprehended
      in the interior of the United States in calendar year
      1978. The importance of such an analysis is twofold:
      (1) to increase our knowledge of the illegal alien
      population and (2) to examine the validity of the I-213
      form as a statistical data-gathering mechanism.

985. Davidson, John. *The Long Road North*. New York: Double-
      day & Co., 1979.

986. Day, Mark. "Illegal Immigrants: A View from the
      Barrio." *The Progressive* (February 1974): 46-48.

987. ———. "Rounding Up the Aliens." *Christian Century*
      (July 18, 1973): 748-49.

988. ———. "Sweeping Up the Aliens." *The Nation* (February
      5, 1977): 146-148.

989. Deedy, John. "Illegal Aliens: Appeal for Legislation
      Granting Amnesty." *Commonweal* (June 20, 1975): 194.

990. Del Olmo, Frank. "The Invasion of the Illegals." *Race Relations Reporter*, 4 (September 1973): 20-25.

991. Di Marzio, Nicholas Anthony, Jr. "Profiling Undocumented Aliens in the New York Metropolitan Area: Social Welfare and Labor Market Implications." Unpublished Ph.D. dissertation. Rutgers University, 1985.

992. Domestic Council, Committee on Illegal Aliens. *Preliminary Report of the Domestic Council*. Washington, D.C.: Department of Justice, 1976.

993. Doudnauth, S. "A Study of Health Problems and Practices Among Guyanese Illegal Alien Families." Unpublished Ed.D. dissertation. Columbia University, Teachers College, 1982.

994. Downes, Richard. "Future Consequences of Illegal Immigration." *Futurist*, 11 (1977): 125-127.

    Predicts that the United States will become increasingly Spanish-speaking because of the unrestrained influx of illegal immigrants. Suggests two possible outcomes: either through peaceful transition, the country becomes entirely and officially Spanish-speaking, or violence occurs between the two language groups and the Spanish-speaking Southwest breaks off to form a separate country.

995. Dupuy, Frank C. "'No Support from Washington': What a Border Agent Tells Carter." *U.S. News & World Report* (April 25, 1977): 35-37.

996. Economic Development Council of New York City, Inc. *The Illegal Alien and the Economy. Looking Ahead in New York City*. New York: Economic Development Council, 1977.

997. *El otro lado. Una guia para los indocumentados*. Albuquerque: New Mexico People and Energy, 1980.

    Intended for undocumented workers; addresses the main concerns of illegal aliens and includes a list of supportive labor unions, legal sources, and other agencies.

998. Elwell, Patricia J. "Haitian and Dominican Undocumented Aliens in New York City: A Preliminary Report." *Migration Today*, 5 (December 1977): 5-9.

999. "Employers May Pay if They Hire Illegals." *Business Week* (June 21, 1982): 38.

1000. "Enlisting Employers in the Alien Hunt." *Business Week* (October 18, 1976): 46.

1001. "Enterprising Border Jumpers." *Time* (May 19, 1975): 14-15.

1002. "Estimating Illegals (Illegal Migrants from Mexico Living in the United States)." *American Demographic*, 5 (August 1983): 14.

1003. "Exploited Illegal Workers Help Create Unfair Price Competition." *Industry Week* (November 8, 1971): 28-29.

1004. "Extended Border Search and Probable Cause." *Washington University Law Quarterly* (Fall 1973): 889-96.

1005. Falasco, Dee. "Economic Fertility Differences Between Legal and Illegal Migrant Mexican Families: The Potential Effects of Immigration Policy Changes." Unpublished Ph.D. dissertation. University of Southern California, 1982.

1006. Farrell, James. *Give Us Your Poor: The Immigration Bomb*. San Francisco: Fulton-Hall, 1976.

1007. Feldman, C. "Uncle Sam's Unwelcomed Boarders." *Nation's Business*, 70 (April 1982): 26-27.

1008. Fenton, R.E. *Illegal Immigration to the United States: A Growing Problem for Law Enforcement*. Newport, Rhode Island: Naval War College, 1983.

   Examines the magnitude and impact of illegal immigration to the United States and possible strategies to reduce the problem.

1009. Fitzgerald, M. "Illegal Aliens Done in by Heartwarming Story." *Editor and Publisher, The Fourth Estate*, 117 (August 4, 1984): 45.

1010. Fitzhugh, David. "The Silent Invasion." *Foreign Service Journal* (January 1976): 7-10+.

1011. Flores, Estevan T. "The Impact of Undocumented Migration on the U.S. Labor Market." *Houston Journal of Inter-*

national *Law*, 5 (Spring 1983): 287-321.

After briefly reviewing the historical role of immigrant labor in this country, (1) treats as a working hypothesis the observation that unfavorable economic conditions and not individuals such as undocumented workers cause unemployment; and (2) examines the positive economic impact of undocumented workers' employment. Concludes that "undocumented immigrants play a vital role in the overall scheme of production and in the most recent societal trend of production reorganization. In production plans as a whole, immigrants filter into the labor market at jobs that are, for the most part, unattractive to the domestic labor force. In terms of production reorganization, mobile and fiscally weighty corporate capital flies from areas of worker strength to areas where cheap labor is available."

1012. ————. "Post-*Bracero* Undocumented Mexican Immigration to the United States and Political Recomposition." Unpublished Ph.D. dissertation. University of Texas (Austin), 1982.

1013. ————. "Research on Undocumented Immigrants and Public Policy: A Study of the Texas School Case." *International Migration Review*, 18 (Fall 1984): 505-523.

The Texas School Case arose over an attempt to deny undocumented immigrant children (irregular status migrants) access to public education. Reviews and evaluates the case and social, political, and educational issues pertinent to it. Further provides social and demographic data from a sample of parents of undocumented children while analyzing the international ramifications of the case.

1014. Fogel, Walter A. "Illegal Alien Workers in the United States." *Industrial Relations*, 16 (1977): 243-263.

Sees the flow of illegal immigration as a continuation of the *bracero* program, augmented by other factors. When the program ended, the needs on both sides of the border did not. Mexico's spiralling population growth and the United States' need for labor in the late 1960s, when the market was tight, encouraged the continuation of the flow of workers north. The 1965 law added its own impetus by including the work certification provision. Places part of the responsibility for large illegal immigration on the Immigration and Naturaliza-

tion Service, which has very little power or incentive
to enforce the law, particularly because it lacks the
support of other institutions. Penalties for hiring
illegal immigrants are so light as to be ineffective.

1015.   ————. *Mexican Illegal Alien Workers in the United
         States.* Los Angeles: University of California, Insti-
         tute of Industrial Relations, 1978.

1016.   ————. "United States Immigration Policy and Unsanc-
         tioned Migrants." *Industrial and Labor Relations
         Review,* 33 (April 1980): 295-311.

1017.   Foster, Doug. "Not So Wonderful World of Disneylandia."
         Progressive, 45 (September 1981): 19-20.

1018.   ————, and Joan Zoloth. "Like Outlaws, Like Thieves:
         How 'Illegal Aliens' Take the Rap for Our Economic
         Problems." *Mother Jones* (April 1976): 11-17.

1019.   Fragomen, Austin T., Jr. "Alien Employment." *Inter-
         national Migration Review,* 13 (Fall 1979): 527-31.

1020.   ————. "Constitutional Rights of Aliens upon Arrest."
         International Migration Review, 7 (Spring 1973):
         67-71.

Congress has delegated to Immigration and Naturalization Service broad power to regulate the flow of aliens
into the United States and to regulate their activities
while in the United States. However, these powers are
tempered by the Constitutional rights of aliens which
flow to them solely as a result of their presence in
the United States. There is a delicate balance between
the power of Immigration and Naturalization Service
Officers to interrogate and arrest without warrant
under Section 287 of the Immigration and Nationality
Act and the right of the alien guaranteed by the Fourth
Amendment to be free of any unreasonable searches or
seizures. The Immigration and Naturalization Services
is charged by law to prevent unlawful entries by aliens
and to detect aliens who enter or remain in the United
States unlawfully. The basic tool to perform this task
is Section 287 of the Immigration and Naturalization
Act which contains several subsections, the first of
which states that any officer or employee of the Immigration and Naturalization Service authorized under
regulations prescribed by the Attorney General shall
have power without warrant to interrogate any alien or

person believed to be an alien as to his right to be
or to remain in the United States. The key words in
the section are contained in the phrase "alien or person *believed* to be an alien." There can be no lawful
interrogation without a reasonable belief or suspicion
that the person is an alien.

1021.   ————. "Criminal Sanctions and Amnesty Bill Passes
         House Judiciary Committee." *International Migration
         Review,* 9 (Winter 1975): 557-563.

1022.   ————. *The Illegal Alien: Criminal or Economic Refu-
         gee.* Staten Island, New York: Center for Migration
         Studies, 1973.

1023.   ————. "President Carter's Amnesty and Sanctions Pro-
         posal." *International Migration Review,* 11 (Winter
         1977): 524-532.

"On August 4, 1977, the Carter Administration announced
its program regarding undocumented aliens and sanctions
to be imposed upon employers. A bill, H.R. 9531, embodying this proposal was introduced on behalf of the
Administration by Congressman Peter Rodino, on October
12, 1977. Specifically the President's proposal covers
the following areas: (1) employer sanctions; (2) border
enforcement; (3) adjustment status; (4) foreign policy;
(5) temporary workers; and (6) general immigration
policy."

1024.   ————. "Rights of Aliens upon Arrest: Revisited."
         International Migration Review, 9 (Fall 1975): 383-
         385.

"On June 24, 1975 the Supreme Court in the case of
United States v. Brignoni-Ponce held that the Fourth
Amendment does not allow a roving patrol or border
patrol to stop a vehicle and question its occupants
about their citizenship and immigration status when
the only ground for suspicion was that the occupants
appeared to be of Mexican ancestry. In 1973, the
Supreme Court in the case of *Almeida-Sanchez v. the
United States,* 413 U.S. 266 (1973), held that the
Fourth Amendment prohibited the use of roving patrols
to search vehicles without a warrant or probable cause
at points removed from the border and its functional
equivalence. Under the rule enunciated in *Almeida-
Sanchez,* it was necessary for the Immigration Service to
demonstrate that either the search took place at the

border or a functional equivalent thereof. Functional
equivalency was determined by whether there was any
access to the particular point where the stop took
place that would have originated in the United States
and not necessitated the automobile crossing the
border."

1025.   ———. "Searching for Illegal Aliens" The Immigration
        Service Encounters the Fourth Amendment." *San Diego
        Law Review*, 13 (December 1975): 82-124.

1026.   ———. "U.S. Supreme Court's Decision on Non-
        Citizenship." *International Migration Review*, 8
        (Spring 1974): 77-78.

On November 19, 1973 the United States Supreme Court
ruled that a rejection of an application for employment
by a private employer because the applicant is an alien
is not a violation of the Civil Rights Act of 1964.
Espinoza v. Farah Manufacturing Company, Inc., Section
703 of Title 7 of the Civil Rights Act makes it unlawful
for an employer to refuse to hire an individual because
of race, color, religion, sex, or national origin.
The facts of the case are uncomplicated. The wife was
a permanent resident alien residing in the State of
Texas married to a United States citizen. She applied
for a job as a seamstress with the Farah Manufacturing
Company and her application was rejected on the basis
of a company policy prohibiting the employment of non-
U.S. citizens. She contended in Court that the Farah
Manufacturing Company had discriminated against her
because of "national origin" in violation of the Civil
Rights Act of 1964, under the above-cited definition.
The District Court, agreeing with her argument, held
that refusal to hire her because of lack of U.S. citizenship constituted discrimination on the basis of
national origin. The Court of Appeals reversed. The
United States Supreme Court granted the writ of certiorari
and affirmed the ruling of the Court of Appeals, with
Mr. Justice Marshall speaking for the majority. The
case was decided on the narrow ground of statutory con-
struction--that is, an interpretation of the terminology
"national origin." The majority pointed out "the term
national origin on its face referred to the country
where a person was born, or more broadly, the country
from which his or her ancestors came." The Court went
on to find the term "national origin" was different
than citizenship and, therefore, discrimination on the

basis of national origin, and the statute does not
prohibit discrimination on the basis of citizenship.

1027. Francke, Linda Bird. "The Mating Game." *Newsweek*
       (January 19, 1976): 48+.

       Discusses fraudulent marriages by illegal aliens.

1028. Fraser, J.C. *Cry of the Illegal Immigrant.* Toronto:
       Williams-Wallace Productions International Inc.,
       1980.

       Joyce Fraser emigrated from Guyana in 1970, entered
       Canada as an illegal immigrant, eventually achieved
       landed immigrant status, and became a Canadian citizen
       in 1976. This is the story of those years between
       emigration and citizenship.

1029. Frisbie, Parker. "Illegal Migration from Mexico: A
       Longitudinal Analysis." *International Migration
       Review*, 9 (Spring 1975): 3-13.

       "Migration is one of the most significant of all
       human behaviors, and a wide range of variables has been
       spanned in the search for possible determinants of the
       redistribution of population. It has been suggested,
       for example, that demographic, political, and psycho-
       logical factors exert a significant causal influence.
       However, regardless of what other variables may be
       operating, migratory streams generally seem to flow
       from a place of origin where economic opportunities
       are restricted to destinations where economic oppor-
       tunities are comparatively great. In the present re-
       search, the economic dimension will constitute the
       basis for an investigation of an intriguing case of
       international migration--the movement of illegal mi-
       grants from Mexico to the United States."

1030. Fuchs, Lawrence H. "Cultural Pluralism and the Future
       of American Unity: The Impact of Illegal Aliens."
       International Migration Review, 18 (Fall 1984):
       800-813.

       Explores the question of the impact of illegal migra-
       tion on American unity and cultural pluralism in the
       United States. Assuming that over time the descendants
       of undocumented workers now in the United States will
       behave substantially like descendants of those who
       immigrate legally, the author concludes that the long-
       term impact of illegal migration barely will be noticeable

provided it is reduced substantially in the future.
The process of acculturation will work in the same way
for both groups as it has for other ethnic groups in
the past, given comparable levels of education and
length of family residence in the United States.
Takes special notice of the illegal migration of
Spanish-speaking workers and hypothesizes that the behavior of their descendants will not differ from the
descendants of other immigrants, legal or illegal, in
ways that disrupt fundamental patterns of American
political unity and cultural pluralism.

1031.   Gall, Norman. "Los indocumentados Colombianos."
        American Universities Field Staff Reports, 16 (Decem-
        ber 1972). [Whole Issue]

1032.   Garcia, Ramon. *Operation Wetback: The Mass Deportation
        of Mexican Undocumented Workers in 1954*. Westport,
        Connecticut: Greenwood Press, 1980.

        Operation Wetback describes the forced repatriation of
        perhaps as many as 1,000,000 Mexican citizens from the
        United States in the summer of 1954. In addition to
        the 4,500,000 workers contracted under the provisions of
        the *bracero* program, there were just as many if not more
        illegal workers, or wetbacks, who crossed the border in
        search of work. This "wetback invasion" was intolerable
        to many groups. Minority organizations such as the
        NAACP and the G.I. Forum believed these workers depressed
        the wage structure and took jobs away from American
        citizens; labor unions shared these beliefs. Church
        and social welfare groups allied with liberal politicans
        and pointed out many instances of inhumane living and
        working conditions which employers forced upon the il-
        legal entrants and many who worked under contractual
        provisions of the international agreement. Growers
        and other employers, fearful that the chorus of criti-
        cisms might ultimately deprive them of cheap, plentiful
        braceros, agreed that something had to be done to check
        the increasing number of wetbacks in the Southwest.
        The report of the President's Commission on Migratory
        Labor in 1951 supported critics when it found proof of
        widespread abuse of workers and exacerbation of existing
        social ills. This imprimatur of the federal government
        then led to full coverage of the "invasion" by the print
        and electronic media. Negative stereotyping of the
        workers, now in the full glare of publicity, further
        heightened perceived dangers because most Americans
        "continued to blame the victims for their status in

society." The Immigration and Naturalization Service's "Operation Wetback" mollified rising public concern, and provided at the same time the best political solution available.

1033. Garcia, Victor Quiroz. *Undocumented Mexicans in Two Los Angeles Communities: A Social and Economic Profile*. La Jolla, California: Center for U.S.-Mexican Studies, University of California, San Diego. Monograph Series, No. 4, 1982.

Based on interviews with some 200 nondetained, undocumented Mexican immigrants living in two neighborhoods of Los Angeles.

1034. Garcia y Griego, Manuel. "El volumen de la migración de Mexicanos no documentados a los Estados Unidos." [Mexico City]: Secretaria de trabajo y previsión social, 1980.

1035. ————. *El volumen de la migración de Mexicanos no documentados a los Estados Unidos. Nuevas hipótesis*. Mexico City: Centro nacional de información y estadísticas del trabajo, 1979.

1036. Gatty, B. "Uncle Sam Wants You--To Help Catch Illegal Aliens." *Hotel and Motel Management*, 198 (June 1983): 17.

1037. Goldman, R.L., and P.J. Connors. "Aliens May File Fiscal Year Returns: What Are the Implications of the Service's New Position?" *Journal of Taxation*, 55 (November 1981): 294-6.

1038. Gonzales, J.L., Jr. "The Contribution of Undocumented Mexican Laborers to the American Economy." Paper presented at the Western Social Science Meeting, San Diego, California, April 27, 1984.

Discussion of the economic contributions of undocumented workers to the American economy begins with a brief review of the characteristics of the "split" or "dual" labor market, composed of undocumented Mexican aliens. Premise of paper is that the tertiary labor market was created and is maintained in an effort to provide American entrepreneurs with a neverending source of cheap labor. At the practical level examples of their economic contributions to U.S. economy are drawn from the persistent and pervasive "wage differen-

tials" that exist in the U.S. market, in the garment
and restaurant industries, motels and hotels, hospitals
and convalescent homes, landscape and construction,
agriculture and horticulture, etc., where heavy concentrations of undocumented workers are commonplace.
Concludes by addressing the issues regarding the type
of social services that are utilized by undocumented
aliens and the various taxes that are paid to the
American economy as a result of their participation
in the tertiary labor market.

1039. Gordon, Charles. "The Problem of Illegal Entries into
the United States." *Interpreter Releases* (December 6,
1971): 352-58.

1040. Gordon, Wendell. "A Case for a Less Restrictive Border
Policy." *Social Science Quarterly*, 56 (December
1975): 485-91.

1041. ————. "The Problem of Illegal Aliens." *Texas Business Review*, 51 (August 1977): 167-70.

1042. Gottron, Martha V. "Illegal Alien Curbs: House Action
Stalled." *Congressional Quarterly Weekly Report*
(March 20, 1976): 637-41.

1043. Graham, Otis L. *Illegal Immigration and the New Reform
Movement*. Washington, D.C.: Federation for American
Immigration Reform, 1980.

Defines the present problem, evaluates the conserva-
tive and liberal restrictionism as well as the political
and international realities and proposes a moral restrictionism.

1044. ————. "Illegal Immigration and the New Restrictionism." *Center Magazine*, 12 (1979): 54-64.

Argues that the old restrictionism of the 1920s and
1950s came from the political right but the new restrictionism of the 1970s and 1980s ought to come from
a centrist or even liberal position. Implies that to
be successful, restrictionism ought to change its
course. Proposes to defend restriction of immigration
on two grounds. First is that of population stabilization. With new concerns about energy use, the question
of population stabilization has changed from "whether
or not to advocate it" to "whom." Since the change is
imminent, limiting immigration could and should take

place within a framework of tolerance and a climate of pluralism. Second argument centers on the effect of immigration on the labor market. Argues that illegal immigration encourages a two-class society. People in the bottom sector suffer from inadequate protection on the job and from poor pay.

1045. ———. "The Problem That Will Not Go Away." *Center Magazine*, 10 (1977): 56-66.

Illegal immigrants are a polyglot group, including particularly large numbers of Mexicans, Jamaicans, Dominicans, Haitians, Koreans, Filipinos, Thais, and Taiwanese who come from countries that experience rapid economic development, displacement of rural populations, explosive urban growth, and high unemployment. The "push" factors are augmented by strong historic links to the United States. Relatively weak sanctions await those who enter illegally and are apprehended: few are actually deported.

1046. Grant, Bruce. *The Boat People*. New York: Penguin Books, 1980.

1047. Grasmuck, Sherri. "Immigration, Ethnic Stratification, and Native Working Class Discipline: Comparisons of Documented and Undocumented Dominicans." *International Migration Review*, 18 (Fall 1984): 692-713.

A number of notions regarding the functions served by international labor immigration, especially the undocumented population, are examined in this article. Comparisons of the working conditions of documented and undocumented Dominicans in New York City are made. Although the two groups resemble one another in terms of organization and industrial sector of employment, the organization of their respective firms is markedly different. It is concluded that one of the most important functions served by the illegal alien population is political and resides in its controllability by employers in the secondary labor market and, consequently, operates to discipline the native labor force.

1048. Greene, Sheldon L. "Immigration Law and Rural Poverty--The Problems of the Illegal Entrant." *Duke Law Journal* (1969): 475-94.

1049. ———. "Public Agency Distortion of Congressional Will: Federal Policy Toward Non-Resident Alien Labor." *George Washington Review*, 40 (March 1972): 440-63.

1050. Griffith, E. "The Alien Meets Some Constitutional
       Hurdles in Employment, Education, and Aid Programs."
       San Diego Law Review, 17 (1980): 201-231.

       Describes the legal obstacles often encountered by
       aliens attempting to take advantage of opportunities
       available to U.S. citizens and examines the major court
       decisions resulting. Finds some inconsistency and
       suggests that the Supreme Court is beginning to take a
       harder look at the role of aliens in the political com-
       munity and is restricting to citizens the functions of
       representative government.

1051. Grossman, J.B. "Illegal Immigrants and Domestic Employ-
       ment." *Industrial Labor Relations Review*, 37 (January
       1984): 240-251.

1052. Hadley, E.M. "A Critical Analysis of the Wetback
       Problem." *Law and Contemporary Problems*, 21 (Spring
       1966): 335-338.

1053. Hager, Barry M. "Illegal Aliens: Carter Prepares His
       Bill." *Congressional Quarterly Weekly Report*
       (April 30, 1977): 822-23+.

1054. Hahn, Richard F. "Constitutional Limits on the Power
       to Exclude Aliens." *Columbia Law Review*, 82 (June
       1982): 957-997.

1055. Hainer, Margaret, ed. "Undocumented Immigrant Workers
       in New York City." *Nacla Report on the Americas*, 13
       (November-December 1979): 2-46.

1056. Halsell, Grace. *The Illegals*. New York: Stein and
       Day, 1978.

       Excerpt: "But if this suggests the great era of Euro-
       pean immigration, there is a difference: the Europeans
       could come in legally, unhampered by quotas. Most
       Mexican immigrants, however, are illegal--'undocumented,'
       as the government euphemistically puts it. In its war
       effort against the illegals, the United States has flung
       men, weapons, and dollars into fruitless tactics to
       stanch the flow. The war has demanded the attention
       of Presidents, cabinet members, legislators, other high
       officials, and the TV and print media. It is a war that
       influences all our daily life--the food we eat, the
       education of our children, the language we speak, the
       taxes we pay. It is a war of mercenaries against a

people expressing their instinct to survive. It is a grim game of life, death, and desperation which both sides realize can never be won as it now is being waged."

1057. Hansen, Christopher T. "Behind the Paper Curtain: Asylum Policy vs. Asylum Practice." *New York University Review of Law and Social Change*, 7 (Winter 1978): 107-141.

1058. Harper, Michael C., and Mitchel Ostrer. "Aliens and the Apple Harvest (Along the Eastern Seaboard)." *New Leader*, 60 (September 12, 1977): 7-9.

1059. Harwood, Edwin. *In Liberty's Shadow: Illegal Aliens and Immigration Law Enforcement.* Stanford, California: Hoover Institution Press, 1986.

1060. Healy, Lynn D. "Meet Mexico's Migrants." *American Demographic*, 6 (February 1984): 40.

1061. Heberton, Craig. "To Educate or Not to Educate: The Plight of Undocumented Alien Children in Texas." *Washington University Law Quarterly*, 60 (Spring 1982): 119-159.

1062. Heer, D.M., and D. Falasco. "Determinants of Earnings Among Three Groups of Mexican-Americans: Undocumented Immigrants, Legal Immigrants and the Native Born." Paper presented at Population Association of America. Annual Meeting. Minneapolis, May 3-5, 1984.

Controversy has arisen concerning whether the earnings of undocumented Mexican workers are lower than those of legal Mexican immigrant workers holding constant other relevant characteristics. Data were obtained from two systematic samples of Los Angeles County birth certificates in which either the mother or the father of the baby was reported to be of Mexican origin and in which the mother was either born in or outside the United States. Multivariate analyses were conducted with three dependent variables: (1) the natural log of annual earnings in hundreds of dollars in 1979; (2) total hours worked in 1979; and (3) the natural log of the average hourly wage in dollars in 1979. For both fathers and mothers it was found that being a legal rather than an undocumented immigrant had a statistically significant positive impact on the hourly wage.

Findings concerning the impact of other independent
variables on the hourly wage and other dependent variables are also reported.

1063. Hendricks, Glenn L. "The Phenomenon of Migrant Illegality: The Case of Dominicans in New York." Paper
presented at the Society for Applied Anthropology
Annual Meeting, Amsterdam, Netherlands, March 19-22,
1975. ERIC microfiche: ED110548.

1064. Herbert, J.D. "Defining Resident Alien Status for Income Tax Purposes." *Virginia Journal of International
Law*, 24 (Spring 1984): 667-694.

Reviews the background of law that has shaped the
present residence guidelines concerning income tax.
Describes and analyzes proposed legislation and suggests
alternative ways of taxing foreigners in the United
States.

1065. Hibbard, Robert L. "Roving Border Searches for Illegal
Aliens: Avoiding the Exclusionary Rule." *Marquette
Law Review*, 59 (1976): 856-75.

1066. "Hiring Penalties: Employing Illegal Aliens May Result
in Fines, Jail." *Engineering News Journal*, 208
(June 10, 1982): 58-59.

1067. Hohl, Donald G., and Michael G. Wenk. "The Illegal
Alien and the Western Hemisphere Immigration Dilemma."
International Migration Review, 7 (Fall 1973): 323-
332.

The House of Representatives Subcommittee on Immigration and Nationality under the new chairmanship of
Representative Joshua Eilberg (D. Pa.) announced the
priorities of its concern for the 93rd Congress as
legislation to control the influx of illegal aliens
into the United States, a preference system for the
Western Hemisphere to regulate the flow of immigration,
and an examination of the functions and operations of
the U.S. Immigration and Naturalization Service in line
with the Subcommittee's oversight role in this area
of governmental operations.

1068. Houstoun, Marion F. "Aliens in Irregular Status in the
United States: Review of Their Numbers, Characteris-
tics and Role in the U.S. Labor Market." *International
Migration*, 21 (1983): 372-414.

Describes aliens in irregular status, mainly from Latin America, especially Mexico. Historical and geographical factors are considered, as are the size of the population, length of stay, characteristics, and role in the U.S. labor market.

1069. "How Illegal Aliens Rob Jobs from Unemployed Americans." *Nation's Business* (May 1975): 18-20+.

1070. "How Millions of Illegal Aliens Sneak into U.S." *U.S. News & World Report* (July 22, 1974): 27-30.

1071. Huddle, Donald L. *Illegals in the Texas Economy.* Department of Economics, Rice University, Houston, 1982.

1072. Huss, John D., and Melanie J. Wirkin. "Illegal Immigration: The Hidden Population Bomb." *Futurist*, 11 (1977): 114-120.

Observes that unmarried males coming north to work are the first immigration installment; later come their wives and families. Once all are established in their new homes, the process is no longer reversible. Recommends employer sanctions and incentives to sending countries to keep their people at home.

1073. "Illegal Aliens: Counting Costs and Benefits (Los Angeles)." *Economist*, 283 (May 8, 1982): 40.

1074. "Illegal Aliens: A Flood of Mail on a Hot Issue." *U.S. News & World Report* (July 4, 1977): 31-32.

1075. "Illegal Aliens: From Their Own Point of View." *U.S. News & World Report* (February 20, 1978): 36.

1076. "Illegal Aliens: A Right to Learn." *Economist*, 283 (June 19, 1982): 46-47.

1077. "Illegal Immigrants: The Problem That Won't Go Away." *The Economist* (August 13, 1977): 29-30.

1078. "Illegal Immigrants: The U.S. May Gain More Than It Loses." *Business Week* (May 14, 1984): 126.

1079. "Illegal Immigration and the Labor Force." In W.B. Littrell and G. Sjoberg, Eds. *Current Issues in Social Policy.* London: Sage Publications, 1976. Pp. 95-157.

Second part of the volume contains the following
chapters which were originally prepared as working
papers for an interdisciplinary conference, "The
Measurement of Social and Economic Data and Public
Policy," held on April 10-11, 1975, at the University
of Texas at Austin; V.S. Martinez, "Illegal Immigration
and the Labor Force: A Historical and Legal View";
V.M. Briggs, Jr., "Illegal Immigration and the Labor
Force: The Use of 'Soft' Data for Analysis"; G. Cardenas,
"Public Data on Mexican Immigration into the United
States: A Critical Evaluation"; J. Bustamante, "Struc-
tural and Ideological Conditions of Undocumented Mexican
Immigration to the United States."

1080.   "Illegal Immigration: NCPA Urges Strong Controls to
        Stem the Tide of Illegal Aliens." *National Parks &
        Conservation Magazine* (July 1978): 26-27.

1081.   Illinois. General Assembly. Legislative Investigating
        Commission. *The Illegal Mexican Alien Problem.*
        [Chicago, 1971.]

1082.   "Immigration: The Alien Wave." *Newsweek* (February 9,
        1976): 56-57.

1083.   [Industrial and Labor Relations] *I.L.R. Report.* "Il-
        legal Immigration from Mexico." 20 (Spring 1983):
        7-28.

        Includes the following articles: "Illegal Immigration
        from Mexico and Its Labor Force Implications" by V.M.
        Briggs; "The Characteristics of Illegal Aliens" by D.S.
        North and M.F. Houston; "Illegal Immigration: Good for
        One and Good for All?" by R.S. Smith; "The AFL-CIO and
        Immigration Reform" by J.F. Otero; "Blaming the Victim"
        by M. Chishti; "S.2222, Employer Sanctions and Civil
        Liberties" by Senator A.K. Simpson.

1084.   "INS Given More Freedom to Search for Illegals." *Res-
        taurant and Institution*, 89 (September 15, 1981): 16.

1085.   "In Search of the Border: Searches Conducted by Federal
        Customs and Immigration Officers." *New York University
        Journal of International Law and Politics*, 5 (Spring
        1972): 93-115.

1086.   "'Invasion' by Illegal Aliens, and the Problems They
        Create." *U.S. News & World Report* (July 23, 1973):
        32-35.

1087. Jackson, Jacquelyne. "Illegal Aliens: Big Threat to Black Workers." *Ebony* (April 1979): 33-40.

1088. Jacoby, Susan. "Immigrants from Mexico: The Struggle to Be Legal." *New Leader* (April 28, 1975): 14-16.

1089. Jaynes, Gregory. "U.S. Announces New Policy for Parole of Some Haitians." *New York Times*, June 15, 1982, p. A-24.

1090. Jenkins, J. Craig. "Push/Pull in Illegal Mexican Migration to the United States." *International Migration Review*, 11 (1977): 178-189.

Concentrates on push factors operating since 1948. Sees Mexican economic developments as relatively unresponsive to the needs of a peasant agriculture.

1091. Johnson, Kenneth F. "Stranded Mexican Aliens in Missouri and Illinois: A Spectrum of Livability and Human Rights Issues." Paper presented to the Annual Convention of the Rocky Mountain Council on Latin American Studies, El Paso, May 5, 1979.

1092. ———, and Nina M. Ogle. *Illegal Mexican Aliens in the United States: A Teaching Manual in Impact Dimensions and Alternative Futures.* Washington, D.C.: University Press of America, 1978.

1093. ———, and Miles W. Williams. *Illegal Aliens in the Western Hemisphere: Political and Economic Factors.* New York: Praeger, 1981.

"In the Western Hemisphere, the focal area of this book, illegal immigration (including clandestine, unsnactioned, fraudulent, and/or undocumented entry) is reaching crisis proportions for some governments. In this study we consider the ideal of creating a hemispheric community-of-nations government as one approach to handling what is clearly a hemispheric dilemma. We devote the majority of our attention to analysis in its various stages and locations." Contents: Population Exchange in the Western Hemisphere; Strategies for Handling Illegal Aliens in the Western Hemisphere and Elsewhere; Illegal Mexican and Other Aliens in North America; Clandestine Migration Between Colombia and Venezuela; Clandestine Immigration into Argentina and Within the Southern Cone; Extralegal Population Transfer: Conclusions and Policy Development.

1094.   Jones, Richard C. "Channelization of Undocumented
        Mexican Migrants to the U.S." *Economic Geography*,
        58 (1982): 156-176.

1095.   ———. "Macro-Patterns of Undocumented Migration
        Between Mexico and the U.S." In Richard C. Jones, ed.,
        *Patterns of Undocumented Migration: Mexico and the
        United States*. Totowa, N.J.: Rowman and Allanheld,
        1984. Pp. 33-57.

        Approximately 100,000 to 300,000 people annually
        come to the United States, constituting between 3 and
        10 percent of total U.S. population growth. It is also
        clear that the typical migrant is young, male, and
        usually unskilled in nonagricultural work. He is poor
        but not among the poorest from his village. He usually
        (in 60 percent of the cases) comes from a small town
        or rural area in Mexico, but is usually (in 70 percent
        of the cases) destined for an urban area in the United
        States. He seldom makes a planned, discretionary
        move but is driven by episodic economic necessity at
        the origin and thus is most properly referred to as an
        "economic refugee." He spends six months to a year
        in the United States before returning to Mexico and
        makes four or five such trips in a lifetime. Therefore,
        he is a temporary as opposed to a permanent migrant.
        Finally, while sending home one third of his earnings
        on the average, he makes few claims on local social
        services and is quite pleased to work at wages below
        the legal minimum. Because of his limited participation
        in skilled occupations, his high productivity in un-
        skilled work, his temporary status, his scant demand
        on social services, and his acceptance of low wages,
        the undocumented Mexican's impact on the host society
        may well be positive or at least neutral.

1096.   ———, ed. *Patterns of Undocumented Migration: Mexico
        and the United States*. Totowa, N.J.: Rowman and
        Allanheld, 1984.

        Jones focuses upon spatial patterns of migrant
        origins, destinations, and flows and the factors which
        explain them. The contributed articles are arranged
        by geographic/political regions, facilitating the com-
        parison of urban areas, regions, and states and en-
        couraging examination of factors operating at those
        scales of analysis. Throughout, the authors are con-
        cerned with the interconnections between regions, in-
        volving such issues as the incidence of step or chain

migration, the relationship between internal and international migration, the flow of repatriated earnings within Mexico, and the displacement of resident Chicanos by undocumenteds within metropolitan areas. Contents: Preface; Introduction; Overview: Changing Patterns of Undocumented Migration from Mexican States in Recent Years, Jorge A. Bustamante; Macro-Patterns of Undocumented Migration between Mexico and the United States, Richard C. Jones; Origins in Mexico: Illegal Mexican Immigration to California from Western Mexico, W. Tim Dagodag; Agricultural Development and Labor Mobility: A Study of Four Mexican Subregions, Kenneth D. Roberts; Patterns of U.S. Migration from a Mexican Town, Joshua S. Reichert and Douglas S. Massey; External Dependency and the Perpetuation of Temporary Migration to the United States, Raymond E. Wiest; Network Migration and Mexican Rural Development: A Case Study, Richard Mines; Destinations in the United States: Occupational and Spatial Mobility of Undocumented Migrants from Dolores Hidalgo, Guanajuato, Richard C. Jones, Richard J. Harris, and Avelardo Valdez; The Channelization of Mexican Nationals to the San Luis Valley of Colorado, Phillip R. Guttierez; Illegal Mexican Aliens in Los Angeles: Locational Characteristics, W. Tim Dagodag; Geographical Patterns of Undocumented Mexicans and Chicanos in San Antonio, Texas: 1970 and 1980, Aveladro Valdez and Richard C. Jones.

1097. ———, et al. "Occupational and Spatial Mobility of Undocumented Migrants from Dolores Hidalgo, Guanajuato." In Richard C. Jones, ed., *Patterns of Undocumented Migration: Mexico and the United States.* Totowa, N.J.: Rowman and Allanheld, 1984. Pp. 159-182.

Recent research on spatial mobility of undocumenteds to and within the United States has shown that over time, undocumented patterns have dispersed northward. This research has not revealed much at all about successive moves of individual migrants. The most popular conception is of undocumented migrants rooted to particular geographic localities year after year, by reason of kinship ties, fear of apprehension, lack of awareness of new opportunities, poverty, and the problems associated with adapting to new surroundings. This article shows that this impression is erroneous. Not only do migrants exhibit substantial geographic mobility, but it is of a highly organized nature. Furthermore, there is significant upward occupational mobility as well.

Subsequent mobility levels off, however, once the migrant reaches the urban sector, despite the fact that undocumenteds continue to travel long distances to undertake new jobs. The basic purpose of this article is to investigate the degree of occupational mobility among a sample of Mexican undocumenteds who have recently migrated to the United States and to examine how spatial mobility as well as other factors are involved in this phenomenon. As such, it fits into the larger theme of economic impacts on U.S. receiving areas.

1098. ———. "Undocumented Migration from Mexico: Some Geographical Questions." *Annals, Association of American Geographers,* 72 (1982): 77-87.

1099. Karkashian, John E. "The Illegal Alien." Paper presented at the 18th Session, Senior Seminar in Foreign Policy, Foreign Service Institute, Department of State, Washington, D.C., 1976.

1100. Keely, Charles B. "Analysis of Methodology Used for the Lesko Associates Study on Illegal Aliens." Paper presented at the American Immigration and Citizenship Conference, January 21, 1976.

1101. ———. "Counting the Untouchable: Estimates of Undocumented Aliens in the United States." *Population and Development Review,* 3 (December 1977): 473-481.

Reviews attempts to estimate the number of undocumented aliens in the United States, concluding that these estimates have been weak. Estimates were based more on budget needs and organizational dynamics than on concern for reliable counts and proper estimation techniques. Suggests that serious problems may result from policies based on inaccurate estimates.

1102. ———, and Ellen Percy. *Profiles of Undocumented Aliens in New York City: Haitians and Dominicans.* Staten Island, New York: Center for Migration Studies, 1978.

1103. ———, and ———. "Recent Net Alien Immigration to the U.S.: Its Impact on Population Growth and Native Fertility." *Demography,* 15 (1978): 267-283.

Shows net immigration to be different from the number of arrivals. Many people come to the United States

declaring their intention to settle. When they change
their minds and leave to reside elsewhere, they are not
counted. The Immigration and Naturalization Service
has not collected statistics on emigration since 1957.
Keely and Percy believe many of the published estimates
to be too low.

1104. ――――, and S.M. Tomasi. "The Disposable Worker:
Historical and Comparative Perspectives on Clandestine
Migration." Paper presented at the Annual Meeting
of the Population Association of America, Montreal,
April 30, 1976.

1105. Kelly, Orr. "Border Crisis: Illegal Aliens out of
Control?" *U.S. News & World Report* (April 25, 1977):
33-39.

1106. ――――. "The Great American Immigration Nightmare."
U.S. News and World Report, June 22, 1981. Pp.
27-31.

"A flood of newcomers to the U.S. threatens to swamp
one of Uncle Sam's most troubled bureaucracies--the
immigration service."

1107. ――――. "Nabbing 29 'Illegals' in One Illinois Town."
U.S. News & World Report (July 4, 1977): 33-34.

1108. Kirsch, Jonathan. "California's Illegal Aliens: They
Give More Than They Take." *New West* (May 23, 1977):
26-28+.

1109. Krauss, M.B. "Unwelcome Guests." *Challenge* (November
1977): 60-61.

1110. Kurzban, Ira J. "Long and Perilous Journey: The Nelson
Decision (Emigration Law)." *Human Rights*, 11 (Summer
1983): 41-44.

1111. Lamm, Richard D., and Gary Imhoff. *The Immigration
Time Bomb: The Fragmenting of America*. New York:
E.P. Dutton, 1985.

Throughout *The Immigration Time Bomb*, the authors
maintain that they are not against moderate levels of
legal immigration, which they feel benefit our country.
They point out the negative social, economic, and
environmental consequences of large-scale legal and
illegal immigration. The methods Lamm proposes to limit

immigration are not designed to "seal the borders,"
"stop illegal immigration," or "end immigration alto-
gether," but to bring it under control: he advocates
strengthening the Border Patrol, computerizing Immigration and Naturalization Service records, limiting family
preferences in legal immigration to immediate relatives
of permanent resident aliens and U.S. citizens, and
setting an annual ceiling on legal immigration and
enforcing it. Lamm also recommends passage of the
Simpson-Mazzoli bill, currently being debated in Congress, that would make it against the law for employers
to knowingly hire illegal alien workers.

1112. Lawrence, Loren E. "The Illegal Immigrant to the
United States: A Profile of the Characteristics and
Techniques and the Impact of His Presence on the
Foreign Service." Paper presented at the 16th Session,
Senior Seminar in Foreign Policy, Foreign Service
Institute, Department of State, Washington, D.C.,
1974.

1113. Leahy, P.J., and S. Castillo. "Making It Illegally."
Unpublished Paper, Department of Sociology, Texas
Christian University, Dallas, Texas, 1977.

1114. "'Legitimate' Discrimination Against Illegitimates: A
Look at *Trimble v. Gordon* and *Fiallo v. Bell*."
Journal of Family Law, 16 (November 1977): 57-75.

1115. Legomsky, S.H. "Suspending the Social Security Benefits
of Deported Aliens: The Insult and the Injury."
Suffolk University Law Review, 13 (Fall 1979): 1235-
83.

1116. Leidigh, Barbara J. "Defense of Sham Marriage Deporta-
tions." *University of California, Davis Law Review*,
8 (1975): 309-22.

1117. [Lesko and Associates]. *Final Report: Basic Data and
Guidance Required to Implement a Major Illegal Alien
Study During Fiscal Year 1976*. Prepared for the
Office of Planning and Evaluation, Immigration and
Naturalization Service, U.S. Department of Justice.
Washington, D.C.: Lesko Associates, 1975.

1118. Lewis, S.G. *Slave Trade Today. American Exploitation
of Illegal Aliens*. Boston: Beacon Press, 1979.

Uncovers "the international network of cut-throat
businessmen--farmers, restauranteurs, industrialists,
and their front men--who thrive on the exploitation
of America's undocumented aliens." Assesses the effect
these immigrants have on American Society and examines
the immigration laws and socioeconomic forces that
create an illegal population.

1119. Lopez, Consuelo Gomez. "Immigrant Status, Security
and Family Role Conflict: A Comparative Study of
Resident Aliens and Undocumented Aliens from Mexico."
Unpublished D.S.W. dissertation, University of
Southern California, 1976.

1120. Los Angeles County Bar Association. Special Committee
on Deportation and Removal of Aliens. *Report on the
Deportation and Removal of Aliens.* Los Angeles, 1976.

1121. Los Angeles Police Department. *Study of the Impact of
Illegal Aliens on Crime in Los Angeles: Ramparts
Division.* Los Angeles, 1974.

1122. Lyman, Stanford M. *Chinese Americans.* New York: Random House, 1974.

Includes discussion of illegal Chinese immigration.

1123. McClellan, Andrew C., and Michael D. Boggs. "Illegal
Aliens: A Story of Human Misery." *American Federationist* (August 1974): 17-23.

1124. Mailman, Stanley. "'Illegal Aliens': A View of the
Employer's Rights and Risks." *Interpreter Releases*
(January 3, 1977): 1-9.

1125. "Majority Would Prosecute Those Who Hire Illegal Aliens."
Gallup Opinion Index (June 1977): 24-28.

1126. Maram, Sheldon L., et al. *Hispanic Workers in the
Garment and Restaurant Industries in Los Angeles
County.* La Jolla, California: Center for U.S.-Mexican
Studies, University of California, San Diego, Working
Papers in U.S.-Mexican Studies, No. 12, October 1980.

Survey study of 499 Hispanic garment workers (81 percent undocumented, 83 percent Mexican nationals) and
327 Hispanic restaurant employees (75 percent undocumented, 85 percent Mexican nationals), interviewed in
workplaces by the staff of the Concentrated Enforcement

Program of the Department of Industrial Relations,
State of California, from June-November 1979.

1127. ———. "The Impact of Undocumented Hispanic Immigration on the Los Angeles Labor Market." Research in
progress, Department of History, California State
University, Fullerton, 1978--.

Survey study of 1,300 undocumented Hispanic workers
conducted between October 1978 and January 1979.

1128. Mariam, Alemazehu Gebre. "The Politics of United
States Immigration Policy: The Case of Recent Undocumented Haitian Entrants." Unpublished Ph.D. dissertation. University of Minnesota, 1984.

1129. Marshall, Dawn I. *The Haitian Problem: Illegal Migration to the Bahamas*. Kingston, Jamaica: Institute
of Social and Economic Research, University of the
West Indies, 1979.

1130. Marshall, F.R. *Illegal Immigration: The Problem, The
Solutions*. Washington, D.C.: Federation for American
Immigration Reform, 1982.

1131. Marshall, Ray. "Inside the Country, Outside the Law."
Worklife (December 1977): 22-26.

1132. Martinez, Vilma S. "Illegal Immigration and the
Labor Force." *American Behavioral Scientist*, 19
(1976): 335-350.

Traces the long record of Spanish-speaking workers
in the Southwest since 1848. During the Depression
of the 1930s, illegal Mexican migrants were deported
and legal ones encouraged to repatriate. Sees the
latest attention on illegal immigration as one more
example in a long history of using Mexican workers as
an elastic labor supply to be sent home when not
needed.

1133. ———. "Illegal Immigration and the Labor Force: A
Historical and Legal View." In W.E. Littrell and
G. Sjoberg, eds. *Current Issues in Social Policy*.
London: Sage Publications, 1976. Pp. 97-112.

Discusses the situation of illegal aliens from a
Mexican-American stance and an historical and legal
perspective.

1134. Massey, D.S., and K.M. Schnabel. "Background and Characteristics of Undocumented Hispanic Migrants to the United States." *Migration Today*, 11 (1983): 46-53.

1135. Maxwell, Evan. "U.S.-Mexico Smuggling: The Buying and Selling of Humans." *Los Angeles Times*, February 22, 1977, pt. 1, p. 3.

1136. Mazón, Mauricio. "Illegal Alien Surrogates: A Psychohistorical Interpretation of Group Stereotyping in Time of Economic Stress." *Aztlan*, 6 (1975): 305-321.

"In the history of United States and Mexican relations, the first illegal aliens were the Anglos who entered Texas in violation of quota restrictions with the expressed intention of aiding legal Anglo aliens in an armed struggle against Mexico." Notes that employment of Mexicans in the United States has depended on the economy but that the image of the Mexican workers has remained much the same. Mexicans are used either as levers for the "personal aggrandizement of native Americans" or as scapegoats for "projected and displaced aggression."

1137. "The Mexican Dream: Al Norte and Home Again." *Los Angeles Times*, April 12, 1981.

1138. "The Mexican Push: Illegal Aliens--Drawn Here or Shoved?" *Human Behavior* (January 1978): 26.

1139. [Mexico]. Interdepartmental Commission for the Study of the Problem of the Clandestine Emigration of Mexican Workers to the United States of America, *Report on Activities and Recommendations*. Tlatelolco, 1972.

1140. Meyer, L. "Aliens Hard to Count." *Washington Post*, February 2, 1975, p. A-12.

1141. Migdail, Carl J. "Mexico's President: No Easy Way to Stop Migration; Interview with José Lopez Portillo." *U.S. News & World Report* (July 4, 1977): 28-30.

1142. ———. "Time Bomb in Mexico: Why There'll Be no End to the Invasion by 'Illegals.'" *U.S. News & World Report* (July 4, 1977): 27-28.

1143. Mines, Richard, and Ricardo Anzaldúa Montoya. *New Migrants vs. Old Migrants: Alternative Labor Market Structures in the California Citrus Industry.* La Jolla, California: Center for U.S.-Mexican Studies, University of California, San Diego. Monographs in U.S.-Mexican Studies, No. 9, 1982.

Study of the changing role of Mexican labor--both legal and illegal migrants--in the Ventura County, California, citrus industry, based on interviews with migrants, citrus growers, personnel managers, labor contractors, and others associated with the citrus harvest, as well as archival data. Fieldwork completed in 1981.

1144. Morales, Rebecca. "Transitional Labor: Undocumented Workers in the Los Angeles Automobile Industry." *International Migration Review,* 17 (Winter 1983/84): 570-596.

Examines the employment of undocumented workers by Los Angeles manufacturers of automobile parts. It suggests that this is part of a broad trend towards primary labor market erosion. The labor force is termed transitional because it is seen as facilitating firms during the current period of industrial change. Insight into the role of these workers is derived from eight case studies representing 926 workers. Regressions on the determinants of wages and the percent undocumented in the workplace are developed from 21 firms and 2,321 workers.

1145. ———. "Unions and Undocumented Workers." *Our Socialism,* 1 (April 1983): 32-37.

1146. Morrison, Patt. "Illegal Aliens: Good Wages, Bad Jobs, Constant Fear." *Los Angeles Times,* January 22, 1977, pp. 1, 24.

1147. Murphy, Michael E. "Personnel Administration and President's Plan on Illegal Aliens." *Personnel Journal,* 56 (November 1977): 550-53.

1148. Nafziger, James A.R. "A Policy Framework for Regulating the Flow of Undocumented Mexican Aliens into the United States." *Oregon Law Review,* 56 (1977): 63-106.

1149. National Council on Employment Policy. *Illegal Aliens: An Assessment of the Issues: A Policy Statement and Conference Report with Background Papers.* Washington, D.C., 1976.

1150. Nelson, E., ed. *Pablo Cruz and the American Dream. The Experiences of an Undocumented Immigrant from Mexico.* Salt Lake City, Utah: Peregrine Smith, 1975.

First-person account of the experiences of an undocumented immigrant from Mexico to the United States recalls Pablo Cruz' "poverty-stricken childhood in central western Mexico, the conflict between his loyalty to Mexico and his desire to relieve his poverty by seeking work in the United States; his journeys north by foot and freight train under cover of darkness and subsequent experiences with 'wetbacks' smugglers, corrupt border officials, and police; his internment for several months in a California prison for illegal entrants, his experiences in a 'wino' farm labor camp in California where workers are kept as slaves in a perpetual alcoholic haze; his love affair with a sympathetic woman who becomes his wife; his decision to become a United States citizen, and the eventual resolution of some of his conflicts as he and his family achieve a somewhat stable life in a small central California town."

1151. New York [State]. Senate Standing Committee on Labor. *The Constitutionality of a State Statute Prohibiting Employers from Hiring Illegal Aliens and Practical Suggestions on Drafting Such a Law.* Albany, 1975.

1152. Norquest, Carrol. *Rio Grande Wetbacks: Mexican Migrant Workers.* Albuquerque, New Mexico: University of New Mexico Press, 1972.

Through a series of individual case studies, Norquest affords the reader a rare composite picture of the illegal entrant, his attitudes toward life and death, the family, marriage, sex, religion, work, and the ever-present border patrol, *la chola*. Carrol Norquest is himself a man of the soil. He is neither academician nor social reformer. He has no axe to grind. As a small farmer in the Rio Grande Valley of Southeast Texas for more than thirty years, Norquest hired the wetback and his family, worked them, fed them, financed and protected them and was, in fact, *el patron*.

1153.   North, David S. *Alien Workers: A Study of the Labor
        Certification Programs.* Washington, D.C.: Trans-
        Century Foundation, 1971.

1154.   ———. *The Border Crossers.* Washington, D.C.:
        Trans-Century Foundation, 1970.

1155.   ———. *Fraudulent Entrants: A Study of Malafide
        Applicants for Admission at Selected Ports of Entry
        on the Southwest Border and at Selected Airports.*
        Washington, D.C.: New TransCentury Foundation,
        1976.

1156.   ———. *Government Records: What They Tell Us About
        the Role of Illegal Immigrants in the Labor Market
        and in Income Transfer Programs.* Washington, D.C.:
        New TransCentury Foundation, 1981.

        Examines governmental records to secure data on the
        intersection between illegal immigrants and the U.S.
        labor market and various income transfer programs.
        Illegal immigrants are likely to pay taxes and are paid
        below-average wages. Findings contradict the assump-
        tion that illegal immigrants rarely seek income trans-
        fer payments and stay in the U.S. labor market only
        briefly.

1157.   ———. "Illegal Aliens: Fictions and Facts." *Work-
        life,* 2 (1977): 17-21.

        Argues that, among the myths associated with illegal
        immigration, the one that all are Mexicans is near the
        top. Illegal aliens are a polyglot group, but the
        concentration of immigration patrol officers on the
        Mexican border distorts the picture. Most of the
        attention on illegal aliens has focused on the Mexican
        border, because most of those detected and deported
        are Mexicans.

1158.   ———. *Keeping Undocumented Workers out of the
        Workforce: Costs of Alternative Work Permit Systems.*
        Washington, D.C.: New TransCentury Foundation, 1979.

1159.   ———, and Marion F. Houstoun. "A Summary of Recent
        Data on and Some of the Public Policy Implications
        of Illegal Immigration." *Illegal Aliens: An Assess-
        ment of the Issues: A Policy Statement and Con-
        ference Report with Background Papers.* National
        Council on Employment Policy, Washington, D.C.,
        1976.

1160. ————, and J.R. Wagner. *Nonimmigrant Workers in the
U.S.: Current Trends and Future Implications*. Report
prepared for the Employment and Training Administration, U.S. Department of Labor, [Washington], May 1980.

Concerned with nonimmigrant workers, who are present
in the U.S. legally and temporarily, and whose rights
in the labor market fall between those of the legal
immigrants and those of the illegal aliens. Focuses
on five groups of nonimmigrants who may work--students,
temporary workers of distinguished merit and ability,
other temporary workers, exchange visitors and intracompany transferees--and gives particular attention to
their role and impact in the labor market.

1161. Ortega, Joe C. "Plight of the Mexican Wetback."
American Bar Association Journal, 58 (March 1972):
251-54.

1162. Orton, Eliot S. "Changes in the Skill Differential:
Union Wages in Construction, 1907-1972." *Industrial
and Labor Relations Review*, 30 (October 1976):
16-24.

Discusses possible effects of illegal alien labor on
wages of skilled workers.

1163. Passel, Jeffrey S., and Karen A. Woodrow. "Geographic
Distribution of Undocumented Immigrants: Estimates
of Undocumented Aliens Counted in the 1980 Census
by State." *International Migration Review*, 18 (Fall
1984): 642-671.

Presents estimates of the number of undocumented
aliens counted in the 1980 census for each state and
the District of Columbia. The estimates, which indicate that 2.06 million undocumented aliens were
counted in the 1980 census, are not based on individual
records but are aggregate estimates derived by a
residual technique. The census count of aliens
(modified somewhat to account for deficiencies in the
data) is compared with estimates of the legally resident alien population based on data collected by the
Immigration and Naturalization Service in January 1980.
The final estimates represent concessions to the state
level of national estimates developed by Warren and
Passel (1984). Estimates are developed for each of
the states for selected countries of birth and for age,
sex, and period of entry categories. Describes the
origins of the undocumented alien population as well

as some of their demographic characteristics. Some of
the implications of the numbers and distribution of
undocumented aliens are also discussed.

1164. "Patrolling the Border: 'At Night the Bushes Come
       Alive.'" *U.S. News & World Report* (April 25, 1977):
       34.

1165. Pear, Robert. "House, by 216-211, Approves Alien Bill
       After Retaining Amnesty Plan in Final Test." *New
       York Times*, June 21, 1984, pp. A-1 and D-21.

1166. ————. "House Votes Plan to Admit Aliens to Harvest
       Crops." *New York Times*, June 28, 1984, p. B-5.

1167. ————. "O'Neill to Delay Debate on Aliens." *New York
       Times*, May 3, 1984, p. A-9.

1168. Peres, G.A. "Dominican Illegals in New York: Selected
       Preliminary Findings." Working Paper. New York
       University. Center for Latin American Studies, May
       1981.

1169. "Personae Non Gratae: Illegal Aliens." *Christian Cen-
       tury* (August 6, 1975): 701.

1170. Piliotis, Anastasios. "Perceptions of Border Patrol
       Agents Toward Their Agency's Degree of Effectiveness
       in Curbing the Illegal Alien Problem." Unpublished
       Ph.D. dissertation. United States International
       University, 1980.

1171. Piore, Michael. "The 'Illegal Aliens' Debate Misses
       the Boat." *Working Papers for a New Society*, 6 (1978):
       60-69.

       Believes that people come to the United States because
       of the labor need and that until legislation recog-
       nizes this fact, reform may worsen rather than ameliorate
       the situation. Industrial societies have always pro-
       duced a variety of jobs that local workers reject, and
       long-distance migrants from relatively less-developed
       areas have moved in to fill them.

1172. ————. "Illegal Immigration in the United States:
       Some Observations and Policy Suggestions." In
       National Council on Employment Policy. *Illegal Aliens
       An Assessment of the Issues*. Washington, D.C.:
       National Council on Employment Policy, 1976. Pp.
       25-35.

1173. ———. "Illegals: Restrictions Aren't the Answer."
       New Republic (February 22, 1975): 7-8.

1174. ———. "Impact of Immigration on the Labor Force."
       Monthly Labor Review, 98 (May 1975): 41-44.

1175. "A Plan to Slow the Flood of Illegal Aliens." *Business
       Week* (August 11, 1975): 67-68.

1176. Portes, Alejandro. "Illegal Immigration and the Inter-
       national System: Lessons from Recent Legal Mexican
       Immigrants to the United States." *Social Problems*,
       26 (April 1979): 245-438.

1177. ———. "Illegal Mexican Immigrants to the United
       States." *International Migration Review*, 12 (Winter
       1978). Special Issue.

1178. ———. "Labor Functions of Illegal Aliens." *Society*,
       14 (1977): 31-37.

       Sees four major consequences: the undermining of es-
       tablished order, the unfair competition with native
       labor, the cost of services, and the creation of a
       different cultural/racial mix. Yet as long as it meets
       a need, illegal immigration will continue.

1179. ———. "Return of the Wetback." *Society* (March
       1974): 40-46.

1180. ———. "Toward a Structural Analysis of Illegal (Un-
       documented) Immigration." *International Migration
       Review*, 12 (Winter 1978): 469-484.

       In his introduction to this issue of IMR which at-
       tempts to understand more fully different aspects of
       undocumented immigration, the guest editor situates the
       articles in the present context of research and policy
       and complements them by summarizing some of the ideas
       common to all and by analyzing, on their basis, the
       significance of the current Administration's plan to
       deal with the illegal flow.

1181. Portman, Robert J. "A Study of Undocumented Mexican
       Workers on a Texas Ranch." Unpublished honors
       thesis, Dartmouth College, June 1979, Department of
       Anthropology. [Hanover, New Hampshire, 1979].

       Ethnographic study of the undocumented Mexican work
       force on a cattle ranch in the Texas borderlands.

1182.   "President Ford Establishes Committee on Illegal
        Aliens: Memorandum, January 6, 1975." *Department
        of State Bulletin* (March 3, 1975): 273.

1183.   "Public Backing Away from Its Hard Stance on Hiring
        Illegal Aliens but Rejects Amnesty." *Gallup Opinion
        Index* (February 1978): 1-5.

1184.   Ramirez, Patricia C. "Living in Fear." *Agenda* (Sep-
        tember-October 1977): 16-18.

1185.   "Reasonable Suspicion of Illegal Alienage as a Precon-
        dition to 'Stop' of Suspected Aliens." *Chicago-Kent
        Law Review*, 52 (1975): 485-502.

1186.   Reichert, Joshua S., and Douglas S. Massey. "Patterns
        of U.S. Migration from a Mexican Sending Community:
        A Comparison of Legal and Illegal Migrants." *Inter-
        national Migration Review*, 13 (Winter 1979): 599-623.

1187.   Reilly, A.M. "Stemming the Tide of Illegal Aliens."
        Dun's Business Month, 118 (October 1981): 44-45.

1188.   "Reporter Charged with Aiding Illegal Aliens (Jack
        Fisher)." *Editor, Publisher, The Fourth Estate*, 117
        (March 10, 1984): 14.

1189.   Research Organizations of Avante Systems, Inc., and Cul-
        tural Research Associates. "A Survey of the Undocu-
        mented Population in Two Texas Border Areas." Unpub-
        lished report. San Antonio, Texas: Research Organiza-
        tions of Avante Systems, Inc., September 1978.

        Based partly on interviews with unapprehended undocu-
        mented immigrants contacted through social service
        agencies in El Paso and Edinburg/McAllen, Texas. The
        total of 600 interviews included an unspecified number
        of illegal migrants who had been detained by the INS and
        were awaiting deportation.

1190.   Reubens, Edwin P. "Aliens, Jobs, and Immigration
        Policy." *The Public Interest*, No. 51 (Spring 1978):
        113-34.

1191.   ———. "Illegal Immigration and the Mexican Economy."
        Challenge (November-December 1978): 13-19.

1192.   Rienow, R., and L. Rienow. *The Great Unwanteds Want
        Us. Illegal Aliens: Too Late to Close the Gate?*

Monterey, California: Viewpoint Books, 1980.

Offers an environmental analysis of the accelerating difficulties caused by the new waves of illegal aliens.

1193. Rios, Omar G. "The Chronic Mexican-Alien Immigration Offender." *Federal Probation*, 34 (September 1970); 57-60.

1194. Ríos-Bustamante, A.J., ed. *Immigration and Public Policy. Human Rights for Undocumented Workers and Their Families*. Los Angeles: University of California, Chicano Studies Center, 1977.

1195. "Rising Flood of Illegal Aliens: How to Deal with It." *U.S. News & World Report* (February 3, 1975): 127-30.

1196. Roberts, Kenneth D. "Agricultural Development and Labor Mobility: A Study of Four Mexican Subregions." In Richard C. Jones, ed., *Patterns of Undocumented Migration: Mexico and the United States*. Totowa, N.J.: Rowman and Allanheld, 1984. Pp. 74-92.

Examines the economic factors that affect labor allocation of rural landholding households in four areas of Mexico. The original research was considerably narrower, focusing on the "push factors" causing illegal migration to the United States. However, it soon became apparent that restricting the analysis to U.S. migration would make it impossible to distinguish between factors that cause members of households to work off-farm in general and those that condition this wage labor to take various forms, such as local labor, circular or permanent migration within Mexico, or migration to the United States. At its broadest level, this is a study of the relationship between rural development and labor mobility. There are a number of interesting theoretical issues involved, especially those raised by the emerging literature on circulation and on peasant household decision-making. This study, however, will keep the issue of undocumented migration as its central theme. Its conclusions challenge the assumption of an inverse relationship between rural economic development and undocumented migration. There are important implications for the effectiveness of development programs in slowing the long-term outflow of rural migrants. This study also sheds light on the suitability of a guest-worker program as an "interim" solution to the current insufficiency of job opportunities in Mexico and high levels of illegal migration to the United States.

1197.   ———, et al. *The Mexican Number Game: An Analysis of
        the Lesko Estimate of the Undocumented Migration from
        Mexico to the United States.* Austin, Texas: Bureau of
        Business Research, University of Texas, 1978.

1198.   Robinson, J.G. "Estimating the Approximate Size of
        the Illegal Alien Population in the United States
        by the Comparative Trend Analysis of Age-Specific
        Death Rates." Paper presented at the Annual Meeting
        of the Population Association of America, April 26,
        1979.

        Reports "the results of the application of compara-
        tive analysis of the trend of age-specific death rates
        to determine approximate size of the illegal alien popu-
        lation in the United States." Results of study are
        compared with other estimates of the number of illegal
        aliens in the United States and contribute "another
        assessment of where this population group may lie along
        the 1 to 12 million continuum."

1199.   ———. "Estimating the Approximate Size of the Il-
        legal Alien Population in the United States by the
        Comparative Trend Analysis of Age-Specific Death
        Rates." *Demography*, 17 (May 1980): 159–176.

        Presents an attempt to determine, through the use of
        demographic analysis, the approximate size of the resi-
        dent illegal alien population in the United States.
        The method used is the comparative analysis of trends
        in age-specific death rates in the United States and in
        selected states from 1950 to 1975. A range of esti-
        mates of the illegal alien population based on the
        analysis is presented and compared with the results
        of other studies.

1200.   Robinson, W.G. "Illegal Immigrants in Canada: Recent
        Developments." *International Migration Review*, 18
        (Fall 1984): 474–485.

        Immigration policies and their management in a country
        like Canada have long been an interesting and instruc-
        tive study for other countries. With borders naturally
        protected by great distance from almost all migrant
        routes; with a long, undefended border with the United
        States and a further 3,000 km to its border on the south
        with a parliamentary system capable of comparatively
        rapid legislative and administrative responses to prob-
        lems; and with a relatively small legal, and even smalle

illegal population, Canada has historically "experimented" with novel, often quite creative, immigration policies and programs to both encourage and control the increases in its population. This article presents a summarized version of what Canada did and is doing in response to an important item of public policy--the entry and presence of illegal immigrants.

1201. ————. "Illegal Immigrants Issue Paper." Discussion paper issued by W.G. Robinson, Special Advisor to the Minister of Employment and Immigration, Hull, Quebec, 1983.

Highlights some issues dealing with illegal immigrants such as exceptional treatment of illegals in Canada, border control, enforcement of immigration laws within Canada, and extended visitor visa requirements.

1202. Rochin, Refugio I. "Illegal Aliens in Agriculture: Some Theoretical Considerations." *Labor Law Journal*, 29 (March 1978): 149-167.

1203. ————. *Illegal Mexican Aliens in California Agriculture: Courses and Implications*. Davis, California: University of California, Department of Agricultural Economics, 1977.

1204. Rodríguez, José Luis. *Los indocumentados*. Barranquilla, Colombia: Tipografía Dovel [1980?].

1205. "The Role of Alien Entrepreneurs in Economic Development." *American Economic Review*, 73 (May 1983): 107-122.

1206. Romo, Harriett Durr. "Status Attainment of Undocumented Mexican Immigrant Children: Language and Education Issues in a Family Context." Unpublished Ph.D. dissertation. University of California (San Diego), 1985.

1207. Rosberg, Gerald M. "Legal Regulation of the Migration Process: The Crisis of Illegal Immigration." In William H. McNeill and Ruth S. Adams, eds. *Human Migrations: Patterns and Policies*. Bloomington, Indiana: Indiana University Press, 1978. Pp. 343-347.

1208. Rosen, Gerald R. "New Curbs on Illegal Aliens?" *Dun's Review* (July 1977): 49.

1209. "Roving Border Patrol Searches for Illegal Aliens: Avoiding the Exclusionary Rule." *Marquette Law Review*, 59 (1976): 856-875.

1210. Salcido, R. "A Proposed Model for Advocacy Services for Mexican Undocumented Aliens with Mental Health Needs." *Exploration in Ethnic Studies*, 4 (July 1981): 56-68.

Discusses studies that have focused on undocumented aliens from Mexico, examines barriers that inhibit their use of mental health services, and outlines ways in which social workers employed in mental health institutions can become actively involved in helping this group.

1211. ———. "Utilization of Community Services and Immigration Experiences of Documented and Undocumented Mexican Families." Unpublished D.S.W. dissertation. University of California (Los Angeles), 1977.

1212. Samuels, Alec. "Legal Recognition and Protection of Minority Customs in a Plural Society in England." *Anglo-American Law Review*, 10 (October-December 1981): 241-256.

1213. Sanchez, G.I., and J. Romo. *Organizing Mexican Undocumented Farm Workers on Both Sides of the Border.* Working Papers in U.S.-Mexican Studies, No. 27, Program in United States-Mexican Studies, University of California, San Diego, 1981.

Documents the work of the Maricopa County Organizing Project--a civil rights organization with a primary concern for the protection and enhancement of the civil and human rights of farm workers and their families-- in organizing Mexican undocumented workers and preparing the groundwork for unionization.

1214. San Diego County. California. *A Study of the Socioeconomic Impact of Illegal Aliens on the County of San Diego.* San Diego: County of San Diego Human Resources Agency, 1977.

1215. Scheuer, James H. "Illegal Immigration: Problems and Proposals." *City Almanac*, 12 (1978): 1-15.

Presents a synthesis of the hearings held by the U.S. House of Representatives' Select Committee on Population under the chairmanship of James H. Scheuer (D-N.Y.).

Summarizes the views and analysis of the issue of illegal immigration as understood by Scheuer. Summarizes the economic and social impact of illegal immigrants with respect to demographic, social services, labor force, balance of payment, and tax revenue factors. Evaluates the proposed policies of the Carter administration concluding that it "appears reasonable--except the amnesty program which is wholly unworkable...."

1216. Schey, Peter A. "Carter's Immigration Proposal--A Windfall for Big Business, Anathema for Undocumented Persons." *Agenda* (September-October 1977): 4-15.

1217. Schroeder, Richard C. "Illegal Immigration." *Editorial Research Reports* (December 10, 1976): 909-26.

1218. Schuck, Peter H., and Rogers M. Smith. *Citizenship Without Consent: Illegal Aliens in the American Polity.* New Haven, Connecticut: Yale University Press, 1985.

The authors take as their point of departure a situation they consider anomalous if not absurd--that under current law children born in the United States to illegal aliens are decreed citizens. To explain and respond to this odd situation, they trace the history of doctrines of citizenship in the United States well back into its English common-law antecedents. They identify two strands of thought and practice on citizenship-- one based on ascriptive principles that supports a birthright standard and one based on consensualist principles that supports a standard more sensitive to the wishes of potential citizens and to the community. The authors trace these two strands through American history and law, arguing that the two have coexisted in uneasy combinations but that the time has come to move toward a more consistent legal standard, one based on the consensualist viewpoint.

1219. Schwartz, L. "Congress to Face Stalled Immigration Bill (Hiring Illegal Aliens)." *Electronic News*, 30, Supp. C (November 12, 1984).

1220. Sciolino, E. "Illegal Aliens' Impact in City Is Uncertain." *New York Times*, September 17, 1984.

1221. "Selected Checklist on Illegal Aliens." *Record*, 34 (December 1979): 775-80.

1222. Shafer, Wilfred A. "Foreign Born Children of Illegal
       Immigrants: A Growing Problem." *Integrated Education*,
       14 (November–December 1976): 18–19.

1223. "Should Illegal Aliens Hold U.S. Jobs?" *Senior Schol-
       astic* (March 27, 1975): 29.

1224. Siegal, Jacob S., et al. *Preliminary Review of Existing
       Studies of the Number of Illegal Residents in the
       United States*. Prepared for the U.S. Bureau of the
       Census. Washington, D.C.: Government Printing
       Office, January 1980.

1225. Simon, Rita J., and Margo C. De Ley. "Undocumented
       Mexican Women: Their Work and Personal Experiences."
       In Rita J. Simon and Caroline B. Brettell, eds.
       International Migration: The Female Experience.
       Totowa, N.J.: Rowman and Allanheld, 1986. Pp. 113–
       131.

1226. ———, and ———. "The Work Experience of Undocu-
       mented Mexican Women Migrants in Los Angeles."
       International Migration Review, 18 (Winter 1984):
       1212–1229.

       Reports the demographic characteristics and labor
       force participation of undocumented and documented
       Mexican women immigrants in Los Angeles County. The
       women were interviewed in their homes, churches, com-
       munity centers, and places of work; not in detention
       centers where other previous studies of illegal migrants
       were conducted.

1227. Simon, T. "Mexican Repatriation in East Chicago,
       Indiana." *The Journal of Ethnic Studies*, 11 (Summer
       1974): 11–23.

       Attempts to relieve the burdens of depression by the
       repatriation of Mexicans.

1228. Singer, James W. "Controlling Illegal Aliens: Carter's
       Compromise Solution." *National Journal* (September 3,
       1977): 1379–83.

1229. Smardz, Zofia J. "The Great Illegal Alien Debate."
       Worldview, 19 (May 1976): 15–20.

       Analysis of the confusion on the immigration policy
       of the United States and how illegal aliens are both
       the beneficiaries and victims of this confusion.

1230. Smith, Anthony Wayne. "Our Undefended Borders."
      National Parks & Conservation Magazine (May 1978):
      2+.

1231. "Soon: A Ban on Hiring Illegal Aliens?" *U.S. News &
      World Report* (February 3, 1975): 30.

1232. Southwest Border Regional Commission. "Border Area
      Development Study: Profile of Undocumented Migration
      to the California Border Region." Final report pre-
      pared under E.D.A. Grant 99-06-09588. Sacramento,
      California: Southwest Border Regional Commission,
      Office of the Lieutenant Governor, State of Califor-
      nia, 1978.

1233. State Prohibitions on Employment Opportunities for
      Resident Aliens: Legislative Recommendations.
      Fordham Urban Law Journal, 10 (1981/82): 699-724.

1234. Stoddard, Ellwyn R. "A Conceptual Analysis of the
      'Alien Invasion': Institutionalized Support of Il-
      legal Mexican Aliens in the U.S." *International
      Migration Review*, 10 (Summer 1976): 157-89.

      Examines the role of Mexican workers in the United
      States since 1848, more particularly after the exclusion
      of Chinese laborers in the 1880s. People stand to gain
      from the exchange: U.S. families need domestic help,
      agribusinesses want seasonal labor, and the Mexican
      government seeks employment for its workers. Until a
      new policy that takes into account the history of Mexican
      employment in the United States and the needs of those
      who support its continuation is instituted, the movement
      will not stop.

1235. ————. "Illegal Mexican Aliens in Borderland Society."
      Paper presented at the Society for the Study of Social
      Problems Conference, San Francisco, California, 1978.

1236. Storer, Desmond, Freda Hawkins, and S.M. Tomasi.
      *Amnesty for Undocumented Migrants: The Experience
      of Australia, Canada, and Argentina*. Staten Island,
      New York: Center for Migration Studies, 1977.

1237. Strickland, B.K. *Analisis de la ley en las Estados
      Unidos de America en relacion con extranjeros indocu-
      mentados. Ensayos 2*. Mexico City: Centro nacional
      de información y estadisticas del trabajo, 1978.

1238. "Surge of Illegal Immigrants Across American Borders."
      U.S. News & World Report (January 17, 1972): 32-34.

1239. Taylor, J. Edward. *Selectivity of Undocumented Mexico-
      U.S. Migrants and Implications for U.S. Immigration
      Reform.* Washington, D.C.: The Urban Institute, 1985.

1240. [Texas]. Department of Community Affairs. *Illegal
      Juvenile Alien Crime Along the Mexico-United States
      Borderland.* Austin, Texas: State Youth Secretariat
      Division, 1975.

1241. Texas Good Neighbor Commission. "Alien Labor and Immi-
      gration." *Texas Migrant Labor.* Annual Report, 1971.
      Austin, Texas: Commission, 1971.

1242. "This Month's Feature: The Problem of Illegal Aliens
      in the United States." *Congressional Digest,* 54
      (January 1975): 3-32.

1243. Toney, W.T. *A Descriptive Study of the Control of
      Illegal Mexican Migration in the Southwestern U.S.*
      San Francisco, California: R & F Research Associates,
      1977.

      Seeks to offer a detailed explanation of the manner
      in which manpower funds and other resources are
      utilized to control Mexican illegal immigration.

1244. "Two Apple Farmers Convicted of Smuggling Mexicans into
      Virginia to Work Their Crops." *Washington Post*
      (November 30, 1983): Sec. C., p. 2.

1245. *Undocumented Workers in the U.S. Labor Market.* Pasadena,
      California: American Friends Service Committee, 1980.

1246. Unger, H. "Illegal Aliens: A Terrible Social Burden
      Provokes an Even Worse Possible Solution (U.S.)."
      Canadian Business, 55 (November 1982): 26.

1247. [U.S.] Comptroller General. "Illegal Aliens: Estimating
      Their Impact on the United States." Report to the
      Congress, March 14, 1980. Washington, D.C.: General
      Accounting Office, 1980.

1248. U.S. Congress. House. Committee on Appropriations.
      *Departments of State, Justice and Commerce, the
      Judiciary, and Related Agencies Appropriations:*

Undocumented Aliens. Hearings before a Subcommittee
on Appropriations, House of Representatives, 95th
Cong., 2nd sess., 1978.

1249. U.S. Congress. House Committee on Banking, Finance and
Urban Affairs. *Development Lending and Illegal Im-
migration*. Hearings before a Subcommittee of the
Committee on Banking, Finance and Urban Affairs,
House of Representatives, 95th Cong., 1st sess.,
1977.

1250. U.S. Congress. House. Committee on Government Opera-
tions. *Law Enforcement on the Southwest Border
(Review of Reorganization Plan No. 2 of 1973 and
Related Developments)*. Hearings before a Subcommittee
of the Committee on Government Operations, House of
Representatives, 93rd Cong., 2nd Sess., 1974.

1251. U.S. Congress. House. Committee on Government Operations. *Law Enforcement on the Southwest Border (Review of Reorganization Plan No. 2 of 1973 and Related
Developments)*. Hearings before a Subcommittee of the
Committee on Government Operations, House of Representatives, 93rd Cong., 2nd Sess., 1974. (Final document)

1252. U.S. Congress. House. Committee on International Re-
lations Subcommittee on Inter-American Affairs.
*Illegal Aliens: Implications for U.S. Policy in the
Western Hemisphere*. Hearings, 95th Cong., 2nd sess.
Washington, D.C.: U.S. Government Printing Office,
1978.

1253. U.S. Congress. House. Committee on Interstate and
Foreign Commerce. *Medical Treatment of Illegal
Aliens*. Hearings before a Subbcommittee of the Com-
mittee on Interstate and Foreign Commerce, House of
Representatives, 95th Cong., 1st sess., 1977.

1254. U.S. Congress. House. Committee on the Judiciary.
*Hearings before Subcommittee No. 1 ... 92nd Congress.
Illegal Aliens*. Part 1, Part 2. 2 vols. Washington,
D.C.: Government Printing Office, 1971.

1255. U.S. Congress. House. Committee on the Judiciary.
*Illegal Aliens and Alien Labor: A Bibliography and
Compilation of Background Materials (1970-June 1977)*.
Committee Print No. 9, 95th Congress, 1st Session,
August 1977. Washington, D.C.: Government Printing
Office, 1977.

Contains listings of government documents and research studies. A separate section provides an access
to newspaper articles and leading editorials.

1256. U.S. Congress. House. Committee on the Judiciary.
*Illegal Aliens: Analysis and Background. Report of
Committee on the Judiciary.* Washington, D.C.: U.S.
Government Printing Office, 1977.

1257. U.S. Congress. House. Select Committee on Population.
*Legal and Illegal Immigration to the United States:
Report.* 95th Congress, 2nd Session. Washington,
D.C.: Government Printing Office, 1979.

1258. U.S. Department of Commerce. Bureau of the Census.
*Preliminary Review of Existing Studies of the Number
of Illegal Residents in the United States.* A paper
prepared by Jacob S. Siegal, et al., for the Research
Staff of the Select Commission on Immigration and
Refugee Policy. January 1980. [Washington, D.C.,
1980]. Final document.

Finds that there are no reliable estimates of the
numbers of illegal residents in the country or of the
net volume of illegal immigration to the United States
in any recent past period. Several analytic studies
now available are subject to major limitations. On
the basis of studies conducted by others, estimates
that "the total number of illegal residents in the
United States for some recent years, such as 1978, is
almost certainly below 6.0 million, and may be substantially less, possibly only 3.5 to 5.0 million....
The Mexican component of the illegally resident population is almost certainly less than 3.0 million, and may
be substantially less, possibly only 1.5 to 2.5 million."

1259. U.S. Domestic Council. *Preliminary Report of the
Domestic Council Committee on Illegal Aliens.*
Washington, D.C.: Government Printing Office, 1976.

This preliminary report was prepared for President
Gerald Ford and was subsequently made the final report
of the committee after Ford's defeat for reelection
in 1976.

1260. U.S. General Accounting Office. *Information on the
Enforcement of Laws Regarding Employment of Aliens
in Selected Countries.* Washington, D.C.; Government
Printing Office, 1982.

1261. ————. *Issues Concerning Social Security Benefits
       Paid to Aliens.* Report to the Congress of the United
       States by the Comptroller General. Gaithersburg,
       Maryland: General Accounting Office, 1983.

       Examines the circumstances under which social security
       benefits are paid to alien retirees and dependents
       living abroad and discusses the characteristics of
       this beneficiary group. Also presents information
       concerning aliens who, while working in violation of
       the Immigration and Nationality Act, can earn social
       security credits.

1262. ————. *Problems and Options in Estimating the Size
       of the Illegal Alien Population.* Report to the
       Chairman of the Subcommittee on Immigration and
       Refugee Policy of the Committee on the Judiciary,
       United States Senate. Gaithersburg, Maryland:
       General Accounting Office, 1982.

       Reviews the previous estimation attempts, describes
       the problems attending the use of alternative estima-
       tion methods, and presents options for acquiring improved
       policymaking information in the illegal alien area.
       Estimates of the resident illegal alien population
       range from 1 million to 12 million, with the most
       widely accepted range being 3.5 to 6 million. The
       most frequently cited estimate of the number who enter
       illegally each year is 500,000. GAO found no single
       previous estimate of either the national illegal alien
       population or its annual flow to be both valid and
       reliable. Current estimates stem from incomplete or
       questionable data bases or untested or demonstrably
       incorrect assumptions or are restricted to a subgroup
       of the illegal alien population.

1263. U.S. Immigration and Naturalization Service. *An Eval-
       uation of the Cost Effectiveness of Repatriating
       Aliens to the Interior of Mexico.* Washington, D.C.:
       U.S. Immigration and Naturalization Service, 1977.

1264. [————]. *Illegal Alien Study Design.* Washington,
       D.C.: Linton & Co., 1976. 3 vols.

1265. "U.S. Job Market Pinched by Alien Trespassers." *U.S.
       News & World Report* (January 26, 1976): 84–85.

1266. U.S. President Jimmy Carter. "Undocumented Aliens:
       Message from the President of the United States."

Weekly Compilation of Presidential Documents, 13 (August 8, 1977): 1170-75.

Preceding President Carter's message to the Congress are his remarks to newsmen at a White House press briefing on the same issue.

1267. U.S. Special Study Group on Illegal Immigrants from Mexico. *Final Report--A Program for Effective and Humane Action on Illegal Mexican Immigrants.* Washington, D.C., 1973.

Often cited as the Cramton Report, after the group's chairman, Roger C. Cramton of the U.S. Department of Justice.

1268. Valdez, Avelardo, and Richard C. Jones. "Geographical Patterns of Undocumented Mexicans and Chicanos in San Antonio, Texas, 1970 and 1980." In Richard C. Jones, ed., *Patterns of Undocumented Migration: Mexico and the United States.* Totowa, N.J.: Rowman and Allanheld, 1984. Pp. 218-235.

Isolates undocumented residential patterns and compares them to those of Chicanos in the early and in the late 1970s. Based on previous research of other immigrant groups, expects that there is a residential succession process occurring among undocumenteds, Chicanos, and Anglos. That is, it is expected that undocumented Mexicans will first settle in lower-income, ethnically homogeneous Chicano neighborhoods. At the same time, Chicanos who have increased their economic status will move into relatively higher-status adjacent subareas, displacing Anglos, who move into areas of still higher status replicating the invasion succession model. Attempts to determine: (a) areas of the city in which undocumenteds and Chicanos cluster; (b) the similarity and dissimilarity of residential patterns between Chicanos and undocumented Mexicans; (c) the relationship between these residential patterns and the socioeconomic status of the areas; and (d) changes in residential patterns of undocumenteds relative to Chicanos during the 1970s. Posits that an understanding of the residential patterns of Chicanos and undocumenteds may explain how this Mexican-origin group maintains its minority status in this society.

1269. Van Arsdol, Maurice D., et al. "Non-apprehended and Apprehended Undocumented Residents in the Los Angeles Labor Market: An Exploratory Study." Report prepared for the Employment and Training Administration, U.S. Department of Labor, under contract No. 20-06-77-16. Los Angeles: Population Research Laboratory, University of Southern California, 1979.

Data refer to the period 1972-1975; 2,905 cases. The data were collected as part of initial screening interviews with potential clients of the One Stop Immigration Center, a legal counseling agency in Los Angeles.

1270. Villalpando, Manuel V. "The Socioeconomic Impact of Illegal Aliens on the County of San Diego." Unpublished Ph.D. dissertation. United States International University, 1976.

1271. ————, et al. *A Study of the Socioeconomic Impact of Illegal Aliens on the County of San Diego.* San Diego, California: Human Resources Agency, County of San Diego, 1977.

1272. Wachter, Michael I. "The Labor Market and Illegal Immigration: The Outlook for the 1980's." *Industry and Labor Relations Review,* 33 (April 1980): 342-354.

1273. ————. "Second Thoughts About Illegal Immigrants." *Fortune* (May 22, 1978): 80-87.

Argues that "illegal aliens may come to be regarded as an important addition to the labor force, welcomed by virtually all Americans, and their number is likely to increase." Attempts to explain why there has been an illegal immigration boom from Mexico, Latin America, and Asia in the 1960s despite powerful contrary trends in the labor market. Explores the impact of deportation of illegals on low-skilled Americans. Maintains that the United States is not about to clamp down on illegal immigration and foresees the possibility that aliens could rescue the financially troubled Social Security System.

1274. Wain, Barry. *The Refused.* New York: Simon and Schuster, 1981.

1275. Warren, R. "Alien Emigration from the United States, 1963-1974." Paper presented at Population Association of American Annual Meeting, Philadelphia, 1979.

1276.   Washington. Inter-Agency Task Force for Agricultural
        Workers. *Investigative Study of the Impact of
        Illegal Aliens on Farmworkers in the State of
        Washington.* Preliminary Report, December 1974.

1277.   Weintraub, Sidney. "Illegal Immigrants in Texas: Im-
        pact on Social Services and Related Considerations."
        International Migration Review, 18 (Fall 1984):
        733-747.

        A survey conducted of undocumented aliens and pro-
        viders of public services showed that the state of
        Texas receives more from taxes paid by undocumented
        persons than it costs the state to provide them with
        such public services as education, health care, correc-
        tions, and welfare. The same survey showed that six
        cities in the state (Austin, Dallas, El Paso, Houston,
        McAllen, and San Antonio) together expended more to
        provide services to undocumented aliens than they re-
        ceived in taxes. The survey concentrated on undocu-
        mented persons not detained by the immigration authori-
        ties and found that this group constituted a distinct
        population from those in detention centers in that the
        former exhibited normal characteristics of settled
        families while the latter were predominantly the familiar
        young, single, and peripatetic males.

1278.   ———. "Illegal Immigration in Texas: Impact on Social
        Services and Other Considerations." Paper presented
        at Annual Conference, American Political Science
        Association, Washington, D.C., August 1984.

1279.   Wenk, Michael G. "The Alien Adjustment and Employment
        Act of 1977: A Summary." *International Migration
        Review*, 11 (Winter 1977): 533-538.

        On August 4, 1977, President Carter sent a message
        to the Congress outlining his initiatives for treating
        the growing undocumented alien problem in the United
        States. Subsequently, the Administration forwarded
        to the Congress the legislative proposals requiring
        enactment if this Presidential initiative is to suc-
        ceed. As outlined in Attorney General Griffin B. Bell's
        letter of transmittal to Congress, the proposed legis-
        lation has three primary objectives: "(1) to adjust
        those undocumented aliens who have resided in the
        United States continuously prior to January 1, 1970,
        to lawful permanent residents; (2) to create a new
        five year temporary resident status for undocumented

aliens who have resided in the United States continuously since January 1, 1977; and (3) to restrict employment opportunities for undocumented aliens in the
United States."

1280. "What Illegal Aliens Cost the Economy." *Business
Week* (June 13, 1977): 86-88.

1281. "What's Employer's Role in Illegal Alien Problems?"
Industry Week (May 23, 1977): 17-19.

1282. Wheeler, C. "Legal Issues and Processes in Preventing
the Deportation of Guatemalan Refugees." Paper
presented at American Anthropological Association.
83rd Annual Meeting. Denver, Colorado, November 14-
18, 1984.

The U.S. policy does not grant the legal status of
refugee to Guatemalans who have left Guatemala in fear
of government violence. Instead, Guatemalans are treated
as undocumented aliens, and the danger of deportation
is real. Based on legal experience in dealing with
Guatemalan cases in Colorado, outlines the major legal
issues and describes the processes by which the Colorado
Rural Legal Services has succeeded in preserving
Guatemalan refugees from deportation.

1283. "When You Catch an Illegal Alien, What Do You Do with
Him?" *U.S. News & World Report* (April 25, 1977): 38.

1284. "Where Two Worlds Meet (Illegal Migration by Mexicans
to U.S. Border States)." *Economist*, 288 (August 20,
1983): 28-31.

1285. "Why the Tide of Illegal Aliens Keeps Rising." *U.S.
News & World Report* (February 20, 1978): 33-35.

1286. Wiessler, J. "Illegal Alien Survey Shelved—Has Already Cost $70,000." *Washington Post*, August 24,
1978.

1287. Wihtol de Wenden, Catherine, and Jacqueline Costa-
Lascoux. "Immigration Reform in France and the
United States: Reflections and Documentation."
International Migration Review, 18 (Fall 1984):
613-622.

Similarities and dissimilarities in France and
American efforts to come to grips with irregular

migration are analyzed. The symbolic importance of
immigration reform is argued to be a key political concern in both nations although the politics of immigration reform has assumed a more partisan flavor in
France particularly since the municipal elections of
1983.

1288. Williams, Jennifer Dingledine. "Legal and Illegal
      Immigration to the United States Since 1965: Recent
      Entrants' Employment and Some Implications for
      Policy." Unpublished Ph.D. dissertation. Ohio
      State University, 1983.

1289. Zazueta, C.H., and F. Mercado. "El mercado de trabajo
      Norteamericano y los trabajadores Mexicanos." Paper
      presented at the Mexico-United States Seminar on Un-
      documented Migration. Centro de estudios económicos
      y sociales del tarcer mundo, Mexico D.F., 1980.

1290. Zero Population Growth, Inc. "Illegal Immigration."
      Fact Sheet (July 1976): 10-15.

                    2. Law Journals and Reviews

1291. Aberson, David F. "Deportation of Aliens for Criminal
      Convictions." *Pepperdine Law Review*, 24 (1974):
      58-82.

1292. "Able-Willing-Qualified-Available Standard of Section
      212 (a) (14) of the Immigration and Nationality
      Act: Method or Madness?" *Southern University Law
      Review*, 9 (1977): 727-45.

1293. Adede, A.O. "Fresh Look at the Meaning of the Doc-
      trine of Denial of Justice Under International
      Law." *Canadian Yearbook of International Law*, 14
      (1976): 73-95.

1294. "Administrative Law--Immigration and Naturalization
      Service Held Estopped from Denying Preference Classi-
      fication." *Fordham Law Review*, 41 (1972): 140-158.

1295. "Administrative Procedure-Immigration-Inapplicability
      of the Administrative Procedure Act to Adjudications
      Before the Board of Immigration Appeals." *Seton
      Hall Law Review*, 8 (1977): 250-87.

1296. "Aftermath of *Almeida-Sanchez v. United States*: Automobile Searches for Aliens Take on a New Look." *California Western Law Review*, 10 (Spring 1974): 657-78.

1297. Aleinikoff, T. Alexander. "Aliens, Due Process and Community Ties: A Response to Martin." *University of Pittsburgh Law Review*, 44 (Winter 1983): 237-260.

1298. "Alien Labor Certification." *Minnesota Law Review*, 60 (May 1976): 1034-60.

1299. "Alien Students in the United States: Statutory Interpretation and Problems of Control." *Suffolk Transnational Law Journal*, 5 (1981): 235-50.

1300. "Alien Teachers: Suspect Class or Subversive Influence?" *Mercer Law Review*, 31 (Spring 1980): 815-24.

1301. "Alien Tort Statute: United States Jurisdiction over Acts of Torture Committed Abroad." *William and Mary Law Review*, 23 (Fall 1981): 103-22.

1302. "Aliens Cannot Be Denied Mental Retardation Services Available to Citizens." *Mental Disability Law Reporter*, 6 (March-April 1982): 89.

1303. "Aliens--Constitutionality of Discrimination Based on National Origin." *Harvard International Law Journal*, 21 (Spring 1980): 467-513.

1304. "Aliens--Fourth Amendment--Examining the Validity of Questioning and Detaining Workers During INS Operations. *ILGWU v. Sureck*. 681 F 2d 624." *Suffolk Transnational Law Journal*, 7 (Fall 1983): 449-62.

1305. "Aliens--Immigration Law--Statutory Waiver of Deportation Is Unavailable to Aliens Who Enter the United States Under a False Claim of U.S. Citizenship." *Virginia Journal of International Law*, 16 (Fall 1975): 187-96.

1306. "Aliens--Immigration and Naturalization--Daily and Seasonal Alien Commuters Who Are Lawfully Admitted for Permanent Residency Are Properly Classified as 'Special Immigrants.'" *Texas International Law Journal*, 10 (1975): 570-578.

1307.   "Aliens--Immigration and Naturalization Service Policy
        of Excluding Homosexual Aliens Without a Medical Cer-
        tificate Is Invalid. *Hill v. United States Immigra-
        tion and Naturalization Service.* 714 F 2d 1470."
        Vanderbilt Journal of Transnational Law, 16 (Summer
        1983): 689-709.

1308.   "Aliens--An Immigration Regulation That Distinguishes
        Among Aliens by National Origin Must Have a Rational
        Basis to Satisfy the Equal Protection Guarantee of
        the Fifth Amendment." *Vanderbilt Journal of Trans-
        national Law,* 13 (Fall 1980): 857-72.

1309.   "Aliens--Labor Relations--National Labor Relations Act.
        Protection of Illegal Aliens." *Suffolk Transnational
        Law Journal,* 4 (1980): 175-83.

1310.   "Aliens' Right to Work: State and Federal Discrimina-
        tion." *Fordham Law Review,* 45 (1977): 835-839.

1311.   "Aliens' Rights--Indigent Alien Has Qualified Right to
        Appointed Counsel at Deportation Hearing." *Vanderbilt
        Journal of Transnational Law,* 9 (1976): 179-186.

1312.   "Aliens--The Secretary of State May Revoke the Visa of
        an Alien Even After an Alien Has Entered the Country.
        Knoetze v. United States. 634 F 2d 207 (5th cir.
        1981)." *New York Law School Journal of International
        and Comparative Law,* 2 (Summer 1981): 531-32.

1313.   "Aliens--Supremacy Clause--Nonimmigrant Alien Students
        Entitled to In-State Status for Reduced Tuition at
        State Institutions. *Toll v. Moreno.* 102 S ct. 2977."
        Suffolk Transnational Law Journal, 7 (Spring 1983):
        157-72.

1314.   "Aliens Under the Federal Venue Statute." *North Carolina
        Central Law Journal,* 10 (Fall 1978): 148-58.

1315.   "Alternative Models of Equal Protection Analysis.
        Plyler v. Doe. 102 S ct. 2382." *Boston College Law
        Review,* 24 (September 1983): 1363-97.

1316.   "*Alvarez v. District Director of U.S. Immigration and
        Naturalization Service.* 539 F 2d 1220." *Georgia
        Journal of International and Comparative Law,* 8
        (Winter 1978): 195-9.

1317. "*Ambach v. Norwick*: A Further Retreat from Graham." *Louisiana Law Review*, 40 (Summer 1980): 997-1011.

1318. "America's Responsibility to Amerasian Children: Too Little, Too Late." *Brooklyn Journal of International Law*, 10 (Winter 1984): 55-82.

1319. Anaya, Stephen James. "Constitutional Law Protection Against Illegal Search and Seizure. *Blackie's House of Beef Inc. v. Castillo*. No. 79-2358 (D.C. cir. July 22, 1981)." *Harvard International Law Journal*, 22 (Fall 1981): 670-676.

1320. Anderson, Kathryn L. "Avoiding Constitutional Challenges to Immigration Policies Through Judicial Deference. *Adams v. Howerton*. 673 F 2d 1036 (9th cir. 1982)." *Golden Gate University Law Review*, 13 (Spring 1983): 318-327.

1321. Appleman, Irving A. "How to Represent a Client Before the BIA (Board of Immigration Appeals)." *Immigration Journal*, 5 (January-February 1982): 11.

1322. ———. "Recommendation Against Deportation." *American Bar Association Journal*, 58 (1972): 1294-1297.

1323. Appleson, Gail. "Court to Review INS Stop-and-Quiz Policy." *ABA Journal*, 68 (July 1982): 791-792.

1324. Aragon, Ellen Weis. "The Factory Raid: An Unconstitutional Act?" *Southern California Law Review*, 56 (January 1983): 605-645.

1325. Ashman, Allan. "Immigration--Detained Aliens." *ABA Journal*, 68 (June 1982): 745.

1326. Asimow, Michael. "Estopped Against the Government: The Immigration and Naturalization Service." *Chicano Law Review*, 2 (19765): 4-39.

1327. Avila, Richard, and James Romo. "The Undocumented Worker: The Controversy Takes a New Turn." *Chicano Law Review*, 3 (1976): 164-94.

1328. "Back to Square One: Estoppel Against the Government After *Immigration and Naturalization Service v. Miranda*. 103 S ct. 281." *Vanderbilt Journal of Transnational Law*, 16 (Fall 1983): 1053-80.

1329. Bacon, Roxana. "Estopping INS--'Affirmative Miscon-
       duct' Makes Positively Bad Law." *Immigration Jour-
       nal*, 5 (January-February 1982): 8.

1330. "Balancing Federal Power over Aliens and Fifth Amend-
       ment Protection." *Notre Dame Lawyer*, 56 (April
       1981): 689-95.

1331. Baldasare, Paul, Jr. "Immigration--in *re* Sandoval:
       Deportation and the Exclusionary Rule. Sandoval,
       In *re* No. 2725 (Board of Immigration Appeals, August
       20, 1979)." *North Carolina Law Review*, 58 (March
       1980): 647-659.

1332. Ballew, Jeff. "Jurisdiction--Aliens, Federal Courts
       and the Law of Nations." *Georgia Journal of Inter-
       national and Comparative Law*, 11 (Summer 1981): 365-
       372.

1333. Bell, Steven C. "Immigration Searches." *Search and
       Seizure*, 9 (September 1982): 65-71.

1334. Benke, Patricia D. "Doctrine of Preemption and the
       Illegal Alien: A Case for State Regulation and a
       Uniform Preemption Theory." *San Diego Law Review*,
       13 (December 1975): 166-74.

1335. Bernsen, Sam. "Search and Seizure on the Highway for
       Immigration Violations: A Survey of the Law." *San
       Diego Law Review*, 123 (December 1975): 69-81.

1336. Bevilacqua, A.J. "Legal Critique of President Carter's
       Proposals on Undocumented Aliens." *Catholic Lawyer*,
       23 (Autumn 1978): 286-300.

1337. "Beyond *United States v. Valenzuela*--Bernal (102 S ct.
       3440): Can the Defendant's Right to Compulsory Process
       Survive in Prosecution for Transportating Illegal
       Aliens?" *Cornell International Law Journal*, 15
       (Winter 1983): 81-120.

1338. Blake, Charles. "Illegal Entrant--Meaning of Expres-
       sion--Function of Courts on Application for Habeas
       Corpus or Judicial Review--Correctness of *Zamir v.
       Secretary of State for the Home Department* (1980)
       A.C. 930 (Great Britain)." *Journal of Social Welfare
       Law* (July 1983): 254-256.

1339. ————. "Immigration: Immigration—Claim by Person
Admitted to United Kingdom for Short-Term Purpose to
Remain as a Refugee Whether Claimant Entitled to
Appeal from Adverse Decision by Adjudicator to Immi-
gration Appeal Tribunal (Great Britain)." *Journal
of Social Welfare Law* (September 1983): 303-4.

1340. ————. "Immigration—Returning Resident—Rights of
Appeal (if Any) of Persons Claiming Entry as Such
but Given Leave to Enter in Another Capacity—Immigration Act 1971 (Great Britain)." *Journal of Social
Welfare Law* (September 1983): 304-5.

1341. Blum, Jeffrey M., and Ralph G. Steinhardt. "Federal
Jurisdiction over International Human Rights Claims:
The Alien Tort Claims Act After *Filartiga v. Pena
Irala*." *Harvard International Law Journal* (Winter
1981): 53-113.

1342. Bonaparte, Ronald H. "The Rodino Bill: An Example of
Prejudice toward Mexican Immigration to the United
States." *Chicano Law Review*, 2 (1975): 40-50.

1343. Bonner, Douglas G. "Filling the Immigration Void: An
Excluded Alien's Right to Be Free from Indeterminate
Detention. Rodriguez—*Fernandez v. Wilkinson*.
654 F 2d 1382 (10th cir. 1981)." *Catholic University
Law Review*, 31 (Winter 1982): 335-363.

1344. "Border Searches in the Fifth Circuit: Constitutional
Guarantees v. Immigration Policy." *Cumberland Law
Review*, 8 (Spring 1977): 107-45.

1345. "Border Searches Revisited: The Constitutional Priority
of Fixed and Temporary Checkpoint Searches." *Hastings
Constitutional Law Quarterly*, 2 (1975): 251-275.

1346. Bowrs, Dana L. "Immigration—Harboring of Illegal
Aliens—New Meaning to the Concept of Shielding from
Detention. *United States v. Rubio-Gonzalez*.
674 F 2d 1067 (5th cir. 1982)." *Suffolk Transnational Law Journal*, 7 (Spring 1983): 255-266.

1347. Brooks, Douglas Montgomery. "Aliens—Civil Rights—
Illegal Aliens Are Inhabitants Within Meaning of
18 U.S.C. 242. *United States v. Otherson*.
637 F 2d 1276 (9th cir. 1980)." *Suffolk Transnational
Law Journal*, 6 (Spring 1982): 117-131.

1348. Bruck, Connie. "Springing the Haitians." *American Lawyer*, 4 (September 1982): 35-40.

1349. Buck, David P. "Legal Complications Arising from Alien Birth or Nationality." *Air Force Law Review*, 22 (Spring 1981): 168-187.

1350. Cagney, Lawrence K. "The Minimum Contacts Standard and Alien Defendants." *Law and Policy in International Business*, 12 (Summer 1980): 783-823.

1351. Carliner, David. "The Right of Aliens to Receive Government Benefits." *Interpreter Releases*, 54 (May 1977): 176-193.

1352. ―――――. "United States Compliance with the Helsinki Final Act: The Treatment of Aliens." *Vanderbilt Journal of Transnational Law*, 13 (Spring/Summer 1980): 397-408.

1353. Casad, Steven J. "Alienage and Public Employment: The Need for an Intermediate Standard in Equal Protection. *Foley v. Connelie.* 435 U.S. 291 (1978)." *Hastings Law Journal*, 32 (September 1980): 163-199.

1354. Catz, Robert S. "Fourth Amendment Limitations on Non-border Searches for Illegal Aliens: The Immigration and Naturalization Service Meets the Constitution." *Ohio State Law Journal*, 39 (1978): 66-95.

1355. ―――――. "Regulating the Employment of Illegal Aliens: *DeCanas* and Section 2805." *Santa Clara Law Review*, 17 (Fall 1977); 751-75.

1356. ―――――, and H.B. Lenard. "Federal Pre-Emption and the 'Right' of Undocumented Alien Children to a Public Education: A Partial Reply." *Hastings Constitutional Law Quarterly*, 6 (Spring 1979): 909-32.

1357. Celebrezze, A.J., Jr., and C.J. Hudak. "Ohio's Non-resident Alien Land Registration Law: A Legislative and Administrative View." *Capital University Law Review*, 9 (1979): 215-39.

1358. Chapman, Robert S., and Robert F. Kane. "Illegal Aliens and Enforcement: Present Practices and Proposed Legislation." *University of California, Davis Law Review*, 8 (1975): 127-61.

1359. "Chinese American Civic Council v. Attorney General.
No. 75-1870. D.C. Cir. October 11, 1977." *Texas
International Law Journal*, 13 (Spring 1978): 372-4.

1360. "Citizenship. Denaturalization--Failure to Disclose
Service as Concentration Camp Guard During Second
World War." *American Journal of International Law*,
74 (January 1980): 186-189.

1361. "Commuters, Illegal and American Farmworkers: The Need
for a Broader Approach to Domestic Farm Labor Problems." *New York University Law Review*, 48 (1973):
439-492.

1362. Conrad, Jane Reister. "Health Care for Indigent Illegal
Aliens: Whose Responsibility?" *University of California, Davis Law Review*, 8 (1975): 107-26.

1363. "A Constitutional Approach to State Regulation of Employment of Illegal Aliens." *Southern California
Law Review*, 46 (1973): 565-584.

1364. "Constitutional Law--Equal Protection--Charge of Tui-
tion to Illegal Alien School Children Pursuant to
Texas Statute Violations Fourteenth Amendment."
St. Mary's Law Journal, 11 (1979): 549-69.

1365. "Constitutional Law--Equal Protection--Citizenship
Requirements for Probation Officers Do Not Deny Resi-
dent Aliens Equal Protection. *Cabell v. Chavez-
Salido.* 102 S ct. 735." *Suffolk Transnational Law
Journal*, 7 (Fall 1983): 463-76.

1366. "Constitutional Law: The Equal Protection Clause: The
Effect of *Plyler v. Doe* (102 S ct. 2382) on Intermediate Scrutiny." *Oklahoma Law Review*, 36 (Spring
1983): 321-37.

1367. "Constitutional Law--Equal Protection--Discrimination
Against Aliens Employed as Public School Teachers Not
Proscribed by the Fourteenth Amendment." *Seton Hall
Law Review*, 10 (1980): 870-86.

1368. "Constitutional Law: Equal Protection and Educating
Illegal Alien Children." *Seton Hall Law Review*, 11
(1981): 499-518.

1369. "Constitutional Law--Equal Protection--Equal Protection
Does Not Protect Nonimmigrant Iranian Students from

Selective Deportation." *Seton Hall Law Review*, 11
(1980): 230-42.

1370. "Constitutional Law--Equal Protection--Public Education
for Undocumented Aliens. *Plyler v. Doe.* 102 S ct.
2382." *Wayne Law Review*, 29 (Summer 1983): 1487-523.

1371. "Constitutional Law: Equal Protection Rights of Illegal
Alien School Children. *Plyler v. Doe.* 102 S ct. 2382."
Harvard International Law Journal, 23 (Winter 1983):
389-95.

1372. "Constitutional Law--Equal Protection--A State Statute
Which Denies an Education to Undocumented Aliens Is
Unconstitutional." *Texas International Law Journal*,
14 (Spring 1979): 289-316.

1373. "Constitutional Law: Equal Protection--A State Statute
Protesting Noncitizens from Serving in All Positions
Classified as 'Peace Officer' Does Not Violate the
Fourteenth Amendment's Equal Protection Clause When
Applied to County Parole Officers: The Citizenship
Requirement Is Not Overbroad and Faces Within the
States Sovereign Authority to Define Its Political
Community. *Cabell v. Chavez-Salido.* 1025 S ct. 735."
Emory Law Journal, 31 (Summer 1982): 707-44.

1374. "Constitutional Law--Equal Protection--Statute Barring
Aliens from Positions as Public School Teachers Is
Within the Exception to Strict Scrutiny Analysis."
Southern Illinois University Law Journal (March 1980):
107-24.

1375. "Constitutional Law--Fourteenth Amendment--Equal Pro-
tection--Aliens' Right--Governmental Function Doctrine."
Duquesne Law Review, 18 (Summer 1980): 957-68.

1376. "Constitutional Law. Fourteenth Amendment--Equal Pro-
tection--Alien's Rights--Governmental Function Doc-
trine--the Supreme Court of the United States Has
Held That a State May Exclude Aliens from Deputy
Probation Officer Positions Which Involve the Exer-
cise of the Sovereign Police Power. *Cabell v. Chavez-
Salido.* 102 S ct. 735." *Duquesne Law Review*, 21
(Fall 1982): 277-93.

1377. "Constitutional Law--Fourteenth Amendment--A State May
Require that Its Public School Teachers Be United States
Citizens." *Tulane Law Review*, 54 (December 1979): 225-
33.

1378. "Constitutional Law--Fourth Amendment--Immigration
       Checkpoint Stops for Questioning Are Reasonable With-
       out Individualized Suspicion." *Brigham Young Univer-
       sity Law Review* (1977): 447-73.

1379. "Constitutional Law--Fourth Amendment Search and
       Seizure--Without Consent, Warrant, or Probable Cause,
       a Roving Patrol Search of a Vehicle Twenty-Five Miles
       from Border Is an Unreasonable Search and Seizure
       Within Meaning of Fourth Amendment." *Vanderbilt Jour-
       nal of Transportation Law*, 7 (Summer 1975): 762-69.

1380. "Constitutional Law--Immigration Law--State Regulation
       of Employment of Illegal Aliens in Not *per se* Pre-
       empted by Federal Control over Immigration or by the
       Immigration and Nationality Act." *Texas International
       Law Journal*, 12 (Winter 1977): 87-96.

1381. "Constitutional Law--Preemption--A University Policy
       Which Denied in State Status to Children of Domiciled
       G-4 Aliens Violated the Supremacy Clause of the Con-
       stitution. *Toll v. Moreno*. 102 S ct. 2977." *Uni-
       versity of Detroit Journal of Urban Law*, 61 (Fall
       1983): 139-53.

1382. "Constitutional Law: Protection Against Illegal Search
       and Seizure." *Harvard International Law Journal*, 22
       (Fall 1981): 670-6.

1383. "Constitutional Law--Resident Alien's Right to Work--
       New York Statute Forbidding Resident Alien to Work
       as Public School Teacher Does Not Violate the Equal
       Protection Clause of the Fourteenth Amendment."
       Vanderbilt Journal of International Law, 20 (Fall
       1979): 219-32.

1384. "Constitutional Law--Right to Trial by Jury--Aliens
       Charged with Non-Military Offenses in a United States
       Court in Berlin Entitled to Jury Trial." *Seton Hall
       Law Review*, 11 (1981): 809-24.

1385. "Constitutional Law--Search and Seizure--Border Patrol
       Vehicular Checkpoints." *New York Law School Law
       Review*, 22 (1976): 354-69.

1386. "Constitutional Law--Search and Seizure--Judicial Limi-
       tations on Warrantless Border Searches Made Without
       Probable Cause Make Fourth Amendment Rights of

Travelers Uncertain." *Vanderbilt Law Review*, 27
(April 1974): 523-37.

1387. "Constitutional Law--Searches and Seizures--Aliens."
New York Law School Law Review, 22 (1977): 1041-52.

1388. "Constitutional Law: State Discrimination Against Resident Aliens in Public Employment--What Standard of
Review?" *Stetson Law Review*, 10 (Fall 1980): 171-84.

1389. "Constitutional Law--Texas Statute's Denial of Free
Education to Illegal Aliens Violates Equal Protection
Clause and Is Preempted by the Immigration and
Nationality Act." *Vanderbilt Journal of Transnational
Law*, 12 (Summer 1979): 787-93.

1390. "Constitutional Law--Undocumented Aliens--State Statute
Denying Undocumented Aliens Access to Free Public
Education Unconstitutional. *Plyler v. Doe*.
102 S ct. 2382." *Suffolk Transnational Law Journal*,
6 (Fall 1982): 367-81.

1391. "Constitutionality of Legislative Restrictions on the
Employment Rights of Legal Resident Aliens in New
York State." *Syracuse Journal of International Law
and Commerce*, 7 (Summer 1979): 109-28.

1392. "*Coriolan v. INS*. 559 F 2d 993." *Brooklyn Journal of
International Law*, 4 (Spring 1978): 285-7.

1393. Cornyn, Michael R. "Constitutional Law--Equal Protection--Statute Barring Aliens from Positions as Public
School Teachers Is Within the Exceptions to Strict
Scrutiny Analysis. *Ambach v. Norwick*. 441 U.S. 68
(1979)." *Southern Illinois University Law Journal*
(Fall 1980): 107-124.

1394. Cottrell, Floyd G. "The Right of Undocumented Aliens
Against Their Employers." *Fordham Urban Law Journal*,
10 (Fall 1981): 683-698.

1395. "Criminal Procedure--The Border Patrol and the Fourth
Amendment." *Annual Survey of American Law* (1976):
148-164.

1396. "Criminal Procedure--Search and Seizure--Aliens and
'Extended' Border Inspections." *Wayne Law Review*, 20
(1974): 1141-1153.

1397. "Criminalizing Employment of Illegal Aliens: Work
      Authorization Cards May Invade Privacy." *Journal
      of Criminal Law,* 72 (Summer 1981): 637-70.

1398. Cunningham, William. "Deportation Based upon Fraudulent
      Entry: A Limitation of the Waiver Provision." *Loyola
      Law Review,* 21 (Fall 1975): 1003-12.

1399. Danilov, Dan P. "Criminal Law and the Foreign Born."
      Washington State Bar News, 30 (1976): 8-11.

1400. ————. "Immigration Today: Rights of Aliens." *Trial,*
      13 (August/September 1977): 8-9, 42-45, 52-57.

1401. "Defense of the Farm Labor Contractor Registration Act."
      Texas Law Review, 59 (March 1981): 531-558.

1402. DeKuiper, Kristin A. "*Santiago vs. Immigration and
      Naturalization Service*--The Ninth Circuit Retreats
      from Its Modern Approach to Estoppel Against the
      Government." *Utah Law Review,* 16 (1976): 371-385.

1403. "Denaturalization and Nationality at the Visa Applica-
      tion Stage. *Fedorenko v. United States.* 101 S ct.
      737." *Santa Clara Law Review,* 22 (Winter 1982):
      255-66.

1404. "Deportation of Aliens--Deportation of Alien Parents
      Resulting in De Facto Deportation of Their Citizen
      Child Is Precluded by the Citizenship Clause of the
      Fourteenth Amendment." *Virginia Journal of Inter-
      national Law,* 17 (1977): 322-328.

1405. "Deportation as Punishment." *Chicago-Kent Law Review,*
      52 (1975): 466-484.

1406. Dernis, Martin M. "Haitian Immigrants: Political Refu-
      gees or Economic Escapees?" *University of Miami Law
      Review,* 31 (1976): 27-41.

1407. "Discrimination Based on Sex and Illegitimacy Is Per-
      missible in the Immigration Area." *DePaul Law Review,*
      27 (Winter 1978): 515-31.

1408. "Discrimination Expectations of Equal Protection.
      Vargas v. Strake. 710 F 2d 190." *The Lawyer of the
      Americas,* 15 (Winter 1984): 521-33.

1409. Dodge, Katharine S. "Immigration: Eligibility for Withholding of Deportation; the Alien's Burden Under the 1980 Refugee Act. (2d Circuit Review--1981-1982 Term) *Stevie v. Sava* 678 F 2d 401 (2d cir. 1982)." *Brooklyn Law Review*, 49 (Summer 1983): 1193-1216.

1410. "Does the Constitution Guarantee a Free Public Education to Undocumented Alien Children?" *Baylor Law Review*, 33 (Summer 1981): 637-55.

1411. "*Dreyfus v. Von Finck*. 534 F 2d 24." *American Journal of International Law*, 71 (January 1977): 149-51.

1412. "Drugs, Databanks and Dignity: Computerized Selection of Travelers for Intrusive Border Searches." *Boston University Law Review*, 56 (1976): 941-969.

1413. "Dual Standard for State Discrimination Against Aliens." *Harvard Law Review*, 92 (May 1979): 1516-37.

1414. "Due Process and the Deportable Alien: Limitations on State Department Participation in Withholding of Deportation Inquiry." *Catholic Lawyer*, 22 (1976): 275-286.

1415. "Due Process Rights for Excludable Aliens Under United States Immigration Law and the United Nations Protocol Relating to the Status of Refugees--Haitian Aliens, a Case in Point." *New York University Journal of International Law and Politics*, 10 (Spring 1977): 203-40.

1416. Durbin, Diana Cabaza. "Collateral Attack of Prior Deportation Orders in Prosecutions for Illegal Reentry." *American Journal of Criminal Law*, 8 (July 1980): 183-197.

1417. "Employer Sanctions: The 'New Solution' to the Illegal Alien Problem." *Arizona State Law Journal* (1979): 439-67.

1418. "Employers of Certain Alien Farm Workers No Longer Need Deposit Unemployment Taxes for Them and May Claim Refund of Taxes." *Wall Street Journal* (December 22, 1982): 1.

1419. "Employment in the Federal Civil Service--Aliens Need Not Apply." *Lawyer of the Americas*, 11 (Summer/Fall 1979): 579-96.

1420.   "Employment of Illegal ALiens--States May Impose Crimi-
        nal and Civil Liabilities on Employer of Illegal
        Aliens if Such Employment Would Have an Adverse
        Effect on Lawful Resident Workers: *DeCanas v. Bica*,
        96 S. Ct. 933, 1976." *Santa Clara Law Review*, 17
        (Winter 1977): 198-214.

1421.   "Enforcement of International Human Rights in the
        Federal Courts After *Filartiga v. Pena-Irala*
        (630 F 2d 876)." *Virginia Law Review*, 67 (October
        1981): 1379-93.

1422.   "Ensuring Due Process in Alien Exclusion Proceedings
        After *Landon v. Plascencia.* 103 S ct. 321." *Hastings
        Law Journal*, 34 (March 1983): 911-39.

1423.   "Equal Protection, Education and the Undocumented Alien
        Child: *Plyler v. Doe.* 102 S ct. 2382." *Houston
        Law Review*, 20 (May 1983): 899-919.

1424.   "Equal Protection--Intermediate Scrutiny Applied to
        Texas Statute Denying Education to Undocumented
        Children. *Plyler v. Doe.* 102 S ct. 2382." *Wake
        Forest Law Review*, 19 (April 1983): 307-29.

1425.   "Equal Treatment of Aliens: Preemption or Equal Protec-
        tion?" *Stanford Law Review*, 31 (July 1979): 1069-91.

1426.   Ericson, Anna-Stina. "The Impact of Commuters on the
        Mexican-American Border Area." *Monthly Labor Review*,
        93 (1970): 18-27.

1427.   "Estoppel and Immigration." *Catholic Lawyer*, 22 (Autumn
        1976): 287-96.

1428.   "European Communities--Migrant Workers--Exclusion of
        Aliens--A Member State May Limit Free Movement of
        Workers on Grounds of Public Policy, Public Security,
        or Health in the Exercise of Discretion Under
        Article 3 (1) of Council Direction No. 64/221."
        Vanderbilt Journal of Transnational Law, 9 (Spring
        1976): 415-23.

1429.   Evans, A.C. "Political Status of Aliens in Internation-
        al Law, Municipal Law and European Community Law."
        International and Comparative Law Quarterly, 30
        (January 1981): 20-41.

1430. Evans, Alona E. "Aliens--Control Over Admission--
      Consular Nonreviewability--Equalization of Admission
      of Aliens from Western and Eastern Hemispheres."
      American Journal of International Law, 74 (January
      1980): 184-185.

1431. Evans, Andrew C. "United Kingdom Courts and European
      Community Law Governing the Exclusion or Expulsion of
      Migrants." *Public Law* (Winter 1981): 497-510.

1432. "Exclusion or Deportation of Aliens for Conviction of
      Foreign Crimes Involving Moral Turpitude: Grand Prob-
      lems with the Petty Offense Exception." *Cornell
      International Law Journal*, 14 (Winter 1981): 135-51.

1433. "Extended Border Search and Probable Cause." *Washing-
      ton University Law Quarterly*, 42 (1973): 889-896.

1434. "Extended Border Searches by Immigration Officers."
      Columbia Journal of Transnational Law, 13 (1974):
      143-154.

1435. "Extent of the Border." *Hastings Constitutional Law
      Quarterly*, 1 (1974): 235-250.

1436. Fawcett, Amelia C. "U.S. Immigration and Refugee Re-
      form: A Critical Evaluation." *Virginia Journal of
      International Law*, 22 (Summer 1982): 805-848.

1437. "Federal Civil Service Employment: Resident Aliens Need
      Not Apply." *San Diego Law Review*, 15 (December 1977):
      171-200.

1438. "Federal Judicial Compulsion of an Alien's Testimony
      Contrary to the Mandate of the Laws of His Native
      Land." *Columbia Journal of Transnational Law*, 16
      (1977): 357-84.

1439. "Federal Jurisdiction of Alleged Torturer Under the
      Alien Tort Statute." *International Trade Law Journal*,
      6 (Spring/Summer 1980/81): 289-95.

1440. "Federalism and a New Equal Protection." *Villanova Law
      Review*, 24 (March 1979): 557-84.

1441. Fernandez, Violette Witwer. "Illegal Aliens as Employ-
      ees Under the National Labor Relations Act. *NLRB v.
      Apollo Tire Co.* 604 F 2d 1180 (9th Cir. 1979)."
      Georgia Law Journal, 68 (February 1980): 851-71.

1442. *"Fernandez v. Wilkinson* (505 F Supp 787): Making the United States Accountable Under Customary International Law." *Denver Journal of International Law and Policy,* 10 (Winter 1981): 360-5.

1443. *"Fiallo v. Bell.* 97 Sup ct. 1473." *Texas International Law Journal,* 13 (Winter 1977): 141-3.

1444. "Fifth Amendment and International Comity as a Basis for Avoiding the Choice Between Conflicting Demands of Two Sovereigns: A Critical Look at *United States v. Field* (352 F 2d 404)." *California Western International Law Journal,* 8 (Spring 1978): 368-83.

1445. *"Filartiga v. Pena-Irala.* 630 F 2d 876. A New Forum for Violations of International Human Rights." *American University Law Review,* 30 (Spring 1981): 807-33.

1446. *"Filartiga v. Pena-Irala.* 630 F 2d 876. Providing Federal Jurisdiction for Human Rights Violations Through the Alien Tort Statute." *Denver Journal of International Law and Policy,* 10 (Winter 1981): 355-9.

1447. Fiorillo, Margaret H. "Immigration--Lawful Unrelinquished Domicile--Deportable Resident Alien Must Accumulate Seven Years of Lawful Domicile Subsequent to Admission for Permanent Residence to Be Eligible for Discretionary Relief. *Castillo-Felix v. Immigration and Naturalization Service.* 601 F 2d 459 (9th Cir. 1979)." *Vanderbilt Journal of Transnational Law,* 12 (Fall 1979): 1009-1017.

1448. Fleischer, Richard I. "Judicial Recommendations Against Deportation." *Kentucky Bench and Bar,* 46 (January 1982): 16.

1449. Flowe, Benjamin H., Jr. "The Illegal Alien Whether to Withhold Deportation to Avoid His Potential Persecution." *Fleurinor v. Immigration and Naturalization Service* 585 F 2d 129 (5th Cir. 1978)." *North Carolina Journal of International Law and Commercial Regulations,* 5 (Spring 1980): 305-318.

1450. Foerstal, Jonathan P. "Suspension of Deportation-- Toward a New Hardship Standard." *San Diego Law Review,* 18 (July-August 1981): 663-683.

1451. Fogel, Walter A. "Illegal Aliens: Economic Aspects and
       Public Policy Alternatives." *San Diego Law Review*, 15
       (December 1977): 63-78.

1452. Fogg, Tamara K. "Adjustment of Status Under Section
       245 of the Immigration and Nationality Act." *San
       Diego Law Review*, 20 (1983): 165-189.

       Aliens who wish to immigrate to the United States
       generally must request a permanent visa from a consular
       office abroad. Sometimes an alien in the United States
       under a temporary visa desires to immigrate. To elim-
       inate the inconvenience of leaving the United States to
       apply for a permanent visa, Section 245 allows qualified
       aliens to remain within the United States and request
       an adjustment of status. This procedure has been
       abused. Discusses the problem of such abuse and solu-
       tion recently proposed in the Simpson-Mazzoli bill.

1453. "*Foley v. Connelie.* 98 Sup. ct. 1067. A New Direction
       in State Discrimination Against Aliens." *Capital Uni-
       versity Law Review*, 8 (1978): 169-82.

1454. Forst, Bradly. "Regulation of Foreign Investment in
       United States Real Estate: State or Federal Preroga-
       tive?" *Southern Illinois University Law Journal*
       (Winter 1981): 21-63.

1455. Foster, Charles C. "The Logic of Adjustment of Status
       to Permanent Residency." *South Texas Law Journal*, 24
       (Winter 1983): 37-68.

1456. "Fourteenth Amendment Equal Protection and Alienage-
       based Discrimination in the Appointment of State
       Police Officers." *Southwestern Law Journal*, 32 (Novem-
       ber 1978): 1027-37.

1457. "Fourth Amendment Applications to Searches Conducted
       by Immigration Officials." *Albany Law Review*, 38
       (1974): 962-975.

1458. "*Francis v. INS.* 532 F 2d 268. Alien on Discretionary
       Relief." *Detroit College Law Review* (Winter 1977):
       893-906.

1459. Franco, Glorene, and Glenn S. Warren. "The Illegal
       Alien Assault: The United States Retreats from the
       Border." *American Criminal Law Review*, 14 (Spring
       1977): 747-79.

1460. Frasch, Brian B. "National Contacts as a Basis for in Personam Jurisdiction over Aliens in Federal Question Suits." *California Law Review,* 70 (May 1982): 686-707.

1461. "Fraud in Nonimmigrating Visitors as Self-serving Waiver of Deportation." *Columbia Journal of Transnational Law,* 13 (1974): 436-451.

1462. Furin, Gary C. "Immigration Law: Alien Employment Certification." *Law Notes,* 14 (Winter 1978): 13-17.

1463. ———. "Immigration Law: Alien Employment Certification." *International Lawyer,* 16 (Winter 1982): 111-119.

1464. Gales, Paul M. "Balancing Federal Power over Aliens and Fifth Amendment Protections. *Mow Sun Wong v. Campbell.* 626 F 2d 739 (9th Cir. 1980)." *Notre Dame Lawyer,* 56 (April 1981): 689-695.

1465. Gallivan, Melissa. "Immigration—A State May Prohibit the Employment of Illegal Aliens." *Vanderbilt Journal of Transnational Law,* 6 (Fall 1976): 907-914.

1466. Garcia, D. "The Coram Nobis Writ in an Immigration Law Context." *Chicano Law Review,* 2 (1975): 92-108.

1467. Garvey, J.L. "Repression of the Political Emigre—the Underground to International Law: A Proposal for Remedy." *Yale Law Journal,* 90 (November 1980): 78-120.

1468. Garza, Daniel. "Tracing the Deadly Tax Drain of Mexican Aliens." *Dallas* (August 1974): 22-25.

1469. Gerber, Barbara Ettlinger. "A Judicial Response to Immigration Service Decision Making (The Second Circuit Review—1979)." *Brooklyn Law Review,* 47 (Spring 1981): 627-660.

1470. "Getting Back In: The Plasencia (*Landon v. Plasencia.* 103 S ct. 321). Decision and the Permanent Resident Alien's Right to Procedural Due Process." *University of Miami Law Review,* 36 (September 1982): 969-85.

1471. Ghezzi, June K. "Toward a Proper Constitutional Approach to the Onehouse Legislative Veto: Atkins and Chadha." *Loyola University of Chicago Law Journal,* 13 (Fall 1981): 171-201.

1472. Gilbert, Jeffrey C., and Steven Kass. "A Stark Pattern of Discrimination. *Jean v. Nelson* No. 82-5772 (11th Cir. April 12, 1983)." *University of Miami Law Review*, 36 (September 1982): 1005-1038.

1473. Goodpaster, Gary S. "Illegal Immigration." *Arizona State Law Journal* (1981): 651-722.

1474. Gordon, Charles. "Powers and Responsibilities of Immigration Officers." *American Bar Association Journal*, 59 (1973): 64-67.

1475. ————. "The Right of Aliens: An Expanding Role for Trial Lawyers." *Trial*, 19 (December 1983): 54-8.

1476. Gough, Arnold G. "Reentry of Aliens Remains Unsettled. *Rosenberg v. Fleuti*. 374 U.S. 449 (1963)." *Notre Dame Lawyer*, 56 (April 1981): 696-703.

1477. Greedon, Kevin T. "Refugee Act of 1980 and the Cuban-Haitian Entrants Status Pending?" *Suffolk Transnational Law Journal*, 5 (June 1981): 213-233.

1478. Green, Mitch. "Unalienable Wrongs--Immigrants and the Law of North of the Rio Grande." *Juris Doctor*, 7 (November 1977): 37-44.

1479. Green, Sheldon L. "Public Agency Distortion of Congressional Will: Federal Policy toward Non-resident Alien Labor." *George Washington Law Review*, 40 (1972): 440-463.

1480. Griffith, Elwin. "The Alien Meets Some Constitutional Hurdles in Employment Education and Aid Programs." *San Diego Law Review*, 17 (March 1980): 201-231.

1481. Grossman, Thomas E. "International Law--International Law (Jurisdiction)--Federal Jurisdiction--Human Rights--Torture Is a Tort in Violation of the Law of Nations, Giving Rise to Federal Jurisdiction Pursuant to 28 U.S.C. 1350 Whenever an Alleged Process by an Alien Within the Borders of the United States. *Filartiga v. Pena-Irala*. 630 F 2d 876 (2d Cir. 1980). *University of Cincinnati Law Review*, 49 (Fall 1980): 880-891.

1482. Hahn, Richard F. "Constitutional Limits on the Power to Exclude Aliens." *Columbia Law Review*, 82 (June 1982): 957-997.

1483. "*Hampton v. Mow Sun Wong.* 96 Sup ct. 1895." *American Journal of International Law,* 70 (October 1976): 846-8.

1484. "*Hampton v. Mow Sun Wong.* 96 Sup ct. 1895." *Texas International Law Journal,* 12 (Winter 1977): 113-16.

1485. Harwood, E. "Arrests Without Warrant: The Legal and Organizational Environment of Immigration Law Enforcement." *University of California-Davis Law Review,* 17 (Winter 1984): 505-48.

1486. Haynes, Jim Tom. "BIA Opinions (Board of Immigration Appeals)." *Immigration Journal,* 5 (January-February 1982): 15.

1487. ————. "A Legitimate Question. (Distinguishing Between Legitimate and Legitimated Children for Immigration Purposes)." *Immigration Journal,* 5 (March-April 1982): 16.

1488. Healy, Lynn D. "Constitutional Law--Right to Trial by Jury--Aliens Charged with Non-Military Offenses in a United States Court in Berlin Entitled to Jury Trial. *United States v. Tiede.* 86 F.R.D. 227 (U.S. Ct. for Berlin 1979)." *Seton Hall Law Review,* 11 (Summer 1981): 809-824.

1489. Healy, Patricia M. "The Materiality Standard in Denaturalization Cases: Concealment by Naturalized Citizen of Service as Nazi Death Camp Guard. *United States v. Fedorenko.* 444 U.S. 1070 (1980)." *The Lawyers of Americas,* 12 (Fall 1980): 757-774.

1490. Heiserman, Robert G., and Jane S. Hazen. "Defense of the Alien Accused of Crime." *Colorado Lawyer,* 11 (April 1982): 950-6.

1491. Helbush, Terry. "INS Violation of Its Own Regulation: Relief for the Alien." *Golden Gate University Law Review,* 12 (Spring 1982): 217-225.

1492. Hennes, Kristin E. "Concealment of Facts Forestalling an Investigation in Denaturalization Proceedings." *University of Chicago Law Review,* 47 (Spring 1980): 588-603.

1493. Henry, Daniel W. "Wetback as Material Witness: Pretrial

Detention or Deposition?" *California Western Law Review*, 7 (Fall 1970): 175-96.

1494. Hiltz, Anne Kirchgassner. "Aliens--Civil Rights--
       Exclusion of Aliens from Federal Civil Service Up-
       held. *Mow Sun Wong v. Campbell.* 626 F 2d 739 (9th
       Cir. 1980)." *Suffolk Transnational Law Journal*, 6
       (Spring 1982): 133-146.

1495. Hing, Bill Ong. "Estoppel in Immigration Proceedings--
       New Life from Akbarin and Miranda." *San Diego Law
       Review*, 20 (December 1982): 11-36.

1496. Hoffheimer, D.J. "Employment Discrimination Against
       Resident Aliens by Private Employers." *Labor Law
       Journal*, 35 (March 1984): 142-147.

1497. Holloway, Jan C. "A Further Retreat from Graham.
       Ambach v. Norwick. 99 S ct. 1589 (1979)." *Loyola
       Law Review*, 40 (Summer 1980): 997-1011.

1498. Hopkins, Joanne P. "Immigration--Adoption by Custom
       Qualifies Beneficiary for Fifth Preference Status.
       *Mila v. District Director-Immigration and Naturaliza-
       tion Service.* 494 F Supp. 998 (D. Utah 1980)."
       Texas International Law Journal, 16 (Summer 1981):
       554-65.

1499. Horwich, Daniel. "Aliens--Labor Relations National
       Labor Relations Act: Protection of Illegal Aliens.
       NLRB v. Apollo Tire Co. 604 F 2d 1180 (9th Cir.
       1979)." *Suffolk Transnational Law Journal*, 4 (Winter
       1980): 174-183.

1500. Houston, Heather A. *"Narenji v. Civiletti:* Expediency
       Triumphs over Alien's Constitutional Rights. *Narenji
       v. Civiletti.* 617 F 2d 745 (D.C. Cir. 1979)."
       Loyola of Los Angeles Law Review, 14 (Spring 1982):
       331-358.

1501. Hull, Elizabeth. "Resident Aliens and the Equal Protec-
       tion Clause: The Burger Court's Retreat from *Graham
       v. Richardson.*" *Brooklyn Law Review*, 47 (Fall 1980):
       1-42.

1502. ――――. "Undocumented Aliens and the Equal Protection
       Clause: An Analysis of *Doe v. Plyler.*" *Brooklyn Law
       Review*, 48 (Fall 1981): 43-74.

1503. "Human Rights—Alien Tort Statute—Internal Deed of Foreign Official Actionable in United States Court." *Suffolk Transnational Law Journal*, 5 (1981): 297-310.

1504. Hurwitz, Gerald S. "Motions Practice Before the Board of Immigration Appeals." *San Diego Law Review*, 20 (December 1982): 79-95.

1505. Hutchinson, D.J. "More Substantive Equal Protection? A Note on *Plyler v. Doe* (102 S ct. 2382)." *Supreme Court Review* (1982): 167-94.

1506. "Ideas Not Welcome: Visa Denials on Ideological Grounds." *Record of the Association of the Bar of the City of New York*, 36 (May-June 1981): 288-298.

1507. "Illegal Aliens with American Families: The Scope of the Statutory Waiver of Deportation in Cases of Fraudulent Entry after *Reid v. Immigration and Naturalization Service*." *Northwestern University Law Review*, 70 (September-October 1975): 673-98.

1508. "Illegal Aliens and the Border Patrol—Reasonable Suspicion Not Required When Occupants of Vehicles Stopped for Questioning at Permanent Inland Checkpoints." *New York University Journal of International Law and Politics*, 9 (Fall 1976): 303-33.

1509. "Illegal Aliens as 'Employees' Under the National Labor Relations Act." *Georgia Law Journal*, 68 (February 1980): 851-71.

1510. "Illegal Aliens and Enforcement: Present Practices and Proposed Legislation." *University of California, Davis, Law Review*, 8 (1975): 127-61.

1511. "Illegal Aliens Have Right to Free Public Education. *Plyler v. Doe*. 102 S ct. 2382." *Washington University Law Quarterly*, 61 (Summer 1983): 591-606.

1512. "Illegal Aliens' Rights Under the NLRA." *Wisconsin Law Review* (1983): 1525-31.

1513. "Illegal Immigration: Short-Range Solution of Employer Sanctions." *Mississippi Law Journal*, 49 (September 1978): 659-87.

1514. "Illegal Immigration in the Tristate Region: New York, New Jersey, Connecticut." *Society* (November 1976): 5-6.

1515. "Immigration--Admissibility--Reentry of Permanent Resident Alien Determined at Exclusion Hearing. *Landon v. Plascencia.* 103 S ct. 321." *Suffolk Transnational Law Journal*, 7 (Fall 1983): 553-64.

1516. "Immigration, Aliens, and the Constitution." *Notre Dame Lawyer*, 49 (1974): 1075-1100.

1517. "Immigration--Aliens--the Invalidation of a Homosexual Marriage for Immigration Purposes. *Adams v. Howerton.* 673 F 2d 1036." *Suffolk Transnational Law Journal*, 7 (Spring 1983): 267-78.

1518. "Immigration--Deportation--Youthful Offender Convicted of Marijuana Possession Is Not Subject to Mandatory Deportation." *Rutgers-Camden Law Journal*, 9 (Fall 1977): 199-206.

1519. "Immigration--Harboring of Illegal Aliens--New Meaning to the Concept of Shielding from Detection. *United States v. Rubio-Gonzales.* 674 F 2d 1067." *Suffolk Transnational Law Journal*, 7 (Spring 1983): 255-66.

1520. "Immigration Law--Deportation Based on an Expunged Marijuana Conviction." *Suffolk University Law Review*, 11 (1977): 378-392.

1521. "Immigration Law: Domicile." *Harvard International Law Journal*, 19 (Fall 1978): 1031-7.

1522. "Immigration Law--Exclusionary Rule--If the Exclusionary Rule Question Is Reached the Civil Nature of a Deportation Proceeding May Preclude Its Applications." *Fordham Urban Law Journal*, 7 (1978-1979): 459-75.

1523. "Immigration Law--Immigration and Nationality Act-- Deportation of an Alien Who Is Charged with Violating Section 212 (a) (20) of the Act by Entering the United States with Invalid Documents Is Waived Under Section 241 (f), Which Grants Relief to Aliens Fraudulently Entering the United States, When the Facts Proving the Section 212 (2) (20) Charge Necessarily Establish Fraudulent Entry in Violation of Section 212 (a) (19)." *George Washington Law Review*, 45 (March 1977): 560-71.

1524. "Immigration Law: Limits on Detention of Excludable Aliens. *Fernandez-Roque v. Smith*. 567 F Supp. 1115." *Harvard International Law Journal*, 25 (Winter 1984): 225-32.

1525. "Immigration Law: Local Enforcement of Federal Immigration Laws. *Gonzales v. Peoria*. 722 F 2d 468." *Harvard International Law Journal*, 25 (Spring 1984): 477-83.

1526. "Immigration Law and the Marijuana User." *University of Toronto Faculty Law Review*, 37 (Fall 1979): 254-65.

1527. "Immigration Law--National Standard, Incorporation of State Law or Hybrid Test--State Definition of Adultery Utilized for Determining 'Good Moral Character' in a Voluntary Departure Proceeding." *New York University Law Review*, 51 (1976): 1021-1049.

1528. "Immigration Law and Procedure--Excludability--Conviction Under British Dangerous Drugs Act of 1965 Is Not a Conviction Under a Law Prohibiting 'Illicit Possession' Within the Meaning of Immigration and Nationality Act Section 212 (a)." *Texas International Law Journal*, 11 (Spring 1976): 345-53.

1529. "Immigration Law: Rights of Detained Aliens. *Jean v. Nelson*. 711 F 2d 1455." *Harvard International Law Journal*, 25 (Winter 1984): 233-9.

1530. "Immigration Law: State Regulation and Equal Protection: Political Asylum Cases; and Exclusion Hearings." *Annual Survey of American Law*, 1983 (March 1984): 837-66.

1531. "Immigration Law--Statutory Citizenship--Ignorance of Statutory Retention Provisions of Immigration and Nationality Act Does Not Excuse Noncompliance." *Texas International Law Journal*, 13 (Summer 1978): 467-73.

1532. "The Immigration Legal Assistance Project." *Los Angeles Lawyer*, 5 (February 1983): 6.

1533. "Immigration and Nationality Law--State Alienage Classifications, Federal Alienage Classifications. Enforcement of the INA and Due Process Rights of

Citizens and Lawful Resident Relatives. State Regulations of Illegal Aliens. Immigration and Nationality Act Amendments of 1976." *Annual Survey of American Law* (1977): 205-37.

1534. "Immigration and Naturalization--The Labor Dispute Regulation and the Status of 'Green Card Commuters.'" *University of Toledo Law Review*, 4 (1973): 305-316.

1535. "*Immigration and Naturalization Service v. Chadha* (103 S ct. 2764): The Legislative Veto Declared Unconstitutional." *West Virginia Law Review*, 86 (Winter 1983/84): 461-78.

1536. "Immigration and Naturalization Service District Director Is Entitled to Broad Discretion in Weighing Criteria for Parole Determination of Unadmitted. *Bertrand v. Sava.* 684 F 2d 204 (2d cir. 1982)." *Vanderbilt Journal of Transnational Law*, 16 (Winter 1983): 263.

1537. "Immigration--State Certificate of Relief from Disabilities Prevents Mandatory Deportation Under 8 USC 1251 (a)(11)." *Fordham Law Review*, 45 (1977): 1247-1253.

1538. "Immigration--a State May Prohibit the Employment of Illegal Aliens." *Vanderbilt Journal of Transnational Law*, 9 (Fall 1976): 907-14.

1539. "Impact of Expungent Relief on Deportation of Aliens for Narcotics Convictions." *Georgia Law Journal*, 65 June 1977): 1325-57.

1540. "The Indefinite Detention of Excludable Aliens. *Palma v. Verdeyen.* 676 F 2d 100." *New York University Journal of International Law and Politics*, 16 (Fall 1983): 119-46.

1541. "Indefinite Detention of Excludable Aliens." *Detroit College Law Review*, 1981 (Fall 1981): 925-46.

1542. "The Indefinite Detention of Excluded Aliens: Statutory and Constitutional Jurisdiction and Limitations." *Michigan Law Review*, 82 (October 1983): 61-89.

1543. "In Search of the Border: Searches Conducted by Federal Custom and Immigration Officers." *New York University*

Journal of International Law and Politics, 5 (1972):
93-115.

1544. "Ins and Outs of Immigration Policy." *Economist*, 280
(August 8, 1981): 17-18.

1545. "INS Surveys of Business Establishments: Reasonable,
Individualized Suspicion of Illegal Alienage."
Northwestern University Law Review, 78 (October
1983): 632-72.

1546. "International Law and Human Rights--Alien Tort Claims
Under 28 U.S.C. Section 1350." *Minnesota Law Review*,
66 (January 1982): 357-75.

1547. "Irrebuttable Presumptions. The Federal Government
and the Rights of Aliens." *Santa Clara Law Review*,
19 (Spring 1979): 465-82.

1548. Jackson, Charles M. "Recent Decisions: Immigration."
Vanderbilt Journal of Transnational Law, 8 (Fall
1974): 231-38.

1549. Jackson, Z.B. "America's Changing Immigration Policy."
Lincoln Law Review, 4 (1968): 72-88.

1550. Jacobson, William A. "Immigration Law: Process Due
Resident Aliens upon Entering the United States.
Landon v. Plasencia. 103 S ct. 321 (1982)." *Harvard
International Law School*, 24 (Summer 1983): 198-205.

1551. Jean v. Nelson. "554 F Supp. 973. A Stark Pattern
of Discrimination." *University of Miami Law Review*,
36 (September 1982): 1005-38.

1552. Joe, Harry J. "The Judicial Recommendations Against
Deportation." *Texas Bar Journal*, 45 (June 1982):
712.

1553. Johnson, C. Donald, Jr. *"Filartiga v. Pena Irala:* A
Contribution to the Development of Customary International Law by a Domestic Court." *Georgia Journal
of International and Comparative Law*, 11 (Summer
1981): 335-341.

1554. Johnson, D.H.N. "Refugees, Deportees and Illegal
Migrants." *Sydney Law Review*, 9 (January 1980):
11-57.

1555. "Judicial Review of Administrative Denials of Immigra-
       tion Visa Preferences Based on Family Relationships:
       *Mila v. District Director of the Immigration and
       Naturalization Service.* 678 F 2d 123." *Utah Law
       Review* (1983): 877-98.

1556. "Judicial Review of Visa Denials: Reexamining Con-
       sumer Nonreviewability." *New York University Law
       Review*, 52 (November 1977): 1137-74.

1557. "Jurisdiction--Aliens,Federal Courts and the Law of
       Nations." *Georgia Journal of International and
       Comparative Law*, 11 (Summer 1981): 365-72.

1558. Jurisdiction--Limitations on Concurrent Jurisdiction--
       Neither Fifth Amendment Protection Against Self-
       Incrimination nor Principles of International Comity
       Preclude a U.S. Court from Compelling Grand Jury
       Testimony. Thereby Subjecting Nonresident Alien to
       Foreign Criminal Liability." *Vanderbilt Journal of
       International Law*, 17 (Winter 1977): 328-43.

1559. "Justice for the Alien: The Adequacy of the Consular
       Visa Issuance System." *Oklahoma City University
       Law Review*, 7 (Fall 1982): 461-87.

1560. Katz, Jerome C. "Extended Border Searches by Immigra-
       tion Officers: *United States v. Thompson*, 5th Cir.,
       1973." *Columbia Journal of Transnational Law*, 13
       (1974): 143-54.

1561. Keener, Dana Marks. "Contesting a Naturalization
       Case." *Immigration Journal*, 5 (March-April 1982):
       9.

1562. Keller, Ken. "Border Searches Revisited: The Consti-
       tutional Propriety of Fixed and Temporary Checkpoint
       Searches." *Hastings Constitutional Law Quarterly*, 2
       (Winter 1975): 251-75.

1563. Kim, C., and B.L.C. Kim. "Asian Immigrants in American
       Law: A Look at the Past and the Challenge Which
       Remains." *American University Law Review*, 26 (Winter
       1977): 373-407.

1564. King, Christopher Qualley. "Aliens--Exclusion of
       Aliens from State Probation Officer Is Not Uncon-
       stitutional Because It Falls Within the Political

Function Exemption. *Cabell v. Chavez-Salido.* 102
S ct. 735 (1982)." *Vanderbilt Journal of Transnational Law,* 15 (Summer 1982): 601-613.

1565. Knoeckel, John F. "Immigration Law: Constitutionality
of One-House Legislative Veto of Stays of Deportation. *Chadha v. INS.* 634 F 2d 408 (9th Cir.
1980)." *Harvard International Law Review,* 22 (Spring
1981): 423-429.

1566. Knudson, David N. "Federal Refugee Resettlement Policy:
Asserting the States' Tenth Amendment Defense."
Hastings Constitutional Law Quarterly, 8 (Summer
1981): 877-921.

1567. Kon, Stephen. "Alleged Discrimination in a Procedure
for the Recovery of Debts. (European Economic Community)." *European Law Review,* 6 (October 1981):
353-368.

1568. Kouri, Gerard M., Jr. "Getting Back In: The Plasencia
Decision and the Permanent Resident Alien's Right
to Procedural Due Process. *Landon v. Plasencia.*
103 S ct. 321 (1982)." *University of Miami Law Review,* 36 (September 1982): 969-985.

1569. Kraiem, Ruben. "Aliens--Constitutionality of Discrimination on National Origin. *Natenji v. Civiletti.*
617 F 2d 745 (D.C. Cir. 1979)." *Harvard International
Law Journal,* 21 (Spring 1980): 467-513.

1570. Kramer, Jane M. "Due Process Rights for Excludable
Aliens under United States Immigration Law and the
United Nations Protocol Relating to the Status of
Refugees--Haitian Aliens, a Case in Point." *Journal
of International Law and Politics,* 10 (1977): 203-
240.

1571. Kurzban, Ira J. "Restructuring the Asylum Process."
South Dakota Law Review, 19 (Winter 1981): 91-117.

1572. Kushnir, Andrei. "Aliens Fraudulently Entering the
U.S. and Establishing Familial Relationships--The
Scope of Section 214(f) of Immigration and National-
ity Act, 8, U.S.C. Section 1251(f)." *Howard Law
Journal,* 18 (1975): 761-82.

1573. "Labor and Administrative Law--Illegal Aliens May
Vote in an Election for Union Representation."

Texas International Law Journal, 14 (Spring 1979):
317-29.

1574. "Labor Law—Illegal Aliens Are Employees Under 29 U.S.C.
Section 152 (3) (1976) and May Vote in Union Certification Elections." *Rutgers-Camden Law Journal*,
10 (Spring 1979): 747-54.

1575. Lansing, Paul, and Javier Alabart. "The Reagan Administration Proposals on Immigration: The Problem of
the Undocumented Alien in the United States." *California Western International Law Journal*, 13 (Winter
1983): 1-36.

1576. "*Laredo-Miranda v. Immigration and Naturalization Service.* 555 F 2d 1242." *Texas International Law Journal*, 13 (Spring 1978): 376-8.

1577. LaRocca, Anthony. "Immigration Law: Control of Immigration into the United States—Immigration Reform
and Control Act of 1982, S. 2222, 97th Congress, 2d
Session (1982)." *Harvard International Law Journal*,
23 (Winter 1983): 410-416.

1578. "*Lav v. Kiley.* 410 F Supp. 221." *Texas International
Law Journal*, 12 (Winter 1977): 109-11.

1579. "Lawful Domicile Under Section 212 (c) of the Immigration and Nationality Act." *University of Chicago
Law Review*, 47 (Summer 1980): 771-802.

1580. Leahy, James E. "Border Patrol Checkpoint Operations
Under Warrants of Inspection: The Wake of *Almeida-
Sanchez v. United States.*" *California Western
International Law Journal*, 5 (Winter 1974): 62-71.

1581. "Legal Lohengrin: Federal Jurisdiction Under the Alien
Tort Claims Act of 1789." *University of San Francisco Law Review*, 14 (Fall 1979): 105-32.

1582. "Legal Problems of Agricultural Labor." *University
of California Davis Law Review*, 2 (1970): 55-69.

1583. "Legal Status of Undocumented Aliens: In Search of a
Consistent Theory." *Houston Law Review*, 16 (1979):
667-709.

1584. "Legalizing the Illegals: A Case for Amnesty." *Columbia Human Rights Law Review*, 12 (Spring/Summer 1980): 65-89.

1585. Leigh, Monroe. "Aliens--Equal Protection. State Requirement of Citizenship for Public Employment." *American Journal of International Law*, 76 (July 1982): 616-617.

1586. ————. "Aliens--Immigration and Nationality Act--Good Moral Character Clause." *American Journal of International Law*, 76 (January 1982): 165-166.

1587. LeMaster, Roger J., and Barmby Zall. "Compassion Fatigue: The Expansion of Refugee Admission to the United States." *Boston College International and Comparative Law Review*, 6 (Spring 1983): 447-74.

1588. Litwin, Edwin. "Labor Certification Report." *Immigration Journal*, 5 (January-February 1982): 14.

1589. Lopez, Gerald P. "Undocumented Mexican Migration: In Search of a Just Immigration Law and Policy." *U.C.L.A. Law Review*, 28 (April 1981): 615-714.

1590. Lopez, Victor Manuel. "Equal Protection for Undocumented Aliens." *Chicago Law Review*, 5 (Winter 1982): 29-54.

1591. Loue, Sana. "What Went Wrong with Wang?: An Examination of *Immigration and Naturalization Service v. Wang*." *San Diego Law Review*, 20 (December 1982): 59-77.

1592. Lowell, Linda. "Constitutional Law: State Discrimination Against Resident Aliens in Public Employment-- What Standard in Review. *Ambach v. Norwick*. 99 S cr. 1598 (1979)." *Stetson Law Review*, 10 (Fall 1980): 171-189.

1593. McCarthy, Mary Kempers. "Evidentiary Proof in Expatriation Proceedings. *Vance v. Perrazas*. 444 U.S. 252 (1980)." *Chicago-Kent Law Review*, 57 (Winter 1981): 323-344.

1594. McCulloch, Kent. "Constitutional Law--Aliens State Statute Excluding Aliens Who Refuse to Declare Intent to Become United States Citizens from Teaching in Public Schools Does Not Violate the Equal Protection Amendment. *Ambach v. Norwick.* 441 U.S. 68 (1979)." *Texas International Law Journal*, 15 (Winter 1980): 203-210.

1595. McFarlane, Karen. "Torture as a Violation of the Law of Nations: Interpreting the Alien Tort Statute. *Filartiga v. Pena-Irala.* 630 F 2d 876 (2d Cir. 1980)." *Brooklyn Journal of International Law*, 7 (Summer 1981): 413-433.

1596. Mackler, I., and J.K. Weeks. "Fleeing Political Refugee's Final Hurdle--the Immigration and Nationality Act." *Northern Kentucky Law Review*, 5 (1978): 9-26.

1597. Mahoney, Dennis J. "A Historical Note on *Hodgson v. Bowerbank.*" *University of Chicago Law Review*, 49 (Summer 1982): 735-740.

1598. Mailman, Stanley. "'Illegal Aliens'--A View of the Employer's Rights and Risks." *Interpreter Releases*, 54 (January 3, 1977): 1-9.

1599. Mancini, Mark. "American the Mazeiful: For Aliens: Land of Plenty Means Plenty of Heartache." *District Lawyer*, 4 (July-August 1980): 35-38.

1600. Manulkin, Gary H., and B. Robert Maghame. "A Proposed Solution to the Problem of the Undocumented Mexican Alien Worker." *San Diego Law Review*, 13 (December 1975): 42-68.

1601. Marcus, Jeffrey. "Access to Discretionary Relief Under the Immigration and Nationality Act. *Castillo Felix v. Immigration and Naturalization Service.* 601 F 2d 459 (9th cir. 1979)." *The Lawyers of Americas*, 12 (Spring 1980): 461-478.

1602. Marinaro, Anna. "Aliens--Regulations--Authority Delegated by Congress to the Attorney General. *Narenji v. Civiletti.* 617 F 2d 745 (D.C. cir. 1979)." *Suffolk Transnational Law Journal*, 5 (March 1980-1981): 115-125.

1603. Mark, Valerie. "Aliens--Forged Passports--Forgery of United States and Foreign Passports Prohibited by U.S.C. 1543. *United States v. Dangdee.* 616 F 2d 1118 (9th cir. 1980)." *Suffolk International Law Journal*, 5 (June 1981): 273-284.

1604. Martin, David A. "Due Process and Membership in the National Community: Political Asylum and Beyond." *University of Pittsburgh Law Review*, 44 (Winter 1983): 165-235.

1605. Martin, Philip L., and Marion F. Houstoun. "European and American Immigration Policies." *Law and Contemporary Problems*, 45 (Spring 1982): 29-54.

1606. Martinez, Vilma S. "Illegal Immigration and the Labor Force: An Historical and Legal View." *American Behavioral Scientist*, 19 (January-February 1976): 335-50.

1607. ————. "Immigration: Entering Through the Back Door." *Columbia Human Rights Law Review*, 15 (Fall 1983): 1-18.

1608. Maters, Adrienne. "Statutory and Constitutional Limitations on the Indefinite Detention of Excluded Aliens." *Boston University Law Review*, 62 (March 1982): 553-600.

1609. Mauro, T. "Will Congress' Veto Power Be Vetoed? (Legislative Power in Deportation Matters)." *National's Business*, 71 (February 1983): 42-43.

1610. "Medical Benefits Awarded to an Illegal Alien: *Perez v. Health and Social Services (NM)*. 573 P 2d 689." *New Mexico Law Review*, 9 (Winter 1978-79): 89-98.

1611. Mestral, A.L.C. de. "Canadian Practice in International Law During 1981: Parliamentary Declaration." *Canadian Year Book of International Law*, 20 (Annual 1982): 305-343.

1612. "Mexican Transmigration: A Case for the Application of International Law." *California Western International Law Journal*, 10 (Winter 1980): 92-122.

1613. "Minority Groups and the Fourth Amendment Standard of Certitude. *United States v. Ortiz* (95 Sup ct. 2585) and *United States v. Brignoni-Ponce* (95 Sup. ct. 2574)." *Harvard Civil Rights Law Review*, 11 (Summer 1976): 733-63.

1614. Moore, M.M., et al. "U.S. Illegal Immigration and Economic Assimilation." Paper presented at the Annual

Meetings of the Pacific Sociological Association,
Victoria, British Columbia, April 16-19, 1975.

1615. Morgan, Rebecca Stein. "Federal Jurisdiction and the
      Protection of International Human Rights." *New York
      University Review Law, Society and Change*, 9 (Winter
      1979-1980): 199-240.

1616. Morris, Edwin G. "Search and Seizure--Border Area
      Stops--Validity of Limited Stops Based upon Facts
      Amounting to Less Than Probable Cause: *United States
      v. Brignoni-Ponce*, --U.S.--, 95 S Ct. 2574, 1975."
      American Journal of Criminal Law, 4 (1975-76):
      203-17.

1617. Morrison, F.L. "Limitations on Alien Investment in
      American Real Estate." *Minnesota Law Review*, 60
      (April 1976): 621-68.

1618. Munoz, Peter S. "The Right of an Illegal Alien to
      Maintain a Civil Action." *California Law Review*, 63
      (May 1975): 762-800.

1619. Musto, Vicki Joiner, and Judith Ruffo. "Are the Borders
      Closing? *Erico* to *Read*: A New Court and an Aging
      Frontier." *University of Miami Law Review*, 31 (Fall
      1976): 1-25.

1620. Myers, Howard S. "A General Practitioner's Guide to
      Principles of Immigration, Non-Immigrant Visas and
      Employment of the Alien." *Bench and Bar of Minnesota*,
      36 (February 1980): 38-59.

1621. Nadin-Davis, R. Paul, and Donna G. White. "Immigration--
      Deportation Order--Foreign Criminal Conviction--Con-
      currency of Meaning." *Canadian Bar Review*, 60 (June
      1982): 363-373.

1622. Nafziger, James A.R. "The General Admission of Aliens
      Under International Law." *American Journal of Inter-
      national Law*, 77 (October 1983): 804-47.

1623. ------. "A Policy Framework for Regulating the Flow
      of Undocumented Mexican Aliens into the United States."
      Oregon Law Review, 56 (1977): 63-106.

1624. ------. "Restating the Rights of Aliens." *Virginia
      Journal of International Law*, 25 (Fall 1984): 125-141.

A restatement of the foreign relations law of aliens. It begins with a description and critique of section 722 of Tentative Draft No. 4 of the Restatement of Foreign Relations Law of the United States (Revised), providing suggestions for revisions in order to reflect recent cases. Analysis focuses on the limited scope of section 722, whose comments and notes largely exclude non-adjudicated interpretations of international law and international legal obligations to protect the rights of aliens.

1625. "National Contacts as a Basis in Personam Jurisdiction over Aliens in Federal Question Suits." *California Law Review*, 70 (May 1982): 686-707.

1626. "New York Statute Requiring State Troopers to Be Citizens Held Constitutional. *Foley v. Connelie*. 98 Sup. ct. 1067." *Connecticut Law Review*, 11 (Fall 1978): 75-93.

1627. Nicol, A. "Illegal Entry After 'Zamir' (R.V. Secretary of State for the Home Department Ex Parte Zamir (1980) 2 All E R 768)." *New Law Journal*, 132 (October 7, 1982): 935-7.

1628. Nieto, Pedro Galindo. "The Undocumented Alien Laborer and *DeCanas v. Bica*: The Supreme Court Capitulates to Public Pressure." *Chicano Law Review*, 3 (1976): 148-63.

1629. O'Hanlon, Kate. "Validity of Entry Certificates-- Change of Circumstances Between Application for and Grant of Certificates--Not Disclosed." *Criminal Law Review* (May 1980): 308-9.

1630. Ortega, J.C. "Plight of the Mexican Wetback." *American Bar Association Journal*, 58 (1972): 251-254.

1631. Ovaska, David E. "Human Rights--Alien Tort Statute-- Internal Deed of Foreign Official Actionable in United States Court. *Filartiga v. Pena-Irala*. 630 F 2d 876 (2d Cir. 1980)." *Suffolk Transnational Law Journal*, 5 (June 1981): 297-310.

1632. Parr, Julie A. "Immigration Law and the Excluded Alien: Potential for Human Rights Violations." *U.C.D. Law Review*, 15 (Spring 1982): 723-740.

1633. Pederson, Donald B., and Dale C. Dahe. "Alien Farm
       Workers and United States Immigration and Naturaliza-
       tion Laws." *Agricultural Law Journal*, 4 (Summer
       1982): 222-246.

1634. Peltz, Joy B. "State Prohibitions on Employment Oppor-
       tunities for Resident Aliens: Legislative Recommenda-
       tions." *Fordham Urban Law Journal*, 10 (Fall 1981):
       699-724.

1635. "Permanent Resident Alien Attempting to Re-Enter the
       United States Is Entitled to Due Process in an Ex-
       clusionary Hearing." *Vanderbilt Journal of Trans-
       national Law*, 16 (Spring 1983): 498-499.

1636. Philips, Deborah Candace. "Constitutional Law--Four-
       teenth Amendment--Equal Protection--Aliens' Rights--
       Governmental Function Doctrine--the Supreme Court
       of the United States Has Held That a State May Exclude
       Aliens from Deputy Probation Officer Positions Which
       Involve the Exercise of the Sovereign Police Power.
       Cabell v. Chavez Salido. 102 S ct. 735 (1982)."
       Duquesne Law Review, 20 (Fall 1982): 277-293.

1637. "*Plyler v. Doe.* 102 S ct. 2382. Broadening the Boun-
       daries of Intermediate Scrutiny in Equal Protection
       Cases." *Arkansas Law Review*, 36 (1983): 383-99.

1638. "*Plyler v. Doe.* 102 S ct. 2382. Education and Illegal
       Alien Children." *Black Law Journal*, 8 (Spring 1983):
       132-7.

1639. "*Plyler v. Doe.* 102 S ct. 2382. Equal Protection for
       Illegal Aliens and Education for Undocumented
       Children." *Southern Texas Law Journal*, 24 (1983):
       350-65.

1640. "*Plyler v. Doe.* 102 S ct. 2382. The Way for Heightened
       Judicial Scrutiny in Constitutional Adjudication of
       Denials of Education." *Journal of Contemporary Law*, 9
       (1983): 235-45.

1641. Potelicki, Victoria L. "United States Asylum Pro-
       cedures: Current Status and Proposals for Reform.
       Haitian Refugee Center v. Civiletti. No. 79-2086
       (S.D. Fla. 1980)." *Cornell International Law Journal*,
       14 (Summer 1981): 405-428.

1642. Pray, Francis X. "Preemption in the Field of Immigration: *DeCanas v. Bica.*" *San Diego Law Review*, 14 (December 1976): 282-300.

1643. Entry deleted.

1644. "Private Consensual Sexual Conduct and the 'Good Moral Character' Requirement of the Immigration and Nationality Act." *Columbia Journal of Transnational Law*, 14 (1975): 357-381.

1645. "Pro Bono Diary: Or Can an Immigration Lawyer Represent 26 Clients in a Single Day and Still Think of It as Due Process?" *Immigration Journal*, 6 (January-March 1983): 11.

1646. "Protecting Aliens from Persecution Without Overloading the INS: Should Illegal Aliens Receive Notice of the Right to Apply for Asylum?" *Virginia Law Review*, 69 (June 1983): 901-30.

1647. "Public School Teachers Covered by the 'Governmental Function Exception' to Strict Security of Alienage Clarifications." *Connecticut Law Review*, 12 (Fall 1979): 137-55.

1648. "Public Schooling Required for Illegal Aliens." *School Law Bulletin*, 13 (July 1982): 16.

1649. "Recent Developments--*United States v. Martinez-Fuerte, DeCanas v. Bica.*" *San Diego Law Review*, 14 (December 1976): 282-325.

1650. "Refugees Under United States Immigration Law." *Cleveland State Law Review*, 24 (1975): 528-571.

1651. "Regulation of Illegal Aliens: Sanctions Against Employers Who Knowingly Hire Undocumented Workers." *Western State University Law Review*, 4 (Fall 1976): 41-62.

1652. Reinhalter, Mark. "Immigration--Extent of Subject Matter Jurisdiction. *United States v. Beliard.* 618 F 2d 886 (1st Cir. 1980)." *Suffolk Transnational Law Journal*, 5 (March 1980): 155-169.

1653. Rendon, J.M., and R. Rendon. "Undocumented Alien: A
       Policy Oriented Approach." *Texas Southern University
       Law Review*, 5 (1978): 7-44.

1654. "The Requirement of Individualized Suspicion: An End
       to INS Factory Sweeps? International Ladies' Garment
       Workers' Union. *AFL-CIO v. Sureck*. 681 F 2d 624."
       Chicago-Kent Law Review, 59 (1983): 1069-97.

1655. "Retaliatory Reporting of Illegal Alien Employee:
       Remedying the Labor-Immigration Conflict." *Columbia
       Law Review*, 80 (October 1980): 1296-1316.

1656. "Rethinking Equal Protection. *Plyler v. Doe* (102 S ct.
       2382)." *Missouri Law Review*, 49 (Winter 1984):
       166-82.

1657. Retter, D. "Look at the 'New' Immigration Law."
       Florida Bar Journal, 53 (July-August 1979): 431-6.

1658. Reza, H.G. "Immigration: Restrictions or Reform?"
       California Lawyer, 2 (December 1982): 32-35.

1659. Rickard, Lisa A. "*Filartiga v. Pena-Irala*: A New
       Form for Violation of International Human Rights.
       Filartiga v. Pena-Irala. 630 F 2d 876 (2d Cir.
       1980)." *American University Law Review*, 30 (Spring
       1981): 817-833.

1660. "Right of Undocumented Aliens Against Their Employers."
       Fordham Urban Law Journal, 10 (1981/82): 683-98.

1661. "The Right of Undocumented Aliens: Balancing Equal
       Protection and Federalism." *New York Law School Law
       Review*, 28 (1983): 431-76.

1662. Rivera, José A. "Aliens Under the Law--A Legal Per-
       spective." *Employee Relations Law Journal*, 3 (1977):
       12-18.

1663. Robinson, Dianne. "State Regulation of the Employment
       of Illegal Aliens: A Constitutional Approach."
       Southern California Law Review, 46 (March 1973):
       565-84.

1664. Robson, Gwendolyn M. "Constitutional Law--Fourteenth
       Amendment--Equal Protection--Alien's Rights--Govern-
       mental Function Doctrine. *Ambach v. Norwick*.

441 U.S. 68 (1979)." *Duquesne Law Review*, 18 (Summer 1980): 957-968.

1665. Rochin, Refugio I. "Illegal Aliens in Agriculture: Some Theoretical Considerations." *Labor Law Journal*, 29 (March 1978): 149-67.

1666. *"Rodrigiez-Fernandez v. Wilkinson*. 654 F 2d 1382. Detention, Due Process and the Excluded Alien." *Boston University International Law Journal*, 2 (Spring 1983): 83-102.

1667. Rogers, Dawn M. "The Indefinite Detention of Excluded Aliens. *Fernandez v. Wilkinson*. 505 F supp. 787 (D Kan. 1980)." *Detroit College Law Review* (Fall 1981): 925-946.

1668. Rohlik, Josef. *"Filartiga v. Pena Irala*: International Justice in a Modern American Court?" *Georgia Journal of International and Comparative Law*, 11 (Summer 1981): 325-334.

1669. Rosenbaum, David B. "The Constitutional Right of Excluded Aliens: Proposed Limitations on the Indefinite Detention of the Cuban Refugees." *Georgia Law Journal*, 70 (June 1982): 1303-1336.

1670. *"Rosenberg v. Fleuti*: Reentry of Aliens Remains Unsettled." *Notre Dame Lawyer*, 56 (April 1981): 696-703.

1671. Rosenberg, Gerald M. "Aliens and Equal Protection: Why Not the Right to Vote?" *Michigan Law Review*, 75 (1977): 1092-1136.

1672. Rosenberg, M.L. "The World After Chadha (*Immigration and Naturalization Service v. Chadha*, 103 S ct. 2764): Can Congress Still Control the Agencies?" *Federal Bar News and Journal*, 30 (September/October 1983): 395-7.

1673. Rosenthal, Paul. "Border Searches: Beyond Almeida-Sanchez." *University of California, Davis Law Review*, 8 (1975): 163-90.

1674. Roth, David. "The Right of Asylum Under United States Immigration Law." *University of Florida Law Review*, 33 (Summer 1981): 539-564.

1675.   "Roving Patrols and Fixed Checkpoints (Criminal Law in
        the Ninth Circuit: Recent Developments)." *Loyola of
        Los Angeles Law Review*, 13 (June 1980): 631-635.

1676.   Rubin, Edwin R., and Mark A. Mancini. "An Overview of
        the Labor Certification Requirement for Intending
        Immigrants." *San Diego Law Review*, 14 (December
        1976): 76-110.

1677.   Rusk, Dean. "A Comment on *Filartiga v. Pena-Irala*
        (Federal Jurisdiction, Human Rights and the Law of
        Nations)." *Georgia Journal of International and Com-
        parative Law*, 11 (Summer 1981): 311-16.

1678.   Rusnak, Michael J., and William H. Satterfield. "Border
        Searches in the Fifth Circuit: Constitutional Guarantees
        v. Immigration Policy." *Cumberland Law Review*, 8
        (Spring 1977): 107-45.

1679.   Salerno, Victor. "Alien Checkpoints and the Troublesome
        Tetralogy: *United States v. Martinez-Fuerte*." *San
        Diego Law Review*, 14 (December 1976): 257-81.

1680.   Salinas, Guadalupe, and Isaias D. Torres. "The Undocu-
        mented Mexican Alien: A Legal, Social and Economic
        Analysis." *Houston Law Review*, 13 (July 1976): 863-
        916.

1681.   Santana, Mark R. "*Almeida-Sanchez* and Its Progeny: The
        Developing Border Zone Search Law." *Arizona Law Re-
        view*, 17 (1975): 214-49.

1682.   Scanlan, John A. "Immigration Law and the Illusion of
        Numerical Control." *University of Miami Law Review*,
        36 (September 1982): 819-864.

1683.   Schenk, Claire M. "The Constitutionality of Legislative
        Restrictions on the Employment Rights of Legal Resi-
        dent Aliens in New York State." *Syracuse Journal of
        International Law and Commerce*, 7 (Summer 1979): 109-
        128.

1684.   Schmid, Alex. "Eligibility for Labor Certification:
        Requisite Intent to Engage in the Certified Employ-
        ment." *Golden Gate University Law Review*, 10 (Fall
        1980): 295-303.

1685.   ————. "Suspension of Deportation: A New Approach
        to the Continuous Physical Presence Requirement."

Golden Gate University Law Review, 10 (Fall 1980): 303-313.

1686. Schneiderwind, Barry. "Constitutional Law--Immigration Law--State Regulation of Employment of Illegal Aliens Is Not *Per Se* Preempted by Federal Control over Immigration or by the Immigration and Nationality Act." *Texas International Law Journal*, 12 (Winter 1977): 87-96.

1687. "School House Door Must Be Open to Children of Illegal Aliens." *Children's Legal Rights Journal*, 3 (June 1982): 19-21.

1688. Schulte, Jeffrey L. "Area Search Warrants in Border Zones: *Almeida-Sanchez* and *Camara*." *Yale Law Journal*, 84 (December 1974): 355-72.

1689. Schwartz, Teresa M. "State Discrimination Against Mexican Aliens." *George Washington Law Review*, 38 (July 1970): 1091-1113.

1690. Scott, Jessye Leigh. "Alien Teachers: Suspect Class or Subversive Influence. *Ambach v. Norwick*. 441 U.S. 68 (1979)." *Mercer Law Review*, 31 (Spring 1980): 815-824.

1691. "The Scope of the Withholding Tax on Payments to Aliens: A Survey." *Columbia Journal of Transnational Law*, 22 (1984): 359-88.

1692. "Secret Law of Immigration and Naturalization Service." *Iowa Law Review*, 56 (1970): 140-151.

1693. "Selected Works on the Rights and Status of Refugees Under United States and International Law, 1960-1980." *Michigan Year Book of International Legal Studies* (Annual, 1982): 589-630.

1694. Sevilla, Charles M. "In Defense of the Alien." *National Journal of Criminal Defense*, 1 (1975): 255-320.

1695. "Sexual Discrimination in the Immigration and Nationality Act--Report of the Special Committee on Sex and Law." *Record of the Association of the Bar of the City of New York*, 31 (1976): 593-596.

1696. Sharp, William M., and Ronald J. Russo. "The New ABA Proposal for Defining a Nonresident Alien for Federal Income Tax Purposes." *Florida Bar Journal*, 56 (October 1982): 732-734.

1697. Sheffield, John F. "Illegal Searches and Arrests of Aliens: The Evolving Standard." *Los Angeles Bar Bulletin*, 49 (July 1974): 375-388.

1698. Sherman, Jeremy P. "Alien Certification Proceedings: The Personal Preference Doctrine and the Burden of Persuasion." *George Washington Law Review*, 43 (1975): 914-935.

1699. Skeen, Randall L. "Unblessed Wedlock: Sham Marriages and Relief from Deportation." *Journal of Beverly Hills Bar Association*, 14 (Spring 1980): 109.

1700. Slaughter, Mark F. "An Isolated Instance of Judicial Activism or an Unwarranted Expansion of Equal Protection? *Plyler v. Doe*. 102 S Ct. 2382 (1982)." *Harvard Journal of Law and Public Policy*, 6 (Summer 1983): 341-352.

1701. Slonim, Scott. "Cuban Refugee Crisis: Quick Test for New Law." *ABA Journal*, 66 (July 1980): 826-27.

1702. ————. "Freedom Flotilla from Cuba: Will the Harbor Stay Open?" *ABA Journal*, 66 (July 1980): 823-25.

1703. Smith, C.D., and J.E. Mendez. "Employer Sanctions and Other Labor Market Restrictions on Alien Employment: The 'Scorched Earth' Approach to Immigration Control." *The North Carolina Journal of International Law and Commercial Regulations*, 6 (Winter 1980): 19-61.

1704. Smith, Shelagh Kiley. "Alien Students in the United States: Statutory Interpretation and Problems of Control." *Suffolk Transnational Law Journal*, 5 (June 1981): 235-250.

1705. Smith, William French. "Let's Stop Illegal Immigration: The Current Policies Are Outdated and Unrealistic—— We Need to Assert Control over Our Borders Again." *California Lawyer*, 2 (February 1982): 11-12.

1706. Sofranko, Andrew J., and Frederick C. Fliegel. "The Neglected Component of Rural Population Growth (Influx of Migrants from Other Rural Areas)." *Growth and Change*, 14 (April 1983): 42-49.

1707. Solomon, Barbara. "The Unauthorized Work Bar of 245 (c). Who Needs It?" *Immigration Journal*, 5 (March-April 1982): 10-11.

1708. Spencer, J.N. "Proof of Illegal Immigration (Great Britain)." *Journal of Criminal Law*, 46 (February 1982): 25-26.

1709. "State Burdens on Resident Aliens: A New Preemption Analysis." *Yale Law Journal*, 89 (April 1980): 940-61.

1710. "State Discrimination Against Mexican Aliens." *George Washington Law Review*, 38 (1970): 1091-1113.

1711. Steel, Richard. "2d and 6th Preference, a Jurisdictional Squabble." *Immigration Journal*, 5 (January-February 1982): 13.

1712. Steel, R.D. "In Defense of the Permanent Resident: Alleged Defects Related to Alien Labor Certifications." *San Diego Law Review*, 19 (December 1981): 119-48.

1713. Stevens, Ronald A. "Reasonable Suspicion of Illegal Alienage as a Precondition to 'Stops' of Suspected Aliens: *Illinois Migrant Council v. Pilliod*, 398 F. Supp. 882 (N.D. Ill. 1975)." *Chicago-Kent Law Review*, 52 (1975): 485-502.

1714. Stevenson, A.B. "Is the Connection Effective? Through the Maze of Section 864." *Northwestern Journal of International Law and Business*, 5 (Summer 1983): 213-68.

1715. Stump, T. Douglas, and Vance Winningham, Jr. "Matrimonial Maladies and the Alien." *Oklahoma Bar Journal*, 54 (April 30, 1983): 1109-1114.

1716. "Suspension of Deportation—Toward a New Hardship Standard." *San Diego Law Review*, 18 (July 1981): 663-83.

1717. Sutis, Robert W. "The Extent of the Border." *Hastings Constitutional Law Quarterly*, 1 (Spring 1974): 235-50.

1718. "Symposium: Immigration and Nationality." [Includes 7 articles]. *South Dakota Law Review*, 19 (Winter 1981): 1-231.

1719. Talmadge, Deborah M. "Videotape Depositions: An Alternative to the Incarceration of Alien Material Witnesses." *California Western International Law Journal*, 5 (Winter 1975): 376-98.

1720. Tamayo, William R. "Do Immigrant Workers in the United States Have a Right to Earn a Living?" *National Lawyer Guild Practice*, 39 (Summer 1982): 84-89.

1721. Tasoff, Ron J., and Malka L. Tasoff. "The Immigrant Last Chance (Suspension of Deportation)." *Los Angeles Lawyer*, 5 (June 1982): 10.

1722. Tawardros, Jerri Blaney. "A Comparative Overview of the Vietnam and Cuban Refugee Crisis: Did the Refugee Act of 1980 Change Anything?" *Suffolk Transnational Law Journal*, 6 (Spring 1982): 25-27.

1723. "A Terminal Approach to Representation for Illegal Aliens. *Federation for American Immigration Reform v. Klutznick*. 486 F Supp. 564 (D.D.C. 1980)." *Michigan Law Review*, 80 (May 1982): 1342-1371.

1724. Terry, James J., Jr. "Reasonable Suspicion for Border Patrol Stops: *United States v. Brignoni-Ponce* (U.S. Sup. Ct. 1975)." *Columbia Journal of Transnational Law*, 15 (1976): 277-312.

1725. Thomas, Robert W. "Criminal Procedure--Search and Seizure--Aliens and 'Extended' Border Inspections." *Wayne Law Review*, 20 (July 1974): 1141-53.

1726. "To Educate or Not to Educate: The Plight of Undocumented Alien Children in Texas." *Washington University Law Quarterly*, 60 (Spring 1982): 119-59.

1727. Toran, J. "Federalism, Personal Jurisdiction, and Aliens." *Tulane Law Review*, 58 (January 1984): 785-90.

1728. "Torture as a Violation of the Law of Nations: An Analysis of 28 USC, Section 1350." *Texas International Law Journal*, 16 (Winter 1981): 117-39.

1729. Traverse, Stephen. "Equal Protection. *Ambach v. Norwick.* 441 U.S. 68 (1979)." *Hastings Constitutional Law Quarterly,* 7 (Winter 1980): 484-496.

1730. Travis, William P. "Migration, Income Distribution, and Welfare Under Alternative International Economic Policies (U.S. Immigration Policy)." *Law and Contemporary Problems,* 45 (Spring 1982): 81-106.

1731. "Treatment of Nonresident Alien's Gain Inconsistent." *Journal of Taxation,* 58 (March 1983): 178-179.

1732. "Undocumented Alien Children and Free Public Education. *Plyler v. Doe* (1025 S ct. 2382)." *Howard Law Journal,* 27 (1984): 301-28.

1733. "Undocumented Alien Laborer and *DeCanas v. Bica;* The Supreme Court Capitulates to Public Pressure." *Chicano Law Review,* 3 (1976): 148-163.

1734. "Undocumented Alien's Rights to Medicaid. *Plyler v. Doe* (102 S ct. 2382)." *Fordham International Law Journal,* 7 (1983/84): 83-117.

1735. "The Undocumented Worker: The Controversy Takes a New Turn." *Chicano Law Review,* 3 (1976): 164-194.

1736. "*U.S. v. McAninch.* 435 F Supp 240." *Lawyer of the Americas,* 10 (Summer-Fall 1978): 636-8.

1737. "*United States v. Martinez-Fuerte.* 96 Sup ct. 3074. The Fourth Amendment Close to the Edge?" *California Western Law Review,* 13 (1977): 333-57.

1738. "University's Restrictive Definition of Domicile, Which Precludes Nonimmigrant Aliens from Attaining Instate Status for Tuition Purposes, Does Not Violate Due Process. *Moreno v. Toll.* 480 F Supp. 1116 (D. Md. 1979)." *Vanderbilt Journal of Transnational Law,* 14 (Winter 1981): 226-227.

1739. "Utilization of Intermediate Scrutiny in Establishing the Right of Education for Undocumented Alien Children. *Plyler v. Doe.* 102 S ct. 2392." *Pepperdine Law Review,* 10 (December 1982): 139-65.

1740. Valby, Scott R. "Aliens--an Immigration Regulation That Distinguishes Among Aliens by National Origin

Must Have a Rational Basis to Satisfy the Equal Protection Guarantee of the Fifth Amendment. *Narenji v.
Civiletti.* 617 F 2d 745 (D.C. Cir. 1979)." *Vanderbilt Journal of Transnational Law*, 13 (Fall 1980):
857-872.

1741. Walls, J. Michael. "The Law of Naturalization: A Uniform Law, Devoid of Uniformity." *Cumberland Law Review*, 7 (1976): 211-231.

1742. Walter, M.P. "Aliens' Right to Work and the Political
Community's Right to Govern." *Wayne Law Review*, 25
(September 1979): 1181-215.

1743. Walter, Rosalind Marshall. "Administrative Law--Aliens.
Yassini v. Crossland. 618 F 2d 1356 (9th cir. 1980)."
Suffolk Transnational Law Journal, 5 (March 1980):
95-104.

1744. "Wandering Between Two Worlds: Employment Discrimination Against Aliens." *Virginia Journal of International Law*, 16 (1976): 355-402.

1745. Watkins, J.J. "Alien Ownership and the Communications
Act." *Federal Communications Law Journal*, 33 (Winter
1981): 1-38.

1746. Weisman, J. "Restrictions on the Acquisition of Land
by Aliens." *American Journal of Comparative Law*, 28
(Winter 1980): 39-66.

1747. Weiss, Michael N. "Immigration by Foreign Businessmen
and Investors." *Florida Bar Journal*, 56 (May 1982):
421-425.

1748. Wenk, Michael G. "The Alien Adjustment and Employment
Act of 1977: A Summary." *International Migration
Review*, 11 (Winter 1977): 533-38.

1749. "Wetback as Material Witness: Pretrial Detention or
Deportation?" *California Western Law Review*, 7
(1970): 175-196.

1750. Wexler, D.B. "Alien Criminal Defendant; an Examination
of Immigration Law Principles for Criminal Practice."
Criminal Law Bulletin, 10 (1974): 287-317.

1751. Wildes, L. "*United States Immigration Service v. John Lennon*: The Cultural Lag." *Brooklyn Law Review*, 40 (1973): 279-313.

1752. Wilner, Gabriel M. "*Filartiga v. Pena-Irala*: Comments on Sources of Human Rights Law and Means of Redress for Violations of Human Rights (Federal Jurisdiction, Human Rights and the Law of Nations)." *Georgia Journal of International and Comparative Law*, 11 (Summer 1981): 317-323.

1753. Wilson, Andrew W. "State Laws Restricting Land Purchases by Aliens: Some Constitutional and Policy Considerations." *Columbia Journal of Transnational Law*, 21 (Winter 1982): 135-156.

1754. Young, Rowland L. "Aliens. State Employment." *ABA Journal*, 68 (March 1982): 342.

1755. ———. "Exclusion Hearing Enough for Illegal Alien Smuggler." *ABA Journal*, 69 (March 1983): 352.

1756. Youngblood, Patricia J. "Provisional Arrest of Foreign Nationals in the United States Requires Showing of Probable Cause--Article XIII of the United States Extradition Treaty with Italy--Right of Party Requested to Enforce Foreign Arrest Warrant to Demand Additional Evidence and Information--Due Process Requirements in Provisional Arrest Cases." *Syracuse Journal of International Law and Commerce*, 8 (Summer 1980): 180-186.

IV. MISCELLANEA

1757. "ABA Delegates to Endorse Section Immigration Proposal." *Human Rights*, 11 (Winter 1983): 11.

1758. Agarwal, V.B., and D.R. Winkler. "Migration of Professional Manpower to the United States." *Southern Economics Journal*, 50 (June 1984): 814-830.

1759. Aguilar, R. *Images of Honduras: The Nicaraguan Refugee.* Baton Rouge, Louisiana: Louisiana State University, Center for Latin American Affairs, 1984.

1760. Aguirre, Benigno E. "Ethnic Newspapers and Politics." *Diario Los Americas* and the Watergate Affair." *Ethnic Groups*, 2 (1979): 155-165.

1761. ———. "The Marital Stability of Cubans in the United States." *Ethnicity*, 8 (December 1981): 387-405.

1762. Alexander, Tom. "Those Amazing Cuban Emigres." *Fortune*, 74 (October 1966): 144-149.

1763. "Ali Baba Strays into the Wrong Fable." *Economist*, 286 (January 29, 1983): 27-28.

1764. American Civil Liberties Union. *Salvadorans in the United States: The Case for Extended Voluntary Departure.* Washington, D.C.: Center for National Security Studies, 1983.

1765. Anderson, Theodore, and Mildred Boyer. *Bilingual Schooling in the United States.* 2 vols. Austin, Texas: Southwest Educational Development Laboratory, 1970; Detroit, Michigan: Blaine Ethridge, 1976.

1766. Arbeláez, Alfonso. "El exodo de Colombianos en el periodo 1963-1973." *Boletín mensual de estadística*, 310 (May 1977): 7-43.

1767. Arguelles, Lourdes. "Miami's Cubans: Illicit Heritage,
       Uncertain Future." *Cubatimes*, 3 (Spring 1982): 12-16,
       27-31.

1768. Ashman, Allan. "Immigration--Homosexual Aliens."
       ABA Journal, 68 (November 1982): 1499.

1769. "The Asian American." *Pacific Historical Review*, 43
       (November 1974): Whole Issue.

       Contents: Roger Daniels--American Historians and
       East Asian Immigrants; Stanford M. Lyman--Conflicts and
       the Web of Group Affiliation in San Francisco's China-
       town, 1850-1910; Harry H.L. Kitano--Japanese Americans:
       The Development of a Middleman Minority; H. Bret Melendy--
       Filipinos in the United States; Lee Houchins and Chang-
       su Houchins--The Korean Experience in America, 1903-
       1924; Gary R. Hess--The Forgotten Asian Americans: The
       East Indian Community in the United States.

1770. Bach, Robert L. "Cuba in Crisis." *Migration Today*, 8
       (April 1980): 15-18.

1771. Baggs, William C. "The Other Miami--City of Intrigue."
       New York Times Magazine (March 13, 1960): 25, 84-87.

1772. Bailey, J., and F. Headlam. *Intercontinental Migra-
       tion to Latin America. A Selected Bibliography.*
       London: Institute of Latin American Studies, University
       of London, 1980.

       The 570 entries focus on the population shifts be-
       tween and within countries of Latin America.

1773. Bailey, Thomas, and Marcia Freedman. "Immigrant Eco-
       nomic Mobility in an Era of Weakening Employment
       Relationships: The Role of Social Networks." Paper
       presented at the Thirty-seventh Annual Meetings of
       the Industrial Relations Research Association.
       San Francisco, California, December 29, 1983.

1774. Barchfield, J.W. *Agrarian Policy and the National
       Development of Mexico.* New Brunswick, New Jersey:
       Rutgers University Press/Transaction Books, 1978.

1775. Bastos de Avila, F.B. *La Immigracion en América Latina.*
       Washington, D.C.: Pan American Union, 1964.

1776. Batista, Laureano F. "Political Sociology of the

Cuban Exile, 1959-1968." Unpublished M.A. thesis. University of Miami, 1969.

1777. Batterson, R.F. "America's Post-War Immigration Policy." *The Journal of Social, Political and Economic Studies*, 9 (Fall 1984): 311-340.

1778. Bean, F.D., and T.A. Sullivan. *Immigration Patterns and Policies in the United States*. Austin, Texas: Texas Population Research Center, 1983.

1779. ———, et al. *Immigration to the United States: Its Volume, Determinants, and Labor Market Implications*. Austin, Texas: Texas Population Research Center, 1984.

1780. Beiler, Ross C. *Links to Government in Greater Miami: The Experience of Three Ethnic Aggregates*. Miami: Division of Continuing Education and Center for Urban Studies, University of Miami, 1969.

1781. Bernard, William S. "Indices of Integration into the American Community." *International Migration*, 11 (1973): 87-101.

Indices of the adjustment of newcomers are examined as they appeared in primary field research done by the author over a period of fifteen years in connection with the major American agencies operating in the resettlement field.

1782. ———. "Refugee Asylum in the U.S.: How the Law Was Changed to Admit Displaced Persons." *International Migration* (Geneva), 13 (1975): 3-20.

Analyzes "the particular process of social action by which some of the world's dispossessed, the so-called Displaced Persons, were given sanctuary in the U.S. after World War II."

1783. Berry, R. Albert, and Ronald Soligo. "Some Welfare Aspects of International Migration." Growth Center Discussion Paper No. 8. Economic Growth Center, Yale University, New Haven, Connecticut, July 7, 1966.

Attempts to analyze the conditions under which loss to the remaining population will occur, considering the possibility of emigration either of skilled or unskilled labor. Concludes that, in general, loss does occur, although there are a few cases where gain (or no change) may result.

1784. ————, and ————. "Some Welfare Aspects of International Migration." *Journal of Political Economy*,
77 (September/October 1969): 778-794.

1785. Bhagwati, Jagdish N. "The Brain Drain." *International
Social Science Journal*, 28 (1976): 691-729.

Places the blame on the United States but notes that
recently Canada, too, has begun to emphasize skills in
evaluating prospective immigrants. Sees the elimination of racial quotas as resulting in an increased flow
of skill and expertise. In "Taxing the Brain Drain"
(*Challenge*, XIX, 1976, 34-38) proposes an income tax
on the earnings of people who leave poorer countries
to live and work in richer ones. The funds so raised
would go to the home countries.

1786. ————. "Taxation and International Migration: Recent
Policy Issues." In Barry R. Chiswick, ed. *The Gateway: U.S. Immigration Issues and Policies* (Washington,
D.C.: American Enterprise Institute, 1982). Pp. 86-
103.

Concerned with two issues. The first is the question
of the appropriate exercise of income tax jurisdiction,
whether it ought to be on the basis of citizenship, as
in the United States and the Philippines, or on the
basis of residence, as in the European countries and
most less-developed countries. This question arises
from the theoretical and policy discussions of the
proposal to tax the "brain drain," or emigration of
skilled labor. The sending countries could impose the
tax on their emigrants. Such a tax would require a
change in U.S. policy only insofar as the sending countries seek bilateral treaties for a sharing of tax information to facilitate their enforcement. The second
issue is one of sharing revenue in proportion to the
taxes paid by the immigrants. Under such a scheme, the
receiving countries, for example, the United States,
would share the tax revenues raised in the normal
course of events from immigrants with the countries of
origin.

1787. Bhatnagar, J., ed. *Educating Emigrants*. New York:
St. Martin Press, 1981.

1788. Bickner, Mie Liang. "The Forgotten Minority: Asian
American Women." *Amerasia Journal*, 11 (Spring 1974):
1-17.

1789. Billitteri, Thomas J. "Why Florida Has a Stake in Reaganizing the Caribbean." *Florida Trend*, 24 (February 1982): 42-46.

1790. Binavince, Emilos. "The Impact of the Mobility Rights: The Canadian Economic Union--A Boom or a Bust?" *Ottawa Law Review*, 14 (Spring 1982): 340-365.

1791. Biondi, Lawrence. *The Italian American Child: His Sociolinguistic Acculturation*. Washington, D.C.: Georgetown University Press, 1975.

1792. Blau, Francine D. "Immigration and Labor Earnings in Early Twentieth Century America." In Julian L. Simon and Julie da Vanzo, eds., *Research in Population Economics*, vol. 2 (Greenwich, Conn.: JAI Press, 1980). Pp. 21-41.

1793. Blumenthal, Sonia D. "The Private Organizations in the Naturalization and Citizenship Process." *International Migration Review*, 5 (Winter 1971): 448-462.

   Naturalization has special significance because in the process of becoming a citizen, the newcomer develops an identification with his new homeland. There is a great psychological difference between carrying an alien identification card and being able to say "I am an American citizen." Naturalization can be a significant step in integration. The importance of this has long been recognized by many public and private organizations. "This article is primarily concerned with the role of private organizations although any discussion of naturalization must include the programs of the United States Immigration and Naturalization Service and the concerns of state and city Boards of Education. Also, there must be included the role of certain courts who have manifested an interest in the ceremonies dignifying the awarding of citizenship."

1794. Bodnar, John E. *The Transplanted: A History of Immigrants in Urban America*. Bloomington, Indiana: Indiana University Press, 1985.

1795. Böhning, W.R. *Basic Aspects of Migration from Poor to Rich Countries: Facts, Problems, Policies*. Geneva: International Labour Organisation, 1976.

1796. ———. *Studies in International Labor Migration.*
       London: Macmillan, 1984.

1797. Boiston, Bernard G. "Immigration Advice to Corporate
       Clients: How to Cope with Foreign Visitors." *Ohio
       State Bar Association Reporter*, 56 (December 12,
       1983): 1786.

1798. Bonaparte, Ronald H. "The Rodino Bill: An Example of
       Prejudice Toward Mexican Immigration to the United
       States." *Chicano Law Review*, 2 (Summer 1975): 40-50.

1799. Borjas, George J. "The Earnings of Male Hispanic Im-
       migrants in the United States." *Industry and Labor
       Relations Review*, 35 (April 1982): 343-53.

1800. Bouscaren, Anthony T. *International Migrations Since
       1945.* New York: Praeger, 1963.

1801. ———. *The Security Aspects of Immigration Work.*
       Milwaukee, Wisconsin: Marquette University Press,
       1959.

1802. Bouvier, Leon F., et al. "International Migration:
       Yesterday, Today, and Tomorrow." *Population Bul-
       letin*, 32 (1977): 3-42.

1803. "A Break with the Past." *The Nation* (March 1, 1975):
       228.

1804. Briggs, Vernon M. "Non Immigrant Labor Policy in the
       United States." *Journal of Economic Issues*, 17 (Sep-
       tember 1983): 609-620.

1805. ———. "Special Labor Market Segments." In *Manpower
       Research and Labor Economics.* Ed. Gordon L. Swanson
       and Jon Michaelson. Beverly Hills, California: Sage
       Publications, 1979. Pp. 243-76.

1806. Broadway, M.J. *U.S. Immigration in the 1970's: Settle-
       ment Patterns and Processes.* Urbana, Illinois: Univer-
       sity of Illinois Press, 1983.

1807. Brock, Daniel. "Movement Seeks Sanctuary for Itself
       as Well as Aliens." *Insight*, 2 (August 11, 1986):
       18-20.

       Summary: The sanctuary movement, which provides
       refuge chiefly for aliens from El Salvador and Guate-

mala, is seeking to have its policies vindicated, thus gaining political asylum for the thousands of aliens its members harbor. At issue is whether the refugees are in danger of political violence. The United States says most of them are coming to the country for economic reasons: No Salvadoran human rights organization has reported a deportee's death since 1982.

1808. Bruck, Connie. "Immigration Lawyer (Daniel Ratter)." *American Lawyer*, 2 (September 1980): 33-34.

1809. Buchanan, Susan Huelsebusch. "The Cultural Meaning of Social Class for Haitians in New York City." *Ethnic Groups*, 5 (1983): 7-29.

1810. ———. "Haitian Women in New York City." *Migration Today*, 7 (September 1979): 19-25, 39.

1811. ———. "Haitians in the Arts." *Migration Today*, 7 (September 1979): 33-38.

1812. ———. "Language and Identity: Haitians in New York City." *International Migration Review*, 13 (Summer 1979): 298-313.

1813. Burkholz, Herbert. "The Latinization of Miami." *New York Times Magazine* (September 21, 1980): 45-46, 84 ff.

1814. Burt, Al. "Cuban Exiles: The Mirage of Havana." *The Nation*, 200 (January 25, 1965): 76-79.

1815. ———. "Miami: The Cuban Flavor." *The Nation*, 212 (March 8, 1971): 299-302.

1816. Bustamante, Jorge A. *Espaldas mojadas: Materia prima para la expansión del capital Norteamericano.* Mexico City: Colegio de Mexico, 1976.

1817. ———. "Migración interna e internacional. La frontera norte de México." *Comercio exterior*, 34 (Septiembre 1984): 849-863.

1818. Caicedo, J.H.P. *Bibliografia comentada sobre migraciones en Colombia.* Bogota: Centro de documentation, Instituto Colombiano para el fomento de la educacion superior, 1980.

1819. Camarillo, Albert. *Chicanos in California: A History
       of Mexican Americans in California*. San Francisco,
       California: Boyd & Fraser, 1985.

1820. Campbell, Duncan A., III, and John C. Taggart. "The
       International Business Client and Nonimmigrant Visas."
       Colorado Lawyer, 11 (October 1982): 2545.

1821. Campbell, Gibson. "The Contribution of Immigration
       to the U.S. Population Growth, 1790-1970." *Inter-
       national Migration Review*, 9 (1975): 157-177.

       Estimates that net immigration to the United States
       in the first 20 federal censuses amounted to 35.5 million
       persons. By 1970 that number had produced about 98
       million of the total population. Resists making pre-
       dictions for the future, saying that the current pic-
       ture is so complicated by variables that the past has
       little relevance for it.

1822. Canada. Employment and Immigration Commission. *Back-
       ground Papers on Future Immigration Levels*. Ottawa:
       Ministry of Supply and Services, 1983.

1823. Cardoso, Lawrence R. *Mexican Emigration to the United
       States 1897-1931: Socio-Economic Patterns*. Tucson,
       Arizona: The University of Arizona Press, 1980.

       Focuses its analysis on the social, political, demo-
       graphic and economic factors in both Mexico and the
       United States that prepared the way for sizeable flows
       of workers across the border beginning in the late
       1890s. Of particular importance was the enforcement
       by the regime of Porfirio Diaz of provisions in the
       Constitution of 1857 that forbade civil corporations
       from owning land. Designed to foster liberal economic
       capitalism, the policies destroyed the *ejido* system
       (involving communal ownership and operation of land
       by the peasantry) and accelerated the growth of large,
       privately owned land holdings, whose economic systems
       of operation effectively and increasingly bound the
       rural masses to the *hacienda*. Concentrated in the
       central plateau region of the country and surrounded
       by mountains on all sides but the north, both *campesino*
       and *peon* families had little hope of escaping abject
       poverty or debt peonage by migration northward, first
       to the northern regions of Mexico and subsequently into
       the southwestern part of the United States.

1824. Carlson, Alvar W. "One Century of Foreign Immigration to the United States, 1880-1979." *International Migration*, 23 (September 1985): 309-333.

1825. Cassidy, Hugh J.B., and Edward Wakin. "Saturday Night Voodoo: Sunday Morning Mass." *U.S. Catholic*, 43 (July 1978): 35-38.

1826. Center for Afroamerican and African Studies, University of Michigan. *Black Immigration and Ethnicity in the United States: An Annotated Bibliography.* Westport, Connecticut: Greenwood Press, 1985.

The stated objective of this book is to "present a comprehensive bibliography of literature, both scholarly and journalistic, related to the issues of Black immigration of recent decades and its effects on the changing composition of the Black population in the United States" (ix). The 1,049 entries are divided into six parts dealing with such topics as immigrant populations, demographics, ecology, race, ethnicity, identity, history, legislation, politics, economic status, and literature. The title of this work does not reflect its contents: 59 percent of the entries are not annotated: many entries deal with Hispanics; and part 6 is devoted to Black immigration to Canada and Great Britain.

1827. Centro estudios migratorios. *Migrantes: Exodo Forcado.* São Paulo: Endicoes Paulinas, 1980.

Eight short essays on different facets of internal and external migrations of Brazilians which attempt an analysis of the political and economic causes of emigration.

1828. Chambers, Larry, and Harry A. Kersey, Jr. "Educating the New Cuban Population." In Neal E. Justin and Harry A. Kersey, Jr., eds., *Florida Education in the 70's.* Dubuque, Iowa: Kendall/Hunt Publishing Company, 1973. Pp. 130-139.

1829. Chang, L.L. "Acculturation and Emotional Adjustment of Chinese Women Immigrants." Unpublished Ph.D. dissertation, Columbia University, 1980.

1830. Chaparro, O., et al. *Emigración de profesionales y técnicos Colombianos y Latinamericanos 1960-1970.* Bogotá: Fondo Colombiano de investigaciones científicas, 1970.

1831. Cheng, Lucie, and Edna Bonacich, eds. *Labor Immigra-
      tion Under Capitalism. Asian Workers in the United
      States Before World War II.* Berkeley: University
      of California Press, 1984.

      The plight of the Asian immigrant worker in the
      United States prior to World War II is well-documented
      in this monograph. This immigration is placed in the
      larger political and economic context in which it arose--
      namely, the development of capitalism in the United
      States and the emergence of imperialism, especially
      in relation to Asia.

1832. Chi, P.S.K., and M.W. Bogan. "Estudio sobre migrantes
      y migrantes de retorno en el Peru." *Notes de pob-
      lacion* (Santiago), 3 (December 1975): 95-114.

      On Peruvian migration (legal and illegal) to the
      United States and elsewhere and the patterns of return.

1833. Chin, A.S. "Adaptive Role of Chinese Women in the
      United States." *Chinese Society of America Bulletin,*
      14 (January 1979): 183-196.

1834. Chiswick, Barry R. "A Longitudinal Analysis of the
      Occupational Mobility of Immigrants." In Barbara
      Dennis, ed., *Proceedings of the 30th Annual Winter
      Meeting, Industrial Relations Research Association.*
      Madison, Wisconsin: University of Wisconsin Press,
      1978. Pp. 32-46.

1835. ————. "Sons of Immigrants: Are They at an Earnings
      Disadvantage?" *American Economic Review,* 133 (Feb-
      ruary 1977): 376-380.

1836. Clark, Garner M. "The Swiss Experience with Foreign
      Workers: Lessons for the United States." *Industry
      and Labor Relations Review,* 36 (July 1983): 606-623.

1837. Coalson, G.O. *The Development of the Migratory Farm
      Labor System in Texas: 1900-1954.* San Francisco,
      California: R & E Research Associates, 1977.

      Presents an outline of the development of the system
      of Mexican migration to the United States.

1838. Cohen, L.M., and M.A. Grossnickle, eds. *Immigrants
      and Refugees in a Changing Nation: Research and
      Training.* Washington, D.C.: The Catholic University
      of America Press, 1983.

1839. Commission on Population Growth and the American Future.
        Final Report. *Population and the American Future.*
        C. Westoff and R. Parke (eds.), Government Printing
        Office, Washington, D.C., 1972.

1840. Conaway, J. "Unwanted Immigrants: Cuban Prisoners in
        America." *The Atlantic Monthly*, 247 (February 1981):
        72-81.

        "The last of America's Cuban refugees, some 6,000
        strong, still live a closely guarded life on an Army
        base in Western Arkansas. If some harbor criminal
        impulses, many others want only the chance to fit into
        the quiltwork of American life."

1841. Congressional Research Service of the Library of Con-
        gress. *Temporary Worker Programs: Background and
        Issues.* Washington, D.C.: U.S. Government Printing
        Office, 1980.

        Prepared at the request of Senator Edward M. Kennedy,
        chairman of the Committee on the Judiciary of the U.S.
        Senate, for the use of the Select Commission on Immigra-
        tion and Refugee Policy, reviews the problems, history,
        and options involved in establishing a temporary worker
        program.

1842. Connolly, Edward. "Refugee Influx Highlights Emergency
        Housing Problems." *Journal of Housing*, 38 (January
        1981): 21-24.

1843. Connor, Walker, ed. *Mexican-Americans in Comparative
        Perspective.* Baltimore, Maryland: Urban Institute
        Press, 1985.

1844. Conroy, Hilery, and T. Scott Miyakawa, eds. *East
        Across the Pacific: Historical and Sociological
        Studies of Japanese Immigration and Assimilation.*
        Santa Barbara, California: ABC-Clio, 1972.

        A collection of essays with important historical back-
        grounds on Japanese communities before 1940 and the
        internment of the Japanese during World War II.

1845. Cordasco, Francesco. "America and the Quest for Educa-
        tional Opportunity: A Prolegomenon and Overview."
        British Journal of Educational Studies, 21 (February
        1973): 50-63.

1846. ————. "Another Face of Poverty: Oscar Lewis's *La
        Vida*." *Phylon: The Atlanta University Review of
        Race & Culture*, 29 (Spring 1968): 88–92.

1847. ————. [Review]. "Arnold B. Cheyney, ed. *The Ripe
        Harvest: Educating Migrant Children* (University of
        Miami Press, 1972)." *International Migration Review*,
        8 (Spring 1974): 83–84.

        The U.S. Dept. of Labor estimates the number of
        migrants to be 500,000, of whom one fourth are 14–17
        years of age. What is not generally realized is
        that public schools, for the most part, were not in-
        volved to any great extent in the education of migrant
        children until the mid-1960s. Involvement occurred
        then only because federal funds under the Economic
        Opportunity Act, and the Elementary and Secondary
        Education Act, principally Title I of the latter act
        became available. Most of the early educational ef-
        forts for migrant children were initiated by church
        and private groups, *e.g.*, the Migrant Ministry, the
        Migrant Children's Fund, etc. Most of the programs
        developed were summer school session and teacher-
        training programs.

1848. ————. "Bilingual Education: An American Dilemma."
        Immigration History Newsletter, 10 (May 1978): 5–8.

1849. ————. "Bilingual Education in American Schools: A
        Bibliographical Essay." *Immigration History News-
        letter*, 14 (May 1982): 1–8.

1850. ————. "Bilingual Education: Overview and Inventory."
        Educational Forum, 47 (Spring 1983): 321–334.

        "The growth of bilingual education in the United
        States invites attention by the academic community....
        This article ... provides a critical overview of the
        origins of bilingual education, contemporary bilingual
        educational practice, bilingual education theory, and
        the evolving controversy which surrounds the social
        context out of which bilingual education emerges.
        [It] also provides an inventory of resources in bi-
        lingual education that are available to the investi-
        gator. Bilingual education is a promising pedagogical
        tool, but it is not without controversy. The passionate
        debate which accompanies the controversy derives from
        a complex set of factors. The implementation of bi-
        lingual programs is perceived as poor, and this charge

is not easily rebutted. There have been few evaluation studies of the bilingual programs, and many programs were hastily undertaken without regard to the
adequacy of staff training, the diagnosis of children's
language needs, and appropriate curricular materials.
Popular support for bilingual education has been
lacking. In the past, public education has served as
the chief vehicle for the assimilation of immigrant
children into the mainstream of American society;
English had always been the sole language of instruction in the schools. The use of native languages in
bilingual education programs in the schools reversed
what was perceived as a national policy. To this
there was (and continues to be) serious resentment by
the progeny of earlier immigrants, who see the new
policy of bilingual education as the first step toward
the official recognition of multilingualism extending
from the schools across all public institutions of
American society. The most dynamic element in the
controversy surrounding bilingual education, however,
is the popular perception that it is a stratagem for
ethnic employment related to the social, political, and
economic aspirations of Hispanic minorities."

1851.   ———. *Bilingual Schooling in the United States: A
Sourcebook for Educational Personnel.* New York:
McGraw-Hill, 1976.

1852.   ———. "Charles Loring Brace and the Dangerous
Classes: Historical Analogues of the Urban Black
Poor." *Journal of Human Relations*, 20 (3rd Quarter
1972): 379-386.

1853.   ———. "Needed: A New Language Policy in the U.S."
USA Today, 113 (July 1984): 67-69.

1854.   ———. "The New Bedford Project for Non-English
Speaking Children." *Journal of Human Relations*, 20
(3rd Quarter 1972): 326-334.

1855.   ———. "Spanish Harlem: The Anatomy of Poverty."
*Phylon: The Atlanta University Review of Race and
Culture*, 26 (Summer 1965): 195-196.

1856.   ———. "Spanish-Speaking Children in American Schools."
International Migration Review, 9 (Fall 1975): 379-
382.

"Latest Census Bureau figures report about 10.8 million persons of Spanish origin in the United States,

comprising nearly 5.2 percent of the nation's population. Persons of Mexican origin make up more than
half of the Spanish group, with some 6.5 million
persons; Puerto Ricans are next with more than 1.5
million, followed by Cubans with 689,000; and, there
are some 2 million other persons of Latin Amercan origin. The N/E child's educational problem begins with a
rejection of his language, reaffirmed in the rejection
of his culture and heritage of which his language is
an extension. And it often results in his effective
exclusion from the processes of education."

1857. ———, and George Bernstein. *Bilingual Education in
       American Schools: A Guide to Information Sources*.
       Detroit, Michigan: Gale Research Co., 1979.

1858. Cornelius, Wayne A. "Migration to the United States:
       The View from Rural Sending Communities." *Develop-
       mental Digest*, 17 (1979): 90-101.

1859. Corwin, Arthur F., and Lawrence A. Cardoso. "Vamos
       al Norte: Causes of Mass Mexican Migration to the
       United States." In *Immigrants--and Immigrants:
       Perspectives on Mexican Labor Migration to the
       United States*. Ed. Arthur F. Corwin. Westport,
       Connecticut: Greenwood Press, 1978. Pp. 46-59.

1860. Cotera, Martha P. *The Chicana Feminist*. Austin,
       Texas: Information Systems Development, 1977.

       Presents material on heritage, role, identity,
       issues, and other areas. Bibliography partially
       annotated.

1861. ———. *The History and Heritage of the Chicana in
       the U.S.* Austin, Texas: Information Systems De-
       velopment, 1976.

       Draws a socioeconomic profile of the Chicana and
       views her as a member of the family and of society
       at large.

1862. Covello, Leonard. *The Social Background of the Italo-
       American School Child: A Study of the Southern
       Italian Mores and Their Effect on the School Situ-
       ation in Italy and America*. Edited by Francesco
       Cordasco. Leiden, Netherlands: E.J. Brill, 1967;
       Totowa, N.J.: Rowman and Littlefield, 1972.

1863. Craig, Richard B. *The Bracero Program.* Austin, Texas: University of Texas Press, 1971.

Study of the *bracero* program within the framework of national and international group processes although most attention is directed toward American political processes. Historical period covered extends from the *bracero* program's legal inception in 1942 to its demise in 1964. Divided into six chapters, with the primary description of intergroup relations appearing in chapters two through four. Chapter one includes a general overview of historical conditions within which the migrant labor program emerged as well as a statement of the arguments for and against the program heard in the United States and Mexico. Chapter six attempts a statement of the implications of this study for "interest group" theory.

1864. Cress, F.D. "Sewing in Spanish: Overcoming a Language Barrier." *Extension Review,* 48 (July 1977): 12-13.

1865. Crist, Raymond E., and Charles M. Nissly. *East from the Andes.* Gainesville, Florida: University of Florida Press, 1973.

1866. Crossitte, Barbara. "Haitians in U.S. May Be Offered Land in Belize." *New York Times,* March 29, 1982, p. A-18.

1867. Dade County, Florida. *Minority-Owned Businesses in Miami, Florida.* Miami: Dade County Planning Department, 1975.

1868. Dade County, Florida. *Statistical Summary of Minority-Owned Business Characteristics, Dade County, Florida, 1977.* Miami: Dade County Planning Department, 1981.

1869. Dahms, F.A. "The Evolution of Settlement Systems: A Canadian Example, 1981-1970." *Journal of Urban History,* 7 (February 1981): 169-204.

Traces the evolution of a carefully defined urban system from its earliest development to the present. Isolates the factors affecting the development of the settlements studied within a theoretical framework.

1870. D'Amato, A.M. "Aliens in Prison—the Federal Re-
       sponse to a New Criminal Justice Emergency."
       Detroit College of Law Review (Winter 1983): 1163-9.

1871. Daniel, Cletus F. *Bitter Harvest: A History of
       California Farmworkers, 1870-1941.* Ithaca, New
       York: Cornell University Press, 1981.

1872. Danilov, D.P. "Gaining Admission into the United
       States for Businessmen and Workers." *Trial*, 15
       (May 1979): 41-6.

1873. Das, M.S. "The 'Brain Drain' Controversy in a Com-
       parative Perspective." *International Review of
       Sociology*, 1 (March 1971): 55-65.

       Examines empirically the attitudes of 1,400 inter-
       national students toward returning to the country of
       origin upon completion of their studies and training
       in the United States and the effect of these attitudes
       on the loss of professional skills by the country of
       origin. The sample represented 31 less developed and
       developed countries of Asia, Africa, and Latin America
       based on Berry's "technological and demographic scales."

1874. Davie, Maurice. *World Immigration with Special Refer-
       ence to the United States.* New York: Macmillan,
       1939.

1875. Davis, Kingsley. "The Migration of Human Populations."
       In *The Human Population.* San Francisco, California:
       W.H. Freeman, 1974. Pp. 55-65.

1876. Davison, L. "Women Refugees: Special Needs and Pro-
       grams." *Journal of Refugee Resettlement*, 3 (May
       1981): 16-26.

       Summarizes the main findings of a study, undertaken
       by the Equity Policy Center with support from the Asia
       Foundation, which identifies the major problems
       facing Indochinese refugee women being resettled in
       the United States, reviews programs available to them,
       and suggests changes in current programs.

1877. Decroos, J.F. *The Long Journey: Integration and
       Maintenance Among Urban Basques in the San Fran-
       cisco Bay Region.* Reno, Nevada: Associated Faculty
       Press, 1983.

1878. Delap, R.L., and J.C. Adams. "Applying the Collapsible Corporation Provisions to Foreign Stockholders." *Journal of Corporate Taxation*, 8 (Winter 1982): 308-22.

1879. de Leeuw, Frank. *The Economic Effects of Immigration: Specification of a Model*. Washington, D.C.: The Urban Institute, 1985.

1880. Departamento administrativo nacional de estadística. "La migración y el proceso de concentración de la población de los departamentos." *Boletin mensual de estadístico*, No. 314 (September 1977): 9-48.

1881. De Veaux, Alexis. "Blood Ties." *Essence*, 13 (January 1983): 62-64, 121.

1882. "Developments in Migrant Worker's Programs: 1982." *Clearinghouse Review*, 16 (January 1983): 776-783. Update of this article can be found in Vol. 17 of the same journal for January 1984: 1058-1070.

1883. Diaz, Guarione M., ed. *Evaluation and Identification of Policy Issues in the Cuban Community*. Miami: Cuban National Planning Council, 1980.

1884. Díaz-Briquets, Sergio, and Lisandro Perez. "Cuba: The Demography of Revolution." *Population Bulletin*, 36 (April 1981): 2-42.

1885. Dickinson, A.E. "Resettlement of Laotian Refugees in Broome County, New York." *Migration News*, 34 (April-June 1985): 3-50.

1886. Dillman, C.D. "Urban Growth Along Mexico's Northern Border and the Mexican National Border Program." *The Journal of Developing Areas*, 4 (July 1970): 487-508.

1887. Dolby, K.K., et al. "Foreign Nationals in U.S." *CPA Journal*, 54 (July 1984): 71-72.

1888. Dominguez, D. "Foreign Investment in Real Property Tax Act of 1980 as It Applies to the Foreign Oil and Gas Investor." *Oil and Gas Tax Quarterly*, 30 (March 1982): 472-84.

1889. Domínguez, Virginia E. *From Neighbor to Stranger: The Dilemma of Caribbean Peoples in the United*

States. New Haven, Connecticut: Yale University,
Antilles Research Program, 1975.

1890. Dorman, James H. "Ethnicity in Contemporary America."
Journal of American Studies, 15 (December 1981):
325-339.

1891. Dumon, W.A. "The Situation of Migrant Women Workers."
International Migration, 19 (1981): 190-209.

1892. Dunbar, Tony, and Linda Kravitz. *Hard Traveling:
Migrant Farm Workers in America.* Cambridge, Massachusetts: Ballinger, 1976.

1893. Durran, Pat H., and R. Cabella-Argaudona, comps.
The Chicana: A Bibliographic Study. Los Angeles:
University of California, Chicano Studies Center,
1973.

1894. "The Economics of Mass Migration from Poor to Rich
Countries." *American Economic Review,* 73 (May
1983): 173-187.

1895. Ehrenpreis, Ralph. "Treaty Status: Immigration Law's
Overlooked Benefit." *Los Angeles Lawyer,* 3 (December
1980): 34.

1896. Eichelberger, F.P. "The Cubans in Miami: Residential
Movements and Ethnic Group Differentiation." Unpublished M.A. thesis, University of Cincinnati,
1974.

1897. Elac, J.C. "The Employment of Mexican Workers in U.S.
Agriculture, 1900-1960: A Binational Analysis."
Ph.D. dissertation, University of California, Los
Angeles, 1961; reprinted by R and F Research Asso-
ciates, San Francisco, 1972.

1898. Emerson, Robert D. *Seasonal Agricultural Labor Markets
in the United States.* Ames, Iowa: Iowa State University Press, 1983.

1899. ———. "Trade in Products and International Migration in Seasonal Labor Markets." *American Journal
of Agricultural Economics,* 64 (May 1982): 339-346.

1900. "Employers Face Penalties Under New Immigration Proposals." *Restaurant and Institution,* 89 (October 15,
1981): 18.

1901. Epstein, Noel. *Language, Ethnicity, and the Schools: Policy Alternatives for Bilingual-Bicultural Education.* Washington, D.C.: George Washington University, Institute for Educational Leadership, 1977.

1902. Estevez, G.A. "Resettling the Cuban Refugees in New Jersey." *Migration Today*, 11 (1983): 27-33.

1903. Fabricio, Roberto. "Miami Goes Latin and Likes It." *Florida Trend*, 18 (April 1976): 140-146.

1904. Fairchild, Gary F. "Socioeconomic Dimensions of Florida Citrus Harvesting." Gainesville: Economic Research Department, University of Florida, December 1975.

1905. Fass, Simon. "Innovations in the Struggle for Self-Reliance: The Hmong Experience in the United States." *International Migration Review*, 20 (Summer 1986): 351-380.

Theory suggests that the process by which traditional societies become more self-reliant involves entrepreneurship in experimenting with different ways to move from known to unknown forms of economic activity. Innovative projects in the United States indicate that Hmong refugees are in the midst of such a movement. Progress to date has been slow and difficult, but the very fact that the projects exist and that participants in many of them are learning how to improve performance provides a basis for cautious optimism about self-reliance outcomes.

1906. Fawcett, J., et al., eds. *Asia-Pacific Immigration to the United States.* Honolulu, Hawaii: East-West Center, 1985.

1907. Feore, R. *Cheap Labour and Racial Discrimination.* Brookfield, Vermont: Gower Publishing, 1984.

1908. *Filipino Immigrants in Hawaii: A Profile of Recent Arrivals.* Honolulu, Hawaii: East-West Center, July 1985.

Describes some essential facts about recent immigrants from the Philippines, especially those who have come since the major changes in U.S. immigration law in 1965.

1909. Fernández, Gastón A. "The Freedom Flotilla: A Legitimacy Crisis of Cuban Socialism?" *Journal of Interamerican Studies and World Affairs*, 24 (May 1982): 183-209.

1910. Fischer, Nancy, and John Marcum. "Ethnic Integration, Socioeconomic Status and Fertility Among Mexican Americans." *Social Science Quarterly*, 65 (1984): 583-593.

1911. Fishman, Joshua A., ed. *Language Loyalty in the United States*. The Hague: Mouton, 1966; New York: Arno Press, 1978.

1912. "Floridians Seek Residency Status for Haitians, Along with Cubans." *New York Times*, February 13, 1984, p. A-15.

1913. Foner, Nancy, and Richard Napoli. "Jamaican and Black-American Migrant Farm Workers: A Comparative Analysis." *Social Problems*, 25 (June 1978): 491-503.

1914. "Foreign Investment in U.S. Real Estate: Federal and State Law Affecting the Foreign Investor--an Update." *Real Property, Probate and Trust Journal*, 16 (Fall 1981): 465-87.

1915. Fornaro, R.J. "Asian-Indians in America: Acculturation and Minority Status." *Migration Today*, 12 (1984): 28-32.

1916. Forst, R.C. "Federal Income Taxation of Foreign Investment in United States Real Estate." *Journal of International Law and Economics*, 13 (1979): 311-27.

1917. Foster, Charles. "An Idea Whose Time Has Come (Legal Specialization in Immigration Law)." *Immigrant Journal*, 5 (January-February 1982): 3.

1918. ————. "We Are Different (Professional Responsibility of Immigration Bar)." *Immigration Journal*, 5 (March-April 1982): 3.

1919. Fox, Robert W., and Jerrold W. Huguet. *Population and Urban Trends in Central America and Panama*. Washington, D.C.: Inter-American Development Bank, 1977.

1920. Fraade, Richard D., and Michael Artan. "Temporary Employment of Foreign Nationals: The 'H' Visa." *International Lawyer*, 14 (Spring 1980): 235-256.

1921. Fradd, S. "Cubans to Cuban Americans: Assimilation in the United States." *Migration Today*, 11 (1983): 34-42.

1922. Fragomen, Austin T. *Immigration Law and Business*. New York: Boardman, 1983.

1923. Franklin, William S. "Cuban Contractors in Miami." *Business and Economic Dimensions* (University of Florida), 10 (November-December 1974): 20-26.

1924. "Free Movement of Workers in the European Economic Community: The Public Exceptions." *Stanford Law Review*, 29 (July 1977): 1283-97.

1925. Freeman, Gary. "Immigrant Labor and Working-Class Politics: The French and British Experience." *Comparative Politics* (October 1978): 29.

1926. Freeman, Lawrence A. "Mandatory Reporting Requirements for Foreigners Who Invest in U.S." *Florida Bar Journal*, 56 (May 1982): 426-31.

1927. Friedland, W.H. "Labor Waste in New York: Rural Exploitation and Migrant Workers." *Trans-Action*, 6 (February 1969): 48-53.

1928. Frittelli, A.T. "Report on Migrant Women in Their Country of Origin." *International Migration*, 29 (1981): 114-128.

1929. Fuchs, Lawrence H. "Immigration Reform in 1911 and 1981: The Role of Select Commissions." *Journal of American Ethnic History*, 3 (1983): 58-89.

1930. Fujii, E.T., and J. Mak. "On the Specification of the Income Equation for Immigrants." *Southern Economics Journal*, 49 (April 1983): 1141-1146.

1931. Fuller, J.P. "Estate and Gift Taxation of Nonresident Aliens." *Southern California Tax Institute*, 31 (1979): 795-809.

1932. Fuller, Varden, and Bert Mason. "Farm Labor." *Annals of the American Academy of Political and Social Science*, 429 (January 1977): 63-80.

1933.   Gaarder, A. Bruce. *Bilingual Schooling and the Sur-*
        vival of Spanish in the United States. Rowley,
        Massachusetts: Newbury House, 1977.

1934.   Gaines-Carter, Patrice. "Boat People Come Ashore."
        Black Enterprise, 9 (November 1979): 21-22.

1935.   Galarza, Ernesto. *Farm Workers and Agri-business in*
        California, 1947-1960. Notre Dame, Indiana: University
        of Notre Dame Press, 1977.

        Includes seven chapters. In introduction, discusses
        the corporate forces which relegated farm workers to
        perpetual migration, and establishes the antecedents to
        the emergence of the NFWU in 1947. Part II details
        the environment of agricultural production and the
        structure of agri-business. Part III recounts the strikes
        organized by the NFLU between 1947 and 1952, the best
        known of which was the DiGiorgio strike of 1942-1950.
        Part IV describes the NAWU's campaign against the
        bracero program, the seasonal contracting of Mexican
        laborers, in the 1950s. Parts V and VI deal with re-
        lations between the NAWU and other labor unions and the
        eventual demise of the NAWU. In the last chapter,
        comments on the union's successes and failures, the
        myths surrounding agri-business, and the continuation
        of social power structures that lay beneath the indus-
        try.

1936.   ————. *Merchants of Labor: An Account of the Managed*
        Migration of Mexican Farm Workers in California
        1942-1960. Santa Barbara, California: McNally and
        Loftin, 1964.

1937.   ————. "The Mexican-American Migrant Worker Culture."
        Integrated Education, 9 (March-April 1971): 17-21.

1938.   Gamio, Manuel. *Mexican Immigrant: His Life Story.*
        Chicago: University of Chicago Press, 1931.

1939.   Garcia, J.R. *Operation Wetback: The Mass Deportation*
        of Mexican Undocumented Workers in 1954. Westport,
        Connecticut: Greenwood Press, 1980.

        Focuses on the large influx of undocumented Mexican
        immigrants who surged into the Southwestern United
        States in the 1940s and early 1950s and the mass depor-
        tations ("Operation Wetback") that resulted. The
        origins of the *bracero* program, the series of conflicting

Mexican and American policy decisions on illegal immigration and the exploitation of undocumented workers are analyzed.

1940. Garcia y Grieco, Manual M. "The Importation of Mexican Contract Laborers to the United States, 1942-1964; Intecedents, Operation and Legacy." Working Papers in U.S.-Mexican Studies, No. 11. Program in United States Mexican Studies, University of California, San Diego, 1981.

Describes the operation of the *bracero* program and assesses its development and legacy in historical context.

1941. Gatty, B. "Change in Visa Laws Means More Guests, Paperwork." *Hotel and Motel Management*, 198 (May 1983): 27.

1942. ———. "A New Twist in the Battle to Draw More Foreign Visitors." *Hotel and Motel Management*, 198 (July 1983): 14.

1943. Geffert, Hannah N., et al. *The Current Status of U.S. Bilingual Education Legislation*. Washington, D.C.: Center for Applied Linguistics, 1975.

1944. Geller, Barry J. "Estate Planning Consideration for the Non-Resident Aliens U.S. Situs Assets." *Trusts and Estates*, 121 (April 1982): 28-32.

1945. Gelnan, R. "Economic Adjustments to the Termination of the Bracero Program." Unpublished Ph.D. dissertation, University of Arkansas, 1967.

1946. Giannola, J.G. "Foreign Money and U.S. Oil and Gas-Tax Considerations." *Oil and Gas Institute*, 30 (1979): 45-65.

1947. "Gift Taxation of Nonresident Aliens: Traps and Opportunities." *CPA Journal*, 53 (July 1983): 57-58.

1948. Gil, R.M. "Issues in the Delivery of Mental Health Services to Cuban Entrants." *Migration Today*, 11 (1983): 43-48.

1949. Glade, W. "The Levantines in Latin America." *American Economic Review*, 73 (May 1983): 118-122.

1950.   Goldfarb, Ronald L. *Migrant Farm Workers: A Caste of*
        Despair. Ames, Iowa: Iowa State University Press,
        1981.

1951.   Goldstein, A. "The Coordinated Use of Data Sources in
        Research on the Demographic Characteristics and Be-
        havior of Jewish Immigrants to the United States."
        American Jewish History, 72 (March 1983): 293-308.

1952.   Goldstein, Eugene. "The Religious Path to Permanent
        Residence." *Immigration Journal*, 5 (Autumn 1982):
        10.

1953.   Goldstein, S., and A. Goldstein. "The Use of the Multi-
        plicity Survey to Identify Migrants." *Demography*, 18
        (1981): 67-83.

1954.   Gonzales, L.S. "Asistencia técnica en legislación
        migratoria." *International Migration*, 11 (1973):
        104-110.

        "Examines the part played, in migration law, by the
        kind of technical assistance that is provided by ICEM
        at the request of governments and reviews the basic con-
        cepts favouring an attempt at unifying Latin American
        law in this field as an instrument of economic, social,
        and cultural development for Latin Americans. Progress
        made toward this type of legislation will permit the
        conclusion of better bilateral or multilateral agreements
        by abolishing, as is done within the European Economic
        Community, any discrimination against the nationals of
        Latin America and other countries. It will, in fact,
        promote the freedom of movement, employment, residence
        and family reunion, and the implementation of an in-
        tegration and social policy insuring the migrant's full
        adaptation in the receiving country."

1955.   Gordon, Charles. "Immigration Problems Confronting
        Foreign Personnel in the United States." *North Caro-*
        lina Journal of International Law and Commercial Rela-
        tions, 7 (Spring 1982): 265-276.

1956.   Gornall, John L., Jr., and Philip L. Wharton. "Briefing
        the Foreign Client on Starting a Business in the
        United States." *North Carolina Journal of Inter-*
        national Law and Commerce Regulations, 6 (Spring
        1981): 235-258.

1957. Gould, J.D. "European Inter-Continental Emigration. The Road Home: Return Migration from the U.S.A." *The Journal of European Economic History*, 9 (Spring 1980): 41-111.

Discusses the differences between the terms immigrant (or emigrant) alien and nonimmigrant (or nonemigrant) alien and explains why these terms may cause the mis-representation of the actual number of migrants who return home from the United States. Points out various reasons U.S. immigrants decide to return to their homeland, emphasizes the distinction between gross and net migration, and offers an alternate method for figuring immigration and emigration rates. Italian emigration from 1876-1914 is highlighted.

1958. Grebler, Leo. "The Naturalization of Mexican Immigrants in the United States." *International Migration Review*, 1 (1966): 17-31.

1959. Greenwood, M.J. "Leading Issues of Fact and Theory." *American Economics Review*, 73 (May 1983): 173-177.

1960. Grifflin, J.P. "Antitrust Constraints on Acquisitions by Aliens in the United States." *The International Lawyer*, 13 (Summer 1979): 427-48.

1961. Grubel, Herbert C. "Reflections on the Present State of the Brain Drain and a Suggested Remedy." *Minerva*, 14 (1976): 209-224.

Believes that the brain drain problem has been exaggerated. Only India and the Philippines appear to be affected by it, and both overproduce professionals in some areas. Suggests that return migration statistics would show that the loss is not so important. A voluntary contribution by skilled workers who choose to leave underdeveloped countries would take care of the problem.

1962. Guest, Avery M. "The Old-New Distinction and Naturalization: 1900." *International Migration Review*, 14 (Winter 1980): 492-510.

"The literature on American immigration frequently distinguishes between the assimilation of the old groups, primarily from Northern and Western Europe, and the new groups, primarily from Southern and Eastern Europe. This article analyzes old-new differences in naturalization, one possible measure of assimilation.

Data described here indicate a clear difference in 1900
between the new and old groups in their rates of assimilation but little difference in eventual degrees
of naturalization among persons who have been in the
United States for some period of time. It is suggested
that some of the remaining differences may be a result
of the social structures of the origin countries."

1963. Gupta, M.L. "Outflow of High-Level Manpower from the
Philippines, with Special Reference to the Period
1965-71." *International Labour Review* (Geneva),
107 (February 1973): 161-191.

1964. Guttierrez, Phillip R. "The Channelization of Mexican
Nationals to the San Luis Valley of Colorado." In
Richard C. Jones, ed., *Patterns of Undocumented
Migration: Mexico and the United States.* Totowa,
N.J.: Rowman and Allanheld, 1984. Pp. 184-198.

Analyzes the migration process of Mexican nationals
to the San Luis Valley of Colorado and identifies the
characteristics of the migrating individuals. Specific
objectives related to the primary purpose are: (a) to
describe areas of origin of this illegal migrant population; (b) to evaluate the validity of the channelization concept for the migration of undocumented Mexicans
from specific areas of origin to the San Luis Valley;
and (c) to identify various social, economic, and personal
characteristics of this migrant population. Demonstrates
that the Mexican migration stream to the San Luis Valley
of Colorado is different, possessing unique characteristics which distinguish it from streams to Texas, to the
West Coast, and to the Midwest and Plains. The study
hypotheses are that (a) the San Luis Valley migration
stream differs from other major migration streams in
the source areas and routes taken by the migrating
Mexicans; and (b) information channels and communication links are the major elements involved in this chan-
nelized migration.

1965. Guzda, M.K. "Routine or Retaliation? [Immigration
Officers at El Diario]." *Editor and Publisher, The
Fourth Estate*, 117 (October 20, 1984): 9.

1966. Guzman, R. "International Migrant Child: An Aspect of
U.S./Mexico Relations." *Educational Research Quarterly*, 6 (Fall 1981): 15-23.

1967. Gwertzman, Bernard. "Policy That Limits Indochina Refugees Is Reversed by U.S." *New York Times,* May 31, 1981, p. A-13.

1968. ————. "U.S. Bids Cuba Take Several Thousand of Its Exiles Back." *New York Times,* May 26, 1983, pp. A-1, A-6.

1969. "The H-2 Enemy: Institutionalized Injustice in Our Fields" [Jamaican Farm Workers in the U.S.]. *Perspectives: The Civil Rights Quarterly,* 15 (Summer 1983): 6-9.

1970. "Haitian Refugees: Reprieved." *Economist,* 284 (July 3, 1982): 25-26.

1971. "Haitians: Black Flotsam." *The Economist,* 269 (December 30, 1978): 23-24.

1972. Hall, Bob, and Jim Clark. "Caribbean Connection." *Southern Exposure,* 10 (May-June 1982): 60-63.

1973. Hall, Joe. *The Cuban Refugee in the Public Schools of Dade County, Florida.* Miami: Dade County Board of Public Instruction, 1965.

1974. Hancock, Richard H. *The Role of the Bracero in the Economic and Cultural Dynamics of Mexico: A Case Study of Chihuahua.* Stanford, California: Stanford University Press, 1959.

1975. Harllee, J., Jr. "U.S. Income Taxation of Aliens on Current and Deferred Compensation." *New York University Institute of Federal Taxation,* 37 (1979): 1-42.

1976. Harper, Elizabeth J. *Immigration Laws of the United States.* 3rd ed. Indianapolis, Indiana: The Bobbs-Merrill Co., 1975.

A textbook integrating statutes, regulations, administrative practices, and leading court and administrative decisions with a comprehensive index and bibliography.

1977. ————, and R.F. Chase. *Immigration Laws of the United States.* Charlottesville, Virginia: Michie, 1978.

1978. Harris, Sara, and Robert Allen. *The Quiet Revolution: How Florida Migrants Changed Their Lives.* New York: New American Library, 1978.

1979.   Hawkins, Freda. *Canada and Immigration.* Montreal:
        McGill-Queen's University Press, 1972.

1980.   ————. "Canada's Green Paper on Immigration Policy."
        International Migration Review, 9 (Summer 1975):
        237-249.

        "The Canadian government's Green Paper on immigration
        policy was finally tabled in the House of Commons on
        February 3rd of this year by the Minister of Manpower
        and Immigration, the Honorable Robert Andras. As in
        Britain, Canadian governments produce green papers in
        order to initiate a national discussion on particular
        issues, and white papers when they wish to make specific
        policy proposals, often leading to legislation. Ac-
        cording to tradition, therefore, this document has been
        presented as a discussion paper and does not make policy
        recommendations."

1981.   Hawley, Ellis E. "The Politics of the Mexican Labor
        Issue, 1950-1965." *Agricultural History* (July 1966).

1982.   "Health Aspects of the Cuban Refugee Problem." *Florida
        Health Notes,* 53 (September 1961): 147-170.

1983.   Hector, G. "The Non-issue of Immigration." *Fortune*
        (July 23, 1984): 91-92.

1984.   Henderson, N. "Foreign Students Salute Old Glory:
        Long May It Waive (Effect of New Immigration Law)."
        Electronic News, 9 (August 1983): 2.

1985.   Henderson, P.V.N. *Mexican Exiles in the Borderlands,
        1910-13.* Southwestern Studies Monograph No. 58.
        El Paso, Texas: Texas Western Press, The University
        of Texas, 1979.

        Focuses on the activities of Mexican political exiles
        and their immediate successors in attempts to overturn
        the incumbent regimes in Mexico from 1910 to 1913.

1986.   Hendrickson, R.A. "American Trusts for Non-resident
        Aliens." *Trusts & Estates,* 123 (February 1984):
        40-48.

1987.   Herrera-Sobek, Maria. *The Bracero Experience: Elite-
        lore Versus Folklore.* Los Angeles: UCLA, Latin Ameri-
        can Center Publications, 1979.

        Less concerned with the *bracero* experience (*braceros*
        were Mexican workers recruited into the United States

during the labor shortage of the 1940s) than with
Mexican perceptions about the program—thus the sub-
title *Elitelore versus Folklore*. "Elitelore," a term
coined by UCLA historian James W. Wilkie, refers to the
lore of societal leaders, including the intelligentsia;
folklore stems from the masses. The two differ in
their depiction of the *bracero* experience, a conflict
that is largely created by class differences: the com-
fortable Mexican middle-class intelligentsia worries
about Mexico's reputation, while the lower-class is
more concerned with the personal gain derived from
working in the United States. Uses limited samples
from both elitelore and folklore to illustrate these
attitudes. Elitelore is represented by several works
of Mexican fiction that appeared mainly in the 1940s
and 50s. Interviews with former *braceros* currently
living in Huecorio, Mexico, and selected folk songs
(*corridos*) constitute the folklore.

1988. Hill, C.E. "Adaptation in Public and Private Behavior
of Ethnic Groups in an American Setting." *Urban
Anthropology*, 4 (Winter 1975): 333-347.

Addresses itself to the problems of adaptation in
both public and private behavior of the ethnic groups
in Atlanta, Georgia, and some of the mechanisms that
aid in their adaptation to an urban setting. Directions
for future research are also briefly explored. Some
notice of undocumented aliens.

1989. Hirschman, C., and M.G. Wong. "Socioeconomic Gains
of Asian Americans, Blacks and Hispanics: 1960-1976."
American Journal of Sociology, 90 (November 1984):
584-607.

Based on the Census of the Population for 1960 and
1970 and the Survey of Income and Education in 1976,
analyzes socioeconomic inequality between five minority
populations—blacks, Hispanics, Japanese, Chinese and
Filipino—and the majority population—white non-Hispanic
—then decomposes ethnic gaps into shares that are ex-
plained by age, nativity, residence, education, and
other social background attributes.

1990. ——, and ——. "Successful Minorities: Socio-
economic Achievement Among Immigrant and Native-Born
Asian Americans." Paper presented at the Annual
Meeting, Population Association of America, Denver,
Colorado, April 10-12, 1980.

Provides a thorough introduction to the structure of
socioeconomic inequalities of the Asian Americans.
Socioeconomic patterns and achievements of three Asian
American communities--Chinese, Japanese and Filipino--
with particular attention to changes from 1960 to 1976.
Analysis contrasts the socioeconomic characteristics
of both immigrants and native born Asian Americans for
three dates for which data are available: 1960, 1970,
and 1976.

1991. Hoffman, Abraham. *Unwanted Mexican Americans in the
Great Depression: Repatriation Pressures 1929-1939.*
Tucson, Arizona: University of Arizona Press, 1974.

1992. Hoffman-Nowotny, H.J. "A Sociological Approach Toward
a General Theory of Migration." In Mary M. Kritz,
Charles B. Keely, and Silvano M. Tomasi, eds., *Global
Trends in Migration: Theory and Research on International Population Movements.* New York: Center
for Migration Studies, 1981. Pp. 240-267.

1993. "House Passage Near: Immigration-reform Bill Relies on
Employer's Help." *Engineering News-Record*, 212
(June 21, 1984): 29.

1994. Howe, Marvine. "Status of Immigrants from India Is
Debated." *New York Times*, April 20, 1986, p. 37.

1995. Hucker, John. "A Synopsis of Canadian Immigration
Law." *Syracuse Journal of International Law and
Commerce*, 3 (Spring 1975): 47-76.

1996. Huffman, W.E. "International Trade in Labor versus
Commodities: U.S. Mexican Agriculture." *American
Journal of Agricultural Economics*, 64 (December
1982): 989-998.

1997. Hutchison, R. "Miscounting the Spanish Origin Population in the United States: Corrections to the 1970
Census and Their Implications." *International Migration*, 22 (1984): 73-89.

Purpose is three-fold: (a) to identify the discrepancies in the 1970 census figures; (b) to suggest
alternative strategies for correcting the original
figures and briefly report on an estimate of the possible "correct" figures for 1970; and (c) to summarize
briefly the implications of the corrected figures for
past and present research. It will be seen that the

revised figures lower the total Spanish Origin population for 1970 by nearly 1,000,000 persons, but in so doing they increase the relative importance of the other (Mexican, Puerto Rican, and Cuban) groups. In addition, the lower base figure resulting from the corrections makes the rate of growth for the Spanish Origin population in the 1970-1980 decade even greater than has previously been thought.

1998. Ignacio, Lemuel. *Asian Americans and Pacific Islanders: Is There Such an Ethnic Group?* San Jose, California: Filipino Development Associates, 1976.

1999. "Immigration and Adoption of Operation Babylift Orphans: Tough Decisions in Family Law." *Orange County Bar Journal*, 4 (Summer 1977): 164-81.

2000. "Immigration: The Black and White of It (Cubans and Haitians)." *Economist*, 290 (February 18, 1984).

2001. "Immigration: The Devil and the Deep Blue Sea." *The Economist*, 281 (October 31, 1981): 38-39.

2002. "Immigration and Nationality Act Amendments of 1976: Implications for the Alien Professional." *Cleveland State Law Review*, 26 (1977): 295-324.

2003. "Immigration: The Price of Purity." *Economist*, 293 (October 6, 1984): 26-27.

2004. "Immigration: Recognition for the Reserve Labor Army." *Economist*, 279 (June 6, 1981); 32-33.

2005. "Immigration: Reducing the Attraction." *Economist*, 284 (August 21, 1982): 20-21.

2006. "Imported from Haiti." *The Economist*, 280 (July 4, 1981): 27.

2007. Isenbergh, J. "The Trade or Business of Foreign Taxpayers in the United States." *Taxes*, 61 (December 1983): 972-85.

2008. Jaco, Daniel E., and George L. Wilber. "Asian Americans in the Labor Market." *Monthly Labor Review*, 98 (July 1975): 33-38.

2009. Jacoby, Susan. "Miami si, Cuba no." *New York Times Magazine* (September 29, 1974): 28, 103-123.

2010. Jadotte, Herard. "Haitian Immigration to Quebec."
       Journal of Black Studies, 7 (June 1977): 485-500.

2011. Jakaboski, Theodore P. "Our Sick Immigration Service:
       How to Cure It." *Commercial Law*, 6 (November-
       December 1981): 2-15.

2012. Japanese-American Project. (University of California,
       Los Angeles, California 90024).
       The largest collection of manuscripts, memorabilia,
       and other materials of the Japanese community. See
       Jyji Ichioka, *A Buried Past: An Annotated Bibliography
       of the Japanese-American Research Project Collection*
       (Berkeley: University of California Press, 1974).

2013. Jaynes, Gregory. "Ruling on Detention of Haitians
       Expected as Miami Suit Concludes." *New York Times*,
       May 16, 1982, p. A-34.

2014. ————. "U.S. Finds a Big Decline in Refugees from
       Haiti." *New York Times*, December 6, 1981, p. A-81.

2015. Jenna, William W. *Metropolitan Miami: A Demographic
       Overview*. Coral Gables, Florida: University of Miami
       Press, 1972.

2016. Jenness, R.A. "Canadian Migration and Immigration
       Patterns and Government Policy." *International
       Migration Review*, 8 (Spring 1974): 5-22.

2017. Jiminez de Arechaga, E. "State Responsibility for the
       Nationalization of Foreign Owned Property." *New York
       University Journal of International Law and Policy*,
       11 (Fall 1978): 179-85.

2018. Johnson, George E. "The Labor Market Effects of Immi-
       gration." *Industry and Labor Relations Review*, 33
       (April 1980): 331-341.

2019. Johnson, Juanita B. *Haitian Directory of Health and
       Social Services*. Miami: Miami-Dade Community Col-
       lege, 1982.

2020. Johnson, Kenneth F. *Mexican Democracy: A Critical View*.
       Rev. ed. New York: Praeger, 1978.

2021. Johnston, H.J. "An Overview of the Growth and Develop-
       ment of the U.S. Migrant Health Program." *Migration
       Today*, 12 (1984): 8-14.

2022. Jones, I.B. "Mexican-American Labor Problems in Texas." Unpublished Ph.D. dissertation, University of Texas, 1965. Reprinted by R and E Research Association, San Francisco, 1971.

2023. Jones, Robert C. *Mexican War Workers in the United States: The Mexico-United States Manpower Recruiting Program, 1942-1944*. Washington, D.C.: Pan American Union, 1945.

2024. Jorge, Antonio, and Raul Moncarz. "International Factor Movement and Complementarity: Growth and Entrepreneurship Under Conditions of Cultural Variation." *R.E.M.P. Bulletin*, 14 (September 1981): 1-63.

2025. "Justice Detained: The Immigration Crisis." *Human Rights*, 11 (Summer 1983): 14.

2026. Kang, T.S. "Name Change and Acculturation: Chinese Students on an American Campus." *Pacific Sociological Review*, 14 (October 1971): 403-412.

Study of social life of 262 Chinese students at the University of Minnesota in 1967. Shows that 36.2% of these students anglicized their names. The change of a person's name is theorized to be a symbolic representation of his identity change. Reveals that those students who changed their names displayed significantly more out-group-oriented attitudes and behaviors than those who did not change their names.

2027. Kasarda, J.D. "Hispanics and City Change." *American Demographic*, 16 (1984): 24-29.

2028. Kelly, Gail P. "The Schooling of Vietnamese Immigrants: Internal Colonialism and Its Impact of Women." In Beverly Lindsay, ed., *Comparative Perspectives of Third World Women: The Impact of Sex, Race and Class*. New York: Praeger Publishers, 1980. Pp. 276-296.

2029. Kerpen, Karen Shaw. "Those Who Left: Two Years Later." *Cubatimes*, 3 (Spring 1982): 1-4.

2030. Keyfitz, N. "Migration as a Means of Population Control." *Population Studies*, 25 (1971): 63-72.

Develops expressions for the effect on ultimate population of a given number of out- or in-migrants, expressed as a function of their age. The main relations

are for one-time migration and for a continuous
stream of migrants, the former affecting only the
level of the ultimate population, the latter affecting
its rate of growth as well. The age effect is ap-
preciable but is not sufficient to encourage a policy
of moving people. Neither internal movement within a
county nor movement to foreign countries is a substitute
for contraception as a means of population control.

2031. Kim, S.D. "Interracially Married Korean Women Immi-
      grants: A Study in Marginality." Unpublished Ph.D.
      dissertation, University of Washington, 1979.

2032. King, T. "Immigration from Developing Countries: Some
      Philosophical Issues." *Ethics*, 93 (April 1983):
      525-536.

2033. Kirstein, Peter N. *Anglo over Bracero: A History of
      the Mexican Worker in the United States from Roosevelt
      to Nixon.* San Francisco, California: R & E Research
      Associates, Inc., 1977.

      Concerned with various aspects of the Mexican
      national worker experience in America. The development
      and implementation of the bi-national *bracero* program
      from the 1940s to the 1960s are examined in a diplomatic,
      social, and economic context. The importance of illegal
      immigration and the impact of the wetback on the *bracero*
      program's demise are analyzed. The role of agribusiness,
      organized labor, and government agencies which had af-
      fected the Mexican worker experience in America is
      examined.

2034. Kloss, Heinz. *The American Bilingual Tradition.*
      Rowley, Massachusetts: Newbury House, 1977.

2035. ————. *Laws and Legal Documents Relating to Problems
      of Bilingual Education in the United States.* Wash-
      ington, D.C.: Center for Applied Linguistics, 1971.

2036. Koppel, Barbara. "The Migrants Stoop, the Growers
      Conquer." *The Progressive*, 46 (March 1982): 42-44.

2037. Krauss, Melvin B., and William J. Baumol. "Guest
      Workers and Income Transfer Programs Financed by Host
      Governments." *Kyklos*, 32 (1979): 36-46.

2038. Kritz, Mary M. "The Impact of International Migration
      on Venezuelan Demographic and Social Structure."
      International Migration Review, 9 (Winter 1975): 513-4

2039.   ————, ed. *Migraciones Internacionales en Las Ameri-
        cas.* Caracas: Centro de estudios de pastoral y
        asistencia migratoria, 1980.

        This collection of 11 essays, several of which were
        previously published in English in the *International
        Migration Review* Fall 1979 issue on International
        Migration in the Americas, represents one of the ef-
        forts to survey the overall situation. One of the
        studies is based on empirical fieldwork done on Latin
        American migrants (a Mexican government study on arrival
        of illegal Mexican immigrants deported from the United
        States).

2040.   ————, et al., eds. *Global Trends in Migration:
        Theory and Research on International Population Move-
        ments.* New York: Center for Migration Studies, 1981.

2041.   Kroll, Monroe. "Needed Now: A Truly Independent Immi-
        gration Court." *Immigration Journal,* 5 (January-
        February 1982): 4-7.

2042.   Kunz, E.F. "The Refugees in Flight: Kinetic Models and
        Forms of Displacement." *International Migration
        Review,* 7 (1973): 125-146.

2043.   Kwok, V. "Economic Model of the Brain Drain (Taiwan)."
        American Economic Review, 72 (March 1982): 91-100.

2044.   ————, and H. Leland. "An Economic Model of the
        Brain Drain." *American Economic Review,* 74 (June
        1984): 533-535.

2045.   "Labor Department Struggles with Live-in Maid Problem."
        Interpreter Releases (November 20, 1969): 273-76.

2046.   Lacefield, Patrick. "These Political Refugees Are from
        the Wrong Place." *In These Times* (November 7-13,
        1979): 11, 13.

2047.   La Franchi, H. "U.S./Mexico Border." *The Christian
        Science Monitor,* December 9, 10, 11, 12 and 13, 1985.

        A five-part article which reports on the interdepen-
        dence that ties border areas together; the efforts to
        stem the flow of illegal immigrants; non-Mexican illegal
        aliens; border economies; and the future of U.S. and
        Mexican border growth.

2048. Laguerre, Michel S. *Voodoo Heritage*. Beverly Hills, California: Sage Publications, 1980.

2049. Lando, Barry. "The Mafia and the Mexicans: Crooked Justice from the INS." *Washington Monthly* (April 1973): 16-21.

2050. Landrigan, Steve. "The Other 'Boat People.'" *Africa*, 103 (March 1980): 89-91.

2051. Lang, Rodney P. "Administrative Law—Constitutional Validity of the One-House Veto. *Chadha v. INS.* 634 F 2D 408 (9th cir. 1980)." *Land and Water Law Review*, 17 (Winter 1982): 241-256.

2052. Lasaga, José I. "La juventud del exilio y la tradicion nacional Cubana." *Exilio*, No. 3-4 (Fall 1969-Spring 1970): 51-81.

2053. "The Latinization of Miami." *Price Waterhouse Review*, 22 (1977): 6-17.

2054. Latortue, Gérard R. "Tyranny in Haiti." *Current History*, 51 (December 1966): 349-353.

2055. "The Law and Procedure of International Adoption: An Overview." *Suffolk Transnational Law Journal*, 7 (Fall 1983): 361-90.

2056. League of United Latin American Citizens. "Analysis of Simpson-Mazzoli Legislation H.R. 1510." Washington, D.C. [July 21, 1983].

      An open letter released by the League's Washington, D.C., office on July 21, 1983.

2057. Lear, Martha Weinman. "New York's Haitians: Working, Waiting, Watching Bébé Doc." *New York Times Magazine* (October 10, 1971): 22-36.

2058. Lee, Everett S. "A Theory of Migration." *Demography*, 3 (1966): 47-57.

2059. Lenoir, Robert L. "Citizenship as a Requirement for the Practice of Law in Ontario." *Ottawa Law Review*, 13 (Summer 1981): 527-548.

2060. Leonard, H.B. "Louis Marshall and Immigration Restriction, 1906-1924." *American Jewish Archives*, 24 (April 1972): 6-26.

To restrict immigration, Louis Marshall believed, would be to destroy "one of the fundamentals of America's national spirit." He did what he could to frustrate restrictionist efforts even when it became a lost cause.

2061. Leonatti, L., and L. Newel-Morris. "Lifetime Patterns of Childbearing and Employment: A Study of Second-Generation Japanese American Women." *Journal of Biosocial Science*, 14 (January 1982): 81-97.

2062. Lescott-Leszczynski, J. *The History of U.S. Ethnic Policy and Its Impact on European Ethnics*. Boulder, Colorado: Westview Press, 1984.

2063. Lewin, Ellen. *Mothers and Children: Latin American Immigrants in San Francisco*. New York: Arno Press, 1980.

The vital role of the mother in the adaptation of the Latin American immigrant family to life in the United States is described in this revealing portrait. The author provides an examination of the experiences of 15 lower-class Mexican and Central American immigrant women in the heavily Latino Mission District of San Francisco. Based on her observations and interviews, the author concludes that, generally, these women have made excellent, rational decisions in the face of relatively adverse circumstances. Originally, Ph.D. dissertation, Stanford University, 1974.

2064. Li, W.L. "A Note on Migration and Employment." *Demography*, 13 (November 1976): 565-570.

Examines the nature of the relation between migration and employment. Preliminary investigation confirms a previous observation that the employment rate of migrants is generally lower than that of nonmigrants. Further analysis suggests that this does not mean that migration has no effect on employment; the two appear to be strongly related. "Migration enables some unemployed and initially disadvantageous persons to improve their employment status, making it more nearly comparable, though not equal to that of the general population."

2065. Lindsey, Robert B. "Change of Immigration Status." *Interpreter Releases* (November 6, 1972): 299-311.

2066. Linehan, Edward J. "Cuba's Exiles Bring New Life to Miami." *National Geographic*, 144 (July 1973): 68-95.

2067. Litwin, Edward. "Live-at-Work." *Immigration Journal*, 5 (March-April 1982): 17.

2068. *Living in Two Cultures: The Socio-Cultural Situation of Migrant Workers and Their Families*. New York: Unipub, 1982.

2069. Lloyd, Robin. "The Boat Stops Here." *In These Times* (February 10-16, 1982): 12-13, 22.

2070. Loney, M. "Canada's Immigration Policy." *Race Today*, 3 (1971): 303-304.

Argues that Canada's immigration policy (1) favors highly-skilled workers; (2) entails a number of political preferences operated by means of the powers of personal assessment of potential immigrants accorded the immigration officers; (3) may allow the racial prejudice of the officer to intrude into decision-making procedures.

2071. Long, J. "Immigration Bill Affects Foreign Students in U.S. Colleges." *Chemical and Engineering News*, 62 (July 2, 1984): 16-17.

2072. Longbrake, David B., and Woodrow W. Nichols. *Sunshine and Shadows in Metropolitan Miami*. Cambridge, Massachusetts: Ballinger, 1976.

2073. Los Angeles County Commission on Human Relations. "Plight of the New Americans: Discrimination Against Immigrants and Refugees." [Los Angeles County Commission on Human Relations, November 1985.]

A digest of 27 presentations at a hearing on discrimination against immigrants and refugees conducted by the Los Angeles County Commission on Human Relations on April 18, 1985. With Los Angeles County the home of 1.6 million foreign-born persons, presenters identified many areas of concern, including education, employment, health care, housing, INS, mental health, image, social services, and intergroup relations. Presenters also cited institutional policies and practices which had a discriminatory and negative effect upon immigrants and refugees.

2074. McBride, J. *Vanishing Bracero*. San Antonio, Texas: Naylor Company, 1963.

2075. McCarthy, K.F., and R.B. Valdez. *Current and Future Effects of Mexican Immigration in California*.

Executive Summary. Santa Monica, California: The
Rand Corporation, November 1985.

The study was undertaken to assess the current situation of Mexican immigrants in California and project
future possibilities. Constructs a demographic profile
of the immigrants, examines their economic effects on
the state, and describes their socioeconomic integration into California society. To unify and interpret
the extensive and varied data on which the study is
based, the authors develop models of both the immigration and integration processes and then use these
models to project future immigration flows.

2076. McCoy, T.L. "The Ambiguities of U.S. Temporary Foreign
Worker Policy." *Population Research and Policy Review,* 4 (February 1985): 31-49.

2077. ————, and C.H. Wood. *Caribbean Workers in the Florida
Sugar Cane Industry.* University of Florida: Center
for Latin American Studies, December 1982.

Reports the findings of a study of a labor program
that has, for the last 39 years, brought workers from
the Commonwealth Caribbean (known as the British West
Indies prior to independence) to south Florida to harvest sugar cane. The eight to nine thousand men in
this work force currently constitute the largest legal
foreign migrant labor program in the United States.

2078. McDonald, J.L. "Income Tax Planning for the Nonresident
Alien Investor." *Southern California Tax Institute,*
31 (1979): 743-94.

2079. McElroy, R.C., and E.E. Gavett. *Termination of the
Bracero Program: Some Effects on Farm Labor and Migrant
Housing Needs.* Agricultural Economic Report No. 77.
Washington, D.C.: U.S. Department of Agriculture,
Economic Research Service, 1965.

2080. McGrath, Peter. "Refugees or Prisoners?" *Newsweek,*
99 (February 1, 1982): 24-29.

2081. MacKenzie, Kyle, et al. "Grandmothers' Stories."
Frontiers, 2 (Summer 1977): 56-58.

At age 85, Grandma Vigil gives her granddaughter the
first threads to be woven with the lives of other grand-
mas, *madres,* and *hijas* into a Hispanic story of mother-
ing.

2082. Mackey, William F., and Von Nieda Beebe. *Bilingual
      Schools for a Bicultural Community: Miami's Adaptation
      to the Cuban Refugees.* Rowley, Massachusetts: New-
      bury House, 1977.

2083. MacMillen, M.J. "Economic Effects of International
      Migration: A Survey." *Journal of Common Market
      Studies,* 20 (March 1982): 245-267.

2084. MacNamara, Mark. "Santeria." *Miami Magazine,* 34 (No-
      vember 1982): 98-101, 109-110, 169-170.

2085. McNeill, William H., and Ruth S. Adams, eds. *Human
      Migrations: Patterns and Policies.* Bloomington,
      Indiana: Indiana University Press, 1978.

2086. Mahoney, Larry. "Inside Krome." *Miami Herald, Tropic
      Magazine* (January 10, 1982): 7-15.

2087. Maldonado, Lionel, and Joan Moore, eds. *Urban Ethnicity
      in the United States. New Immigrants and Old Minori-
      ties.* Beverly Hills, California: Sage Publications,
      1985.

2088. Malone, Patrick. "In Defense of Voodoo." *Miami
      Herald, Tropic Magazine* (September 20, 1981): 8-14,
      36-41.

2089. Mamer, G.W. "The Use of Foreign Labor for Seasonal
      Farm Work in the United States: Issue Involved and
      Interest Groups in Conflict." *Journal of Farm Eco-
      nomics,* 43 (December 1961): 1204-10.

2090. "Many Hands Make Light Deficits." *American Demograph-
      ics,* 5 (January 1983): 12.

2091. Mármora, Lelio. "Labor Migration Policy in Colombia."
      International Migration Review, 13, 3 (Fall 1979):
      440-54.

2092. Marrus, Michael R. *The Unwanted: European Refugees in
      the Twentieth Century.* New York: Oxford University
      Press, 1986.

      Argues that the appearance of masses of refugees is
      a recent phenomenon, a product of modern politics.
      Central theme is "the emergence of a new variety of
      collective alienation, one of the hallmarks of our
      time." The refugee is described as a person who has

fled what he regards as intolerable conditions in his homeland, and the flight of tens or hundreds of thousands of people is part of the history of that homeland; but a special problem is created and a special history is engendered if these people, once they have gotten out, find that there is nowhere to go. It is this latter condition that is "the peculiar condition of the refugee of the 20th century."

2093. Martin, L., and D.S. North. "Nonimmigrant Aliens in American Agriculture." Paper presented at the U.S. Department of Labor/University of Florida Conference on Seasonal Agricultural Labor Markets, Arlington, Virginia, January 1980.

2094. Martin, Philip L. *Guest-Worker Programs: Lessons from Europe.* Prepared for the Bureau of International Labor Affairs, U.S. Department of Labor. Washington, D.C.: Government Printing Office, 1980.

2095. ———. *Illegal Immigration and the Colonization of the American Labor Market.* Washington, D.C.: Center for Immigration Studies, 1968.

The report (1) finds that the ready availability of illegal alien workers in major industries and geographical regions is having far-reaching and often unanticipated consequences for patterns of investment, employment, and business competition in the United States; (2) documents the displacement of American workers by illegal immigrants in agriculture, food processing, services and construction, analyzing the processes of network recruiting and subcontracting that lead ultimately to the exclusion of American citizens and legal residents from many work places; and (3) concludes that our acquiescence in illegal immigration has become a selective labor subsidy that has contributed in the last two decades to distorted investment decisions, slower growth, and the proliferation of low-skill, low-productivity jobs in the American labor market.

2096. ———, and Mark J. Miller. "Guestworkers: Lessons from Western Europe." *Industrial and Labor Relations Review*, 33 (1980): 142-154.

2097. Martin, W.E. "Alien Workers in United States Agriculture: Impacts on Production." *Journal of Farm Economics*, 48 (December 1966): 1137-45.

2098. Martínez, Oscar J. *Border Boom Town: Ciudad Juárez
        Since 1848*. Austin: University of Texas Press,
        1975.

2099. Maselli, G. "Immigration as an Essential Element for
        the Development of Latin America." *International
        Migration*, 2 (1967): 108-26.

2100. [Masonz, S.D.]. *History of the Immigration and Natural-
        ization Service*. Washington, D.C.: U.S. Government
        Printing Office, 1980.

        Prepared by S.D. Masonz of the Library of Congress
        at the request of Senator E.M. Kennedy. The chrono-
        logical development of INS within the context of U.S.
        immigration policy.

2101. Mathewson, Marie A. "Is Crazy Anglo Crazy Haitian?"
        Psychiatric Annals, 5 (August 1975): 79-83.

2102. Meislan, Richard J. "Trial in Haiti Puts the Focus on
        Rights." *New York Times*, August 27, 1982, p. A-3.

2103. Melom, Gail B., and Robert S. Bixby. "The Pros and
        Cons of Specialization in Immigration Law." *Immi-
        gration Journal*, 5 (January-February 1982): 6.

2104. Melville, Margarita B. "Mexican Women Adapt to Migra-
        tion." *International Migration Review*, 12 (Summer
        1978): 225-236.

        A study of recent Mexican female migrants to Houston,
        Texas, which seeks to determine the strategies used by
        these migrants to cope with the stress of migration.

2105. Mene, G.J. "Estate Planning for Nonresident Aliens."
        Texas, 59 (September 1981): 617-33.

2106. Merricks, Walter. "Removing a Blot on British Justice
        (Emigration and Immigration Law)." *New Law Journal*,
        132 (November 4, 1982): 1019.

2107. [Mexico, Consejo nacional de población]. *Reunion
        nacional sobre distribución de la población, migración
        y desarrollo*. Mexico, D.F.: Consejo nacional de
        población, 1984.

2108. Meyer, Sylvan. "Cuban Power: Cracking the Anglo Struc-
        ture." *Miami Magazine*, 28 (August 1977): 22-27, 47.

2109. "Miami: Haven for Terror." *The Nation*, 224 (March 19, 1977): 326-331.

2110. Migdail, Carl. "In Haiti, Desperation Is a Way of Life." *U.S. News and World Report* (November 30, 1981): 39-40.

2111. "Migrant Laborers in Virginia Are Part of 'Guest Worker' Program That May Spread If Immigration Restrictions Are Relaxed." *Washington Post*, May 23, 1983, Sec. C, p. 1.

2112. "Migrating Out of Work." *Economist*, 283 (May 1, 1982): 83.

2113. Miles, Robert. *Racism and Migrant Labour: A Critical Text.* Boston: Routledge and Kegan Paul, 1983.

2114. Miller, Mark J., and Philip L. Martin. *Administering Foreign-Worker Programs: Lessons from Europe.* Lexington, Massachusetts: D.C. Heath and Co., 1982.

2115. ————, and D.J. Yeres. *A Massive Temporary Worker Programme for the U.S.: Solution or Mirage?* Geneva: International Labour Office, World Employment Programme Research, 1979.

2116. Millott, Dan. "Cuban Thrust to the GOP." *New Florida*, 1 (September 1981); 70-71.

2117. Mines, Richard. "Network Migration and Mexican Rural Development: A Case Study." In Richard C. Jones, ed., *Patterns of Undocumented Migration: Mexico and the United States.* Totowa, N.J.: Rowman and Allanheld, 1984. Pp. 136-155.

United States migration policies and enforcement practices have adapted to the changing labor supply-demand situation. In the 20 years after World War II, Mexican immigrants were desired principally as field laborers in agriculture. The contract labor system of 1942-64, the *"Bracero"* program, and the deportation drive of 1954 (Operation Wetback) made it difficult for nonimmigrant Mexicans to find nonagricultural work. Operation Wetback cleared the undocumented migrants from the cities, forcing those interested in U.S. work to come as contract laborers in agriculture. By the late 1960s, however, as the demand for Mexican workers spread from agriculture to urban employment, immigration

law enforcement could not keep up with events. Social
security cards were easily obtained by undocumented
workers until recently. Now the ebb and flow of hundreds of thousands of Mexicans across the border occurs
largely outside the purview of U.S. immigration law.

2118. ———, and P.L. Martin. "Immigrant Workers and California Citrus Industry." *Industrial Relations*, 23
(Winter 1984): 139-149.

2119. Miracle, M.P., and S.P. Berry. "Migrant Labor and Economic Development." *Oxford Economic Papers*, 22 (March
1970): 86-108.

2120. Moncarz, Raul. "Professional Adaptation of Cuban
Physicians in the United States, 1959-1969." *International Migration Review*, 4 (Spring 1970): 80-86.

"This study analyzes the extent of utilization or
underutilization of the education and training brought
by Cuban physicians, describing the adaptation process
and how much of their competencies were transferable
under conditions existing in the United States since
January 1, 1959. Basic to the study is an analysis of
the readaptation of the human capital involved in the
skills brought by the Cuban physicians to the United
States. The objective is to discover (1) the types of
individuals in terms of occupational or personal characteristics who adjusted better to the new environment
and (2) the barriers to absorption encountered by the
Cuban physicians who tried to remain in their same
Cuban professions."

2121. ———. "Professional Adaptation of the Cuban Teachers
in the United States, 1959-1969." *International
Migration*, 8 (1970): 110-116.

Analyzes the extent of utilization or underutilization
and training of male Cuban teachers, who have gone
through the special programs sponsored by the different
states and universities, under the guidance and sponsorship of the U.S. Department of Health, Education and
Welfare, to fully accredit their Cuban degrees.

2122. Monroy, D. "An Essay on Understanding the Work Experience of Mexicans in Southern California, Between
1900 and 1930." *Aztlán*, 12 (Spring 1981): 59-74.

Discusses the status of Mexican workers in Southern
California between 1900 and 1930, describing the

Mexican's position on the social ladder, the hierarchy
within the strata and the movement up from agricultural
to industrial labor.

2123. Moore, O. Ernest. "Haiti: The Tragic Island." *Revista/
Review Interamericana*, 10 (Fall 1980): 305-319.

2124. Mora, Magdalena, and Alelaida R. De Castillo, eds.
*Mexican Women in the United States: Struggles Past
and Present*. Los Angeles: University of California
Chicano Studies Research Center Occasional Paper No.
2, 1980.

The primary objective of this book is to document and
appraise Mexican women's activism in struggles against
"national oppression, class exploitation, and sexism."
The essays, case studies, and profiles of individual
women indicate the extent to which women of Mexican
heritage have been involved in such struggles and the
dilemmas they face when they are active.

2125. Morris, Milton D. *Immigration--The Beleaguered Bureaucracy*. Washington, D.C.: The Brookings Institution,
1985.

Centers on the administration of U.S. immigration
policy. After noting the importance of having adequate
means to implement alternative new immigration actions
that have recently been debated in Congress, the book
explores the history of U.S. immigration policy and the
record and roots of migration to the United States.

2126. Nathan, K.S. "Legal Aid for Immigration Civil Cases."
(Great Britain). *Solicitor's Journal*, 127 (September
9, 1983): 587.

2127. [National Commission for Manpower Policy]. *Foreign
Workers: Dimensions and Policies*. Special Report (34).
Washington, D.C.: National Commission for Manpower
Policy, March 1979.

Sets out a set of broad policy options with respect
to the temporary importation of foreign labor to the
United States and evaluates the options.

2128. National Lawyers Guild. *Immigration Law and Defense*.
New York: Clark Boardman Co., 1984.

2129. Navarro, G.R. "Federal Estate Tax Planning and the
Nonresident Alien: The Costly Privilege of Dying an

American." *Lawyer of the Americas*, 12 (Fall 1980):
503-32.

2130. Newdick, Christopher. "Immigrants and the Decline of
       Habeas Corpus." (Great Britain). *Public Law* (Spring
       1982): 89-109.

2131. Newland, K. *International Migration: The Search for
       Work*. Worldwatch Paper 33. Washington, D.C.: World-
       watch Institute, November 1979.

       Discusses the international problem of voluntary,
       economically motivated migrants who cross borders in
       search of work. Significance of migration as an eco-
       nomic and political issue between countries is explored
       as a graphic phenomenon of global interdependence.

2132. Niejolt, G. Thomas-Lycklama. *On the Road for Work:
       Migratory Workers on the East Coast of the U.S.*
       Hingham, Massachusetts: Kulwer Academic Publishers,
       1980.

2133. Norment, Lynn. "Are Black Refugees Getting a Dirty
       Deal?" *Ebony*, 38 (October 1983): 132-136.

2134. North, David S. *Alien Legalization and Naturalization:
       What the United States Can Learn from Down Under*.
       Washington, D.C.: New TransCentury Foundation, 1984.

       A commentary and critical essay on any useful lessons
       to be learned for U.S. immigration policy-makers in
       Australia and New Zealand, regarding legalization pro-
       grams and the granting of citizenship.

2135. ————. "Labor Market Rights of Foreign-Born Workers."
       Monthly Labor Review, 105 (May 1982): 32.

2136. ————. "The Non-sense of Immigration and Welfare
       Policies." *Public Welfare* (Winter 1982): 28-35.

2137. Oliver, A.T., Jr., and B.D. May. "Immigration and Em-
       ployer Liability." *Personnel Journal*, 63 (October
       1984): 19.

2138. Orton, Eliot S. "Changes in Skill Differential: Union
       Wages in Construction, 1907-1972." *Industrial and
       Labor Relations Review*, 30 (1976): 16-24.

       Traces remuneration paid to both skilled and unskilled
       workers in the United States and finds that the premium

paid to skilled workers stopped its steady decline
after 1960. Concludes that illegal immigrants depressed the wages of unskilled workers in the 1960s
and widened the gap between the earnings of skilled
and unskilled construction workers.

2139. Packman, B.B., and M. Rosenberg. "How Foreigners (Un-
intentionally) Become U.S. Residents." *Taxes*, 57
(February 1979): 85-96.

2140. Page, John Bryan. "The Children of Exile: Relationships Between the Acculturation Process and Drug Use
Among Cuban Youth." *Youth and Society*, 11 (June
1980): 431-447.

2141. ————, et al. *The Ethnography of Cuban Drug Use*.
Miami: University of Miami, Center for Social Research
on Drug Abuse, 1981.

2142. Paine, P. *Exporting Workers*. New York: Cambridge
University Press, 1974.

2143. Papademetriou, D.G. "Immigration Reform, American
Style." *International Migration*, 22 (1984): 265-280.

2144. Parai, Louis. "Canada's Immigration Policy, 1962-
1974." *International Migration Review*, 9 (Winter
1975): 449-78.

2145. Parsons, J.J. "The Migration of Canary Islanders to
the Americas: An Unbroken Current Since Columbus."
Americas, 39 (April 1983): 447-481.

2146. Pastor, Robert A., ed. *Migration and Development in
the Caribbean: The Unexplored Connection*. Boulder,
Colorado: Westview Press, 1985.

Is emigration from the Caribbean area to the United
States an essential escape valve, releasing de-stabilizing
population pressures and permitting space for economic
development? Or do the talented, skilled, and professional people exit, reducing the possibilities for
development? In answering these questions, the contributors to this volume offer an in-depth analysis of
the unexplored relationship between two crucial phenomena
shaping the region: migration and development. The
contributors break new ground in challenging old assumptions that underlie current policies, offering new
proposals that aim to multiply the benefits of migration

to Caribbean development while reducing the costs.
They examine the impact of various development strategies on migration and suggest projects and strategies
that could reduce the pressures of migration. Finally,
they assess the impact of U.S. immigration policies on
Caribbean economic development and U.S.-Caribbean relations and offer proposals to modify policies.

2147.   ———. "U.S. Immigration Policy and Latin America:
          In Search of the 'Special Relationship.'" *Latin
          American Research Review*, 19 (1984): 35-56.

2148.   Patchett, K.W., and J.R. Young. "Tourist Divorces and
          the Abuse of a Small States Legal System: The Mont-
          serrat Matrimonial Causes for Foreigners Ordinance,
          1978." *American Journal of Comparative Law*, 30 (Fall
          1982): 654-677.

2149.   Paulston, Christina B. *Bilingual Education: Theories
          and Issues*. Rowley, Massachusetts: Newbury House,
          1980.

2150.   Payne, Karen. "Haiti: An Inside Report." *Miami News*
          (August 1, 1981). Special Supplement. Pp. 1-16.

2151.   Pear, Robert. "Aliens Who Stay in Clusters Are Said
          to Do Better." *New York Times*, March 11, 1982, p.
          A-24.

2152.   ———. "Cuban Aliens, but Not Haitians, Will Be Of-
          fered Residency Status." *New York Times*, February 13,
          1984, p. A-1.

2153.   ———. "Final Action on Immigration Bill Seen as Un-
          likely before Late July." *New York Times*, June 22,
          1984, p. A-11.

2154.   ———. "House to Debate Immigration Bill Despite
          Pleas of Hispanic Groups." *New York Times*, June 12,
          1984, p. A-1.

2155.   ———. "House Girds to Take Up Touchy Immigration
          Bill." *New York Times*, June 8, 1984, p. A-14.

2156.   ———. "Stockman Warns Immigration Bill May Be Too
          Costly." *New York Times*, January 19, 1984, p. A-19.

2157.   ———. "What the House Said in Not Voting an Immigra-
          tion Bill." *New York Times*, December 27, 1982, p.
          B-12.

2158. Penalosa, Fernando. "Education Income Discrepancies between Second and Later Generation Mexican-Americans in the Southwest." *Sociology and Social Research*, 16 (July 1969): 448-454.

2159. Perusek, Glenn. "Haitian Emigration in the Early Twentieth Century." *International Migration Review*, 18 (Spring 1984): 4-18.

Standard migration theories see receiving countries as the dynamic agent which pull migrants to them. These theories, while useful for explaining many cases, appear inadequate for the case of labor migration from Haiti to Cuba and the Dominican Republic in the early twentieth century. This article examines this history and offers an alternative theoretical framework for explaining this migration flow. It is argued that the prime causes of migration from Haiti are factors in the sending country.

2160. Petersen, W. "A General Typology of Migration." *American Sociological Review*, 23 (June 1958): 256-266.

2161. Peterson, M.F. "Work Attitudes of Mariel Boatlift Refugees." *Cuban Studies*, 14 (Summer 1984): 1-20.

2162. Pido, Antonio. "Brain Drain Philipinos." *Society*, 14 (1977): 50-53.

2163. Pietrodangelo, Danny. "The Caribbean Refugees." *Access: A Human Services Magazine*, 3 (June-July 1980): 9-11.

2164. Pifer, Alan. *Bilingual Education and the Hispanic Challenge*. New York: Carnegie Corporation of New York, 1980.

2165. Poitras, Guy, ed. *Immigration and the Mexican National: Proceedings*. San Antonio, Texas: Trinity University, Border Research Institute, 1978.

2166. ———. *Return Migration from the United States to Costa Rica and El Salvador*. San Antonio, Texas: Border Research Institute, Trinity University, 1980.

Based on a binational research project. Aims to describe the personal and demographic characteristics of Costa Rican and Salvadorian samples of return migrants,

to describe the patterns of migration to the United
States, and to examine the return of the migrants to
their home countries.

2167.   Pomp, R.D., and O. Oldman. "Tax Measures in Responses
        to the Brain Drain." *Harvard International Law
        Journal*, 20 (Winter 1979): 1-60.

2168.   Porteus, Sandra McClure. *A State of the Field Study of
        Child Welfare Services for Migrant Children and Their
        Families Who Are In-Stream, Home-Based, or Settled-
        Out*. Washington, D.C.: InterAmerica Research Associa-
        tes, 1977. ERIC microfiche: ED135562.

2169.   Porter, Patricia A. *The Health Status of Migrant Farm
        Workers*. New York: Field Foundation, 1980.

2170.   Portes, Alejandro, et al. "Immigrant Aspirations."
        Sociology of Education, 51 (October 1978): 241-260.

2171.   ————. "Migration and Underdevelopment." *Politics
        and Society* (August 8, 1978): 1-48.

2172.   ————. "The Rise of Ethnicity: Determinants of Ethnic
        Perceptions Among Cuban Exiles in Miami." *American
        Sociological Review*, 49 (June 1984): 383-397.

2173.   Poulson, B.W., and T.N. Osborn, eds. *U.S.-Mexico
        Economic Relations*. Boulder, Colorado: Westview
        Press, 1979.

2174.   Ramirez, D.M. "Legal Residents and Naturalization: A
        Pilot Study." Report prepared for the Mexican Ameri-
        can Legal Defense and Educational Fund. Davis, Cali-
        fornia: University of California, 1979.

2175.   Rawitz, Sidney B. "The Efficiency Bill and Its Legis-
        lative Odyssey." *Immigration Journal*, 5 (March-
        April 1982): 4.

2176.   "Regulation of Foreign Investment in U.S. Real Estate."
        The Tax Lawyer, 33 (Winter 1980): 586-629.

2177.   Reichert, Joshua S. *The Agricultural Labor System
        in North Carolina: Recommendations for Change*.
        Raleigh, North Carolina: Department of Administration,
        June 1980.

2178. ———. "Guestworker Programs: Evidence from Europe
and the United States and Some Implications for U.S.
Policy." Paper presented at Population Association
of America Annual Meeting, Washington, D.C., March
26-28, 1981.

Considers the implications of a temporary worker program by examining the social and economic effects of
previous guestworker programs in the United States and
Western Europe from the perspective of both sending
and receiving societies. Attention is paid to the
efficacy of these programs in promoting temporary vs.
long-term immigration of foreign workers as well as
their developmental impact on sending countries.

2179. ———, and Douglas S. Massey. "Patterns of U.S. Migration from a Mexican Town." In Richard C. Jones, ed.,
*Patterns of Undocumented Migration: Mexico and the
United States.* Totowa, N.J.: Rowman and Allanheld,
1984. Pp. 93-109.

Explores how legal status affects the demographic
profile of migrants from Guadalupe. How demographic
characteristics interact with legal status to produce
distinct patterns of movement within the United States
will also be examined. Begins by describing the nature
of the data and how they were gathered and used to document Guadalupe's intense involvement in the U.S. labor
market. Compares legal and illegal migrants to demonstrate and explain basic demographic differences between the two groups--differences in the size of migration units, their age-sex composition, and the amount
of time spent away from home each year. Shows how
legal status affects patterns of migration. Concludes
by summarizing the findings and discussing their relevance to broader patterns within Mexico.

2180. Reinhold, Robert. "Flow of 3rd World Immigrants Alters
Weave of U.S. Society." *New York Times*, June 30,
1986, pp. A-1, B-5.

2181. Reisler, M. "Mexican Unionization in California Agriculture, 1927-1936." *Labor History*, 14 (1973): 562-
579.

Factors which stimulated Mexican workers to establish
unions, how the growers reacted to this development,
the part left-wing organizers played in California
strikes, the response of the federal and local govern-

ments to farm labor unrest, and why no permanent Mexican agricultural union survived.

2182. ———. *By the Sweat of Their Brow: Mexican Immigrant Labor in the United States, 1900-1940.* Westport, Connecticut: Greenwood Press, 1976.

Reisler has synthesized existing data and has clarified little known subjects through extensive use of U.S. government documents. There is here, for example, a far clearer picture of such important events as the World War I temporary admissions program and the role of the U.S. State Department in lobbying against the inclusion of Mexicans in the immigration quotas for diplomatic reasons.

2183. Retter, Daniel. "Immigration Law Practice." *Florida Bar Journal*, 47 (1973): 370-373.

2184. Reubens, E.P. "International Migration Models and Policies." *American Economic Review*, 73 (May 1983): 178-182.

2185. Rice, Berkely. "New Gangs of Chinatown." *Psychology Today*, 10 (1977): 60-69.

Documents the expansion of New York's Chinatown. Before 1965 the city's Chinese population had been fairly stable. Then it began to climb rapidly, putting great pressure on the small area known as Chinatown to provide housing, schools, and recreation facilities. The Fifth Precinct of the New York City Police Department, covering Chinatown, reported fewer than 10 arrests a year of young people before 1966. By 1977 that figure grew to 200.

2186. Richards, D.A. "Real Estate Counsel, Contract and Closing for the Foreign Investor." *Real Property Probate and Trust Journal*, 14 (Winter 1979): 757-846.

2187. Riche, M.F. "Immigration Statistics (Statistical Sources)." *American Demographic*, 5 (October 1983): 38-39.

2188. Richmond, Anthony H. *Aspects of the Absorption and Adaptation of Immigrants.* Ottawa: Information Canada, 1974.

2189. ———, and Ravi P. Verma. "The Economic Adaptation of Immigrants: A New Theoretical Perspective." *Internation Migration Review*, 12 (1978): 3-38.

2190. Richmond, Marie L. "Beyond Resource Theory: Another Look at Factors Enabling Women to Affect Family Interaction." *Journal of Marriage and the Family*, 38 (May 1976): 257-265.

The changing roles of Cuban women in immigrant families.

2191. ———. *Immigrant Adaptation and Family Structure Among Cubans in Miami, Florida.* New York: Arno Press, 1980.

Modifications in the structure of Cuban exile families have occurred as a result of adaptation to life in Miami. This study explores the special impact of two factors--the presence of Americans as a new reference group and the considerable employment of Cuban exile women. Particular emphasis is placed on the resulting socialization of children and the changing role and status of women. Originally, Ph.D. dissertation, Florida State University, 1973.

2192. ———. "Immigration Adaptation and Family Structure Among Cubans in Miami, Florida." Unpublished Ph.D. dissertation, Florida State University, 1973.

2193. Rivera-Batiz, F.L. "Trade Theory, Distribution of Income, and Immigration." *American Economic Review*, 73 (May 1983): 183-187.

2194. Robertson, J. "Government Closeup: Send Me Your Brains (Foreign Engineering Students)." *Electronic News*, 28 (June 14, 1982): 14.

2195. Robinson, C. "Physical and Emotional Health Care Needs of Indo-Chinese Refugees." Washington, D.C.: Indochina Refugee Action Center, 1980.

Identifies the physical and emotional needs of Indo-chinese refugees; describes the efforts being made to respond to these needs, both in the United States and overseas; discusses the lags, complications and gaps that still exist in the systems of physical and mental health care delivery to the refugees; and assesses the recommendations made by public and private agencies to improve these services.

2196. Rockett, I.R.H. "American Immigration Policy and
       Ethnic Selection: An Overview." *Journal of Ethnic
       Studies*, 10 (Winter 1983): 1-26.

2197. ————. "Ethnicity, Immigration Process, and Short-
       Term Occupational Mobility." *International Migration*,
       21 (1983): 358-371.

2198. Rodriguez, Jacobo. "Alienation of a New Generation of
       Chicanos." *Aztlán*, 4 (Spring 1973): 147-54.

2199. Rose, Peter I. *Working with Refugees*. Staten Island,
       N.Y.: Center for Migration Studies, 1986.

       Working with Refugees provides new insights into the
       complex and often contradictory world of refugee settle-
       ment. The edited proceedings of the Simon Shargo con-
       ference on refugee resettlement, *Working with Refugees*
       delves into current data, procedures, and refugee
       research to offer an invaluable tool to those working
       in resettlement and refugee studies. The topics include:
       the protection and assistance of refugees; the initial
       stage of resettlement; the ways services to refugees
       might be improved; the problems inherent in learning
       to adapt to a new society; the rules governing selection
       for relocation, and the means by which refugees are to
       be admitted to "third countries" such as the United
       States. Authors of the papers include UNHCR officials,
       foreign service officers, administrators of key voluntary
       agencies, immigration lawyers, social workers, case
       managers, volunteers, and several academic specialists.

2200. Rosenberg, M., and B.B. Packman. "Taxation of Foreign
       Executives in the U.S." *Taxes*, 57 (September 1979):
       563-75.

2201. Ross, Jane. "The Latin Hustle." *Miami Magazine*, 30
       (April 1979): 96-97.

2202. Ross, Stanley R., ed. *Views Across the Border: The
       United States and Mexico*. Albuquerque, New Mexico:
       University of New Mexico Press, 1978.

2203. Rowe, Leslie. "Immigration Reform and International
       Students." *Fletcher Forum*, 7 (Winter 1983): 109-119.

2204. Ruiz, V. "Working for Wages: Mexican Women in the
       Southwest, 1930-1980." Tucson, Arizona: Southwest

Institute for Research on Women, The University of
Arizona, Working Paper No. 19, 1984.

Presents both a statistical profile of Mexican women
workers and a narrative examination of their relationship with trade unions. Using the 1980 Census, as well
as other materials, it compares occupational distribution, median incomes, and educational levels of Chicanas
with those of Anglo, black, and American Indian women.
Comparison of the median earnings of ethnic and Anglo
women with those of Mexican and Anglo men reveals significant gender disparities. These cross-cultural and
cross-gender perspectives illuminate the socioeconomic
vulnerability of Chicana workers in particular and women
in general. An analysis of obstacles facing female
Hispanic industrial operatives illustrates their economic precariousness.

2205. Rumbaut, Ruben G., and John R. Weeks. "Fertility and
Adaptation: Indochinese Refugees in the United States."
International Migration Review, 20 (Summer 1986):
428-465.

Levels of fertility among Indochinese refugees in the
United States are explored in the context of a highly
compressed demographic transition implicit in the move
from high-fertility Southeast Asian societies to a low-
fertility resettlement region. A theoretical model is
developed to explain the effect on refugee fertility
of social background characteristics, migratory history
and patterns of adaptation to a different economic and
cultural environment controlling for marital history
and length of residence in the United States. Multiple
regression techniques are used to test the model which
was found to account for nearly half of the variation
in refugee fertility levels in the United States.
Fertility is much higher for all Indochinese ethnic
groups than it is for American women; the number of
children in refugee families is in turn a major deter-
minant of welfare dependency. Adjustments for rates of
natural increase indicate a total 1985 Indochinese
population of over one million, making it one of the
largest Asian-origin populations in the United States.
This remarkable phenomenon has occurred in less than
a decade. Implications of these findings for public
policy are discussed, focusing on family planning,
maternal and child health needs, and the attainment of
refugee economic self-sufficiency.

2206. Russo, R.J., and W.M. Sharp. "A New Definition of Non-residency: The ABA Proposal." *Taxes*, 60 (November 1982): 779-790.

2207. Sachs, Carolyn E. *The Invisible Farmers. Women in Agricultural Production.* Totowa, N.J.: Rowman and Allanheld, 1983.

U.S. agricultural policy has always emphasized the importance of the "family farm," but research has focused on the male of that family, relegating the female to only minor roles--invisible, as the title suggests. Sachs's study fills this gap. It documents the extensive participation of rural women (including immigrant) in U.S. agriculture as owners, workers, and household producers, paid and unpaid, farm and off-farm.

2208. Samora, Julian. *Los Mojados: The Wetback Story.* South Bend, Indiana: University of Notre Dame Press, 1971.

2209. Sanderson, S.R.W. "Migration, Economic Opportunity, and Land Distribution in Mexico." In *Land Reform in Mexico: 1910-1980.* Orlando, Florida: Academic Press, Inc., 1984. Pp. 72-89.

Analyzes the complex interaction of push-pull factors in Mexican emigration. A linear systems model of Mexican emigration to the United States is presented in which the strength and direction of Mexican agricultural policy, U.S. immigration policy, and U.S. economic development are principal determinants of the volume and flow of migrants. Model describes schematically the influences among the variables in the system.

2210. Sansaricq, Guy. "The Haitian Apostolate in Brooklyn." *Migration Today*, 7 (February 1979): 22-25.

2211. Sassen-Koob, Saskia. "Economic Growth and Immigration in Venezuela." *International Migration Review*, 13 (Fall 1979): 455-74.

2212. Scanlan, John A., and G.D. Loescher. "Mass Asylum and Human Rights in American Foreign Policy." *Political Science Quarterly*, 97 (Spring 1982), 39-56.

2213. Schachter, J. "Net Immigration of Gainful Workers into the United States, 1870-1930." *Demography*, 9 (February 1972): 87-105.

Presents socioeconomic occupational grouping of the foreign-born gainful workers of the United States at each census from 1870 through 1930. Series is then used to estimate the net immigration of gainful workers into the United States during each of the six decades from 1870 to 1930 cross classified by occupational group and sex. Three conclusions are drawn from the above series. First, the socioeconomic position of the foreign-born population of the United States remained relatively stable from 1870 to 1910 but then increased appreciably from 1910 to 1930. Second, although most of the contribution that immigration made to the United States labor force was in the form of semiskilled and unskilled workers, the relative importance of professional, clerical, and skilled workers increased almost continuously from 1870 to 1930. Third, the "new immigration" was actually more skilled than the "old immigration."

2214. Schander, Edwin R. "Immigration Law and Practice in the United States: A Selective Bibliography." *International Migration Review*, 12 (Spring 1978): 117-127.

Includes brief section on illegal immigration. Lists State statutes pertaining to employment of illegal aliens.

2215. Schechtman, Joseph B. *The Refugee in the World: Displacement and Integration.* New York: A.S. Barnes & Co., 1963.

2216. Scheinman, Ronald S., and Norman L. Zucker. "Refugee Policy." *New York Times*, May 24, 1981, p. E-19.

2217. Schey, Peter A. "The Black Boat People." *Migration Today*, 9 (1981): 6-10.

2218. Schmitz, J.W. "Immigration Possibilities for Foreign Investors." *Practical Lawyer*, 25 (June 1979): 73-81.

2219. Schultheis, M.J. *Refugees: The Structures of a Global Justice Issue.* Washington, D.C.: The Center of Concern, 1983.

Probes the structural dimensions of the contemporary refugee problem. The thesis of the analysis is that the main refugee flows in the world today are the direct or indirect result of forces which lie outside the countries where the refugee originates. In most instances these forces are the extension of the conflict between the Soviet Union and the United States and the efforts by them to extend or maintain their areas of influence.

2220. Schultz, T.P. "The Schooling and Health of Children of U.S. Immigrants and Natives." *Research in Population Economics*, 5 (1984): 251-288.

2221. Schwartz, Abba. "Migration, Age and Education." *Journal of Political Economy*, 16 (August 1976): 701-719.

2222. Scott, Clarissa S. "Health and Healing Practices Among Five Ethnic Groups in Miami, Florida." *Public Health Reports*, 89 (November-December 1974): 524-532.

2223. Scurrah, N.J., and A. Montalvo. "Migración interna, movilidad social y actitudes y orientaciones de trabajadores permanos." *Demografía y Economía*, 11 (1975): 244-258.

    Studies the differences between rural and urban workers in the migration process.

2224. "Second Seminar on Adaptation and Integration of Permanent Immigrants." *International Migration* (Geneva), 14 (1976). [Whole Issue].

    Considers the problems confronting immigrants, migrants, and the nations which receive them; makes recommendations on the migration of family units and family return; makes recommendations on problems of migrants returning to their country.

2225. Secretariado nacional de pastoral social, Colombia. *Estudio sobre deportados Colombianos desde Venezuela: 1973-1975.* [Bogota, 1976]

2226. Segal, Aaron Lee, ed. *Population Policies in the Caribbean.* Lexington, Massachusetts: D.C. Heath and Company, 1975.

2227. Segalman, Ralph. *Army of Despair: The Migrant Worker Stream.* Washington, D.C.: Educational Systems Corp., 1968.

2228. Seggar, John. "Italian Migration to the U.S., 1966-1978: The Transition Period and a Decade Beyond Public Law 89-236." In Lydio F. Tomasi, ed., *Italian*

Americans: New Perspectives in Italian Immigration and Ethnicity. Staten Island, New York: Center for Migration Studies, 1985. Pp. 32-56.

2229. Seligson, Mitchell A., and Edward J. Williams. *Maquiladoras and Migration.* Tucson: Department of Political Science, University of Arizona, 1980.

2230. Semler, Michael. "Temporary Foreign Labor: The Administration's Guest-worker Proposal." *Clearinghouse Review*, 15 (December 1981): 642-645.

2231. Severo, Richard. "The Flight of the Wetbacks." *New York Times Magazine* (March 10, 1974): 77-84.

2232. Silva, H. *The Children of Mariel: Cuban Refugee Children in South Florida Schools.* Washington, D.C.: The Cuban American National Foundation, Inc., 1985.

Details the Mariel experience of the Dade County Public School System, which accepted 11,000 Cuban children in just seven months. "Because they had spent all their lives in a regimented, economically stagnant communist society, the adaptation of the children of Mariel to democracy, free enterprise and a consumer society was a long journey from shock to integration," writes Silva. She shows how that journey was carried out with help from the Dade County schools. Silva describes how the Dade County school system quickly devised a summer English immersion program that served 9,000 students, hired hundreds of bilingual teachers and other personnel for the fall, and opened several new facilities to be ready in the 1980-81 academic year for the massive influx.

2233. Silvers, A.L., and P. Crosson. "Urban Bound Migration and Rural Investment: The Case of Mexico." *Journal of Regional Science*, 23 (February 1983): 33-47.

2234. Simon, Rita J. *Public Opinion and the Immigrant: Print Media Coverage, 1880-1980.* Lexington, Massachusetts: Lexington Books, 1985.

Part 1 provides a brief statistical overview, broken down by country of origin and year; a succinct and informative summary of major immigration legislation enacted between 1880 and 1980; and an analysis of public opinion on immigrants and immigration, based on national

polls from the time such data were first collected in
1937 to 1980. Part 1 sets the stage for and provides
an introduction to part 2, which is really the heart
of the book. Part 2 looks at how fifteen leading magazines in the United States covered the issue of immigration between 1880 and 1980. The following magazines
were included in the survey: *North American Review*,
Saturday Evening Post, *Literary Digest*, *Harpers*, *Scrib-
ners*, *Atlantic Monthly*, *The Nation*, *Reader's Digest*,
Christian Century, *Commentary*, *Commonweal*, *Time*, *Life*,
Newsweek, and *U.S. News & World Report*. In addition to
the magazines, a sample of editorials from the *New York
Times* dealing with immigration was also analyzed.

2235. "Simpson-Mazzoli Immigration Bill: Back to the Bracero
       Fiasco." *New York Times*, October 2, 1982, p. A-26.

       Letter to the editor from Joaquin G. Avila, president
       and general counsel of the Mexican American Legal De-
       fenses and Education Fund.

2236. Smith, B., and R. Newman. "Depressed Wages Along the
       U.S.-Mexico Border." *Economic Inquiry*, 15 (January
       1977): 51-66.

2237. Smith, Frederick, Jr. "The Department of State and
       U.S. Consular Officers Abroad in Citizenship Determina-
       tions." *International Migration Review*, 5 (Winter
       1971): 436-446.

       Some ten years after *Perez v. Brownell* (356 U.S. 44),
       a majority of the Supreme Court, in *Afroyim v. Rusk*
       (387 U.S. 253), decided that the minority in *Perez* was
       right after all. But in holding that a U.S. citizen
       (at least a citizen "born or naturalized in the United
       States") has "a constitutional right to remain a citizen
       in a free country unless he voluntarily relinquishes
       that citizenship," the Court provided little in the way
       of guidance for determining what constitutes voluntary
       relinquishment. This task was left to the administering
       agencies--the Department of State and the Department of
       Justice. And there were widely differing views within
       and between those departments as to what *Afroyim* meant.

2238. Smith, William French. "A Look at Immigration Laws."
       Texas Bar Journal, 45 (February 1982): 224-225.

2239. Sosa, Juan J. "La Santeria: A Way of Looking at Reality."
       Unpublished M.A. thesis, Florida Atlantic University,
       1981.

2240. Spero, A. *In America and In Need: Immigrant, Refugee,
        and Entrant Women.* Washington, D.C.: American Asso-
        ciation of Community and Junior Colleges, 1985.

        Objective of the study was to collect information
        about certain members of the "new wave" immigrant
        population, specifically, Southeast Asian women,
        Haitian women, and Hispanic women, to find out what
        is known, and what is not known about women, with
        special emphasis given to their labor force status.
        Another objective was to use these findings as the
        basis for recommendations for improving the policies
        and programs that relate to the women's economic and
        social adjustment.

2241. Steel, Richard. "Foreign MD's--Sugarcoating for a
        Bitter Pill." *Immigration Journal*, 5 (March-April
        1982): 8.

2242. Steif, William. "Hopeless in Haiti." *The Progressive*,
        43 (October 1979): 34-40.

2243. Steinman, Clay. "Scapegoats of Unemployment." *The
        Nation* (April 17, 1972): 497-500.

2244. Stepick, Alex, et al. "Haitian Refugees in Miami: An
        Assessment of Their Background and Potential."
        Occasional Papers Series, Dialogue No. 12. Miami:
        Latin American and Caribbean Center, Florida Inter-
        national University, 1982.

2245. ————. "Structural Determinants of the Haitian Refu-
        gee Movement: Different Interpretations." Occasional
        Papers Series, Dialogue No. 4. Miami: Latin American
        and Caribbean Center, Florida International Univer-
        sity, 1981.

2246. ————, and Alejandro Portes. "Flight into Despair: A
        Profile of Recent Haitian Refugees in South Florida."
        International Migration Review, 20 (Summer 1983):
        329-350.

        Based on a random sample survey of recently arrived
        Haitians, participant observation, and intensive inter-
        viewing, this article examines the following areas:
        (a) individual background characteristics of Haitian
        immigrants; (b) their arrival and early resettlement
        experiences; (c) their education, knowledge of English,
        and information about the United States; (d) current

employment status and occupation; (e) income and use
of public assistance; (f) predictors of employment,
occupation, and income; and (g) beliefs and orienta-
tions. These results are presented after discussion
of the methodology of the study and the context of
outmigration from Haiti.

2247. Stewart, J.B., and T. Hyclak. "An Analysis of the
       Earnings Profiles of Immigrants." *Review of Economics
       and Statistics*, 66 (May 1984): 292-296.

2248. Stoddard, Ellwyn R. "Illegal Mexican Labor in the
       Borderlands: Institutionalized Support of an Unlaw-
       ful Practice." *Pacific Sociological Review*, 19 (April
       1976): 175-210.

       "The upsurge in numbers of illegal Mexican aliens
       (IMAs) entering the United States is traditionally
       explained in legalistic terms. This study presents
       the view that the IMAs are a natural, functional
       phenomenon in the U.S.-Mexico Borderlands, overtly
       and covertly supported by political, economic, social,
       religious, and cultural Borderland institutions."

2249. ————. "Selected Impacts of Mexican Migration on
       the U.S. Mexican Border." Paper presented to the
       U.S. Department of State Select Panel on U.S.-
       Mexican Border Issues, Washington, D.C., October 23,
       1978.

2250. Stolz, James. "The Dangerous Chemistry of Dade
       County." *GEO Magazine*, 3 (August 1981): 88-111.

2251. Strand, Paul J., and Woodrow Jones, Jr. *Indochinese
       Refugees in America: Problems of Adaptation and
       Assimilation*. Durham, North Carolina: Duke Univer-
       sity Press, 1984.

       After a brief discussion of international migration,
       forced migration, and governmental policy regarding
       refugees, the book provides a short historical and
       cultural snapshot of the Lao, Hmong, Cambodians, and
       Vietnamese. With this background, turns to federal
       and state resettlement policy. An account of how the
       first and second waves of refugees were processed is
       coupled with a description of federal refugee legisla-
       tion and funding and the use of voluntary agencies
       and sponsorships to resettle the refugees. Since the
       refugees have tended to settle or resettle in selected

states such as California and Texas, the book discusses these states' policies, agencies, programs, and
funding for refugees.

2252. Stuart, Reginald. "Cuban's Lawyers Question Deportation Plans." *New York Times*, May 29, 1983, p.
A-22.

2253. Sung, Betty Lee. *Chinese Immigrant Children in New
York City. The Experience of Adjustment.* Staten
Island, New York: Center for Migration Studies,
1985.

2254. Sutton, Horace. "The Curious Intrigues of Cuban Miami."
Saturday Review (September 11, 1973): 24-31.

2255. Sutton, Susan B., and Tracy Brunner. "Life on the
Road: Midwestern Migrant Farmworker Survival Skills."
Migration Today, 11 (1983): 24-31.

2256. Szulc, Tad. "Foreign Policy Aspects of the Border."
Views Across the Border. Edited by Stanley R. Ross.
Albuquerque: University of New Mexico Press, 1978.
Pp. 43-62.

2257. Tarver, J.D., and R.D. McLeod. "Trends in the Distance
of Movement of Interstate Migrants." *Rural Sociology*,
41 (Spring 1976): 119-126.

2258. "Taxing Time for Foreigners." *Economist*, 290 (March
24, 1984): 17-19.

2259. Taylor, R.C. "Migration and Motivation: A Study of
Determinants and Types." In J.A. Jackson, ed.,
Migration. Cambridge: The University Press, 1969.
Pp. 99-133.

2260. Teitelbaum, Michael S. "Right versus Right: Immigration and Refugee Policy in the United States." *Foreign
Affairs* (Fall 1980): 52-53.

2261. Texas. Good Neighbor Commission of Texas. *Texas Migrant Labor Annual Report 1975*. Austin, Texas: Good
Neighbor Commission, 1976.

2262. Thomas, Frinley. *Economics of International Migration*.
London: Macmillan, 1958.

2263. Thomas, Jo. "Florida's Refugees Challenging Plan to
       Use West Indies in Cane Harvesting." *New York Times*,
       October 11, 1981, p. 22.

2264. Thompson, Bill. "Mangoes Don't Grow in Brooklyn."
       Revista/Review Interamericana (1972): 84-90.

2265. Thompson, Elvia Hernandez. "Can Cuban Culture Last
       Through the Next Generation." *Miami Magazine*, 28
       (April 1977): 25-27, 54-55.

2266. Thompson, Roger. "Migrants: Enduring Farm Problem."
       Editorial Research Reports (June 3, 1983): 415-432.

2267. Tidwick, Kathryn. "Need for Achievement, Social
       Class, and Intention to Emigrate in Jamaican Stu-
       dents." *Social and Economic Studies*, 32 (March
       1976): 52-60.

2268. Tienda, M., and L.J. Neidert. *Segmented Markets and
       Earnings Inequality of Native and Immigrant Hispanics
       in the United States*. Madison, Wisconsin: Center
       for Demography and Ecology, University of Wisconsin,
       1980.

       Investigates the relationship between market segmen-
       tation and the work earnings of native and foreign-
       born Hispanic origin workers. Assesses how earnings
       differentials among four Spanish birthplace groups are
       shaped by the differential allocation of native and
       immigrant workers to core and periphery labor market
       sectors and the differential evaluation of worker
       characteristics according to market sector. Analysis
       found "sectoral location to be important in stratifying
       and differentiating native and foreign born. Results
       show that it is inappropriate to study income in-
       equality only in terms of individual worker charac-
       teristics. This is because both nativity and market
       sector interact with individual worker characteristics
       and labor market characteristics in determining earn-
       ings."

2269. "To Be or Not To Be a Resident--Tax Is the Question."
       San Diego Law Review, 17 (December 1979): 149-72.

2270. Tolchin, Martin. "Democrats Bar Action in House on
       Immigration," p. A-31; see also Martin Tolchin, "Re-
       publicans Push Immigration Bill." *New York Times*,
       October 19, 1983, p. A-25.

2271. ———. "Democrats Bar Action in House on Immigration." *New York Times*, October 2, 1983, p. A-1; and Robert Pear, "O'Neill Says Bill on Illegal Aliens Is Dead for 1983," *ibid.*, October 5, 1983, p. A-1.

2272. ———. "O'Neill, in a Reversal, Supports Immigration Bill." *New York Times*, December 1, 1983, p. A-19.

2273. Torrado, Susana. "International Migration Policies in Latin America." *International Migration Review*, 13 (Fall 1979): 428-39.

2274. "Trapped from Dawn to Dark: Exploited Immigrant Women in Canada." *Migration Today*, 28 (1981): 21-22.

2275. Turack, Daniel C. "Brief Reviews of the Provision in Recent Agreements Concerning Freedom of Movement Issues in the Modern World." *Case Western Reserve Journal of International Law*, 11 (Winter 1979): 95-115.

2276. ———. "Freedom of Movement in the Caribbean Community." *Denver Journal of International Law and Policy*, 11 (Fall 1981): 37-49.

2277. ———. "Freedom of Transnational Movement: The Helsinki Accord and Beyond." *Vanderbilt Journal of Transnational Law*, 11 (Fall 1978): 585-608.

2278. Ugalde, A., et al. "International Migration from the Dominican Republic: Findings from a National Survey." *International Migration Review*, 13 (Summer 1979): 235-254.

2279. ———, and T. Langham. "International Return Migration: Socio-Demographic Determinants of Return Migration to the Dominican Republic." Paper presented at the Fifth Annual Meetings of Caribbean Studies Association, Curacao, Netherlands Antilles, May 7-10, 1980.

Analyzes some sociodemographic determinants of international return migration to the Dominican Republic and looks at the characteristics of those migrants who returned because they had difficulties in adjusting in the country of immigration.

2280. *Undocumented Aliens in the New York Metropolitan Area: An Exploration into Their Society and Labor Market*

Incorporation. Staten Island, N.Y.: Center for Migration Studies, 1986.

This final report of a five-year project conducted under the auspices of the Center for Migration Studies probes many aspects of the undocumented alien population. Unique for its examination of unapprehended, undocumented aliens, this text also presents new data on the much-contested questions of rates of payment of taxes and utilization of the social infrastructure by undocumented aliens. Voluntary agency personnel, legislators, policy-makers, research analysts, and academicians will find *Undocumented Aliens* valuable for its critical review of literature on undocumented immigration and the methodologies used in this field, 363-question interview schedule, and a summary of the policy implications of the research study.

2281.   U.S. Commission on Civil Rights. *Civil Rights Issues of Asian and Pacific Americans: Myths and Realities.* Washington, D.C.: U.S. Commission on Civil Rights, 1980.

2282.   U.S. Commission on Civil Rights. Idaho Advisory Committee. *A Roof over Our Heads: Migrant and Seasonal Farmworker Housing in Idaho.* Washington: The Commission, 1980.

2283.   U.S. Congress. House Committee on the Judiciary. Subcommittee on Immigration, Citizenship, and International Law. *The Use of Temporary Alien Labor on Guam.* Washington, D.C.: Government Printing Office, 1979.

2284.   U.S. Congress. House. Select Committee on Population. *Final Report.* Washington, D.C.: Government Printing Office, 1978.

2285.   U.S. Congress. Senate Committee on the Judiciary. *Hearings, U.S. Refugee Programs, 1981.* Washington, D.C.: Government Printing Office, 1980.

2286.   U.S. Congress. Senate. Subcommittee on Immigration and Refugee Policy. *Refugee Problems in Central America.* Washington, D.C.: U.S. Government Printing Office, 1984.

2287.   U.S. Department of Commerce. Bureau of the Census. *Persons of Spanish Origin in the United States.*

Washington, D.C.: Government Printing Office, [March] 1979.

Presents advance data on selected demographic, social, and economic characteristics of persons of Spanish origin in the United States for March 1979.

2288. U.S. Department of Labor. *Seven Years Later: The Experience of the 1970 Cohort of Immigrants in the United States.* Washington, D.C.: U.S. Department of Labor, 1979.

Gives answers to questions about the labor force characteristics of recent immigrants and what happened to them in the labor market. Analysis of the 1970 cohort is set in a legal, demographic, and historical context. Concludes with a series of recommendations regarding immigration, employment, and training policies.

2289. U.S. Department of State. "Active Immigrant Visa Applicants Registered at Consular Offices as of January 1, 1982." Report ICRR49. Washington, D.C., April 19, 1982.

2290. U.S. General Accounting Office. *Illegal Aliens: Information on Selected Countries' Employment Prohibition Laws.* Washington, D.C.: U.S. Government Printing Office, 1985.

"Most countries reported that employer sanction laws have helped to deter illegal alien employment. For example, five of the eight countries and Hong Kong reported that these laws were a moderate or great deterrent against illegal alien employment. This group included Germany and France which reported in 1982 that their laws were not an effective deterrent. The three countries that reported their laws were less of a deterrent (Italy, Canada, and Spain) acknowledged that various problems with the enforcement of these laws had lessened their effectiveness. Nevertheless, Hong Kong and six of the eight countries reported that if they had not enacted employer sanction laws, the problem of aliens working illegally would be greater than it is. Two countries (Italy and Canada) reported the problem would be about the same as it is. From 1981 through September 1985, the estimated number of aliens working illegally reportedly decreased in Hong Kong and one country, remained about the same in three countries, and increased in four countries (Italy, Canada,

France, and Spain). All respondents reported that little or no discrimination against citizens or legal aliens has resulted from employer sanction laws."

2291. United States Immigration and Naturalization Service. *Annual Report*. 1892–

Began as the *Annual Report* of the United States Commissioner General of Immigration in 1892. Also, the USINS publishes the quarterly *I and N Reporter*.

2292. Velie, Lester. "Poverty at the Border: Mexican Labor Brought in by Greedy U.S. Employers." *Reader's Digest* (August 1970): 92–97.

2293. Velikonja, Joseph. "Italian Immigrants in the United States in the Sixties." In Silvano M. Tomasi and Madeline H. Engel, eds., *The Italian Experience in the United States*. Staten Island, New York: Center for Migration Studies, 1970. Pp. 23–38.

2294. Verdet, Paule. "Trying Times: Haitian Youth in an Inner City School." *Social Problems*, 24 (December 1976): 228–233.

2295. "The View of Migrant Women." *Language for Living*, 7 (1977): 22–40.

2296. Vigro, J.M. "Economic Impacts of International Manpower Flows: A Consideration of the Bracero Program." Unpublished Ph.D. dissertation, Claremont Graduate School, Claremont, California, 1972.

2297. Villars, C. "Social Security for Farm Workers in the Framework of the Council of Europe." *International Labour Review*, 120 (May/June 1981): 291–302.

2298. Villegas, A. "Migrations and Economic Integration in Latin America: The Andean Group." *International Migration Review*, 11 (Spring 1977): 59–76.

2299. Villegas, Jorge. "Condiciones del trabajador migrante, documentos de trabajo." Bogotá: Organization of American States, 1974.

2300. Walsh, Bryan O. "The Church and the City: The Miami Experience." *New Catholic World*, 225 (May–June 1982): 107–110.

2301. Walter, I. "One Year Arrival. The Adjustment of Indochinese Women in the United States: 1979-1980."
International Migration, 19 (1981): 129-152.

2302. "Warmer Welcome for Foreign Technicians." *Business
Week* (August 17, 1981): 31-32.

2303. Warren, W.B. "Personal Trusts for Nonresident Aliens."
Trusts and Estates, 121 (April 1982): 36-42.

2304. Weber, A.R. "With U.S. Immigration Policy in Crises,
Businessmen Must Speak Out." *Dun's Review*, 118
(July 1981): 11.

2305. Weil, R.H. "International Adoptions: The Quiet Migration." *International Migration Review*, 18 (Summer
1984): 276-293.

2306. Weiss, Fagan P. *Applying for Political Asylum in New
York: Law, Policy, and Administrative Practice.*
New York: Center for Latin American and Caribbean
Studies, 1984.

2307. ————. "Immigration, Emigration, and Asylum Policies
in Cuba." *Migration News*, 33 (1984): 21-29.

2308. ————. *Refugees and Displaced Persons in Central
America.* Washington, D.C.: Refugee Policy Group,
1984.

2309. Weissbrodt, D. *Immigration Law and Procedure in a Nutshell.* St. Paul, Minnesota: West Publishing Co.,
1984.

2310. White, R., and F.J. Hampson. "The British Nationality
Act 1981--*Civitas in Trespartes Divisa Est.*" *Public
Law* (Spring 1982): 6-20.

2311. Wiest, Raymond E. "External Dependency and the Perpetu-
ation of Temporary Migration to the United States."
In Richard C. Jones, ed., *Patterns of Undocumented
Migration: Mexico and the United States.* Totowa,
N.J.: Rowman and Allanheld, 1984. Pp. 110-135.

Analyzes migration from a single rural community in
northern Michoacán in terms of recent theoretical
development that for general purposes may be referred
to as dependency theory. First treats the explanation

of migration and its effects. Deals briefly with the
essential elements of the "dependency" approach and
argues for attention to long-term structural features
of social systems based in the production process which
involves all humans. The specific context of migration
dealt with in this essay is then treated. This provides some sense of the history of the process as well
as the peculiarities of the case discussed. The main
part of the essay details several specific impacts of
migration that perpetuate and increase external dependency. Various elements of this increased dependency are discussed.

2312. ————. *Mexican Farm Laborers in California: A Study
       of Intragroup Social Relations*. Palo Alto, Cali-
       fornia: R & E Research Associates, 1977.

2313. Wilkening, David. "Pluck and Luck in Little Havana."
       Florida Trend, 23 (December 1980): 46-48.

2314. Williams, D.V. "New Zealand Immigration Policies and
       the Law--A Perspective." *Otago Law Review*, 4 (1978):
       185-200.

2315. Wilson, Kenneth L., and W. Allen Martin. "Ethnic En-
       claves: A Comparison of the Cuban and Black Econo-
       mies in Miami." *American Journal of Sociology*, 88
       (July 1982): 135-160.

2316. Winsberg, Morton D. "Ethnic Competition for Residen-
       tial Space in Miami, Florida, 1970-80." *American
       Journal of Economics and Sociology*, 42 (July 1983):
       305-314.

2317. ————. "The Latin Melting Pot Is Boiling Over."
       American Journal of Economics and Sociology, 40
       (October 1981): 349-352.

2318. Women, Immigration and Nationality Group. *Worlds
       Apart: Women Under Immigration and Nationality Law*.
       London: Pluto Press, 1985.

       Discusses the way that women have been defined under
       successive immigration and nationality Acts. Shows how
       racism and sexism are combined in the law so that to
       this day women are defined as dependents of men.
       Analyzes the political context of these policies and
       describes some of the campaigns that are currently
       being mounted against them.

2319. "The World Confederation of Labour and Migration Ques-
       tions." *International Migration Review*, 7 (Fall
       1973): 289-321.

       The Commission "Migrant Workers and Refugees," set
       up at the Geneva Congress of the W.C.L., has been en-
       trusted with the survey of the problems arising from
       the migrations of the workers in the world in general.
       The participation of the regional organizations
       affiliated to the W.C.L. in this work of meditation
       will offer the possibility of defining the problems in
       the countries from which departure takes place as well
       as in the countries of arrival and of defining a trade
       union strategy, taking into account this historic and
       present reality of the migration phenomenon.

2320. [World Council of Churches]. *Filipino Workers: A Case
       of Exported Women Workers*. Geneva: Migration Secre-
       tariat, World Council of Churches, 1980.

2321. Wortham, Jacob. "The Black Boat People." *Black Enter-
       prise*, 10 (April 1980): 32-36.

2322. Wyden, Peter. *Bay of Pigs: The Untold Story*. New York:
       Simon and Schuster, 1979.

2323. Yoshika, Robert, et al. "Asian American Women." *Civil
       Rights Digest*, 6 (Spring 1974): 43-53.

       On Chinese, Japanese, and other Asian-American women.

2324. Yu, Elena S.H., and William T. Liu. "Methodological
       Problems and Policy Implications in Vietnamese Refu-
       gee Research." *International Migration Review*, 20
       (Summer 1986): 483-501.

       Written with two objectives: First, to describe some
       of the critical methodological problems encountered
       in research with Vietnamese refugees in San Diego,
       California, about which few studies have been conducted
       previous to their arrival in 1975. Second, to discuss
       the policy implications of research beset with these
       difficulties, some of which are unique to studies of
       refugee populations *per se*, while others are common to
       research on small ethnic minorities in general. This
       article focuses on four major issues: the quality of
       refugee studies; the purpose and functions of such
       research; the ethical dilemmas of studying refugees;
       and public policy implications of refugee research.

Recommendations are offered to resolve some of these
issues which would call for policy changes both in the
ways refugee research are conducted and in the training
of researchers themselves.

2325.   Zagaris, B. "Investment by Nonresident Aliens in
         United States Real Estate." *University of Miami Law
         Review*, 31 (Spring 1977): 566-613.

2326.   Zazueta, Carlos H., and Rodolfo Corona. *Los trabajadores
         Mexicanos en los Estados Unidos: Primeros resultados
         de la encuesta nacional de emigración*. Mexico City:
         Centro nacional de información y estadísticas del
         trabajo, 1979.

2327.   ————, and C. Zazueta. *En las puertas del Paraiso*.
         Mexico City: Centro nacional de información
         estadísticas del trabajo, 1980.

2328.   Zucker, Naomi Flink. "Some Boat People Are More Equal
         Than Others." *The Progressive*, 46 (March 1982):
         39-41.

APPENDIX

Select Commission on Immigration
and Refugee Policy

*U.S. Immigration Policy
and the National Interest (1981)*

Introduction
Recommendations

Introduction to the Final Report
of the Select Commission on Immigration
and Refugee Policy

If I am not for myself, who will be
for me? But if I am for myself
only, what am I? And if not now,
when?

Hillel
Sayings of the Fathers 1:14

Our history is largely the story of immigration. Even the
Indians were immigrants. The ancestors of all other Americans--
when measured in terms of world history--came here only yester-
day.

As a refuge and a land of opportunity, the United States
remains the world's number one magnet. This fact reaffirms
the faith of our founding fathers and the central values we
have adopted as a nation--freedom, equality under the law,
opportunity and respect for diversity. Throughout our history,
our leaders have seen in immigration the articulation of these
deeply held and religiously based values. President Ronald W.
Reagan, in his speech accepting the Republican nomination for
the presidency, reminded us of that fact when he said:

I ask you to trust that American spirit which knows
no ethnic, religious, social, political, regional or
economic boundaries: the spirit that burned with zeal
in the hearts of millions of immigrants from every
corner of the earth who came here in search of
freedom....

Then, examining the events of the recent past, the President
asked:

Can we doubt that only a divine Providence placed this
land--this island of freedom here as a refuge for all
those people in the world who yearn to breathe free?
Jews and Christians enduring persecution behind the
Iron Curtain, the boat people of Southeast Asia, Cuba,

and Haiti, the victims of drought and famine in Africa,
the freedom fighters in Afghanistan and our own countrymen held in savage captivity.

Letters and oral testimony to the Select Commission affirm
the continuing vitality of President Reagan's characterization of the United States as a land of opportunity and as a
beacon of liberty for immigrants. We have listened carefully
to these moving voices, but we have also been faced with the
reality of limitations on immigration. If it is a truism to
say that the United States is a nation of immigrants, it is
also a truism that it is one no longer, nor can it become a
land of unlimited immigration. As important as immigration
has been and remains to our country, it is no longer possible
to say as George Washington did that we welcome all of the
oppressed of the world, or as did the poet, Emma Lazarus, that
we should take all of the huddled masses yearning to be free.

The United States of America--no matter how powerful and
idealistic--cannot by itself solve the problems of world migration. This nation must continue to have some limits on immigration. Our policy--while providing opportunity to a portion
of the world's population--must be guided by the basic national
interests of the people of the United States.

The emphasis in the Commission's recommendations, which
are themselves complex, can be summed up quite simply: We
recommend closing the back door to undocumented/illegal migration, opening the front door a little more to accommodate legal
migration in the interests of this country, defining our immigration goals clearly and providing a structure to implement
them effectively, and setting forth procedures which will lead
to fair and efficient adjudication and administration of U.S.
immigration laws.

The United States and the World

In emphasizing that our recommendations must be consistent
with U.S. national interests, we are aware of the fact that
we live in a shrinking, interdependent world and that world
economic and political forces result in the migration of
peoples. We also are aware of how inadequately the world is
organized to deal with the dislocations that occur as a result
of such migrations. None of the great international issues
of our time--arms control, energy, food, or migration--can be
solved entirely within the framework of a nation-state world.
Certainly, there is no unilateral U.S. solution to any of these
problems; we must work with a world organized along nation-
state lines and with existing international organizations.
As a nation responsible for the destiny of its people and

their descendants, we can better deal with these problems by
working with other nations to build more effective international mechanisms. That is why we begin our recommendations with
a call for a new emphasis on internationalizing world migration issues. Since many, large-scale, international migrations are caused by war, poverty, and persecution within
sending nations, it is in the national interests of the
United States to work with other nations to prevent or ameliorate those conditions.

Immigration and the National Interest

That immigration serves humanitarian ends is unquestion-
able: most immigrants come to the United States seeking reunion
with their families or as refugees. But in examining U.S.
immigration policy and developing its recommendations, the
Select Commission also asked another question: Is immigration
and the acceptance of refugees in the U.S. national interest?
That question was asked by many in this country when Fidel
Castro pushed his own citizens out of Cuba knowing that their
main destination would be the United States. Nothing about
immigration--even widespread visa abuse and illegal border
crossings--seems to have upset the American people more than
the Cuban push-out of 1980. But these new entrants were
neither immigrants nor refugees, having entered the United
States without qualifying as either. Their presence brought
home to most Americans the fact that U.S. immigration policy
was out of control. It also brought many letters to the
Select Commission calling for restrictions on U.S. immigration.
It is easy to understand the feelings which motivated these
opinions, but in the light of hard-headed U.S. interests it
would be a mistake to let the emotion generated by an unusual,
almost bizarre episode guide national policy. While the
Cuban push-out should not be permitted to happen again, the
fact that it happened once should not blind us to the advantages of legally accepting a reasonable number of immigrants
and refugees.
To the question: Is immigration in the U.S. national interest?, the Select Commission gives a strong but qualified
yes. A strong yes because we believe there are many benefits
which immigrants bring to U.S. society; a qualified yes because we believe there are limits on the ability of this country to absorb large numbers of immigrants effectively. Our
work during the past 19 months has confirmed the continuing
value of accepting immigrants and refugees to the United
States, in addition to the humanitarian purpose served. The
research findings are clear: Immigrants, refugees and their

children work hard and contribute to the economic well-being
of our society; strengthen our social security system and manpower capability; strengthen our ties with other nations;
increase our language and cultural resources and powerfully
demonstrate to the world that the United States is an open
and free society.

New immigrants benefit the United States and reaffirm its
deepest values. One can see them in New Orleans, where Indochinese refugees, hard at work during the day, crowd class-
rooms at night to learn English; in Fall River, Massachusetts,
a city with more than 20 identifiable ethnic groups whose an-
cestral flags fly in front of City Hall and which has been
restored to economic health by recent Portuguese immigrants;
in Koreatown in Los Angeles, where Korean-Americans have taken
an inner-city slum and transformed it into a vital community;
in Florida, where Cuban Americans have renewed the City of
Miami, through economic ties to Latin America; in Chicago,
where young Jewish immigrants from the Soviet Union work two
jobs in addition to attending high school; in San Antonio,
where new Mexican immigrants are taking advantage of English-
literacy classes and have joined Mexican-Americans with many
generations of U.S. residence to create a healthy economy and
to strengthen trade and cultural ties with our border neighbor;
and in Denver, where, in a third-grade class, students from
five countries are learning the history of the United States
and are learning to count in two foreign languages in addition
to English, and where, in February 1980, a Vietnamese-American
third grader who had been in this country for only six months,
identified George Washington as "the father of our country."

But even though immigration is good for this country, the
Commission has rejected the arguments of many economists,
ethnic groups, and religious leaders for a great expansion in
the number of immigrants and refugees to be accepted by the
United States. Many of those in favor of expanded immigration
have argued that the United States is capable of absorbing
far greater numbers of immigrants than are now admitted. They
contend that:

- The United States has the lowest population density of any
  wealthy, industrial nation in the world, with the exceptions of Canada and Australia; and

- The United States, with only 6 percent of the world's
  population, still accounts for 25 percent of the world's
  gross national product.

They further point out that the United States faces serious
labor shortages in the decade to come, particularly of young
and middle-aged workers. Greatly expanded immigration, they
believe, will go a long way towards providing needed workers.

Religious leaders have presented some of these same arguments from a different perspective. They, too, note the vast resources and relatively low population density of the United States but argue that this nation has a humanitarian responsibility to provide immigration opportunities to those seeking entry on the basis of family reunification or as refugees. They wish the United States to preserve its role as a country of large-scale immigration, despite fears about the entry of the foreign-born.

Historians, in their support of increased immigration, have cautioned against overly restrictionist tendencies. They point out that U.S. citizens have always been concerned about the arrival of immigrants but note that immigrants have always made contributions to U.S. society. These scholars also state that the proportion of foreign-born citizens in the United States is now at an all-time low since 1850, when the government began to keep such statistics. If immigration did no harm to U.S. society when foreign-born citizens accounted for 14 to 15 percent of the population, they argue it should certainly cause no internal problems now.

The Select Commission is, however, recommending a more cautious approach. This is not the time for a large-scale expansion in legal immigration--for resident aliens or temporary workers--because the first order of priority is bringing undocumented/illegal immigration under control while setting up a rational system for legal immigration.

The Commission is, therefore, recommending a modest increase in legal immigration sufficient to expedite the clearance of backlogs--mainly to reunify families--which have developed under the current immigration system and to introduce a new system, which we believe will be more equitable and more clearly reflect our interests as a nation.

Such a modest increase will continue to bring the benefits of immigration to the United States without exacerbating fears--not always rational--of competition with immigrants. Such an increase recognizes that immigrants create as well as take jobs and readily pay more into the public coffers than they take out, as research completed for the Select Commission shows. It also recognizes that immigrants in some locales do compete for jobs, housing, and space in schools with citizens and previously entered resident aliens. In the case of refugees, there is an immediate competition with needy U.S. citizens for a variety of services which must be paid for by U.S. taxpayers. In many communities, local officials have complained about the strains which a sudden influx of refugees has placed on their capabilities to provide health services, schooling, and housing.

The American people have demonstrated that they are willing to do what must be done to save a portion of the world's

refugees from persecution and sometimes even from death.
That is why the Select Commission has endorsed the Refugee
Act of 1980 even while questioning aspects of its administration. But it is impossible for the United States to absorb
even a large proportion of the 16 million refugees in this
world and still give high priority to meeting the needs of
its own poor, especially those in its racial and ethnic minorities. Our present refugee policy may seem unduly harsh and
narrow to many, particularly when a terribly poor country
such as Somalia has more than one million refugees in its
care. But we must be realistic about our obligations as a
society to persons in need who already live in this country.

Undocumented/Illegal Migration

Illegal migrations of persons in search of work occur
extensively throughout Europe and Latin America as well as
in Canada and the United States. Such migration to the United
States is so extensive that hundreds of thousands of persons
annually enter this country outside of the law. Although these
migrants usually do not stay, each year tens of thousands of
other aliens remain in the United States illegally after coming
here originally as students or other nonimmigrant aliens.
The Select Commission is well aware of the widespread dis-
satisfaction among U.S. citizens with an immigration policy
that seems to be out of control.

Some have argued before the Select Commission that there
is virtually nothing that can be done about the tidal movements of people that are propelled by economic forces. They
believe this is particularly true in a country such as ours,
with land and coastal borders which are easy to cross and
where millions of tourists and students, having entered, find
it easy to stay. Some have further testified that the United
States has nothing to fear from illegal migration since immigrants who come or remain outside of the law are self-selected,
hard-working, highly creative persons who, even if they remain
in this country, aid rather than harm U.S. society. This is a
view that the Commission believes does not sufficiently consider the serious problems created by illegal migration.

One does not have to be able to quantify in detail all
of the impacts of undocumented/illegal aliens in the United
States to know that there are some serious adverse effects.
Some U.S. citizens and resident aliens who can least afford
it are hurt by competition for jobs and housing and a reduction of wages and standards at the workplace. The existence
of a fugitive underground class is unhealthy for society as a
whole and may contribute to ethnic tensions. In addition,

widespread illegality erodes confidence in the law generally,
and immigration law specifically, while being unfair to those
who seek to immigrate legally.

The Select Commission's determination to enforce the law
is no reflection on the character or the ability of those who
desperately seek to work and provide for their families.
Coming from all over the world, they represent, as immigrants
invariably do, a portion of the world's most ambitious and
creative men and women. But if U.S. immigration policy is to
serve this nation's interests, it must be enforced effectively.
This nation has a responsibility to its people--citizens and
resident aliens--and failure to enforce immigration law means
not living up to that responsibility.

The strong desire to regain control over U.S. immigration
policy is one of several reasons for the Commission's unanimous
vote to legalize a substantial portion of the undocumented/
illegal aliens now in our country. Another is its acknowledg-
ment that, in a sense, our society has participated in the
creation of the problem. Many undocumented/illegal migrants
were induced to come to the United States by offers of work
from U.S. employers who recruited and hired them under protection of present U.S. law. A significant minority of undocu-
mented/illegal aliens have been part of a chain of family
migrants to the United States for at least two generations.
Often entering for temporary work, these migrants began
coming to the United States before this nation imposed a
ceiling on legal immigration from the Western Hemisphere in
1968 and a 20,000 per-country visa ceiling on legal immigration
for each Western Hemisphere country in 1976.

But that is not the main reason for legalizing a substantial portion of those who are here. Legalizing those who have
settled in this country and who are otherwise qualified will
have many positive benefits for the United States as a whole:

- Hard-working, law-abiding persons with a stake in U.S.
  society will come out into the open and contribute much
  more to it.

- No longer exploitable at the workplace, they no longer will
  contribute to depressing U.S. labor standards and wages.

- New and accurate information about migration routes and the
  smuggling of people into the United States will contribute
  to the targeting of enforcement resources to stop illegal
  migrations in the future.

- New and accurate information about the origins of migration
  will enable the United States to work with large sending
  countries in targeting aid and investment programs to deal
  with migration pressures at the source, in the villages and
  provinces of those countries.

• New and accurate information about patterns of visa abuse
  by those who entered as nonimmigrant aliens will help to
  make our visa issuance process and control at ports of
  entry more effective.

The recommended legalization program will help to enforce
the law, however, only if other enforcement measures designed
to curtail future illegal migration to the United States are
instituted. That is why the Commission has linked the
legalization program to the introduction of such measures.
Recognizing that future migration pressures could lead to even
higher levels of illegal migration to the United States, the
Commission has emphasized the development of effective enforcement strategies, including a new law to penalize employers who
hire undocumented/illegal aliens and new measures to control
the abuse of non-immigrant status.

No one on this Commission expects to stop illegal migration *totally* or believes that new enforcement measures can be
instituted without cost. But we do believe that we can reduce
illegal entries sharply and that the social costs of not doing
so may be grave. What is a serious problem today could become
a monumental crisis as migration pressures increase.

The Reunification of Families

A better immigration system may help to reduce the pressures
for illegal migration to some extent. A look at present U.S.
immigration statistics reveals one relatively small but important source of illegal migration. Of the more than one million
persons now registered at consular offices waiting for visas,
more than 700,000 are relatives of U.S. citizens or resident
aliens, including spouses and minor children of resident
aliens. There is something wrong with a law that keeps out—
for as long as eight years—the small child of a mother or
father who has settled in the United States while a nonrelative
or less close relative from another country can come in immediately. Certainly a strong incentive to enter illegally
exists for persons who are separated from close family members
for a long period of time.

What is basically wrong is that we have not made clear our
priority to reunify the immediate relatives of U.S. residents
regardless of their nationality. Among our recommendations are
two which would help to do just that. The first puts immigrants whose entry into the United States would reunify families on a separate track from other immigrants. The second
puts spouses and minor children of lawful permanent resident
aliens under a separate, numerically limited category without
country ceilings. Eliminating country ceilings in this cate-

gory, should help assure the reunification of the families of permanent resident aliens on a first-come, first-served basis within a fixed world ceiling.

Independent Immigrants

The creation of a separate category for nonfamily immigrants--the independent category--may also somewhat reduce illegal immigration by broadening immigration opportunities. It reaffirms the importance to the United States of traditional "new seed" immigrants who come to work, save, invest, and plan for their children and grandchildren and creates an immigration channel for persons who cannot enter the United States on the basis of family reunification. It is the Commission's hope that this category will provide immigration opportunities for those persons who come from countries where immigration to the United States has not been recent or from countries that have no immigration base here.

Many other important issues have also been addressed by the Select Commission, including an upgrading of our system for administering U.S. immigration laws, the need to streamline deportation proceedings, and the importance of English-language acquisition. We have tried to address these and other issues with open minds, recognizing that few of them can be resolved easily.

That there is disagreement on some issues among Commissioners is not surprising since we represent a great variety of perspectives and since the complex issues of immigration are charged with emotion and special interest. Even though we have disagreed among ourselves in formulating some answers, we have reached consensus on a great many of the questions which faced us. Our basic concern has been the common good which must characterize good U.S. law, and we have tried to recommend policies that would be responsible, equitable, efficient, and enforceable.

We have not, of course, answered every question and our answers are far from perfect, but we believe we asked the right questions and that the answers are free from the cant, hypocrisy, and racism which have sometimes characterized U.S. immigration policy in years gone by. With that in mind, we hope that our recommendations, in the words of George Washington, "set a standard to which the wise and honest can repair."

The Reverend Theodore M. Hesburgh

EXECUTIVE SUMMARY
Recommendations of the Select Commission
on Immigration and Refugee Policy

SECTION I. INTERNATIONAL ISSUES

Better Understanding of International Migration

The Select Commission recommends that the United States continue to work with other nations and principal international
organizations that collect information, conduct research,
and coordinate consultations on migratory flows and the
treatment of international migrants to develop a better understanding of migration issues.

Revitalization of Existing International Organizations

The Select Commission recommends that the United States initiate discussion through an international conference on ways
to revitalize existing institutional arrangements for international cooperation in the handling of migration and refugee
problems.

Expansion of Bilateral Consultations

The Select Commission recommends that the United States expand
bilateral consultations with other governments, especially
Mexico and other regional neighbors regarding migration.

The Creation of Regional Mechanisms

The United States should initiate discussions with regional
neighbors on the creation of mechanisms to:

- Discuss and make recommendations on ways to promote regional cooperation on the related matters of trade, aid, investment, development, and migration.

- Explore additional means of cooperation for effective
  enforcement of immigration laws.

- Establish means for mutual cooperation for the protection
  of the human and labor rights of nationals residing in each
  other's countries.

- Explore the possibility of negotiating a regional convention on forced migration or expulsion of citizens.

- Consider establishment of a regional authority to work
  with the U.N. High Commissioner for Refugees and the
  Intergovernmental Committee on Migration in arranging for
  the permanent and productive resettlement of asylees who
  cannot be repatriated to their countries of origin.

SECTION II. UNDOCUMENTED/ILLEGAL ALIENS

II.A.   Border and Interior Enforcement

II.A.1.   Border Patrol Funding

           The Select Commission recommends that Border Patrol
           funding levels be raised to provide for a substan-
           tial increase in the numbers and training of per-
           sonnel, replacement sensor systems, additional light
           planes and helicopters, and other needed equipment.

II.A.2   Port-of-Entry Inspections

           The Select Commission recommends that port-of-entry
           inspections be enhanced by increasing the number of
           primary inspectors, instituting a mobile inspections
           task force, and replacing all outstanding border-
           crossing cards with a counterfeit-resistant card.

II.A.3.   The Select Commission recommends that regional bor-
           der enforcement posts be established to coordinate
           the work of the Immigration and Naturalization
           Service, the U.S. Customs Service, the Drug Enforce-
           ment Administration, and the U.S. Coast Guard in
           the interdiction of both undocumented/illegal mi-
           grants and illicit goods, specifically narcotics.

II.A.4.   Enforcement of Current Law

           The Select Commission recommends that the law be
           firmly and consistently enforced against U.S. citi-
           zens who aid aliens who do not have valid visas to
           enter the country.

II.A.5.   Nonimmigrant Visa Abuse

           The Select Commission recommends that investiga-
           tions of overstays and student visa abusers be
           maintained regardless of other investigative priori-
           ties.

II.A.6.   Nonimmigrant Document Control

           The Select Commission recommends that a fully
           automated system of nonimmigrant document control
           should be established in the Immigration and Natural-
           ization Service to allow prompt tracking of aliens
           and to verify their departure. U.S. consular posts
           of visa issuance should be informed of nondepartures.

II.A.7.   Deportation of Undocumented/Illegal Migrants

           The Select Commission recommends that deportation
           and removal of undocumented/illegal migrants should

be effected to discourage early return. Adequate
funds should be available to maintain high levels
of alien apprehension, detention, and deportation
throughout the year. Where possible, aliens should
be required to pay the transportation costs of deportation or removal under safeguards.

II.A.8.   Training of INS Officers

The Select Commission recommends high priority be
given to the training of Immigration and Naturalization Service Officers to familiarize them with the
rights of aliens and U.S. citizens and to help them
deal with persons of other cultural backgrounds.
Further, to protect the rights of those who have
entered the United States legally, the Commission
also recommends that immigration laws not be selectively enforced in the interior on the basis of
race, religion, sex, or national origin.

II.B.   Economic Deterrents in the Workplace

II.B.1.   Employer Sanctions Legislation

The Select Commission recommends that legislation
be passed making it illegal for employers to hire
undocumented workers.

II.B.2   Enforcement Efforts in Addition to Employer Sanctions

The Select Commission recommends that the enforcement of existing wage and working standards legislation be increased in conjunction with the enforcement of employer responsibility legislation.

II.C.   Legalization

The Select Commission recommends that a program to
legalize illegal/undocumented aliens now in the
United States be adopted.

II.C.1.   Eligibility for Legalization

The Select Commission recommends that eligibility
be determined by interrelated measurements of
residence—date of entry and length of continuous
residence—and by specified groups of excludability
that are appropriate to the legalization program.

II.C.2.   Maximum Participation in the Legalization Program

The Select Commission recommends that voluntary
agencies and community organizations be given a
significant role in the legalization program.

II.C.3.   Legalization and Enforcement

The Select Commission recommends that legalization
begin when appropriate enforcement mechanisms have
been instituted.

II.C.4.   Unqualified Undocumented/Illegal Aliens

The Select Commission recommends that those who are
ineligible for a legalization program be subject to
the penalties of the Immigration and Nationality
Act if they come to the attention of immigration
authorities.

SECTION III. THE ADMISSION OF IMMIGRANTS

III.A.   Numbers of Immigrants

III.A.1.   Numerical Ceilings on Total Immigrant Admissions

The Select Commission recommends continuing a system where some immigrants are numerically limited
but certain others--such as immediate relatives
of U.S. citizens and refugees--are exempt from any
numerical ceilings.

III.A.2.   Numerically Limited Immigration

The Select Commission recommends an annual ceiling
of 350,000 numerically limited immigrant visas with
an additional 100,000 visas available for the first
five years to provide a higher ceiling to allow
backlogs to be cleared.

III.B.   Goals and Structure

III.B.1.   Categories of Immigrants

The Select Commission recommends the separation
of the two major types of immigrants--families and
independent (nonfamily) immigrants--into distinct
admissions categories.

III.C.   Family Reunification

The Select Commission recommends that the reunification of families continue to play a major and
important role in U.S. immigration policy.

III.C.1.   Immediate Relatives of U.S. Citizens

The Select Commission recommends continuing the
admission of immediate relatives of U.S. citizens
outside of any numerical limitations. This group

should be expanded slightly to include not only
the spouses, minor children, and parents of adult
citizens but also the adult unmarried sons and
daughters and grandparents of adult U.S. citizens.
In the case of grandparents, petitioning rights for
the immigration of relatives do not attach until
the petitioner acquires U.S. citizenship.

III.C.2.   Spouses and Unmarried Sons and Daughters of Permanent
Resident Aliens

The Select Commission recognizes the importance of
reunifying spouses and unmarried sons and daughters
with their permanent resident alien relatives.   A
substantial number of visas should be set aside for
this group and it should be given top priority in
the numerically limited family reunification category.

III.C.3.   Married Sons and Daughters of U.S. Citizens

The Select Commission recommends continuing a
numerically limited preference for the married sons
and daughters of U.S. citizens.

III.C.4.   Brothers and Sisters of U.S. Citizens

The Select Commission recommends that the present
policy of admitting all brothers and sisters of
adult U.S. citizens within the numerical limitations
be continued.

III.C.5.   Parents of Adult Permanent Residents

The Select Commission recommends including a
numerically limited preference for certain parents
of adult permanent resident aliens.   Such parents
must be elderly and have no children living outside
the United States.

III.C.6   Country Ceilings

The Select Commission recommends that country ceilings apply to all numerically limited family reunification preferences except to that for the
spouses and minor children of permanent resident
aliens, who should be admitted on a first-come,
first-served basis within a worldwide ceiling set
for that preference.

III.C.7.   Preference Percentage Allocations

The Select Commission recommends that percentages
of the total number of visas set aside for family

reunification be assigned to the individual preferences.

III.D. Independent Immigration

The Select Commission recommends that provision
should be made in the immigrant admissions system
to facilitate the immigration of persons without
family ties in the United States.

III.D.1. Special Immigrants

The Select Commission recommends that "special"
immigrants remain a numerically exempt group but
be placed within the independent category.

III.D.2. Immigrants with Exceptional Qualifications

The Select Commission recognizes the desirability
of facilitating the entry of immigrants with exceptional qualifications and recommends that a small,
numerically limited category be created within the
independent category for this purpose.

III.D.3. Immigrant Investors

The Select Commission recommends creating a small,
numerically limited subcategory within the independent category to provide for the immigration of
certain investors. The criteria for the entry of
investors should be a substantial amount of investment or capacity for investment in dollar terms,
substantially greater than the present $40,000
requirement set by regulation.

III.D.4. Retirees

The Select Commission recommends that no special
provision be made for immigration of retirees.

III.D.5. Other Independent Immigrants

The Select Commission recommends the creation of a
category for qualified independent immigrants other
than those of exceptional merit or those who can
qualify as investors.

III.D.6. Selection Criteria for Independent Immigrants

The Select Commission believes that specific labor
market criteria should be established for the selection of independent immigrants but is divided over
whether the mechanism should be a streamlining and
clarification of the present labor certification
procedure plus a job offer from a U.S. employer,

or a policy under which independent immigrants
would be admissible unless the Secretary of Labor
ruled that their immigration would be harmful to
the U.S. labor market.

III.D.7.   Country Ceilings

The Select Commission recommends a fixed-percentage
limit to the independent immigration from any one
country.

III.E.   Flexibility in Immigration Policy

III.E.1.   Suggested Mechanism

The Select Commission recommends that ranking members of the House and Senate subcommittees with
immigration responsibilities, in consultation with
the Departments of State, Justice, and Labor, pre-
pare an annual report on the current domestic and
international situations as they relate to U.S.
immigration policy.

SECTION IV. PHASING IN NEW PROGRAMS RECOMMENDED BY THE SELECT
COMMISSION

The Select Commission recommends a coordinated
phasing-in of the major programs it has proposed.

SECTION V. REFUGEE AND MASS FIRST ASYLUM ISSUES

V.A.   The Select Commission endorses the provisions of
the Refugee Act of 1980 which cover the definition
of refugee, the number of visas allocated to refugees, and how these numbers are allocated.

V.A.1.   Allocation of Refugee Numbers

The Select Commission recommends that the U.S.
allocation of refugee numbers include both geographic considerations and specific refugee characteristics. Numbers should be provided--not by
statute but in the course of the allocation process
itself--for political prisoners, victims of torture, and persons under threat of death.

V.B.   Mass First Asylum Admissions

V.B.1.   Planning for Asylum Emergencies

The Select Commission recommends that an interagency
body be established to develop procedures, including

contingency plans for opening and managing federal
processing centers, for handling possible mass
asylum emergencies.

V.B.2.   Determining the Legitimacy of Mass Asylum Claims

The Select Commission recommends that mass asylum
applicants continue to be required to bear an individualized burden of proof. Group profiles should
be developed and used by processing personnel and
area experts (see V.B.4.) to determine the legitimacy of individual claims.

V.B.3   Developing and Issuing Group Profiles

The Select Commission recommends that the responsibility for developing and issuing group profiles
be given to the U.S. Coordinator for Refugee Affairs.

V.B.4.   Asylum Admissions Officers

The Select Commission recommends that the position
of asylum admissions officer be created within the
Immigration and Naturalization Service. This
official should be schooled in the procedures and
techniques of eligibility determinations. Area
experts should be made available to these processing
personnel to provide information on conditions in
the source country, facilitating a well-founded
basis for asylum determinations.

V.B.5.   Asylum Appeals

The Select Commission holds the view that in each
case a simple asylum appeal be heard and recommends
that the appeal be heard by whatever institution
routinely hears other immigration appeals.

V.C.   Refugee Resettlement

The Select Commission endorses the overall programs
and principles of refugee resettlement but takes
note of changes that are needed in the areas of
cash and medical assistance programs, strategies
for resettlement, programs to promote refugee self-
sufficiency, and the preparation of refugee sponsors.

V.C.1.   State and Local Governments

The Select Commission recommends that state and
local governments be involved in planning for initial refugee resettlement and that consideration
be given to establishing a federal program of impact
aid to minimize the financial impact of refugees
on local services.

V.C.2.   Refugee Clustering

The Select Commission recommends that refugee clustering be encouraged. Mechanisms should be developed, particularly within the voluntary agency
network, to settle ethnic groups of similar backgrounds in the same areas.

V.C.3.   Resettlement Benefits

The Select Commission recommends that consideration
be given to an extension of federal refugee assistance reimbursement.

V.C.4.   Cash-Assistance Programs

The Select Commission recommends that stricter
regulations be imposed on the use of cash-assistance
programs by refugees.

V.C.5.   Medical-Assistance Programs

The Select Commission recommends that medical assistance for refugees should be more effectively
separated from cash-assistance programs.

V.C.6.   Resettlement Goals

The Select Commission recommends that refugee
achievement of self-sufficiency and adjustment to
living in the United States be reaffirmed as the
goal of resettlement. In pursuance of this goal,
"survival" training--the attainment of basic levels
of language and vocational skills--and vocational
counseling should be emphasized. Sanctions (in the
form of termination of support and services) should
be imposed on refugees who refuse appropriate job
offers if these sanctions are approved by the voluntary agency responsible for resettlement, the cash-
assistance source, and, if involved, the employment
service.

V.C.7.   Sponsors

The Select Commission recommends that improvements
in the orientation and preparation of sponsors be
promoted.

V.D.   Administration of U.S. Refugee and Mass Asylum
           Policy

V.D.1.   Streamlining of Resettlement Agencies

The Select Commission recommends that the Administration, through the office of the Coordinator for

Refugees, be directed to examine whether the program of resettlement can be streamlined to make
government participation more responsive to the
flow of refugees coming to this country. Particular attention should be given to the question of
whether excessive bureaucracy has been created,
although inadvertently, pursuant to the Refugee
Act of 1980.

V.D.2.   U.S. Coordinator for Refugee Affairs

The Select Commission recommends that the office
of the U.S. Coordinator for Refugee Affairs be
moved from the State Department and be placed in
the Executive Office of the President.

SECTION VI. NONIMMIGRANT ALIENS

VI.A.   Nonimmigrant Adjustment to Immigrant Status

The Select Commission recommends that the present
system under which eligible nonimmigrants and
other aliens are permitted to adjust their status
into all immigrant categories be continued.

VI.B.   Foreign Students

VI.B.1.   Foreign Student Employment

The Select Commission recommends that the United
States retain current restrictions on foreign student
employment but expedite the processing of work
authorization requests; unauthorized student employment should be controlled through the measures
recommended to curtail other types of illegal employment.

VI.B.2.   Employment of Foreign Student Spouses

The Select Commission recommends that the spouses
of foreign students be eligible to request employment authorization from the Immigration and
Naturalization Service under the same conditions
that now apply to the spouses of exchange visitors.

VI.B.3   Subdivision of the Foreign Student Category

The Select Commission recommends dividing the
present all-inclusive F-1 foreign student category
into subcategories: a revised F-1 class for foreign
students at academic institutions that have foreign
student programs and have demonstrated their capacity

for responsible foreign student management to the
Immigration and Naturalization Service; a revised
F-2 class for students at other academic institutions authorized to enroll foreign students that
have not yet demonstrated their capacity for responsible foreign student management; and a new
F-3 class for language or vocational students. An
additional F-4 class would be needed for the spouses
and children of foreign students.

VI.B.4.   Authorization of Schools to Enroll Foreign Students

The Select Commission recommends that the responsibility for authorizing schools to enroll foreign
students be transferred from the Immigration and
Naturalization Service to the Department of Education.

VI.B.5.   Administrative Fines for Delinquent Schools

The Select Commission recommends establishing a
procedure that would allow the Immigration and
Naturalization Service to impose administrative
fines on schools that neglect or abuse their foreign
student responsibilities (for example, failure to
inform INS of changes in the enrollment status of
foreign students enrolled in their schools).

VI.C.   Tourists and Business Travelers

VI.C.1.   Visa Waiver for Tourists and Business Travelers
           from Selected Countries

The Select Commission recommends that visas be
waived for tourists and business travelers from
selected countries who visit the United States for
short periods of time.

VI.C.2.   Improvement in the Processing of Intracompany
           Transferee Cases

The Select Commission recommends that U.S. consular
officers be authorized to approve the petitions
required for intracompany transfers.

VI.D.   Medical Personnel

VI.D.1.   Elimination of the Training Time Limit for Foreign
           Medical School Graduates

The Select Commission recommends the elimination
of the present two- to three-year limit on the
residency training of foreign doctors.

VI.D.2. Revision of the Visa Qualifying Exam for Foreign Doctors

The Select Commission recommends that the Visa Qualifying Exam (VQE) be revised to deemphasize the significance of the Exam's Part I on basic biological science.

VI.D.3. Admission of Foreign Nurses as Temporary Workers

The Select Commission recommends that qualified foreign nurses continue to be admitted as temporary workers but also recommends that efforts be intensified to induce more U.S. nurses who are not currently practicing their professions to do so.

VI.D.4. Screening of Foreign Nurses Applying for Visas

The Select Commission recommends that all foreign nurses who apply for U.S. visas continue to be required to pass the examination of the Commission on Graduates of Foreign Nursing Schools.

VI.E. H-2 Temporary Workers

The Department of Labor should recommend changes in the H-2 program which would improve the fairness of the program to both U.S. workers and employers. Proposed changes should:

- Improve the timeliness of decisions regarding the admission of H-2 workers by streamlining the application process.

- Remove the current economic disincentives to hire U.S. workers by requiring, for example, employers to pay FICA and unemployment insurance for H-2 workers; and maintain the labor certification by the U.S. Department of Labor.

- The Commission believes that government, employers, and unions should cooperate to end the dependence of any industry on a constant supply of H-2 workers.

The above does not exclude a slight expansion of the program.

VI.F. Authority of the Attorney General to Deport Non-immigrants

The Select Commission recommends that greater statutory authority be given to the Attorney General to institute deportation proceedings against nonimmi-

grant aliens when there is conviction for an offense subject to sentencing of six months or more.

SECTION VII. ADMINISTRATIVE ISSUES

VII.A.   Federal Agency Structure

The Select Commission recommends that the present
federal agency structure for administering U.S.
immigration and nationality laws be retained with
visa issuance and the attendant policy and regulatory mechanisms in the Department of State and
domestic operations and the attendant policy and
regulatory mechanisms in the Immigration and
Naturalization Service of the Department of State.

VII.B.   Immigration and Naturalization Service

VII.B.1.   Service and Enforcement Functions

The Select Commission recommends that all major
domestic immigration and nationality operations be
retained within the Immigration and Naturalization
Service, with clear budgetary and organizational
separation of service and enforcement functions.

VII.B.2.   Head of the INS

The Select Commission recommends that the head of
the Immigration and Naturalization Service be up-
graded to director at a level similar to that of
the other major agencies within the Department of
Justice and report directly to the attorney general
on matters of policy.

VII.B.3.   Professionalism of INS Employees

The Select Commission recommends the following
actions be taken to improve the responsiveness and
sensitivity of Immigration and Naturalization Service employees:

-   Establish a code of ethics and behavior for all
    INS employees.

-   Upgrade employee training to include meaningful
    courses at the entry and journeymen levels on
    ethnic studies and the history and benefits of
    immigration.

-   Promote the recruitment of new employees with
    foreign-language capabilities and the acquisition
    of foreign-language skills in addition to Spanish

in which all officers are now extensively trained—for existing personnel.

- Sensitize employees to the perspectives and needs of the persons with whom they come in contact and encourage INS management to be more sensitive to employee morale by improving pay scales and other conditions of employment.

- Reward meritorious service and sensitivity in conduct of work.

- Continue vigorous investigation of and action against all serious allegations of misfeasance, malfeasance, and corruption by INS employees.

- Give officers training to deal with violence and threats of violence.

- Strengthen and formalize the existing mechanism for reviewing administrative complaints, thus permitting the Immigration and Naturalization Service to become more aware of and responsive to the public it serves.

- Make special efforts to recruit and hire minority and women applicants.

VII.C. Structure for Immigration Hearings and Appeals

Article I Court

The Select Commission recommends that existing law be amended to create an immigration court under Article I of the U.S. Constitution.

VII.C.2 Resources for Article I Court

The Select Commission urges that the court be provided with the necessary support to reduce existing backlogs.

VII.D. Administrative Naturalization

The Select Commission recommends that naturalization be made an administrative process within the Immigration and Naturalization Service with judicial naturalization permitted when practical and requested. It further recommends that the significance and meaning of the process be preserved by retaining meaningful group ceremonies as the forum for the actual conferring of citizenship.

VII.E. Review of Consular Decisions

The Select Commission recommends that the existing

informal review system for consular decisions be
continued but improved by enhancing the consular
post review mechanism and using the State Department's visa case review and field support process
as tools to ensure equity and consistency in consular decisions.

VII.F.　　Immigration Law Enforcement by State and Local
Police

The Select Commission recommends that state and
local law enforcement officials be prohibited from
apprehending persons on immigration charges, but
further recommends that local officials continue
to be encouraged to notify the Immigration and
Naturalization Service when they suspect a person
who has been arrested for a violation unrelated to
immigration to be an undocumented/illegal alien.

SECTION VIII. LEGAL ISSUES

VIII.A.　　Powers of Immigration and Naturalization Officers

VIII.A.1.　Temporary Detention for Interrogation

The Select Commission recommends that statutes
authorizing Immigration and Naturalization Service
enforcement activities for other than activities
on the border clearly provide that Immigration and
Naturalization Service Officers may temporarily
detain a person for interrogation or a brief investigation upon reasonable cause to believe (based
upon articulable facts) that the person is unlawfully
present in the United States.

VIII.A.2.　Arrests with and Without Warrants

The Select Commission recommends that:

- Arrests, effected with or without the authority
  of a warrant, should be supported by probable
  cause to believe that the person arrested is an
  alien unlawfully present in the United States.

- Warrantless arrests should only be made when an
  INS officer reasonably believes that the person
  is likely to flee before an arrest warrant can
  be obtained.

- Arrest warrants may be issued by the Immigration
  and Naturalization Service District Directors or
  Deputy District Directors, the heads of suboffices

and Assistant District Directors for Investigations acting for the Attorney General.

• Persons arrested outside the border area without a warrant should be taken without unnecessary delay before the Immigration and Naturalization Service District Director, Deputy District Director, head of suboffice or Assistant Director for Investigations acting for the Attorney General or before an immigration judge who will determine if sufficient evidence exists to support the initiation of deportation proceedings. With respect to arrests at the border, persons arrested without a warrant should be taken without unnecessary delay before an immigration judge or a supervisory responsible Immigration and Naturalization Service official who will determine whether sufficient evidence exists to support the initiation of deportation proceedings.

VIII.A.3. Searches for Persons and Evidence

The Select Commission recommends that the Immigration and Nationality Act include provisions authorizing Immigration and Naturalization Service officers to conduct searches:

• With probable cause either under the authority of judicial warrants for property and persons or in exigent circumstances.

• Upon the receipt of voluntary consent at places other than residences.

• When searches pursuant to applicable law are conducted incident to a lawful arrest.

• At the border.

VIII.A.4 Evidence Illegally Obtained

The Select Commission recommends that enforcement officials using illegal means to obtain evidence should be penalized. The evidence thus obtained should not be excluded from consideration in deportation cases.

VIII.B. Right to Counsel

VII.B.1. The Right to Counsel and Notification of That Right

The Select Commission recommends that the right to counsel and notification of that right be mandated

at the time of exclusion and deportation hearings
and when petitions for benefits under the INA are
adjudicated.

VIII.B.2   Counsel at Government Expense

The Select Commission recommends amending the current law to provide counsel at government expense
only to permanent resident aliens in deportation
or exclusion hearings and only when those aliens
cannot afford legal counsel and alternative sources
of free legal services are not available.

VIII.C.   Limits on Deportation

VIII.C.1.   Revision of Section 244 of the Immigration and
Nationality Act

The Select Commission recommends that the words
"extreme hardship" in Section 244 of the Immigration and Nationality Act be changed to "hardship."
And that the reference to congressional confirmation
of suspension of deportation be eliminated from
this section.

VIII.C.2.   Long-Term Permanent Residence As a Bar to Deportation

The Commissioners did not reach a consensus on this
issue.

VIII.D.   Exclusions

VIII.D.1.   Grounds for Exclusion

The Select Commission believes that the present
exclusionary grounds should not be retained.   The
Select Commission recommends that Congress re-
examine the grounds for exclusion set forth in the
INA.

VIII.D.2.   Reentry Doctrine

The Select Commission recommends that the reentry
doctrine be modified so that returning lawful
permanent resident aliens (those who have departed
from the United States for temporary purposes) can
reenter the United States without being subject to
the exclusion laws, except the following:

• Criminal grounds for exclusion (criminal convictions while abroad).

• Political grounds for exclusion.

- Entry into the United States without inspection.

- Engaging in persecution.

SECTION IX. LANGUAGE REQUIREMENT FOR NATURALIZATION

The Select Commission recommends that the current
English-langauge requirement for naturalization
be retained but also recommends that the English-
language requirement be modified to provide a
flexible formula that would permit older persons
with many years of permanent residence in the
United States to obtain citizenship without reading, writing, or speaking English.

SECTION X. TREATMENT OF U.S. TERRITORIES UNDER U.S. IMMIGRATION AND NATIONAL LAWS

The Select Commission recommends that U.S. law permit, but not require, special treatment of all U.S.
territories.

This book is indexed by the last name and the identifying initials of the authors of the works cited herein. Substantive references (organizations, etc.) are indexed by first letter of first word in normal word order. The numbers after the name (or substantive reference) are the entry numbers.